ARTIST'S NOTE

D0662546

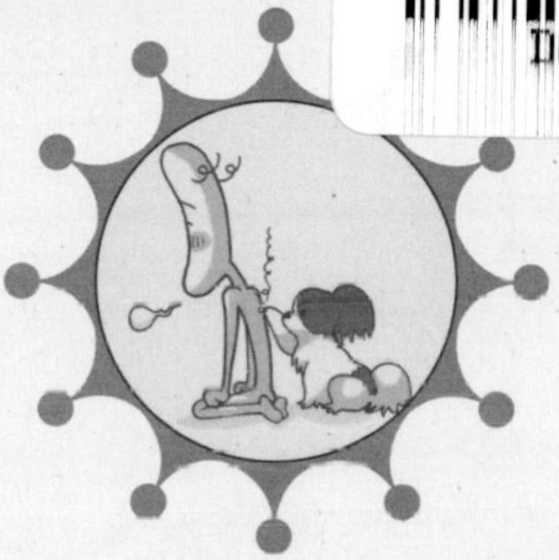

It's Volume 2!

With each installment being released in 100-page segments, it didn't take long for this book to come together. However, due to unexpected circumstances, it might be a while until the next volume comes out. But don't worry! Shinji Wada-sensei assures me that there are still plenty of surprising twists and turns in store, so I hope you can be patient as you wait for it. It'll be worth it!

You Higuri

Visit You Higuri online at
www.youhiguri.com

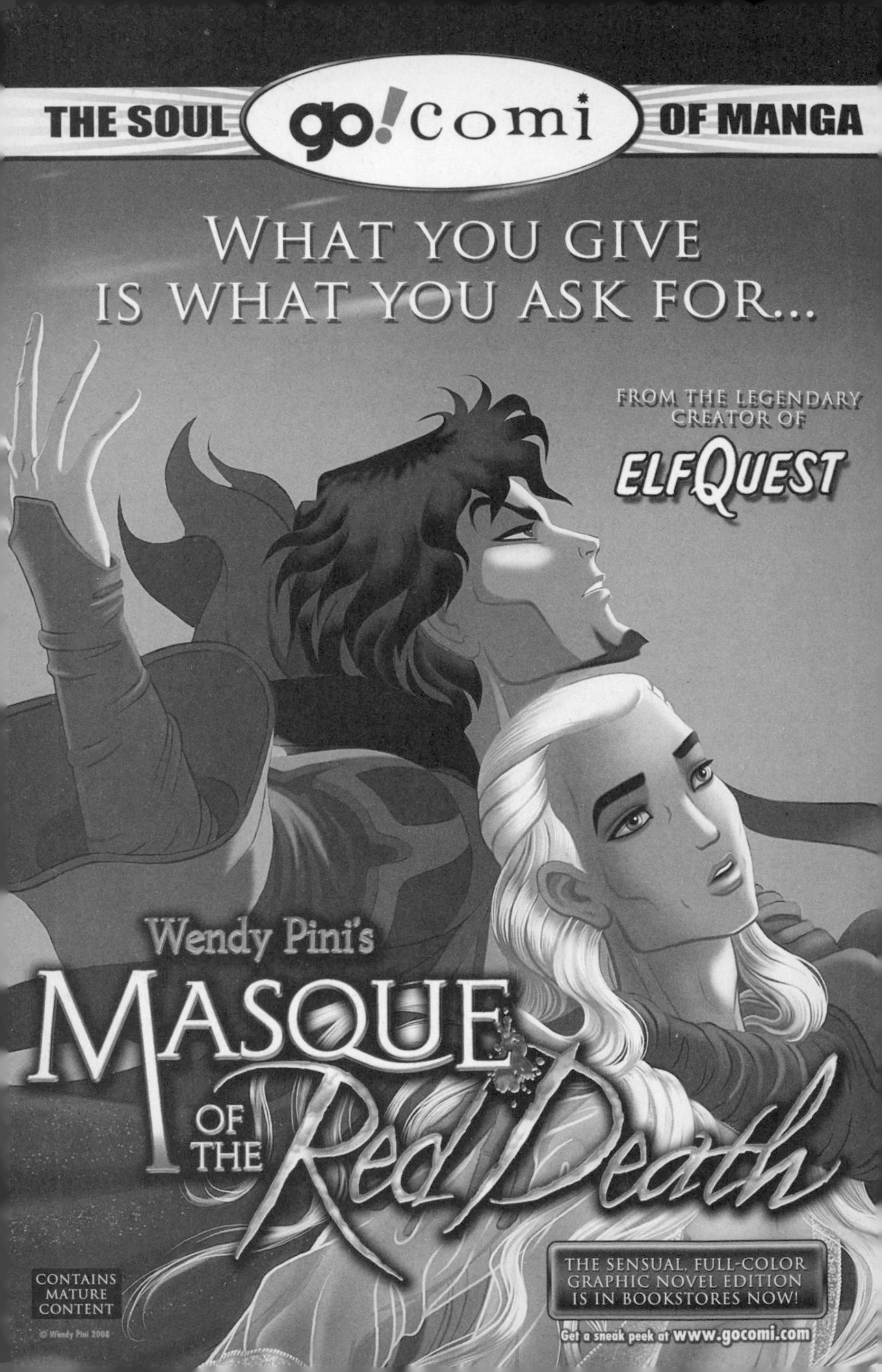
THE SOUL go!comi OF MANGA
WHAT YOU GIVE
IS WHAT YOU ASK FOR...
FROM THE LEGENDARY CREATOR OF
ELFQUEST
Wendy Pini's
MASQUE OF THE Red Death
THE SENSUAL, FULL-COLOR GRAPHIC NOVEL EDITION IS IN BOOKSTORES NOW!
Get a sneak peek at www.gocomi.com
CONTAINS MATURE CONTENT
© Wendy Pini 2008

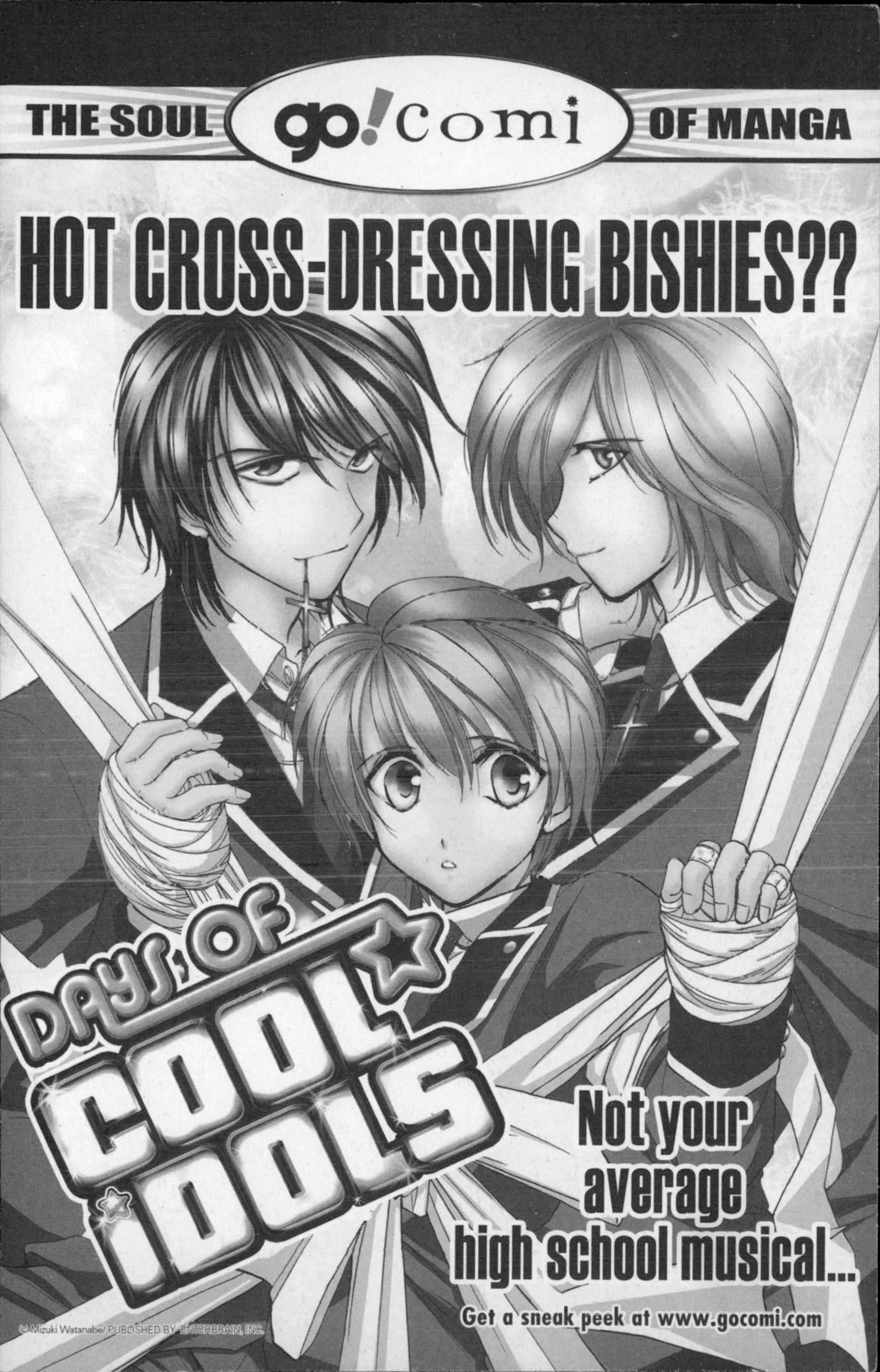
THE SOUL go!comi OF MANGA
HOT CROSS-DRESSING BISHIES??
DAYS OF COOL IDOLS
Not your average high school musical...
Get a sneak peek at www.gocomi.com
© Mizuki Watanabe/ PUBLISHED BY ENTERBRAIN, INC.

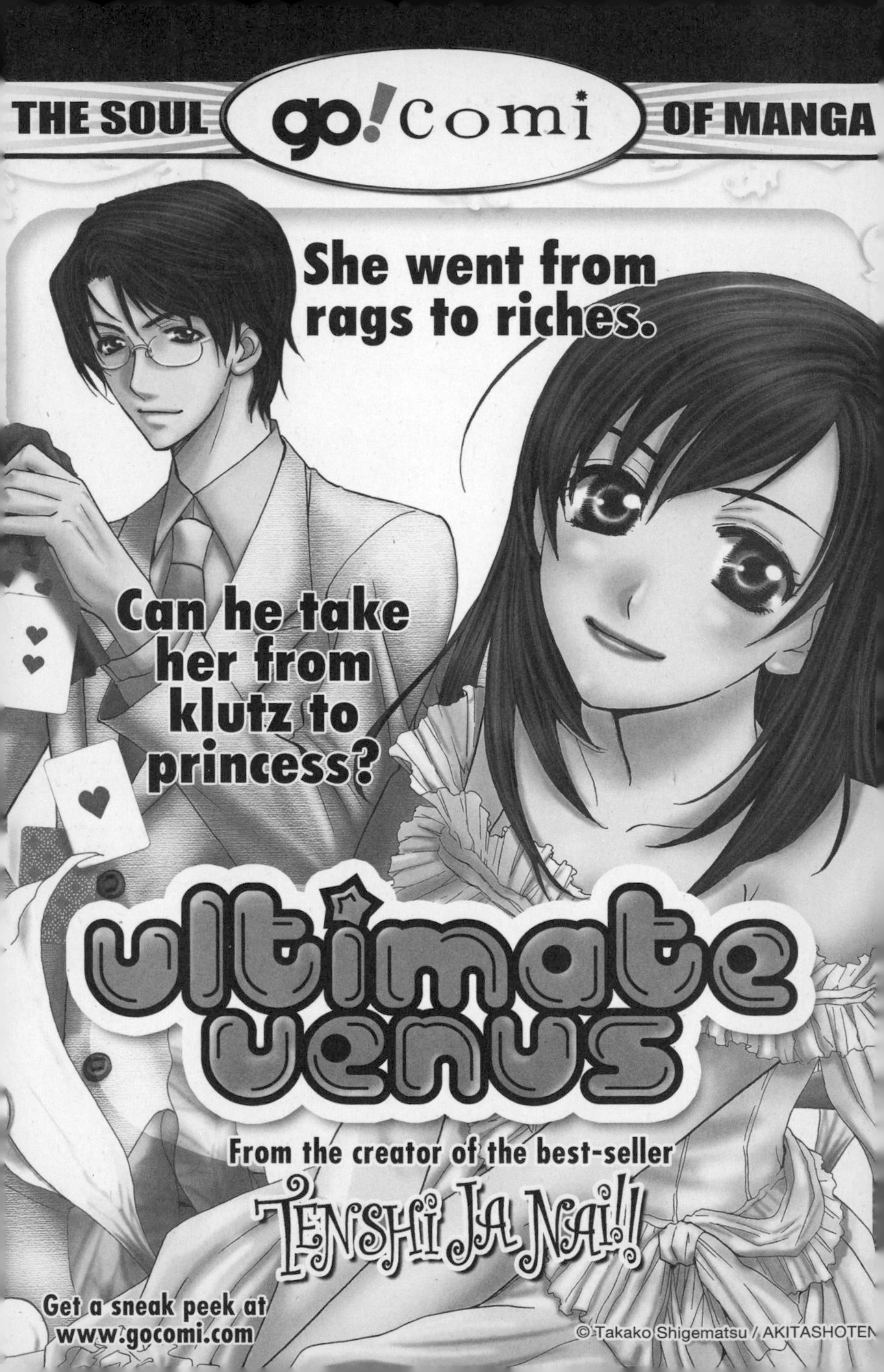
THE SOUL go!comi OF MANGA
She went from rags to riches.
Can he take her from klutz to princess?
ultimate venus
From the creator of the best-seller
TENSHI JA NAI!!
Get a sneak peek at www.gocomi.com
© Takako Shigematsu / AKITASHOTEN

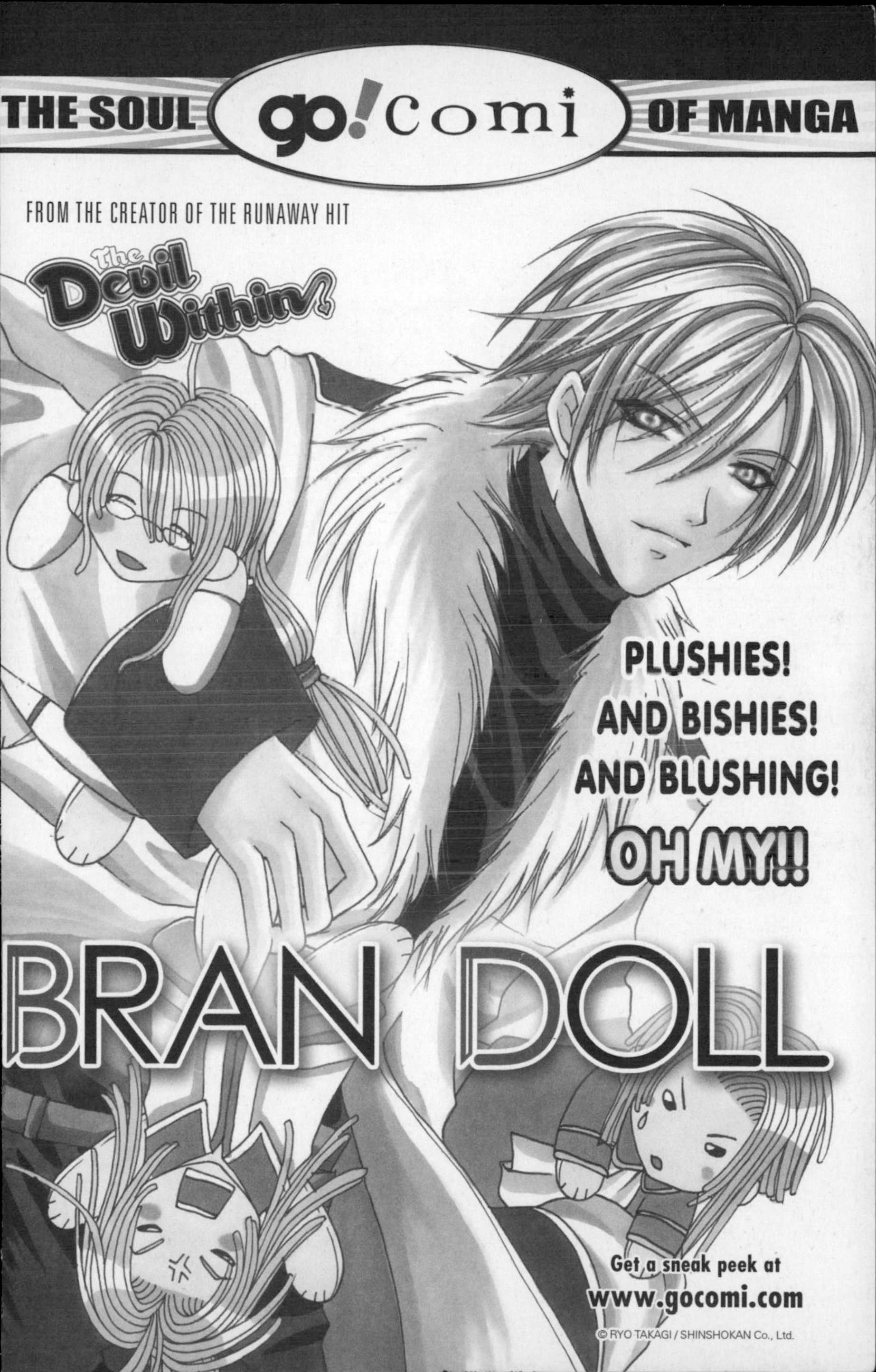
THE SOUL
go!comi
OF MANGA
FROM THE CREATOR OF THE RUNAWAY HIT
The Devil Within!
PLUSHIES!
AND BISHIES!
AND BLUSHING!
OH MY!!
BRAN DOLL
Get a sneak peek at
www.gocomi.com
© RYO TAKAGI / SHINSHOKAN Co., Ltd.

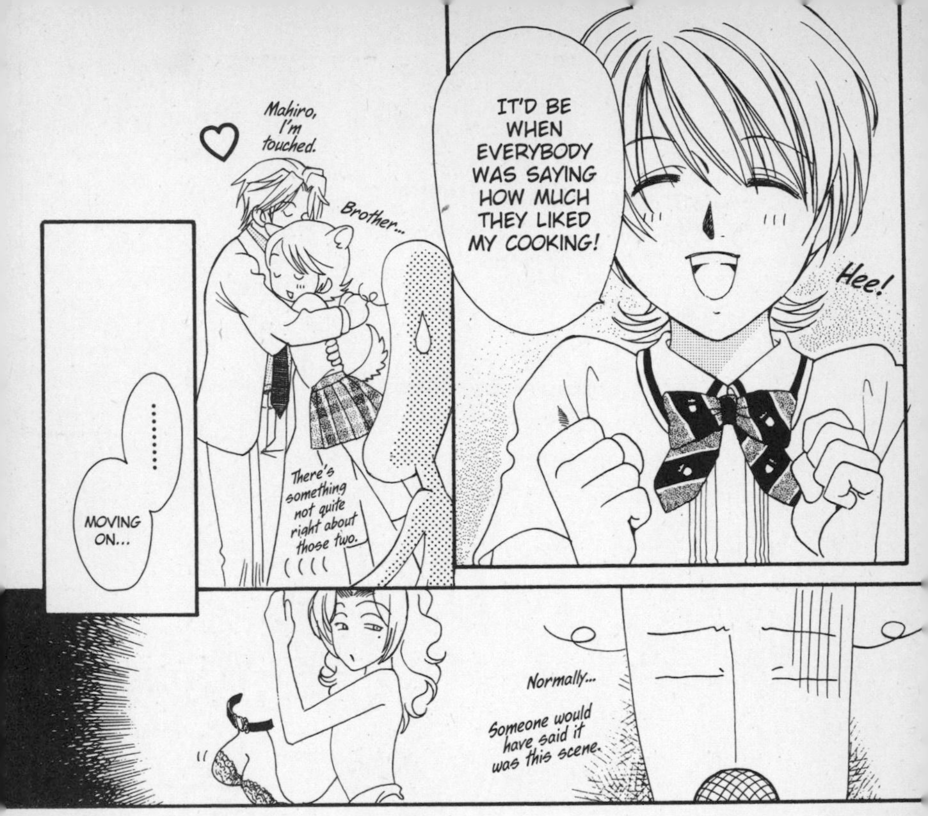
IT'D BE WHEN EVERYBODY WAS SAYING HOW MUCH THEY LIKED MY COOKING!
Hee!
Mahiro, I'm touched.
Brother...
There's something not quite right about those two.
......
MOVING ON...
Normally...
Someone would have said it was this scene.

SPECIAL THANKS

To Hijiri Izumi-san, Naoko Nakatsuji-san, Kazumi Onishi-san, Akiyoshi-san, Mitsuru Fuyutsuki-san, Akito Aizawa-san, Asakura-san, Kiyo-chan, my Chief Oda, my editors at Princess Comics like H'no-san, Sumiyoshi-san from Fake Graphics, and all you readers: thank you very much!

You Higuri's official website: Digital Higurin Database TIARA
www.youhiguri.com

Please send your fan letters and fan art to:

Go! Comi
28047 Dorothy Dr. Suite 200
Agoura Hills, CA 91301

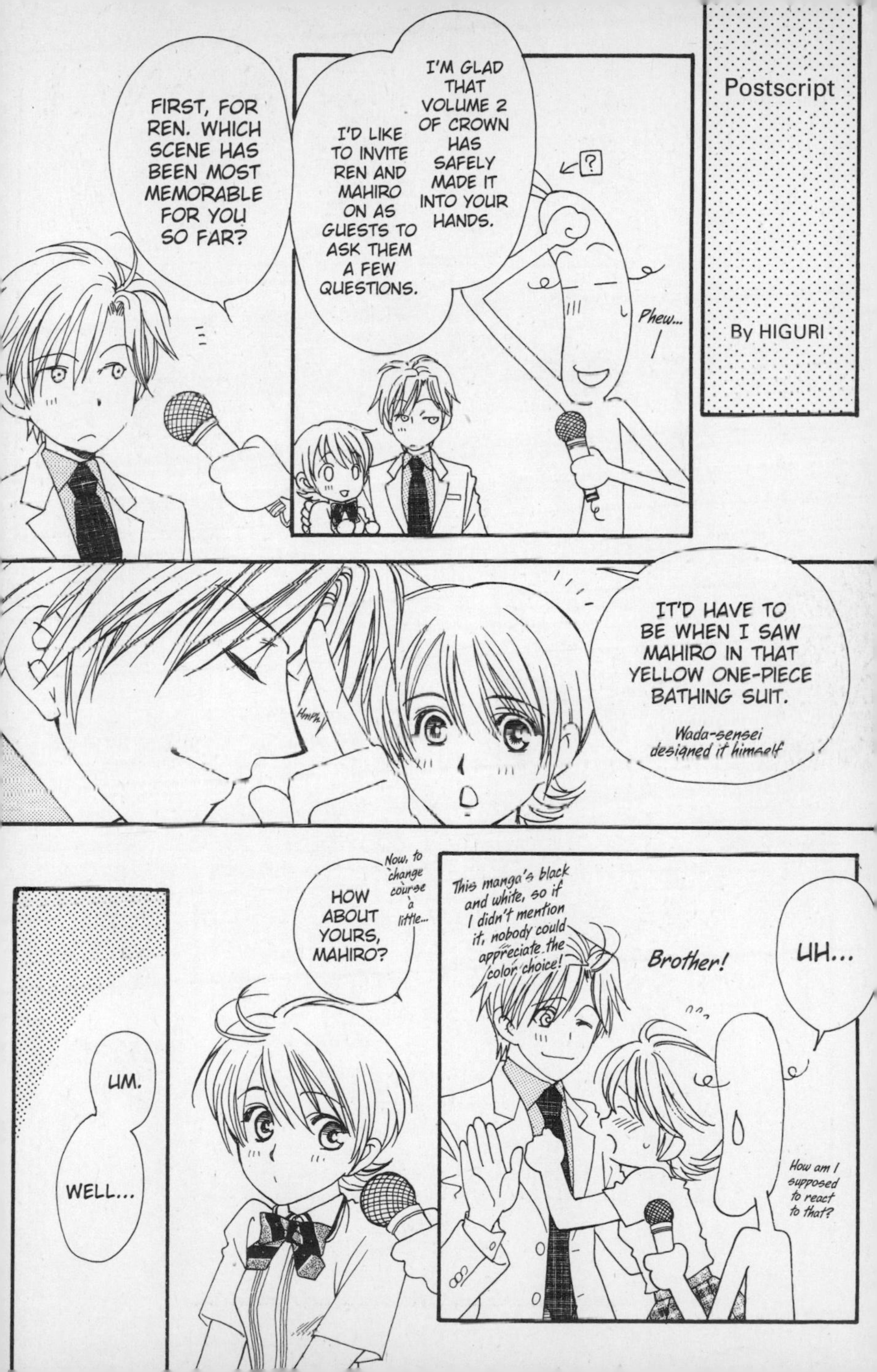
Postscript
By HIGURI
I'M GLAD THAT VOLUME 2 OF CROWN HAS SAFELY MADE IT INTO YOUR HANDS.
I'D LIKE TO INVITE REN AND MAHIRO ON AS GUESTS TO ASK THEM A FEW QUESTIONS.
?
Phew...
FIRST, FOR REN. WHICH SCENE HAS BEEN MOST MEMORABLE FOR YOU SO FAR?
IT'D HAVE TO BE WHEN I SAW MAHIRO IN THAT YELLOW ONE-PIECE BATHING SUIT.
Wada-sensei designed it himself
Hmph.
UH...
Brother!
This manga's black and white, so if I didn't mention it, nobody could appreciate the color choice!
How am I supposed to react to that?
Now, to change course a little...
HOW ABOUT YOURS, MAHIRO?
UM.
WELL...

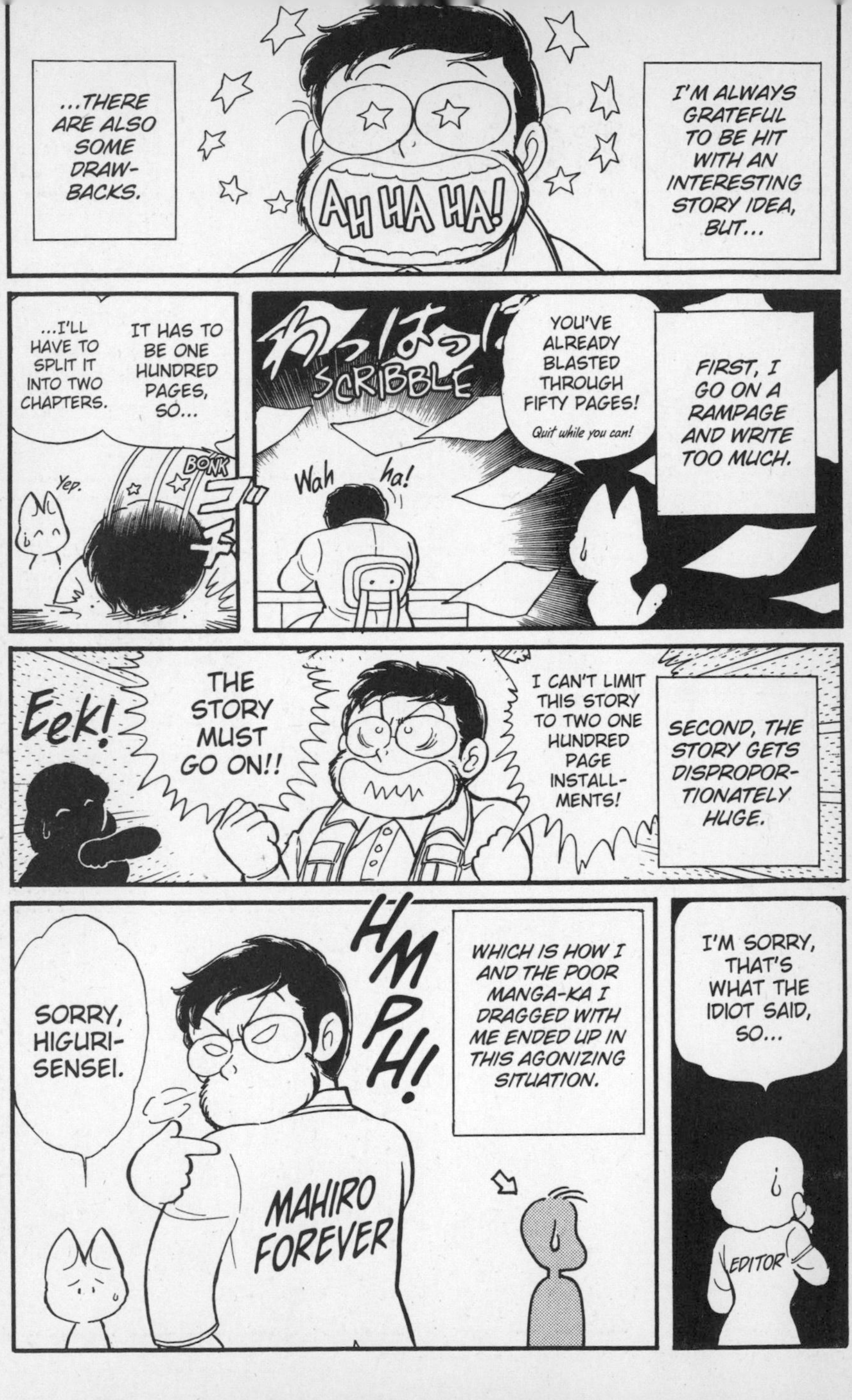
I'M ALWAYS GRATEFUL TO BE HIT WITH AN INTERESTING STORY IDEA, BUT...
AH HA HA!
...THERE ARE ALSO SOME DRAW-BACKS.
FIRST, I GO ON A RAMPAGE AND WRITE TOO MUCH.
YOU'VE ALREADY BLASTED THROUGH FIFTY PAGES!
Quit while you can!
わっはっ!
SCRIBBLE
Wah ha!
IT HAS TO BE ONE HUNDRED PAGES, SO...
...I'LL HAVE TO SPLIT IT INTO TWO CHAPTERS.
BONK
Yep.
SECOND, THE STORY GETS DISPROPORTIONATELY HUGE.
I CAN'T LIMIT THIS STORY TO TWO ONE HUNDRED PAGE INSTALLMENTS!
THE STORY MUST GO ON!!
Eek!
I'M SORRY, THAT'S WHAT THE IDIOT SAID, SO...
EDITOR
WHICH IS HOW I AND THE POOR MANGA-KA I DRAGGED WITH ME ENDED UP IN THIS AGONIZING SITUATION.
HMPH!
SORRY, HIGURI-SENSEI.
MAHIRO FOREVER

The Making of

"CROWN"

By the Author
Shinji Wada

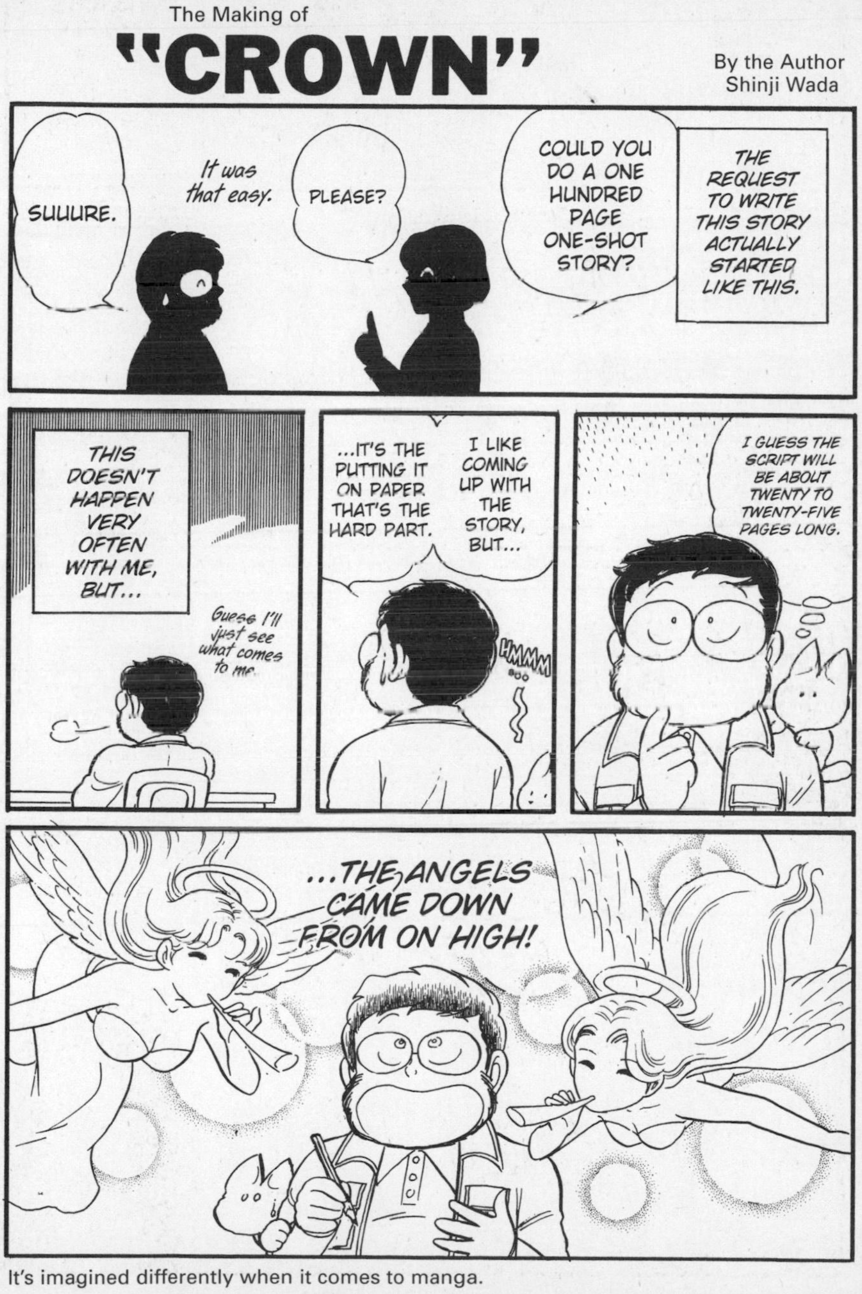
THE REQUEST TO WRITE THIS STORY ACTUALLY STARTED LIKE THIS.
COULD YOU DO A ONE HUNDRED PAGE ONE-SHOT STORY?
PLEASE?
It was that easy.
SUUURE.
I GUESS THE SCRIPT WILL BE ABOUT TWENTY TO TWENTY-FIVE PAGES LONG.
I LIKE COMING UP WITH THE STORY, BUT...
...IT'S THE PUTTING IT ON PAPER THAT'S THE HARD PART.
HMMM
THIS DOESN'T HAPPEN VERY OFTEN WITH ME, BUT...
Guess I'll just see what comes to me...
...THE ANGELS CAME DOWN FROM ON HIGH!

It's imagined differently when it comes to manga.

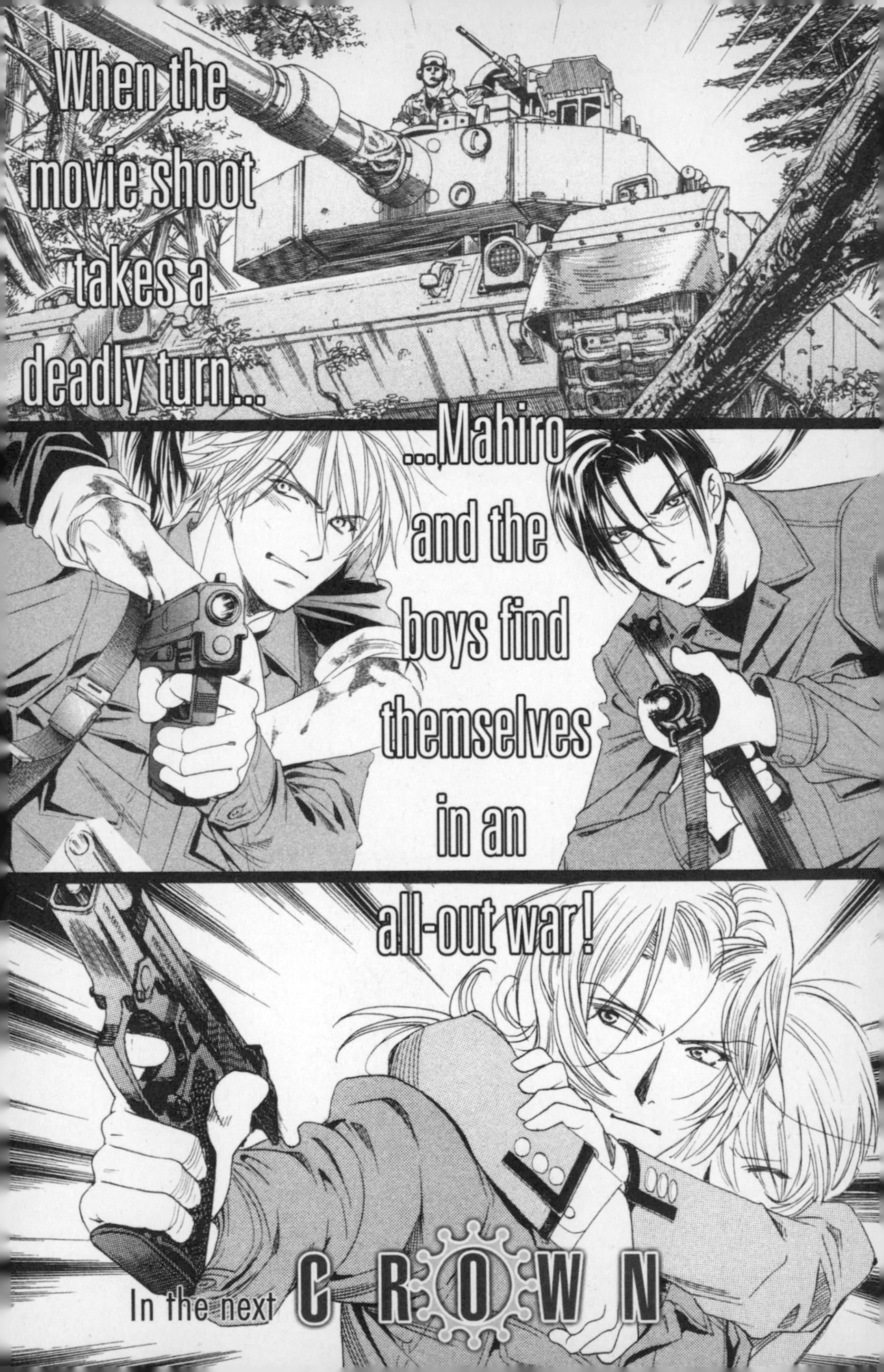
When the movie shoot takes a deadly turn...
...Mahiro and the boys find themselves in an all-out war!
In the next CROWN

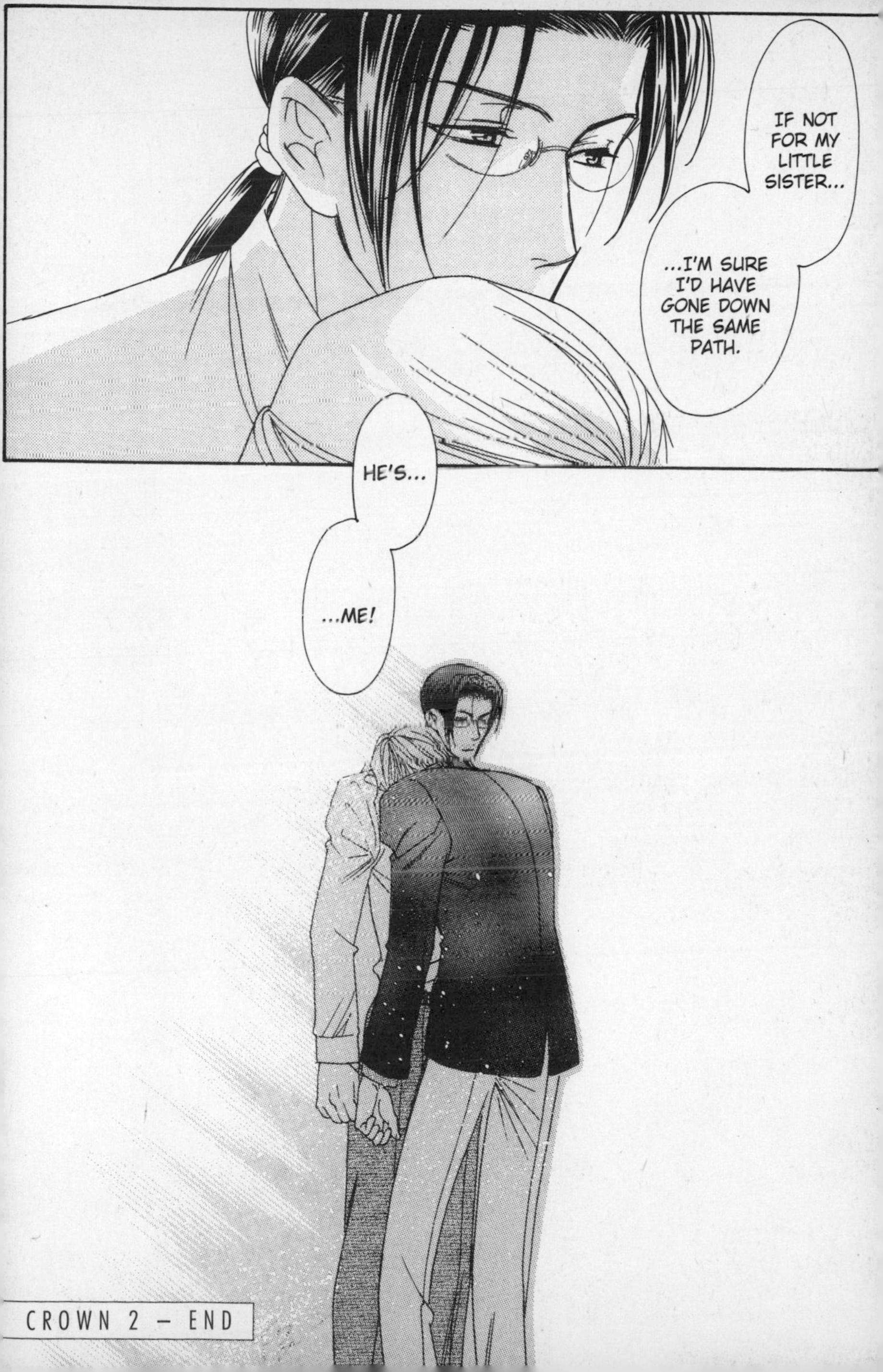
IF NOT FOR MY LITTLE SISTER...
...I'M SURE I'D HAVE GONE DOWN THE SAME PATH.
HE'S...
...ME!

CROWN 2 – END

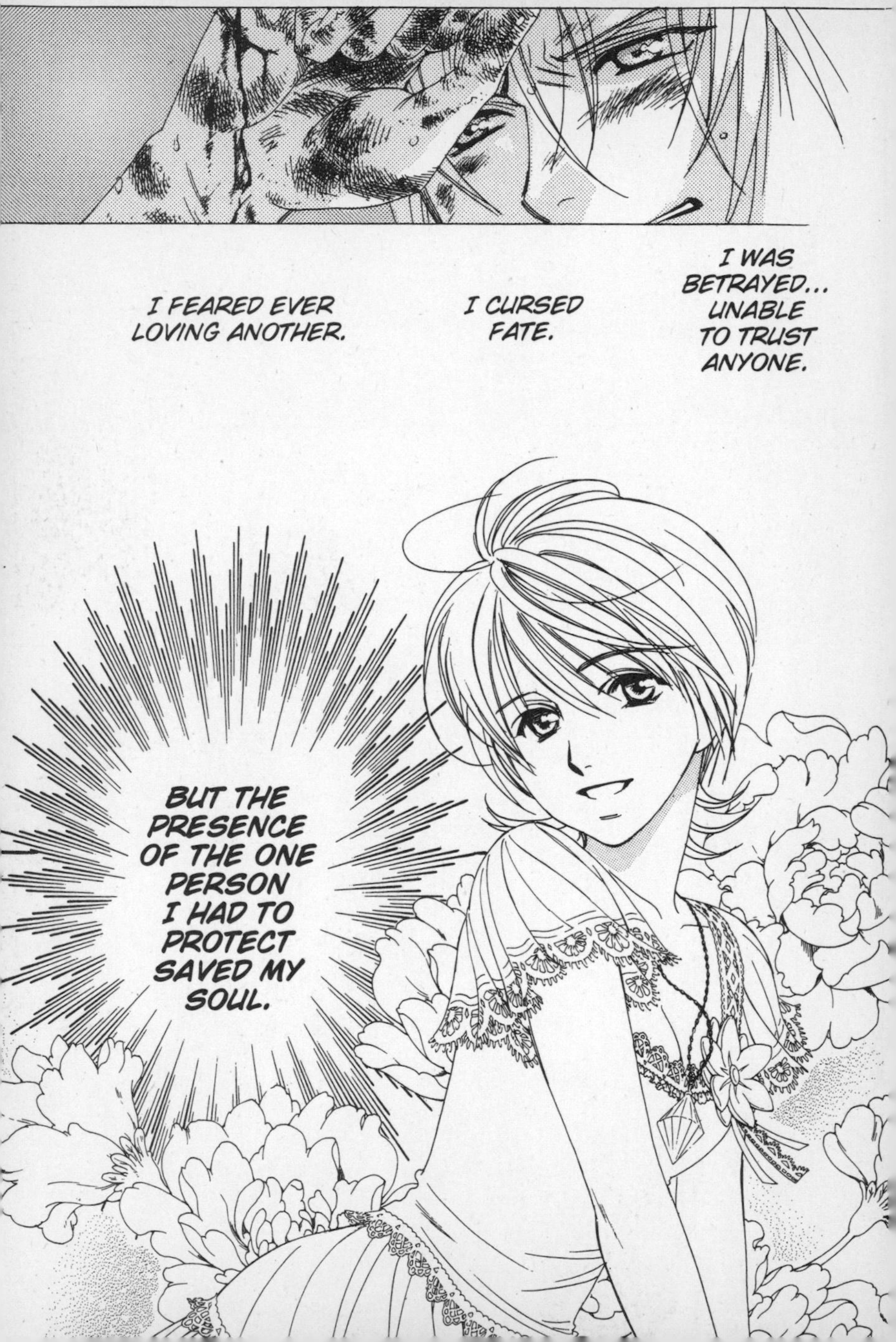
I WAS BETRAYED... UNABLE TO TRUST ANYONE.
I CURSED FATE.
I FEARED EVER LOVING ANOTHER.
BUT THE PRESENCE OF THE ONE PERSON I HAD TO PROTECT SAVED MY SOUL.

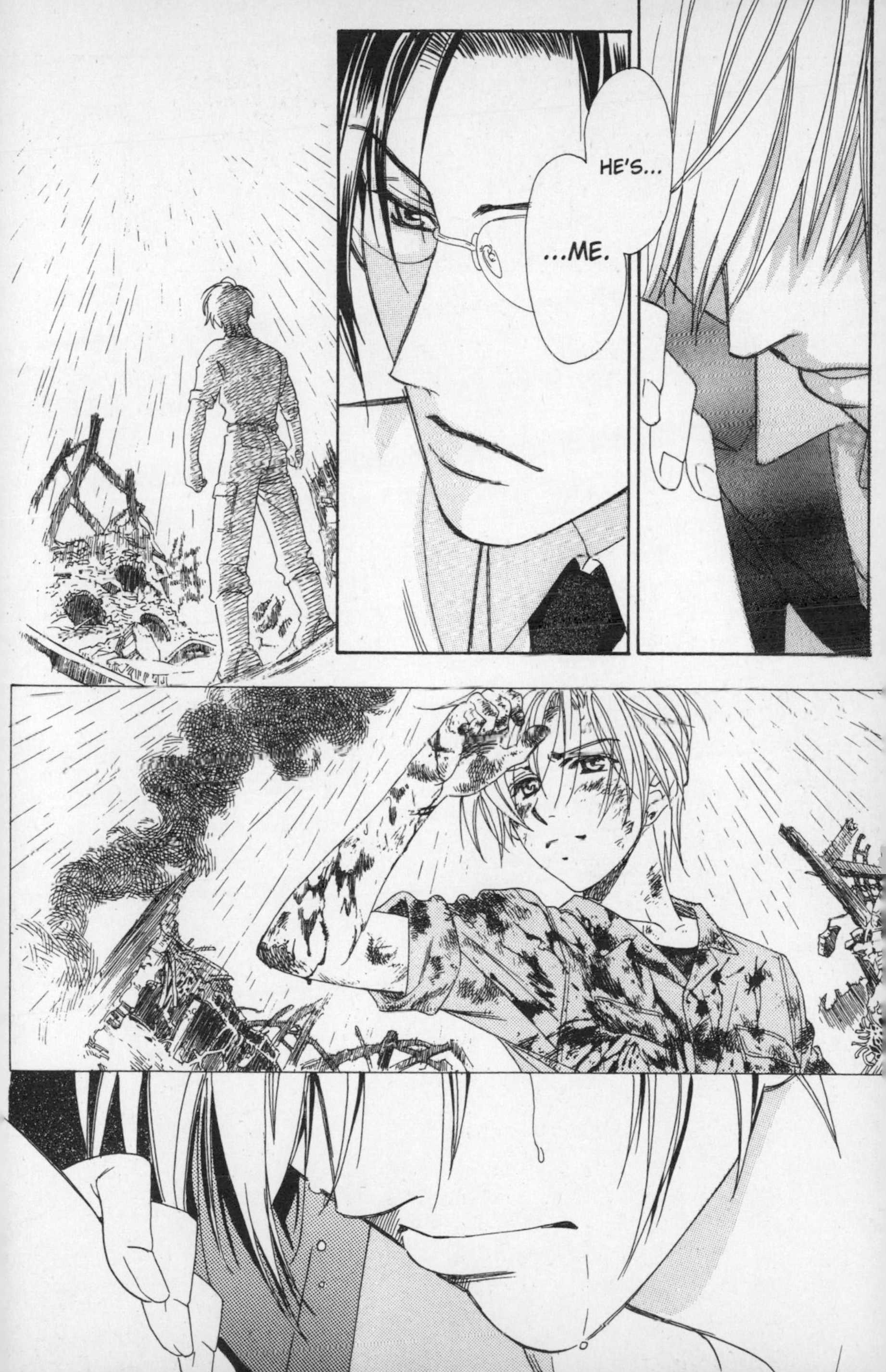
HE'S...
...ME.

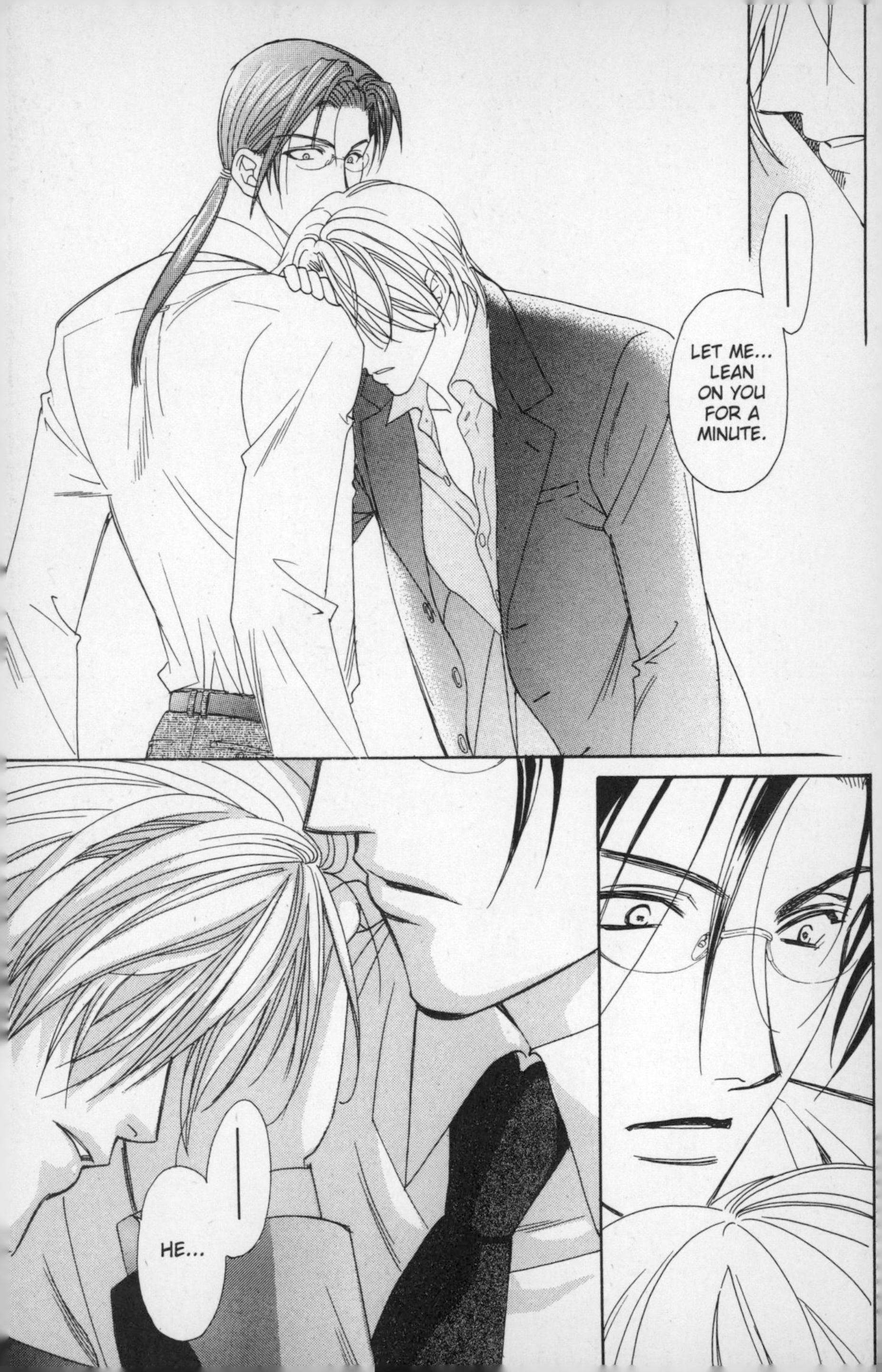

—
LET ME... LEAN ON YOU FOR A MINUTE.
—
HE...

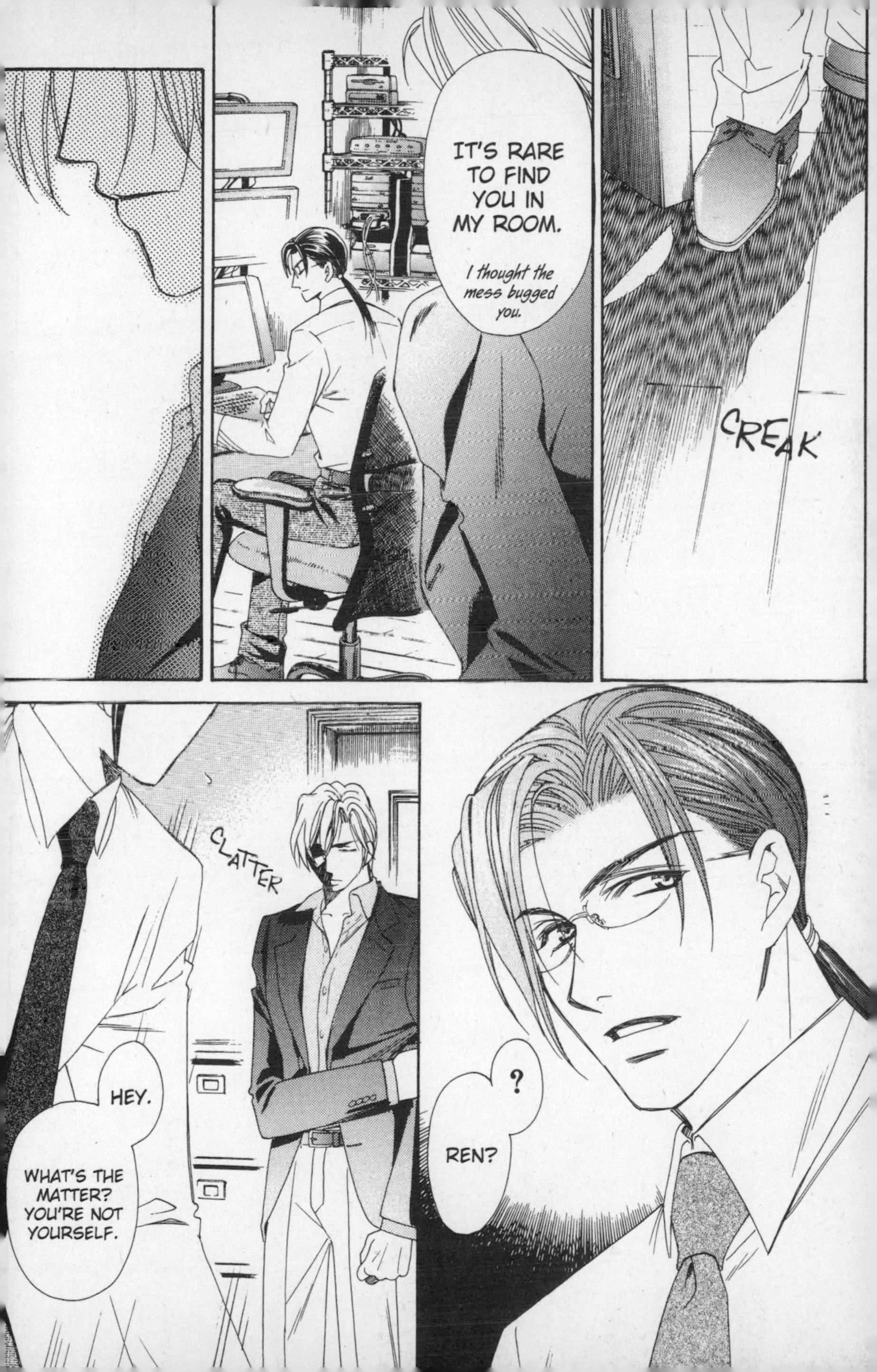

IT'S RARE TO FIND YOU IN MY ROOM.
I thought the mess bugged you.
CREAK
CLATTER
?
REN?
HEY.
WHAT'S THE MATTER? YOU'RE NOT YOURSELF.

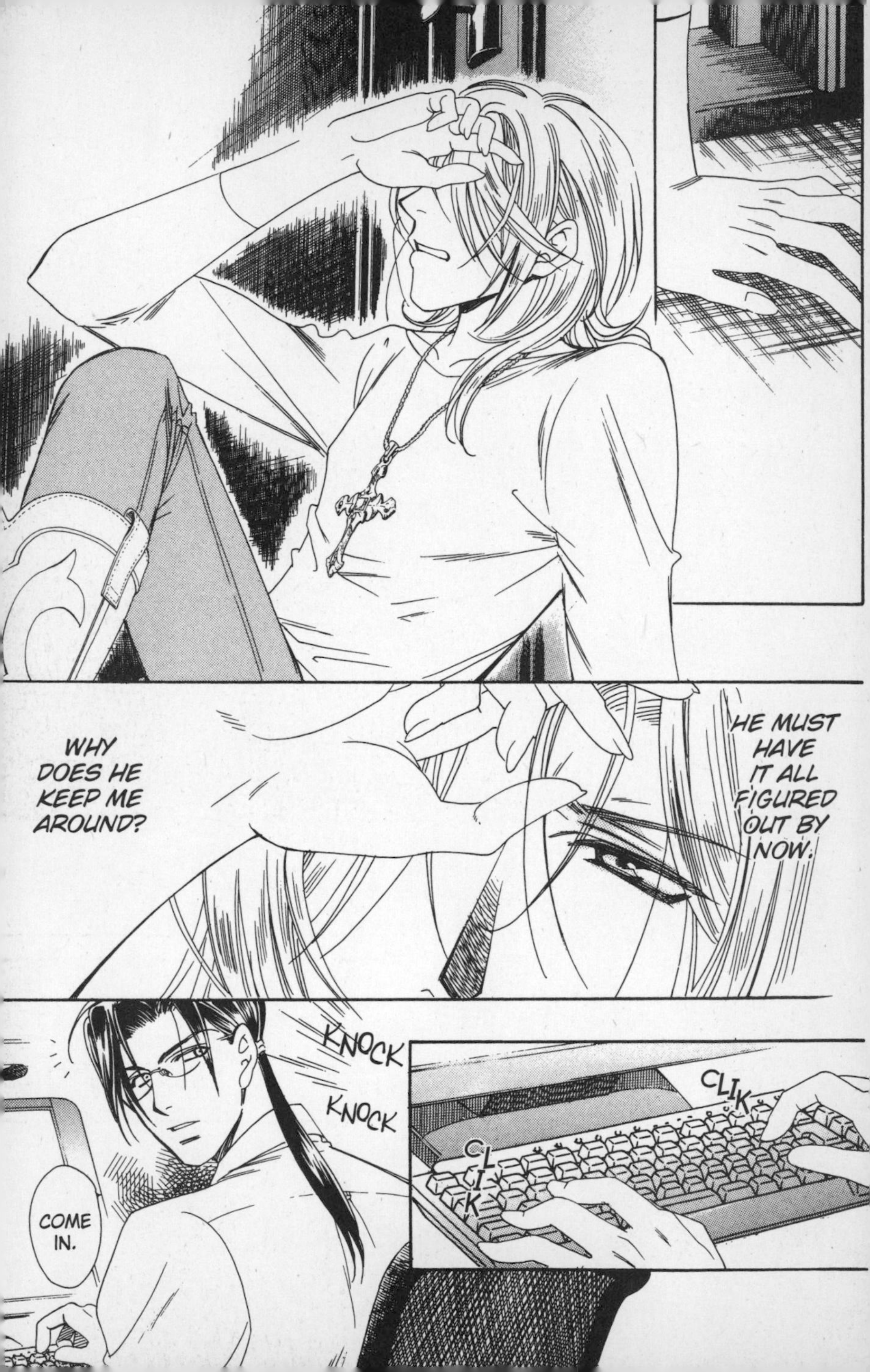
HE MUST HAVE IT ALL FIGURED OUT BY NOW.
WHY DOES HE KEEP ME AROUND?
CLIK
CLIK
KNOCK
KNOCK
COME IN.

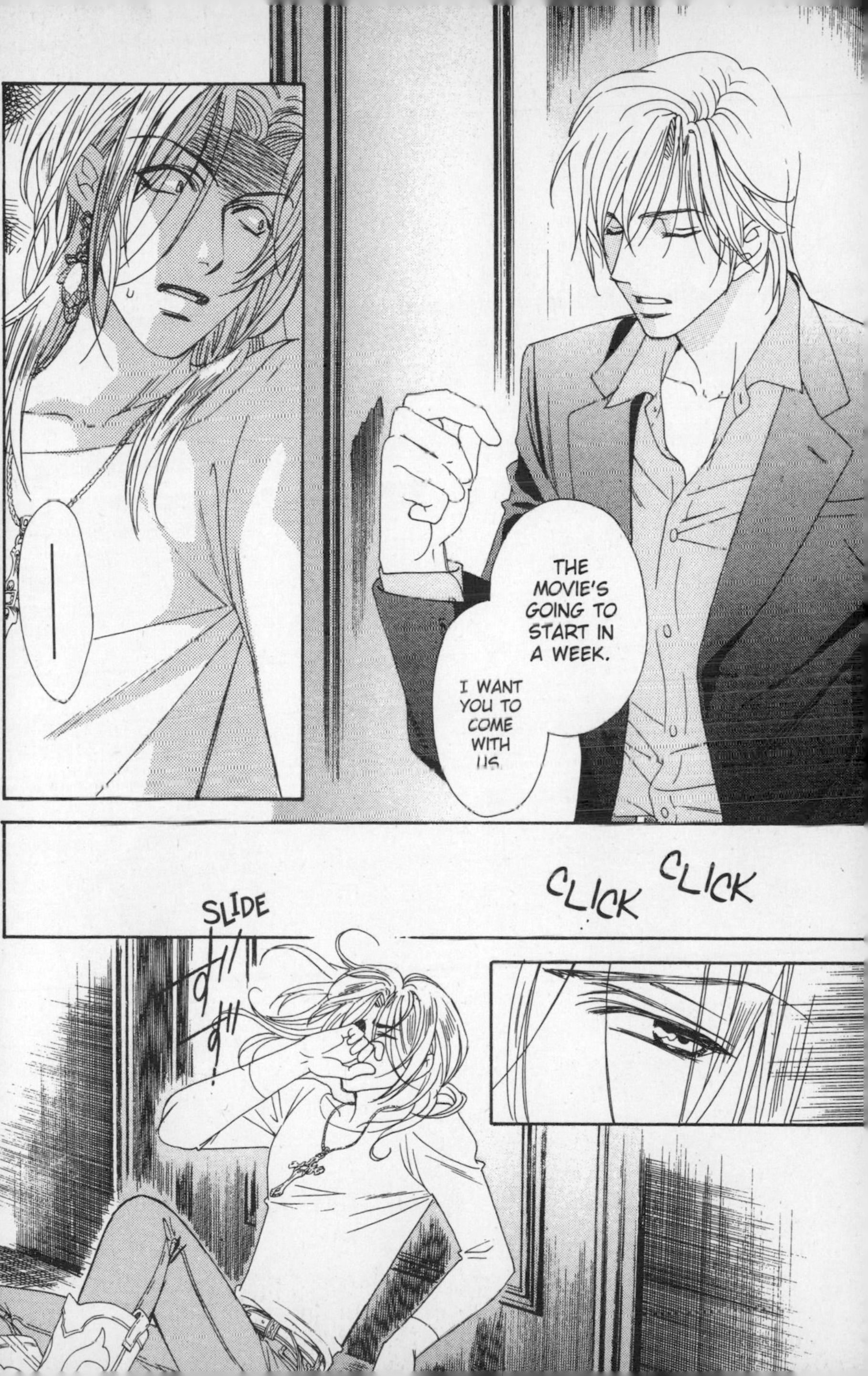

THE MOVIE'S GOING TO START IN A WEEK.
I WANT YOU TO COME WITH US.
CLICK
CLICK
SLIDE

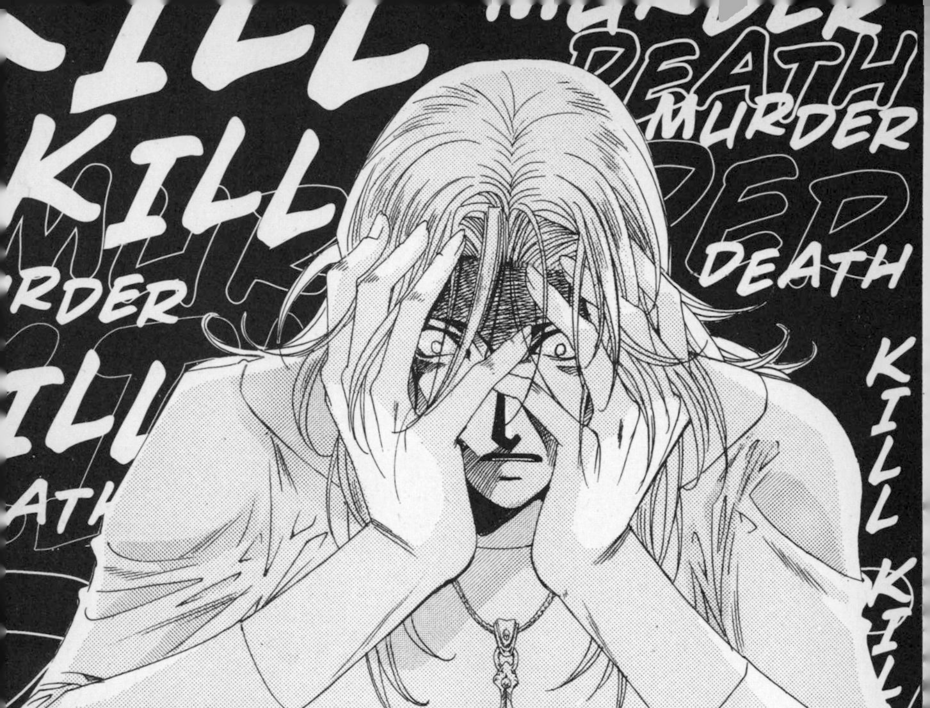
KILL
MURDER
DEATH
MURDER
DEATH
KILL
RDER
DEATH
KILL KILL
KILL THEM ALL

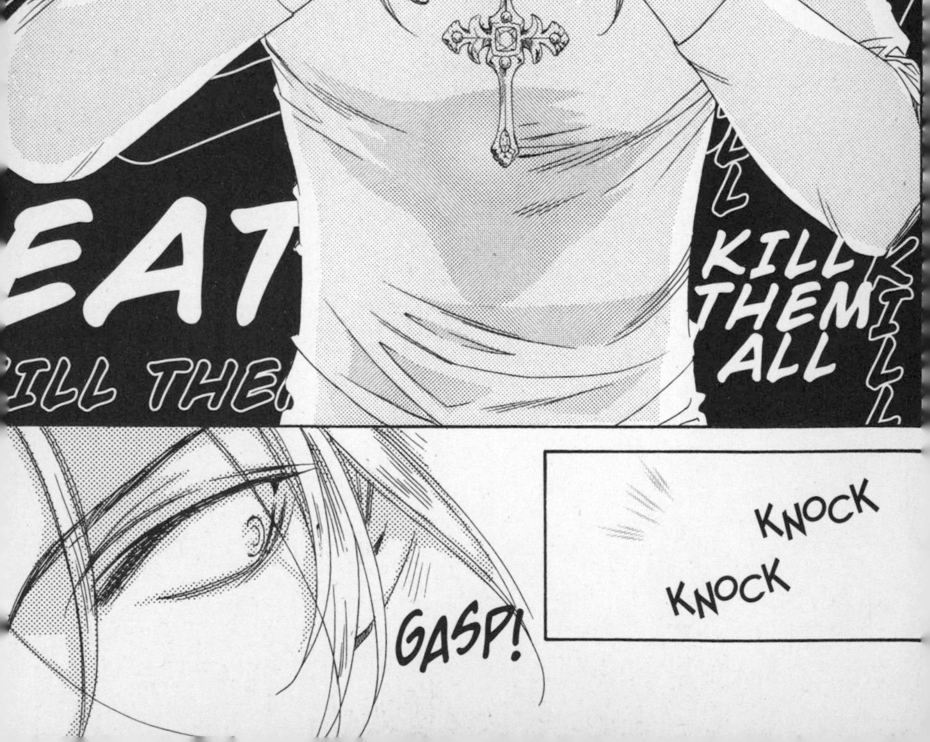
KNOCK
KNOCK
GASP!

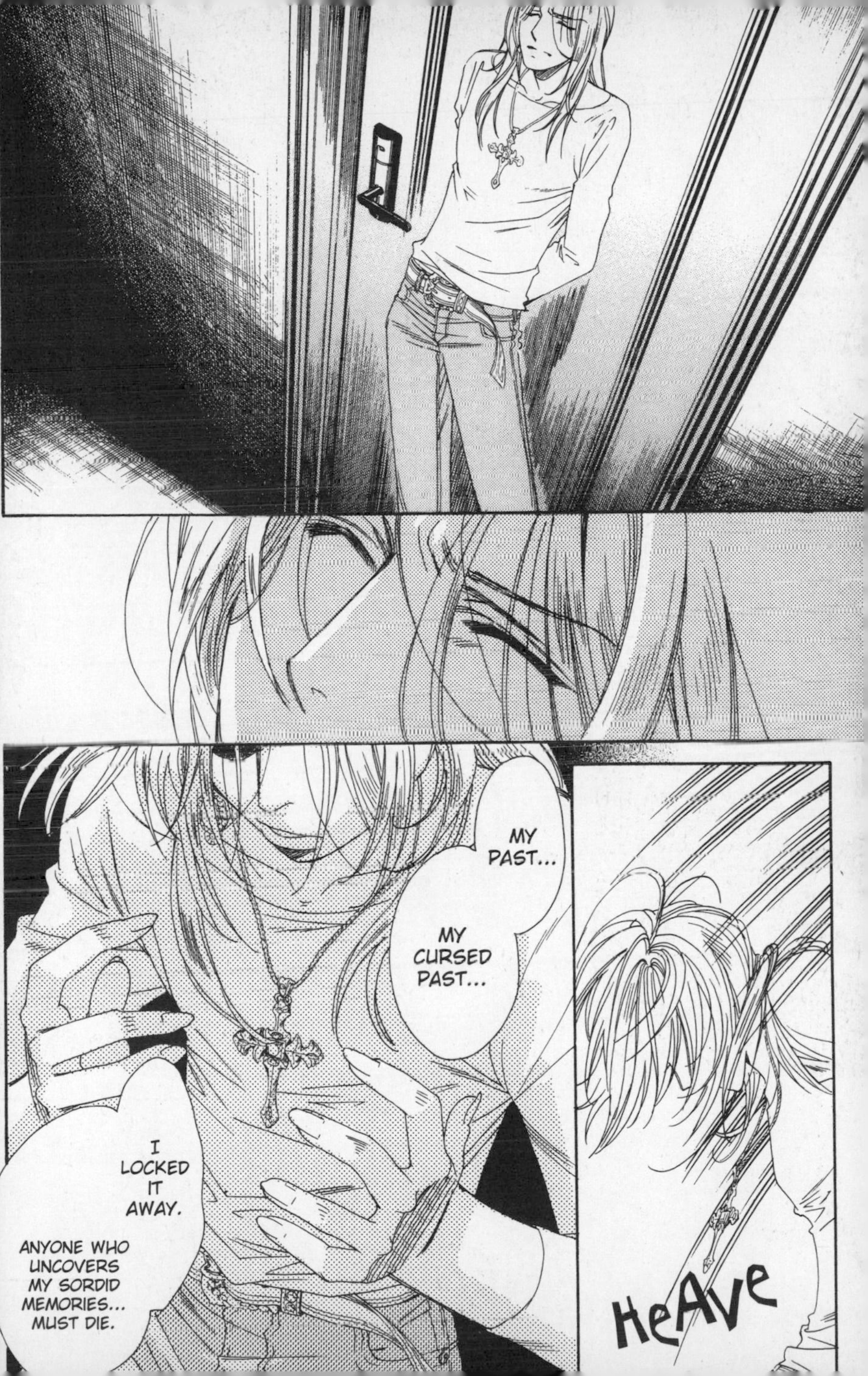
MY PAST...
MY CURSED PAST...
I LOCKED IT AWAY.
ANYONE WHO UNCOVERS MY SORDID MEMORIES... MUST DIE.
HEAVE

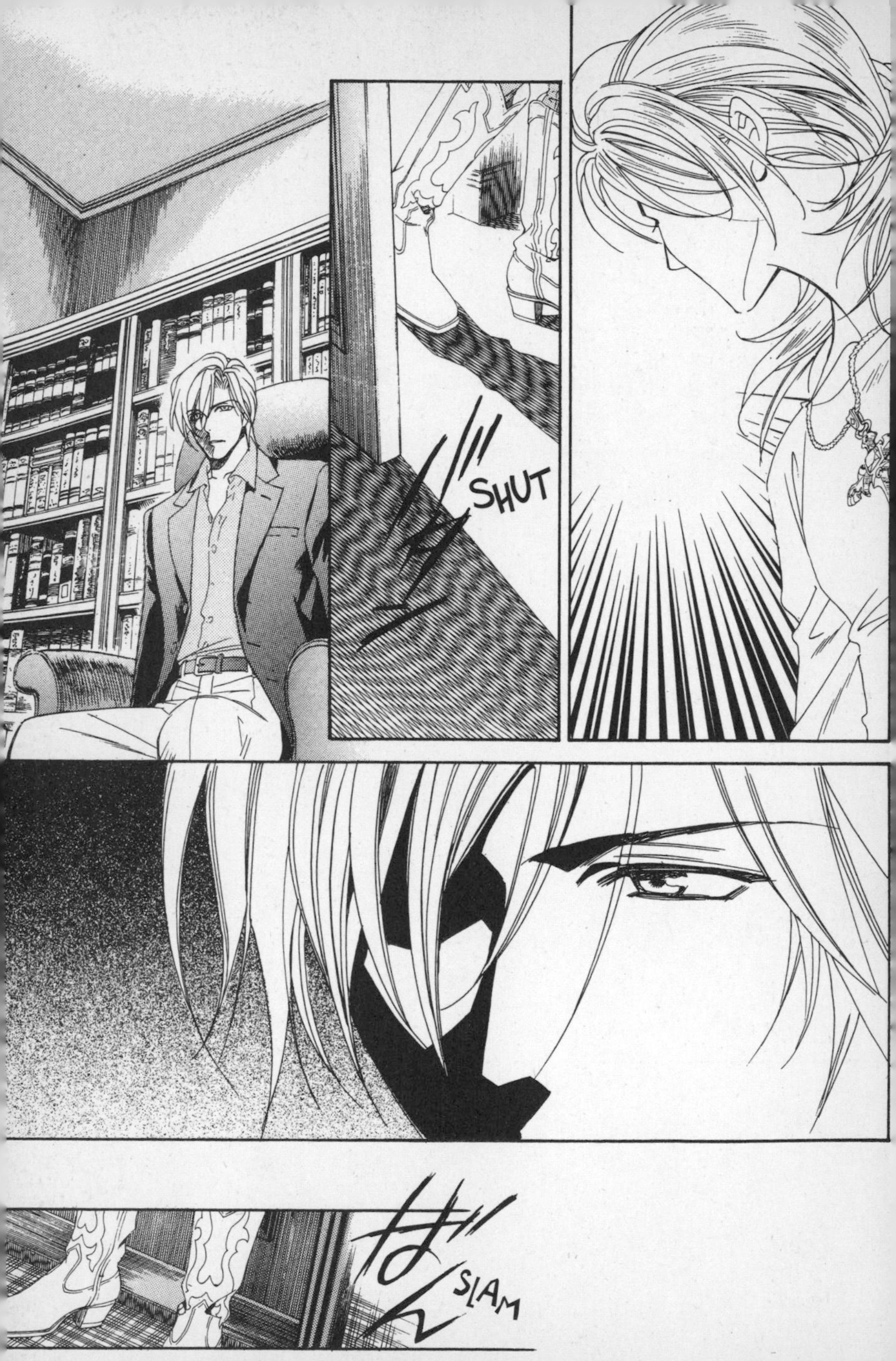
SHUT
SLAM

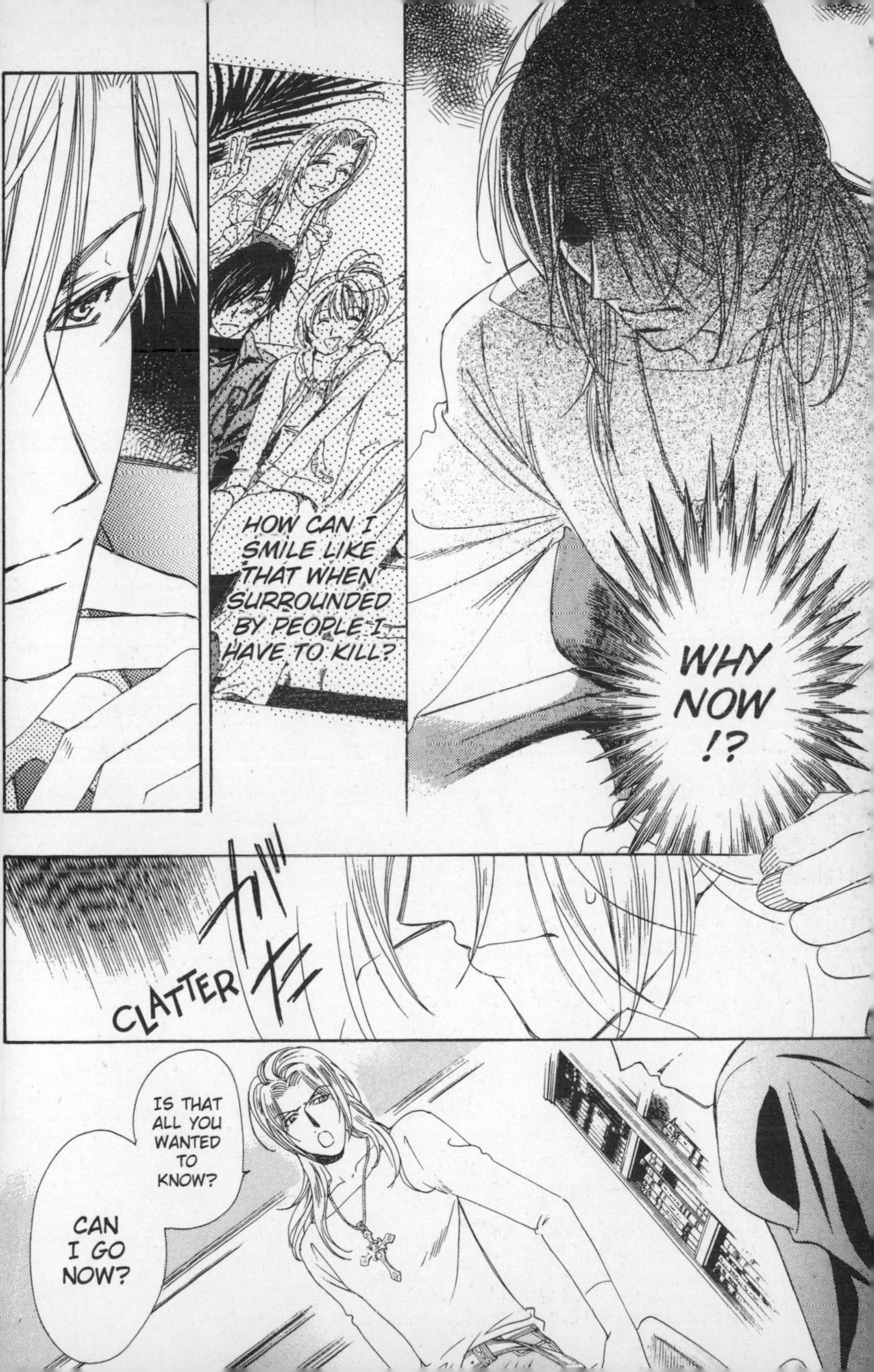
WHY NOW !?
HOW CAN I SMILE LIKE THAT WHEN SURROUNDED BY PEOPLE I HAVE TO KILL?
CLATTER
IS THAT ALL YOU WANTED TO KNOW?
CAN I GO NOW?

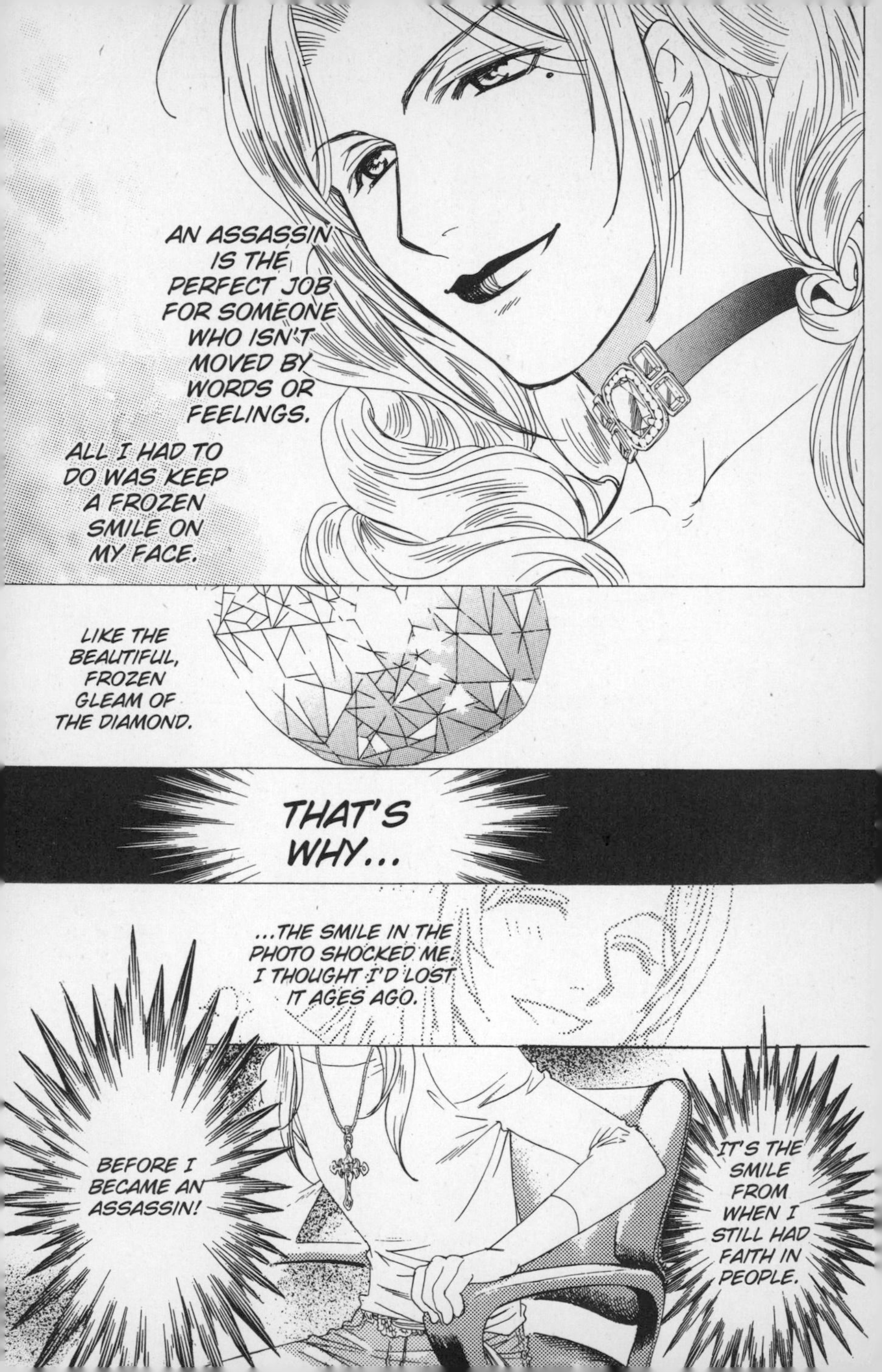
AN ASSASSIN IS THE PERFECT JOB FOR SOMEONE WHO ISN'T MOVED BY WORDS OR FEELINGS.
ALL I HAD TO DO WAS KEEP A FROZEN SMILE ON MY FACE.
LIKE THE BEAUTIFUL, FROZEN GLEAM OF THE DIAMOND.
THAT'S WHY...
...THE SMILE IN THE PHOTO SHOCKED ME. I THOUGHT I'D LOST IT AGES AGO.
IT'S THE SMILE FROM WHEN I STILL HAD FAITH IN PEOPLE.
BEFORE I BECAME AN ASSASSIN!

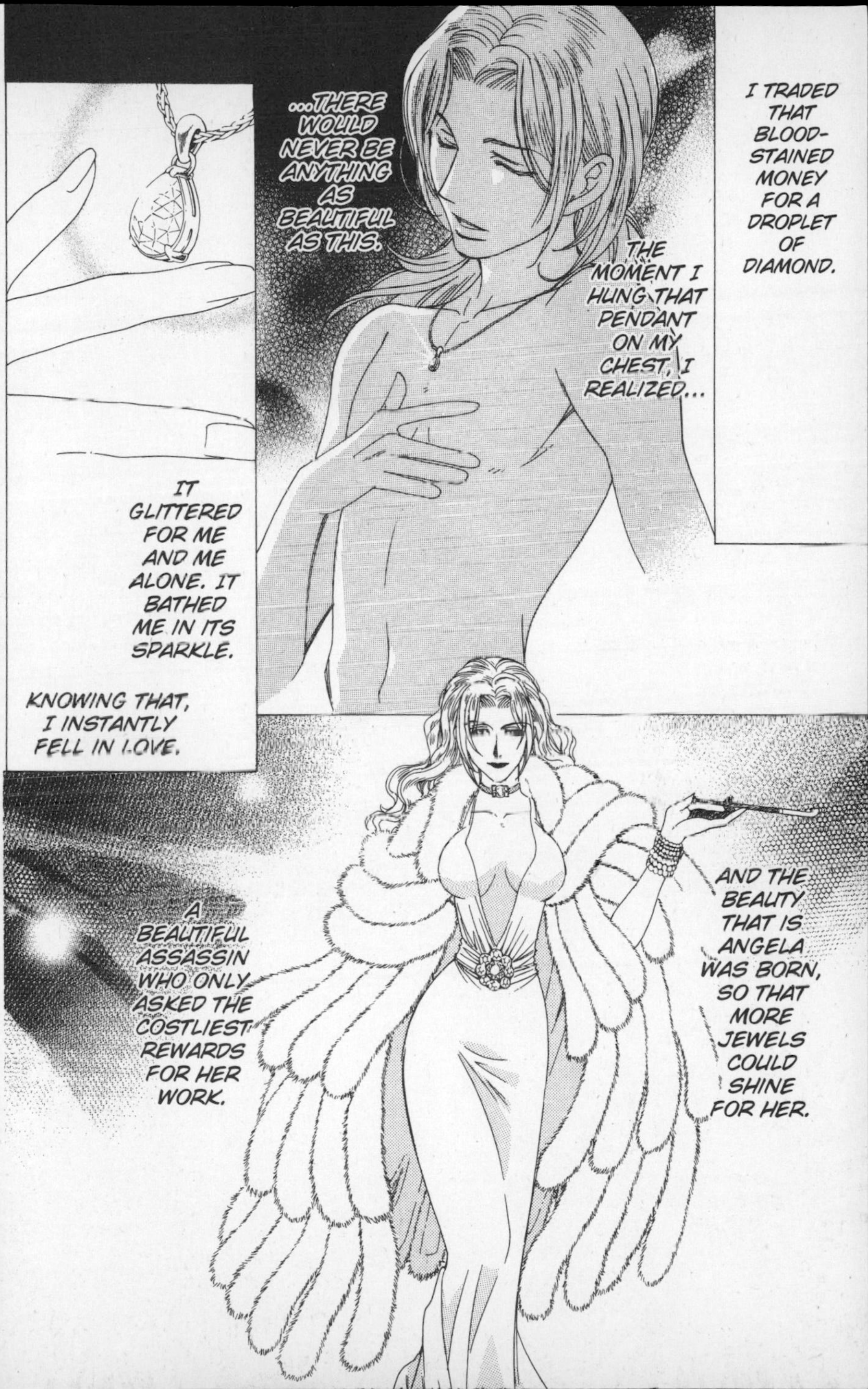
I TRADED THAT BLOOD-STAINED MONEY FOR A DROPLET OF DIAMOND.
THE MOMENT I HUNG THAT PENDANT ON MY CHEST, I REALIZED...
...THERE WOULD NEVER BE ANYTHING AS BEAUTIFUL AS THIS.
IT GLITTERED FOR ME AND ME ALONE. IT BATHED ME IN ITS SPARKLE.
KNOWING THAT, I INSTANTLY FELL IN LOVE.
AND THE BEAUTY THAT IS ANGELA WAS BORN, SO THAT MORE JEWELS COULD SHINE FOR HER.
A BEAUTIFUL ASSASSIN WHO ONLY ASKED THE COSTLIEST REWARDS FOR HER WORK.

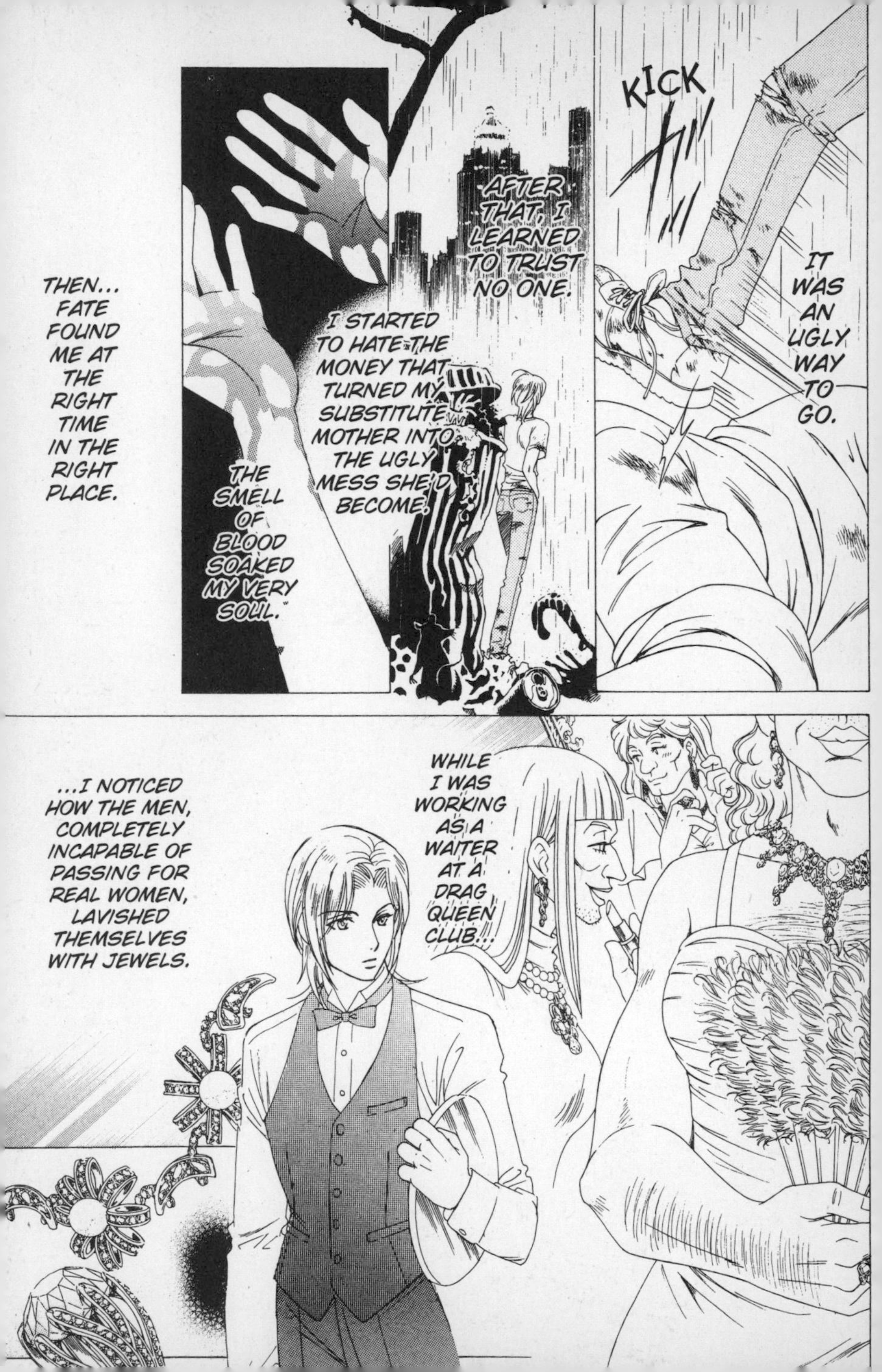
KICK
IT WAS AN UGLY WAY TO GO.
AFTER THAT, I LEARNED TO TRUST NO ONE.
I STARTED TO HATE THE MONEY THAT TURNED MY SUBSTITUTE MOTHER INTO THE UGLY MESS SHE'D BECOME.
THE SMELL OF BLOOD SOAKED MY VERY SOUL.
THEN... FATE FOUND ME AT THE RIGHT TIME IN THE RIGHT PLACE.
WHILE I WAS WORKING AS A WAITER AT A DRAG QUEEN CLUB...
...I NOTICED HOW THE MEN, COMPLETELY INCAPABLE OF PASSING FOR REAL WOMEN, LAVISHED THEMSELVES WITH JEWELS.

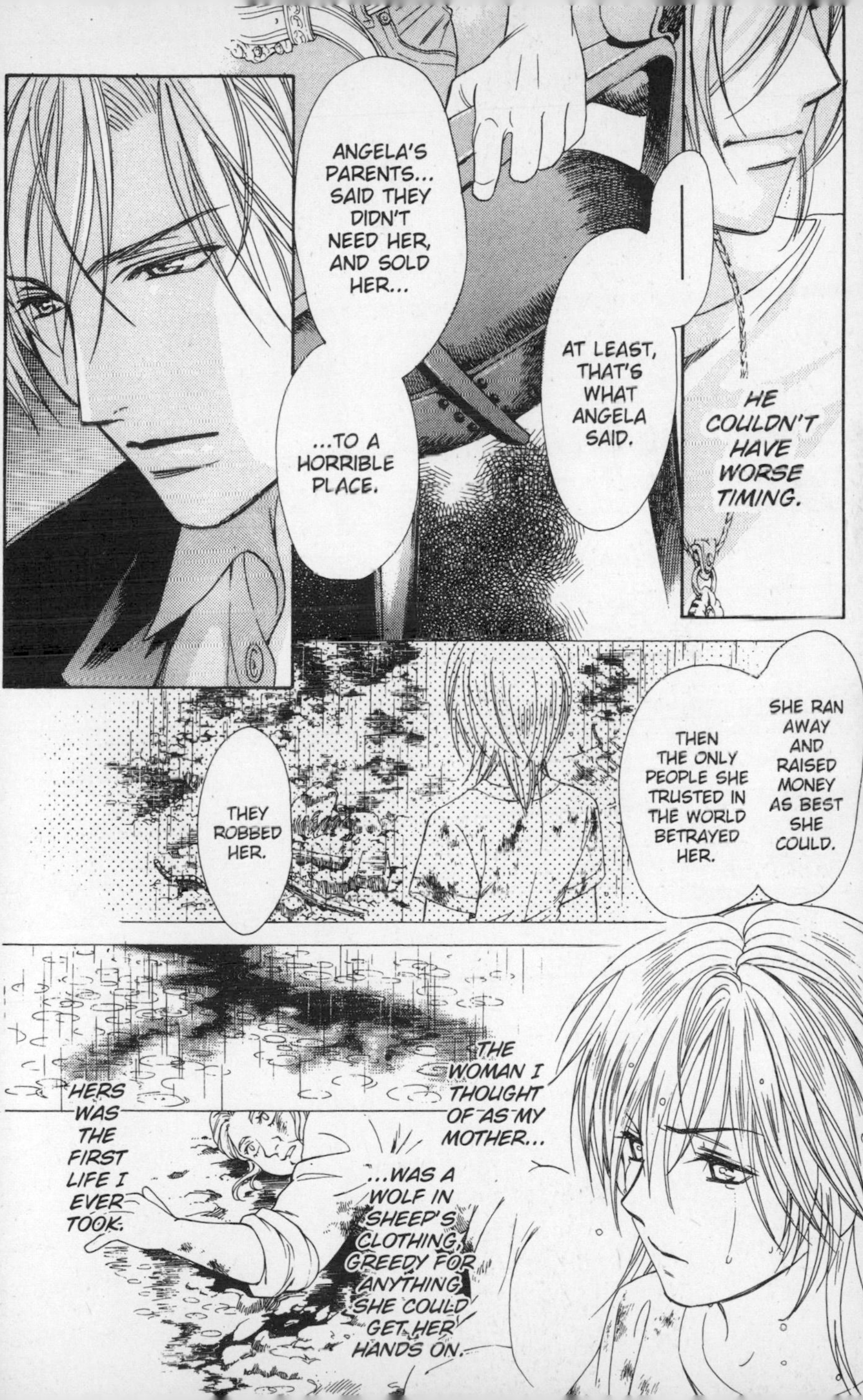
HE COULDN'T HAVE WORSE TIMING.
AT LEAST, THAT'S WHAT ANGELA SAID.
ANGELA'S PARENTS... SAID THEY DIDN'T NEED HER, AND SOLD HER...
...TO A HORRIBLE PLACE.
SHE RAN AWAY AND RAISED MONEY AS BEST SHE COULD.
THEN THE ONLY PEOPLE SHE TRUSTED IN THE WORLD BETRAYED HER.
THEY ROBBED HER.
THE WOMAN I THOUGHT OF AS MY MOTHER...
...WAS A WOLF IN SHEEP'S CLOTHING, GREEDY FOR ANYTHING SHE COULD GET HER HANDS ON.
HERS WAS THE FIRST LIFE I EVER TOOK.

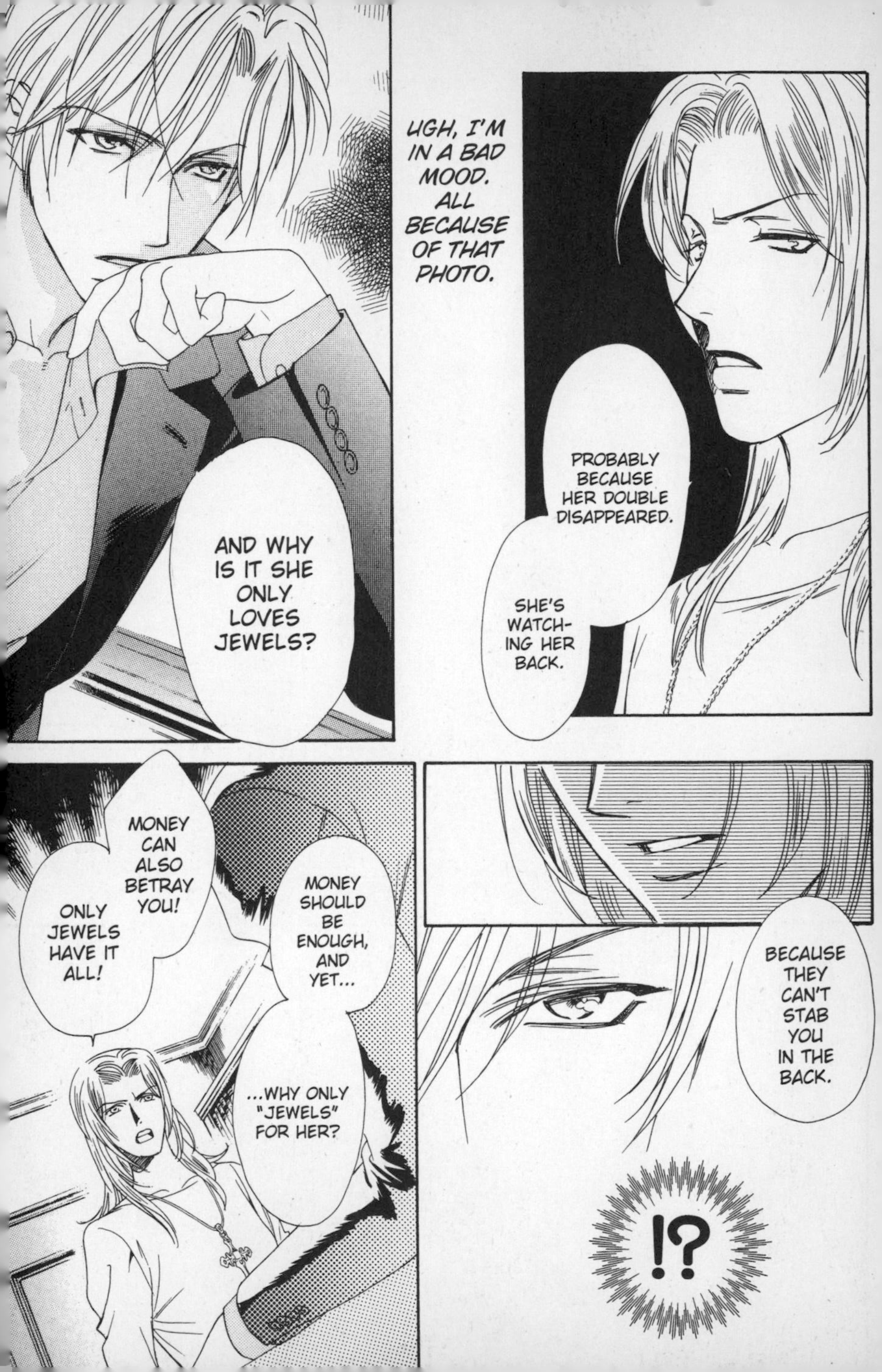
UGH, I'M IN A BAD MOOD. ALL BECAUSE OF THAT PHOTO.
PROBABLY BECAUSE HER DOUBLE DISAPPEARED.
SHE'S WATCH-ING HER BACK.
AND WHY IS IT SHE ONLY LOVES JEWELS?
BECAUSE THEY CAN'T STAB YOU IN THE BACK.
!?
MONEY SHOULD BE ENOUGH, AND YET...
...WHY ONLY "JEWELS" FOR HER?
MONEY CAN ALSO BETRAY YOU!
ONLY JEWELS HAVE IT ALL!

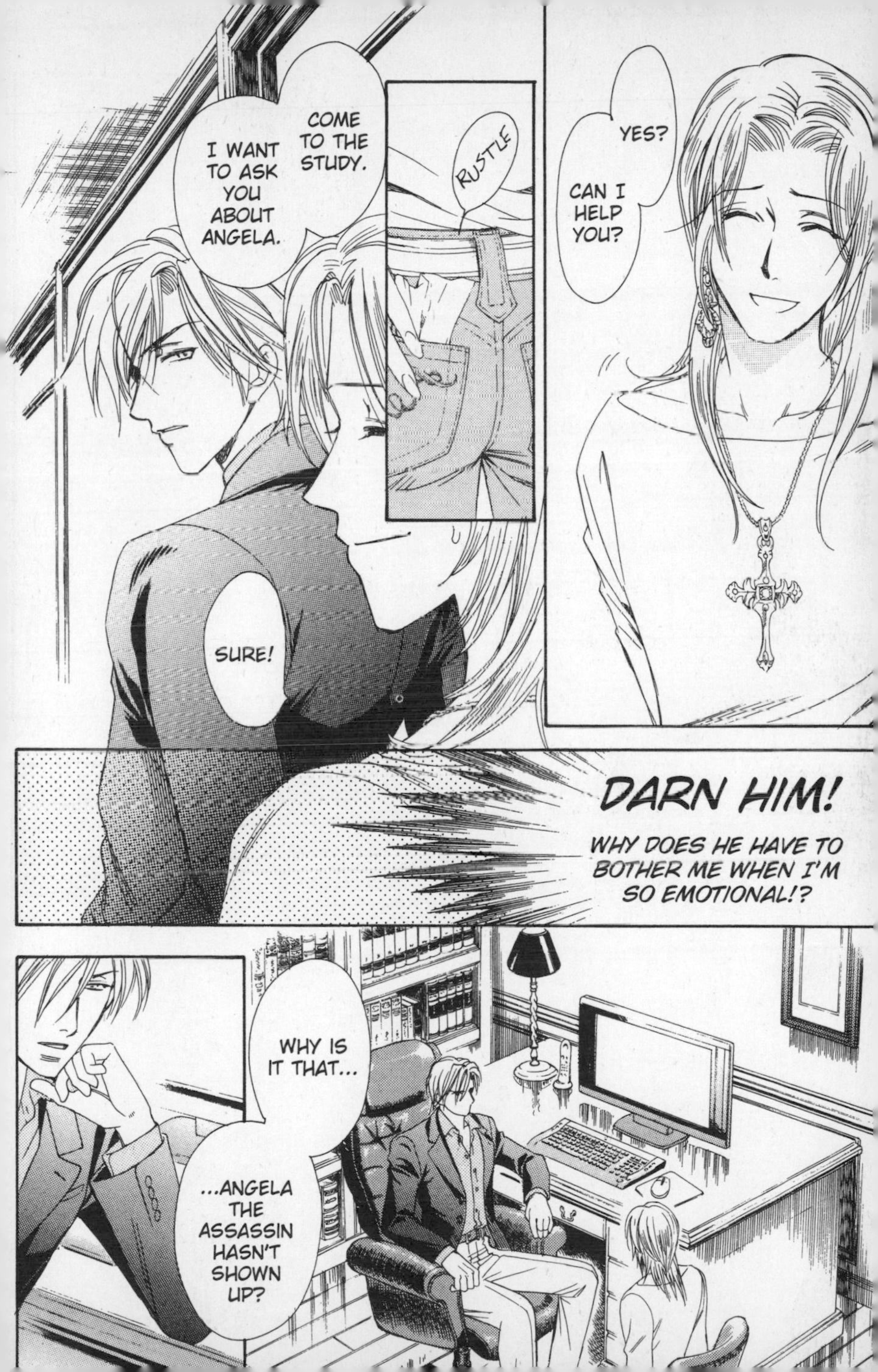
YES?
CAN I HELP YOU?
RUSTLE
COME TO THE STUDY.
I WANT TO ASK YOU ABOUT ANGELA.
SURE!
DARN HIM!
WHY DOES HE HAVE TO BOTHER ME WHEN I'M SO EMOTIONAL!?
WHY IS IT THAT...
...ANGELA THE ASSASSIN HASN'T SHOWN UP?

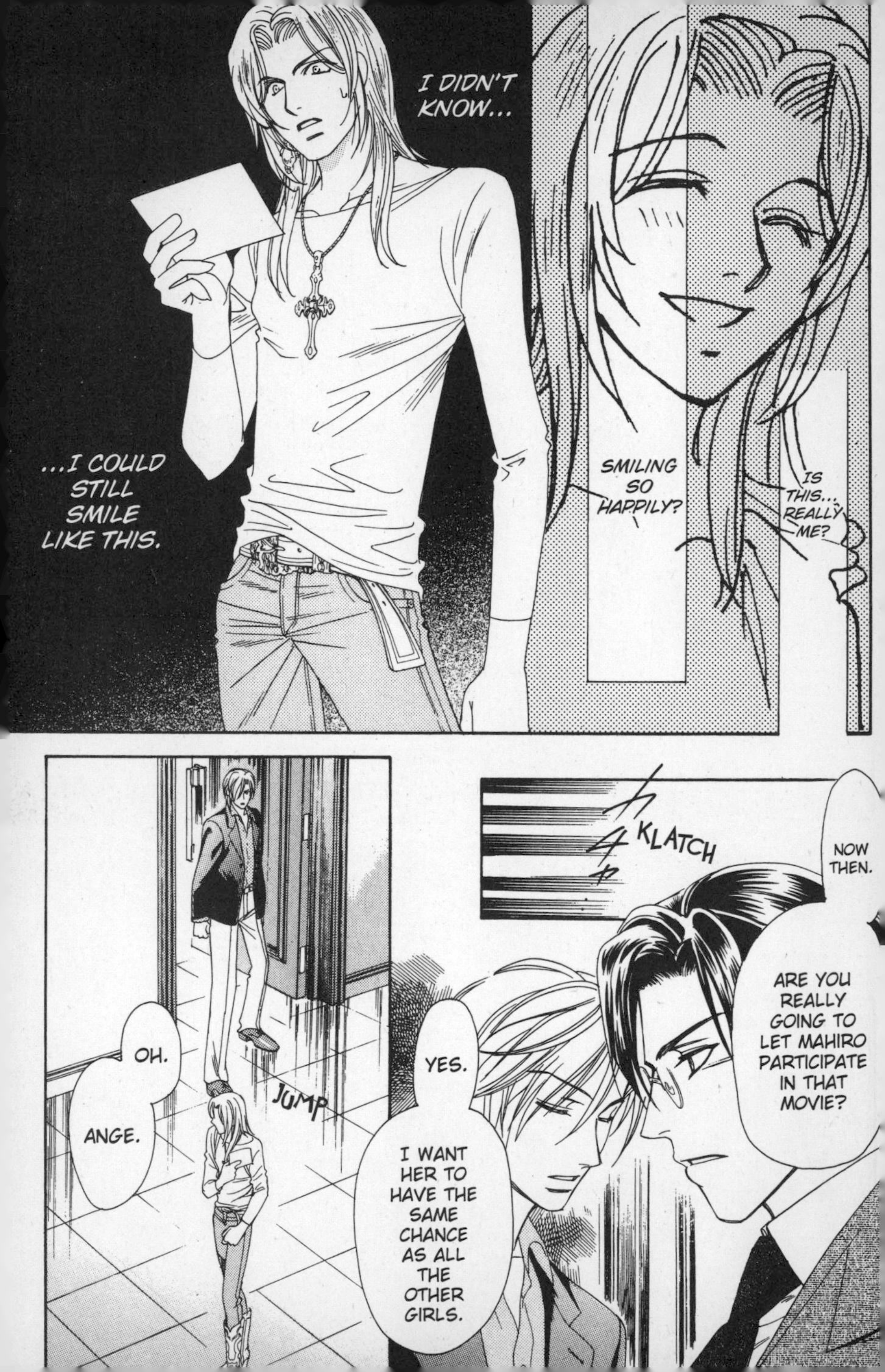
IS THIS... REALLY ME?
SMILING SO HAPPILY?
I DIDN'T KNOW...
...I COULD STILL SMILE LIKE THIS.
KLATCH
NOW THEN.
ARE YOU REALLY GOING TO LET MAHIRO PARTICIPATE IN THAT MOVIE?
YES.
I WANT HER TO HAVE THE SAME CHANCE AS ALL THE OTHER GIRLS.
JUMP
OH.
ANGE.

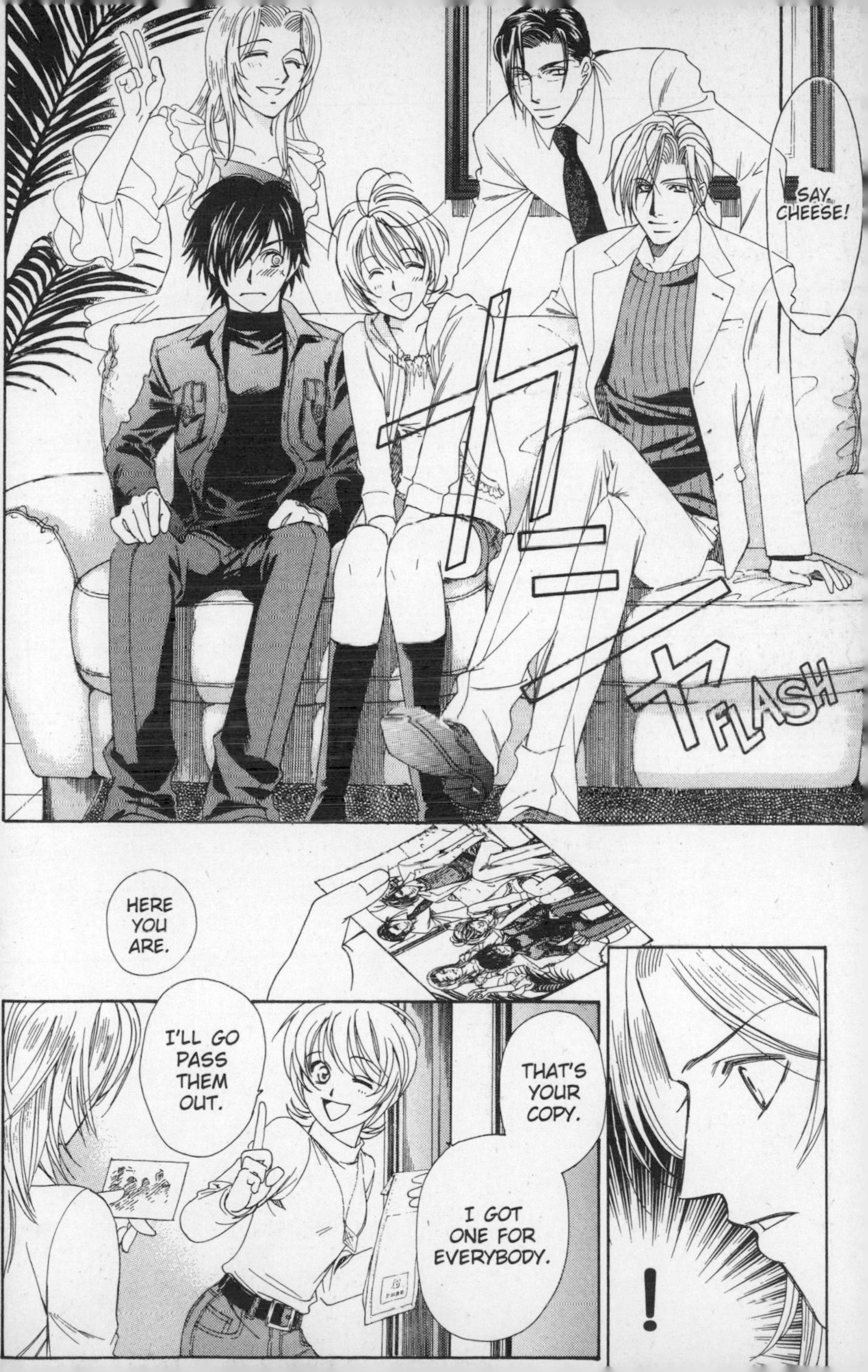

SAY CHEESE!
FLASH
HERE YOU ARE.
THAT'S YOUR COPY.
I GOT ONE FOR EVERYBODY.
I'LL GO PASS THEM OUT.
!

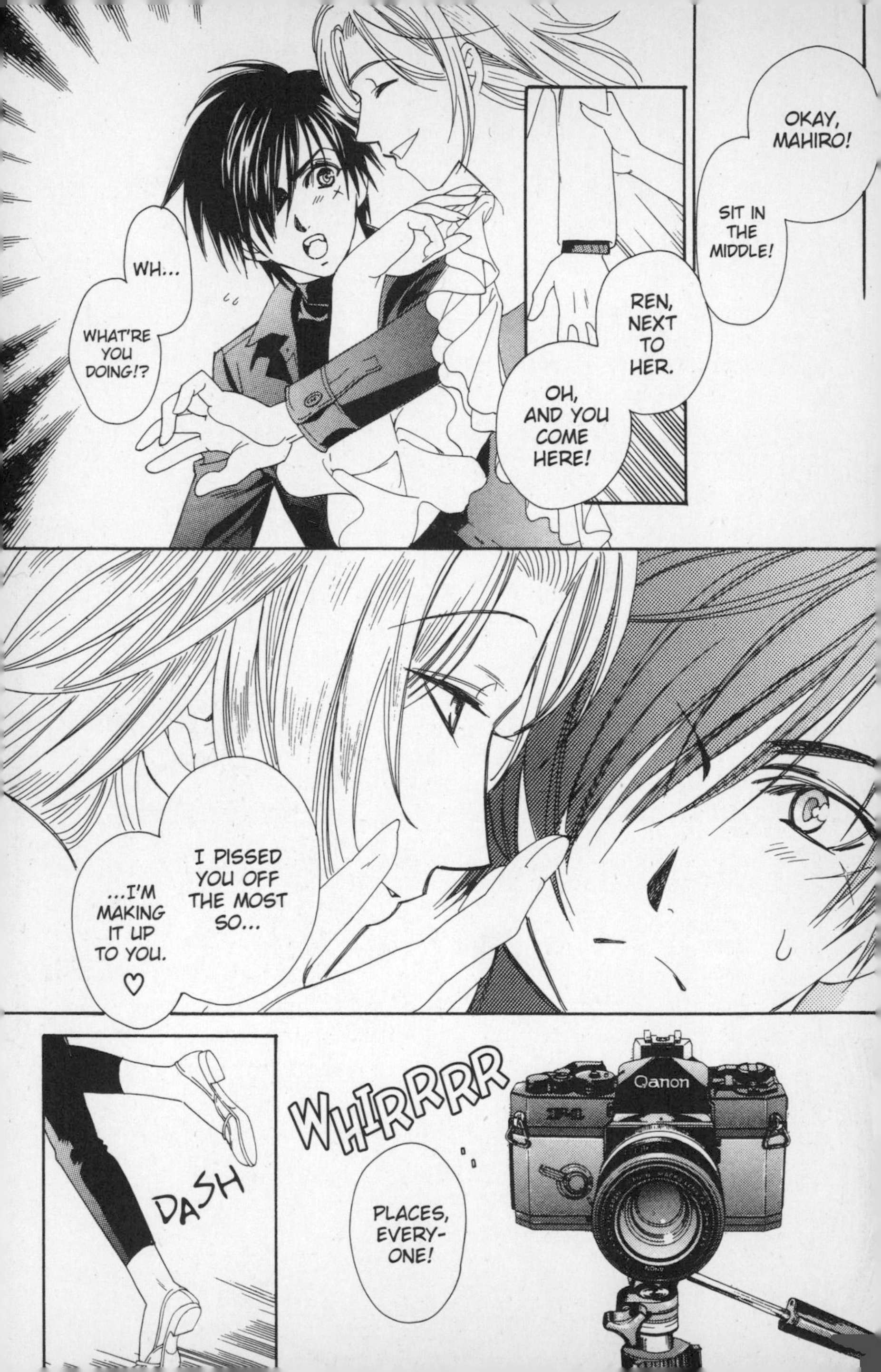
OKAY, MAHIRO!
SIT IN THE MIDDLE!
REN, NEXT TO HER.
OH, AND YOU COME HERE!
WH...
WHAT'RE YOU DOING!?
I PISSED YOU OFF THE MOST SO...
...I'M MAKING IT UP TO YOU. ♡
Qanon
WHIRRRR
PLACES, EVERY-ONE!
DASH

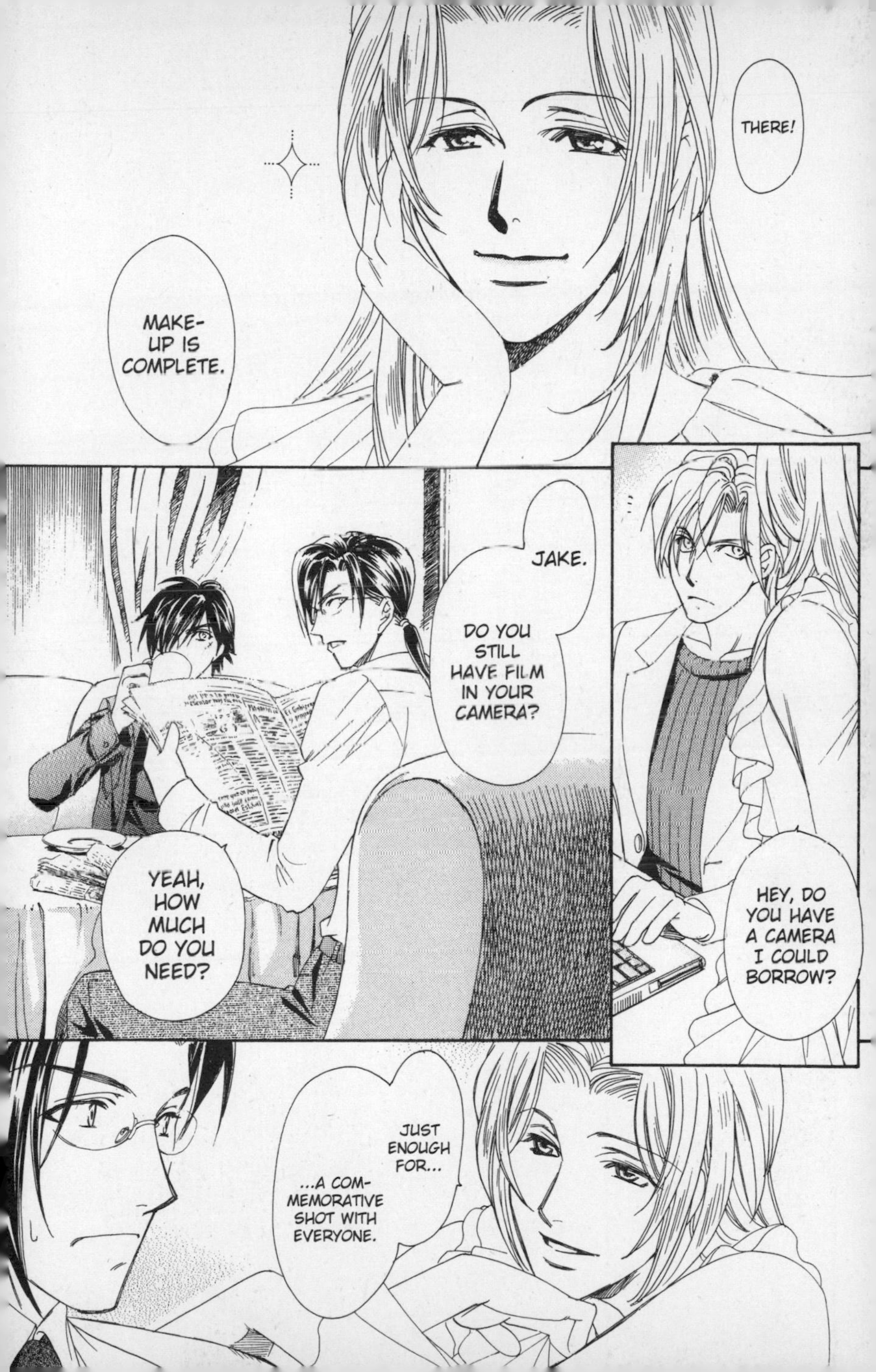
THERE!
MAKE-UP IS COMPLETE.
HEY, DO YOU HAVE A CAMERA I COULD BORROW?
JAKE.
DO YOU STILL HAVE FILM IN YOUR CAMERA?
YEAH, HOW MUCH DO YOU NEED?
JUST ENOUGH FOR...
...A COM-MEMORATIVE SHOT WITH EVERYONE.

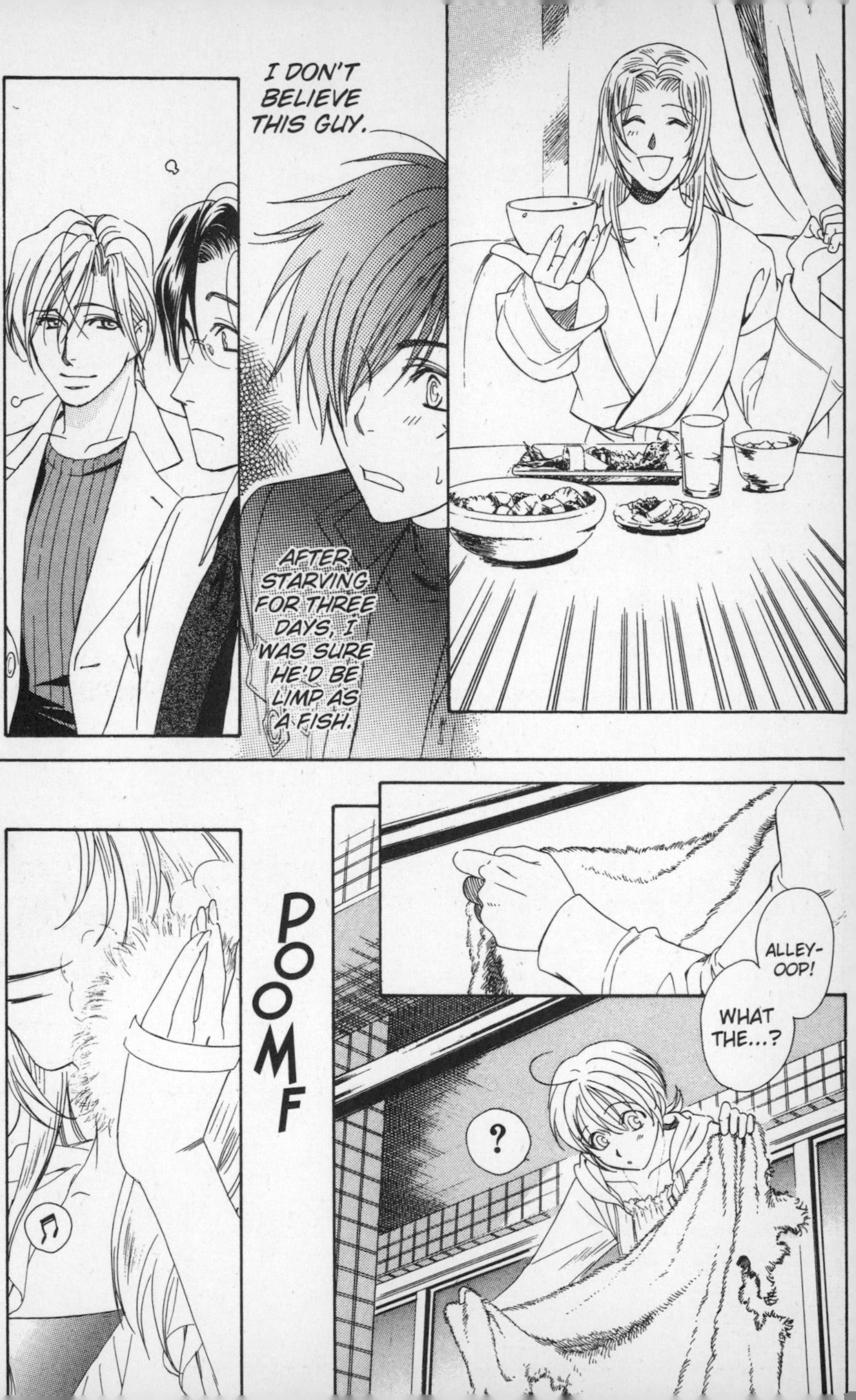
I DON'T BELIEVE THIS GUY.
AFTER STARVING FOR THREE DAYS, I WAS SURE HE'D BE LIMP AS A FISH.
ALLEY-OOP!
WHAT THE...?
?
POOMF
♫

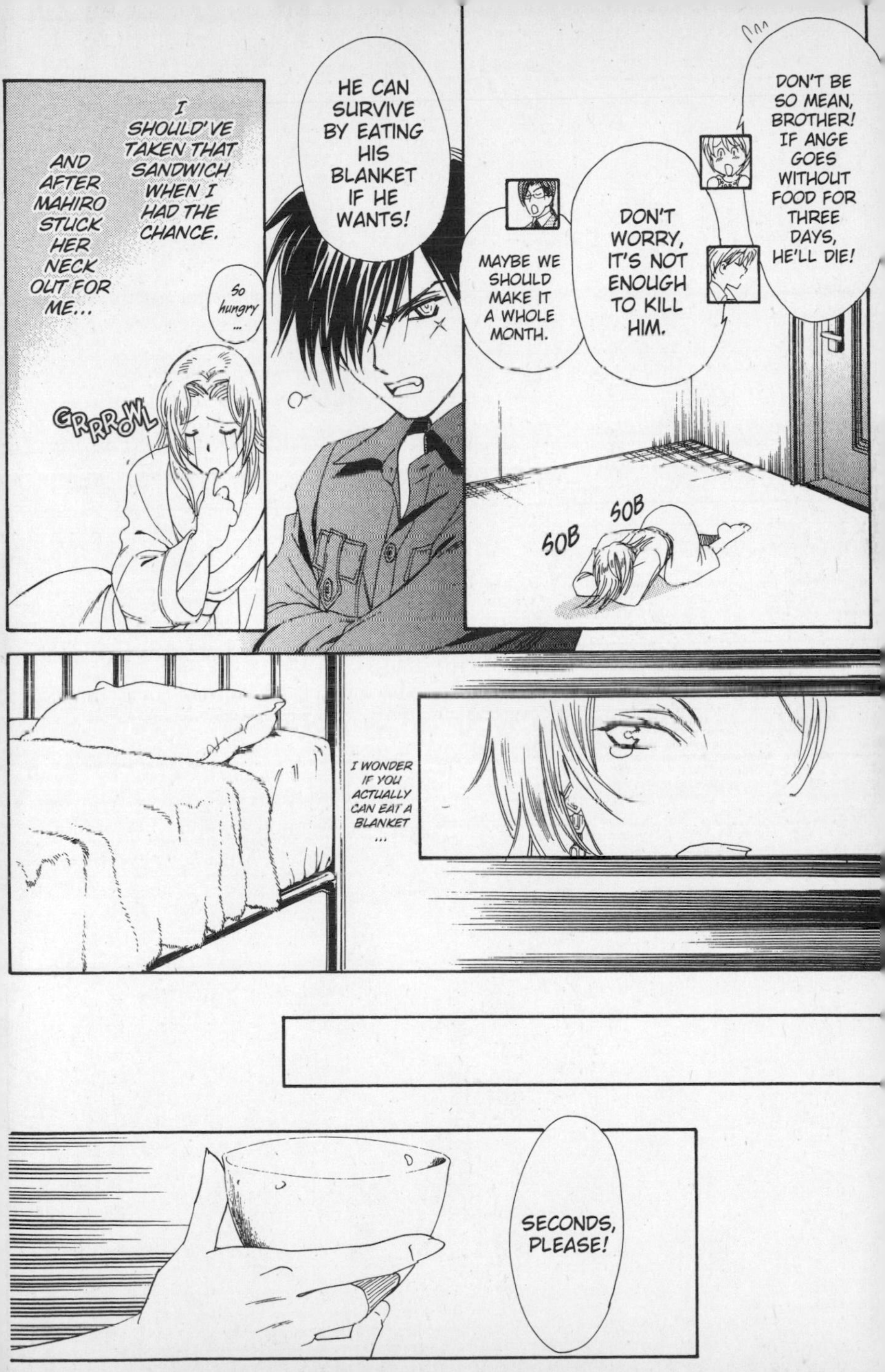
DON'T BE SO MEAN, BROTHER! IF ANGE GOES WITHOUT FOOD FOR THREE DAYS, HE'LL DIE!
DON'T WORRY, IT'S NOT ENOUGH TO KILL HIM.
MAYBE WE SHOULD MAKE IT A WHOLE MONTH.
SOB
SOB
HE CAN SURVIVE BY EATING HIS BLANKET IF HE WANTS!
I SHOULD'VE TAKEN THAT SANDWICH WHEN I HAD THE CHANCE.
AND AFTER MAHIRO STUCK HER NECK OUT FOR ME...
So hungry ...
GRRROWL
I WONDER IF YOU ACTUALLY CAN EAT A BLANKET ...
SECONDS, PLEASE!

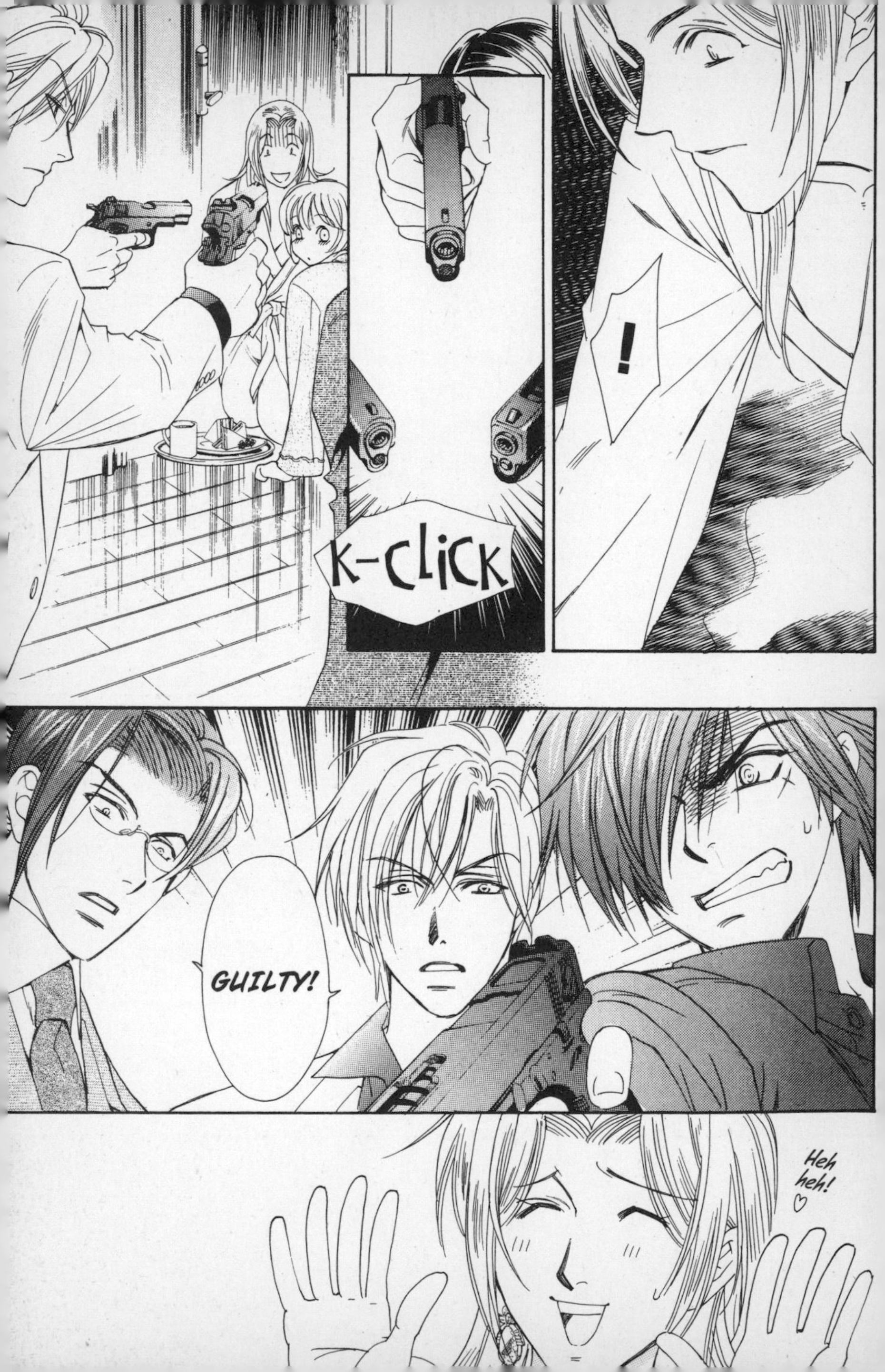
!
K-CLICK
GUILTY!
Heh heh! ♡

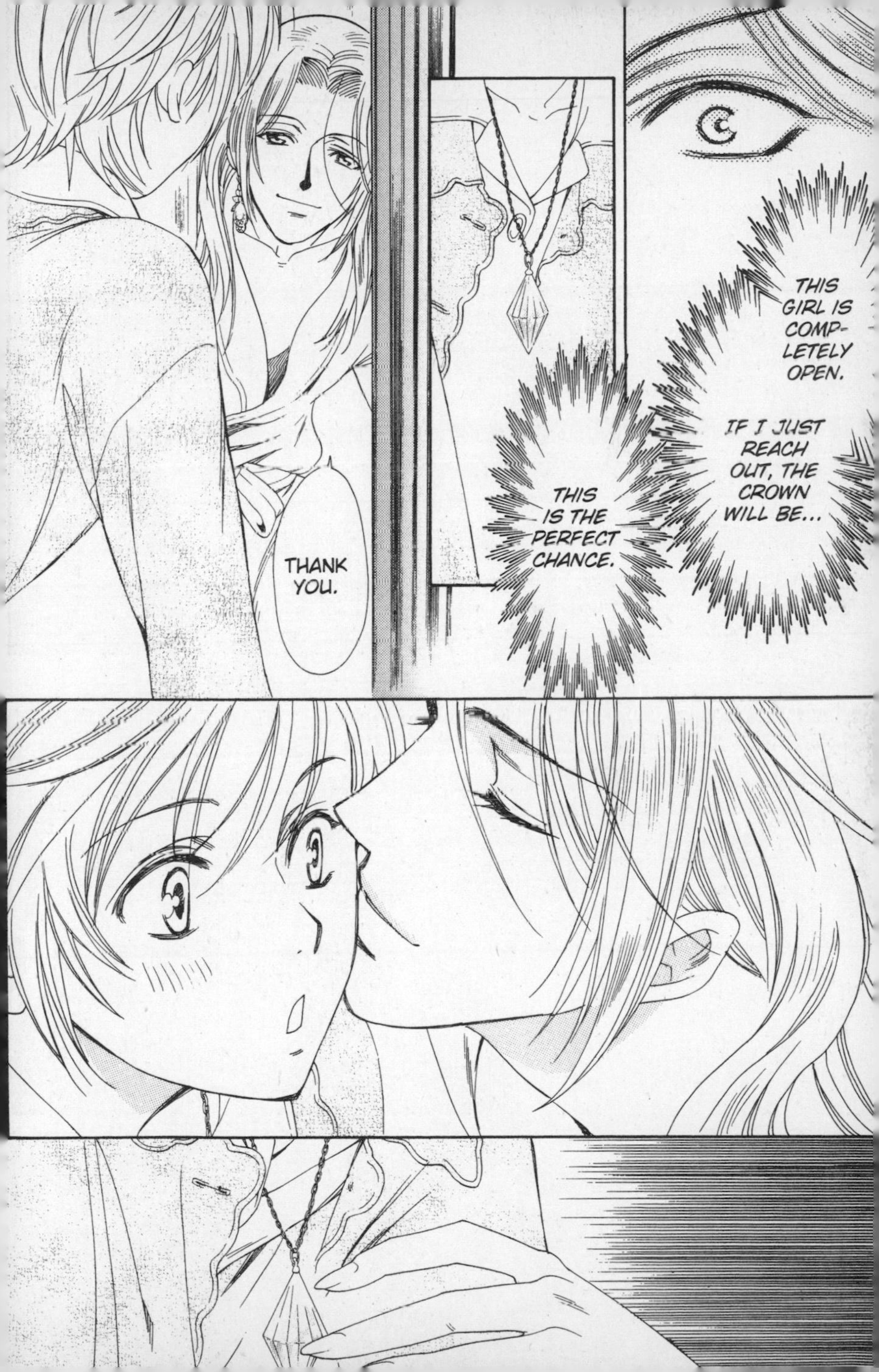
THIS GIRL IS COMP-LETELY OPEN.
IF I JUST REACH OUT, THE CROWN WILL BE...
THIS IS THE PERFECT CHANCE.
THANK YOU.

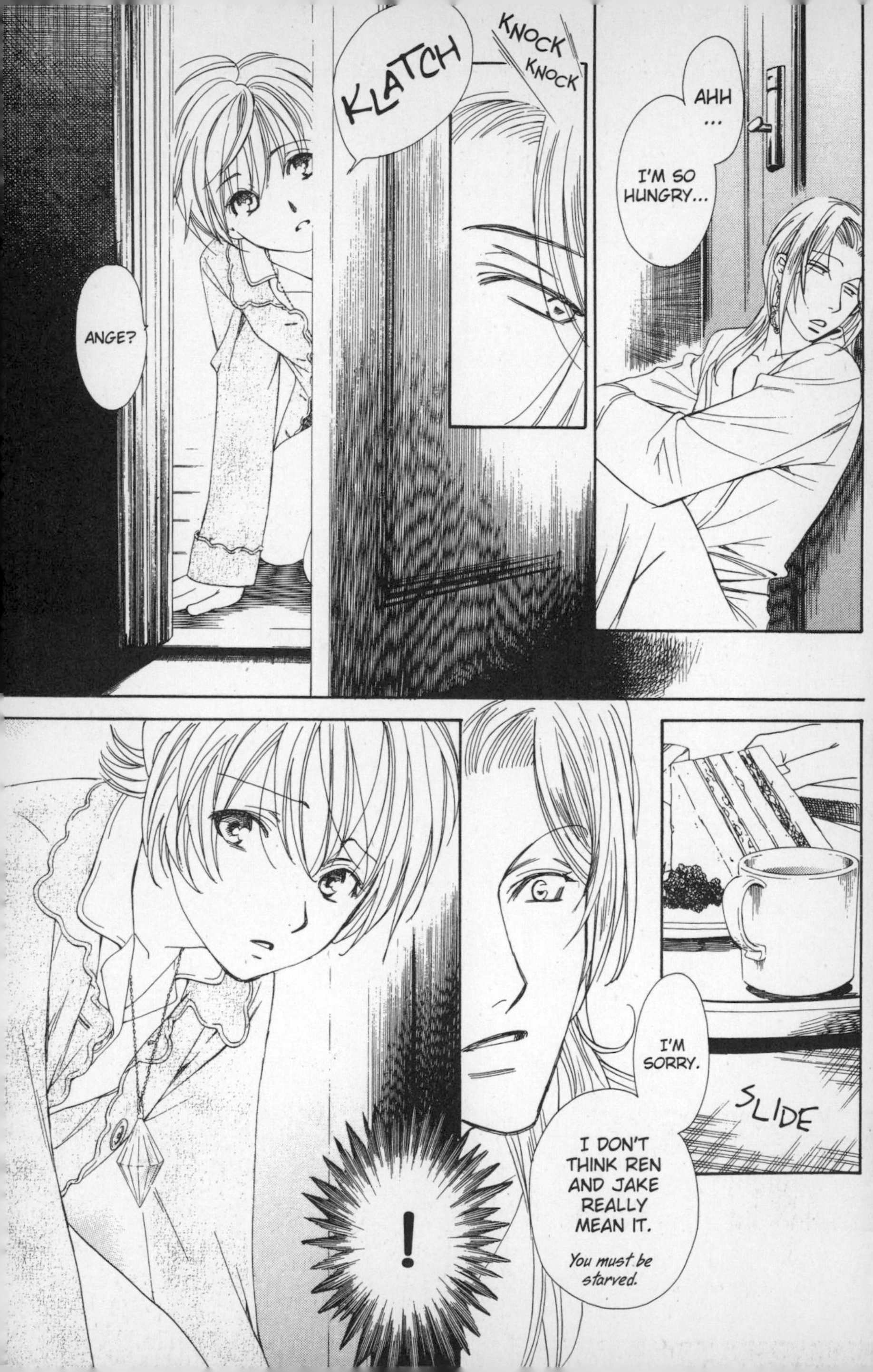
AHH ...
I'M SO HUNGRY...
KNOCK KNOCK
KLATCH
ANGE?
SLIDE
I'M SORRY.
I DON'T THINK REN AND JAKE REALLY MEAN IT.
You must be starved.
!

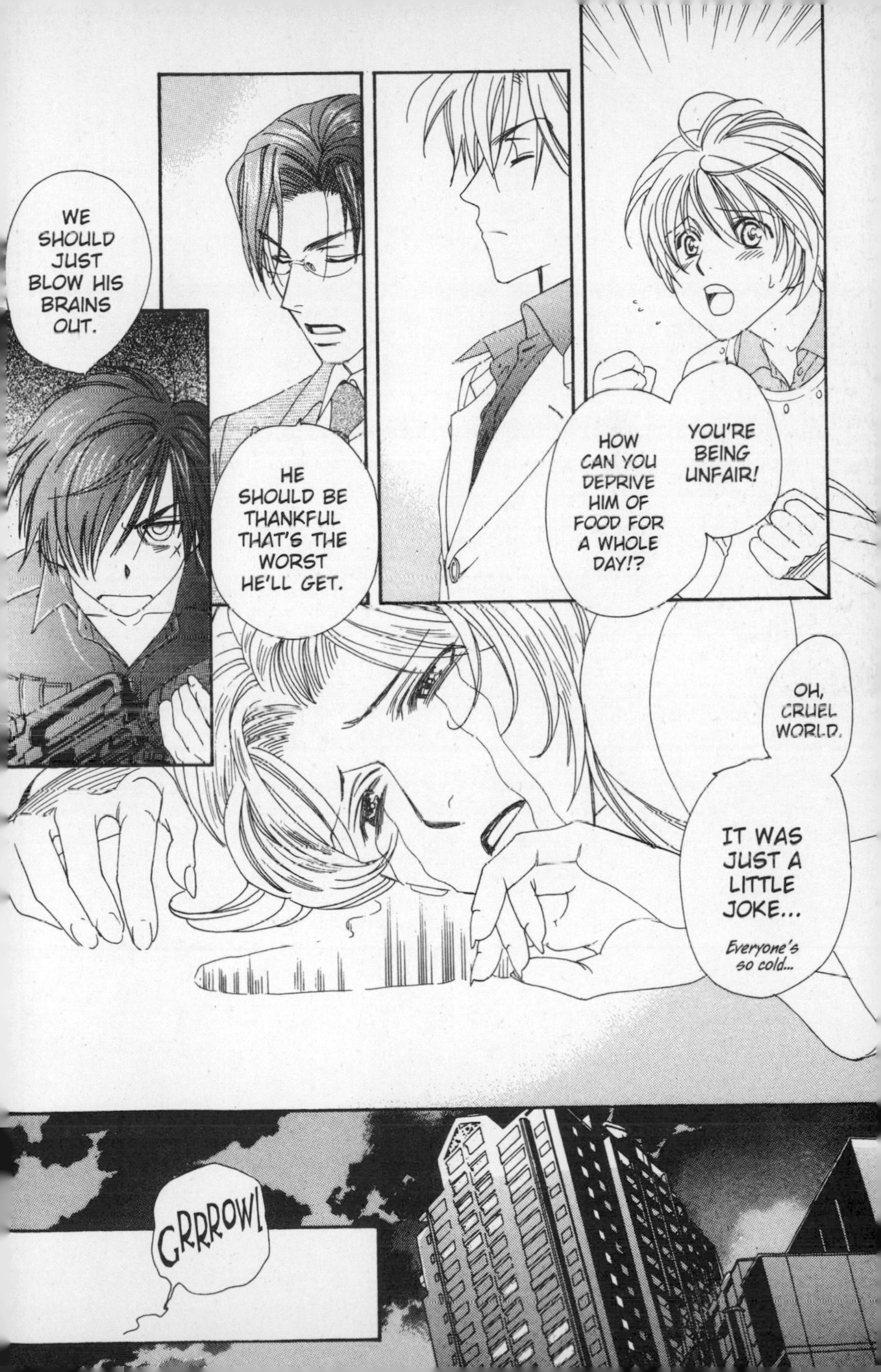
YOU'RE BEING UNFAIR!
HOW CAN YOU DEPRIVE HIM OF FOOD FOR A WHOLE DAY!?
HE SHOULD BE THANKFUL THAT'S THE WORST HE'LL GET.
WE SHOULD JUST BLOW HIS BRAINS OUT.
OH, CRUEL WORLD.
IT WAS JUST A LITTLE JOKE...
Everyone's so cold...
GRRROWL

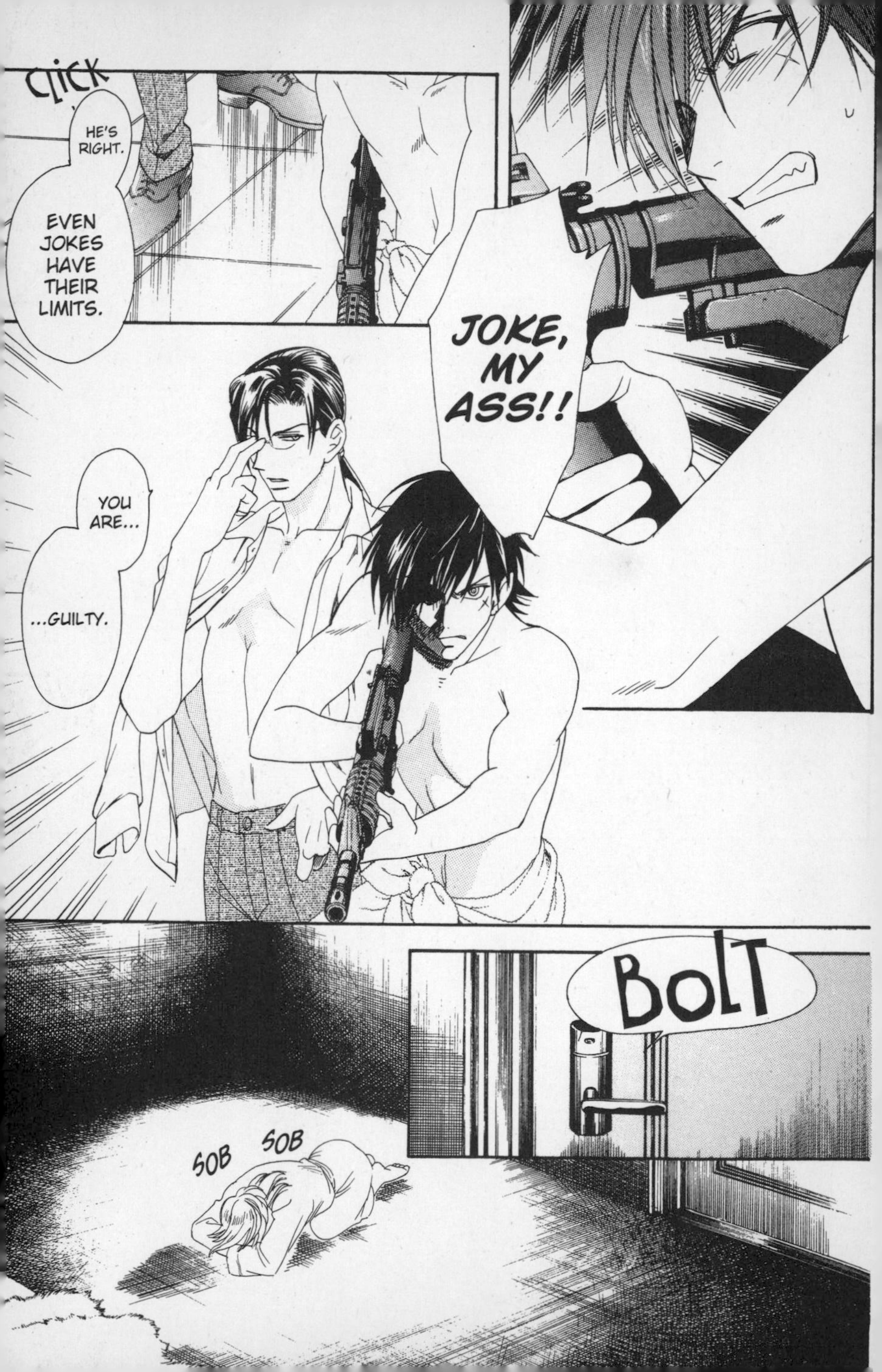
JOKE, MY ASS!!
CLICK
HE'S RIGHT.
EVEN JOKES HAVE THEIR LIMITS.
YOU ARE...
...GUILTY.
BOLT
SOB SOB

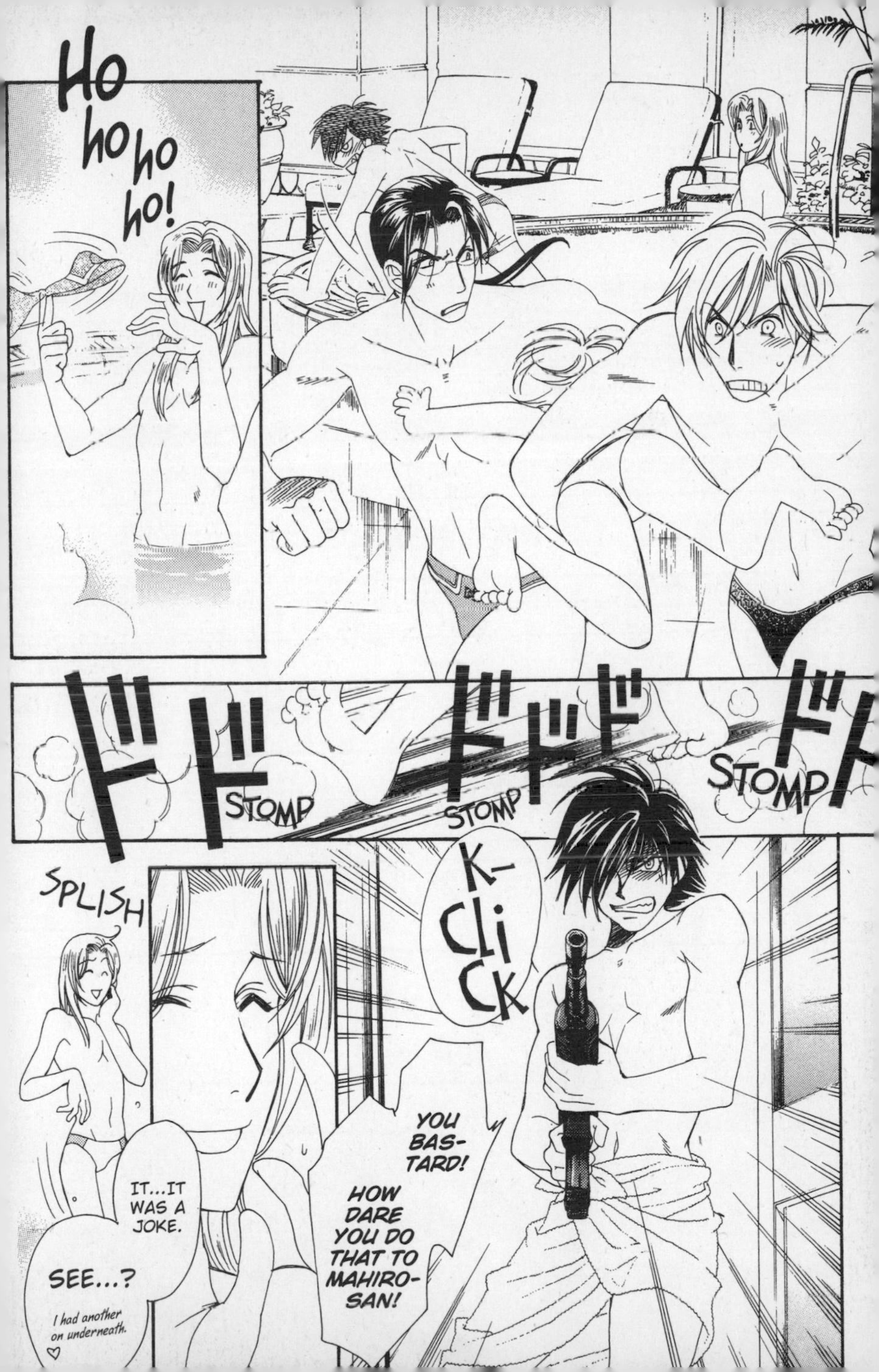

Ho ho ho ho!
ドドドドドドド
STOMP
STOMP
STOMP
SPLISH
K-CLICK
YOU BASTARD!
HOW DARE YOU DO THAT TO MAHIRO-SAN!
IT...IT WAS A JOKE.
SEE...?
I had another on underneath. ♡

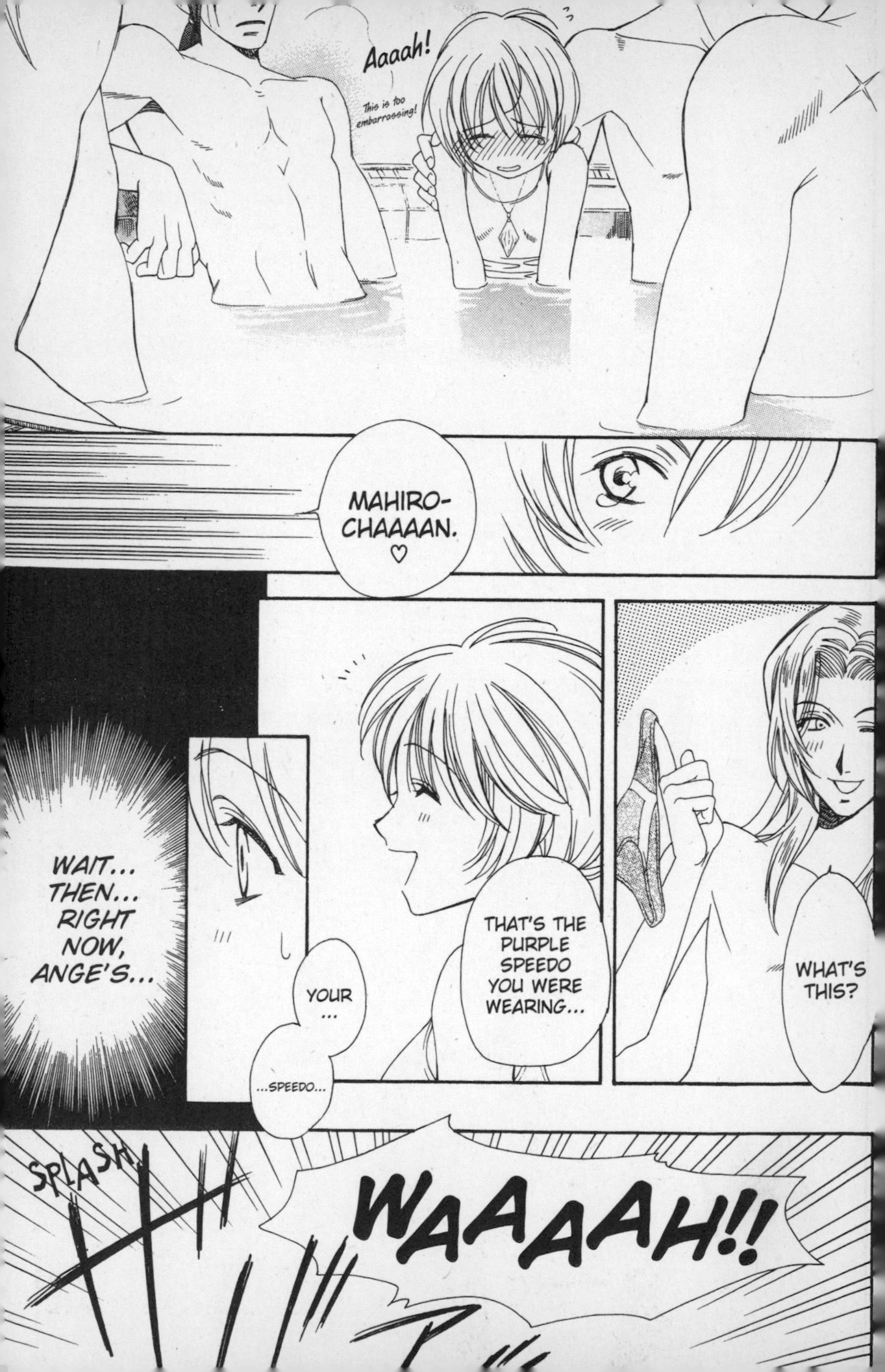
Aaaah!
This is too embarrassing!
MAHIRO-CHAAAAN. ♡
WHAT'S THIS?
THAT'S THE PURPLE SPEEDO YOU WERE WEARING...
YOUR ...
...SPEEDO...
WAIT... THEN... RIGHT NOW, ANGE'S...
WAAAAH!!
SPLASH

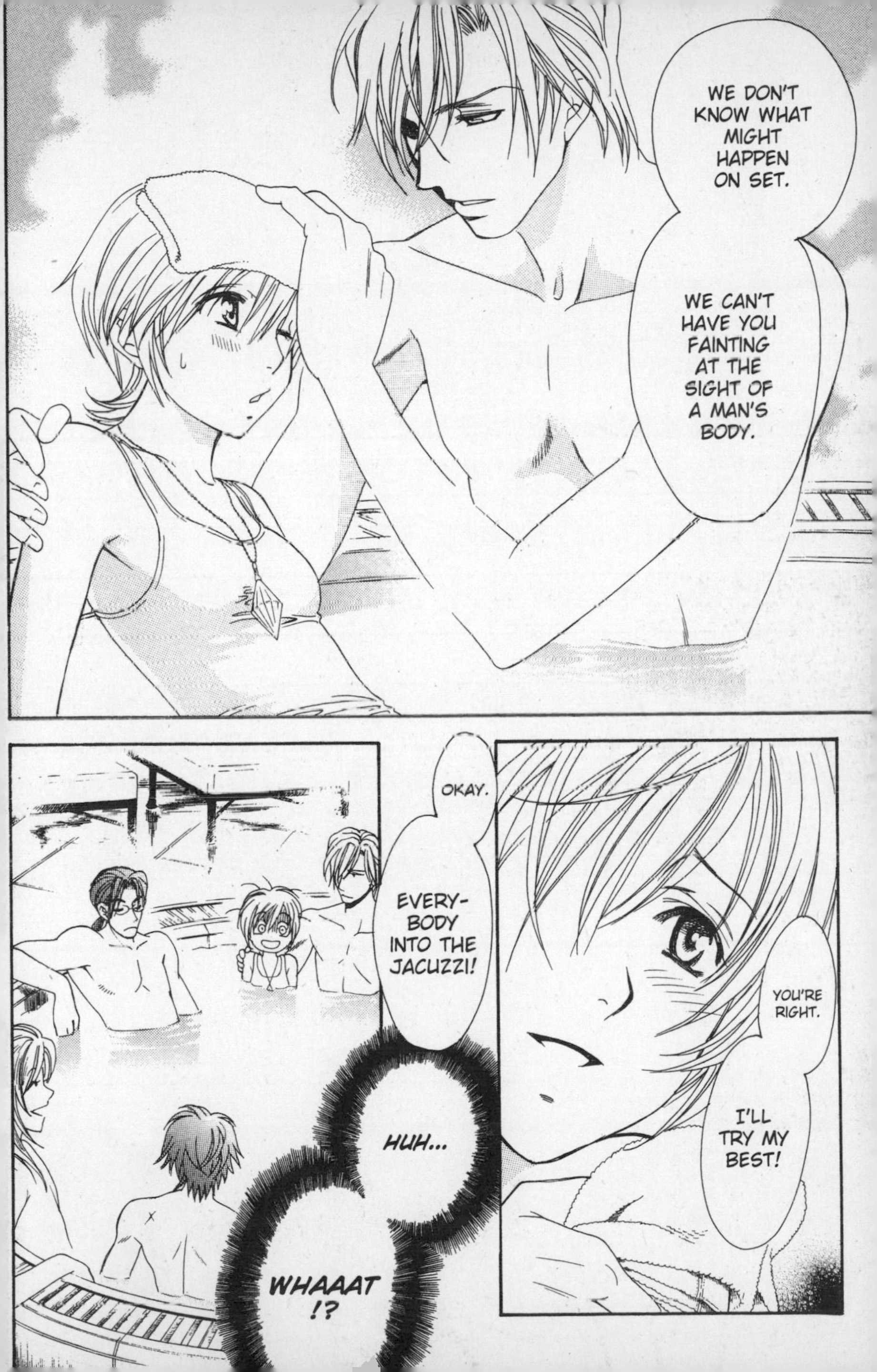
WE DON'T KNOW WHAT MIGHT HAPPEN ON SET.
WE CAN'T HAVE YOU FAINTING AT THE SIGHT OF A MAN'S BODY.
YOU'RE RIGHT.
I'LL TRY MY BEST!
OKAY.
EVERY-BODY INTO THE JACUZZI!
HUH...
WHAAAT!?

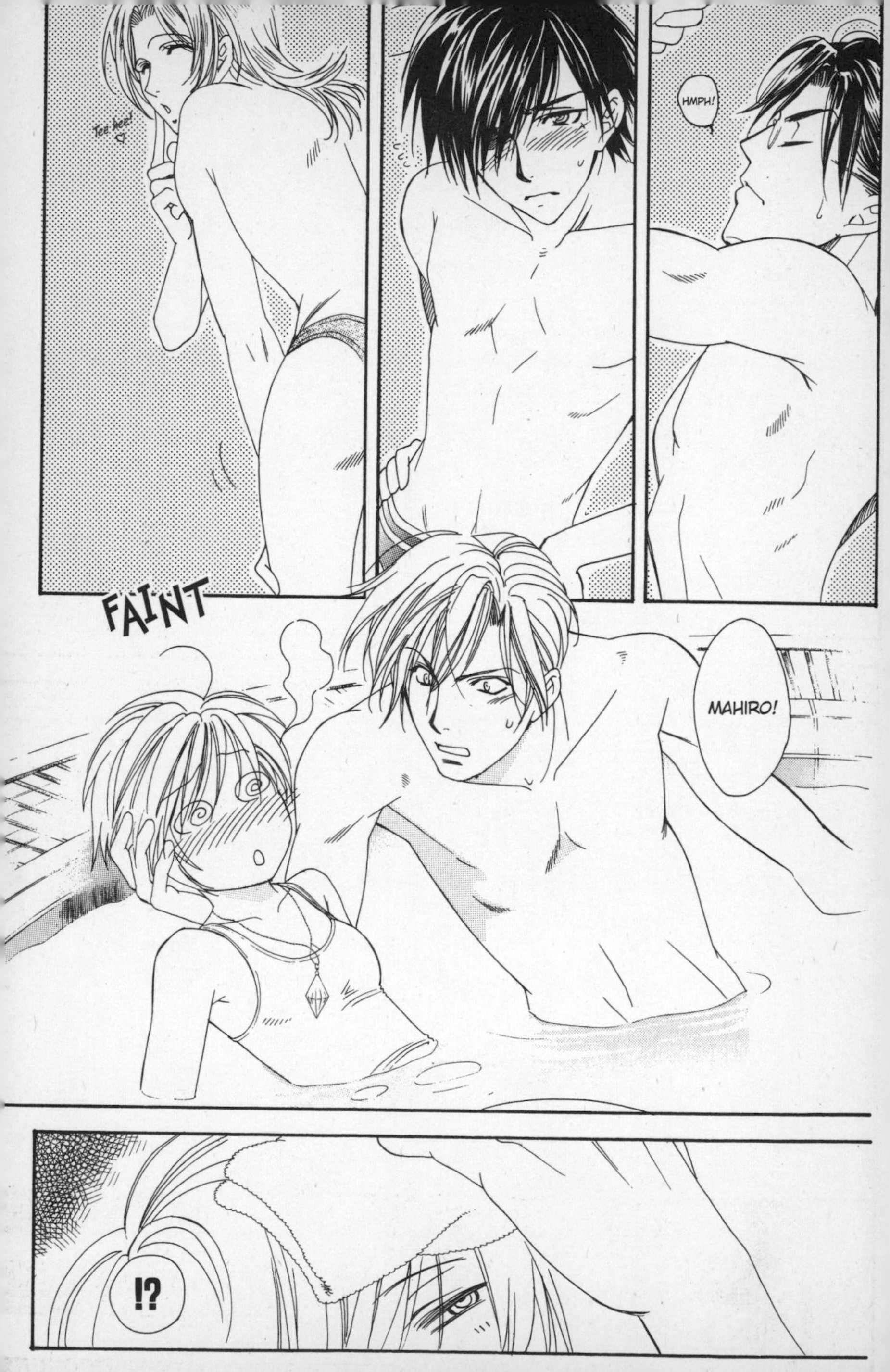
HMPH!
Tee hee! ♡
MAHIRO!
FAINT
!?

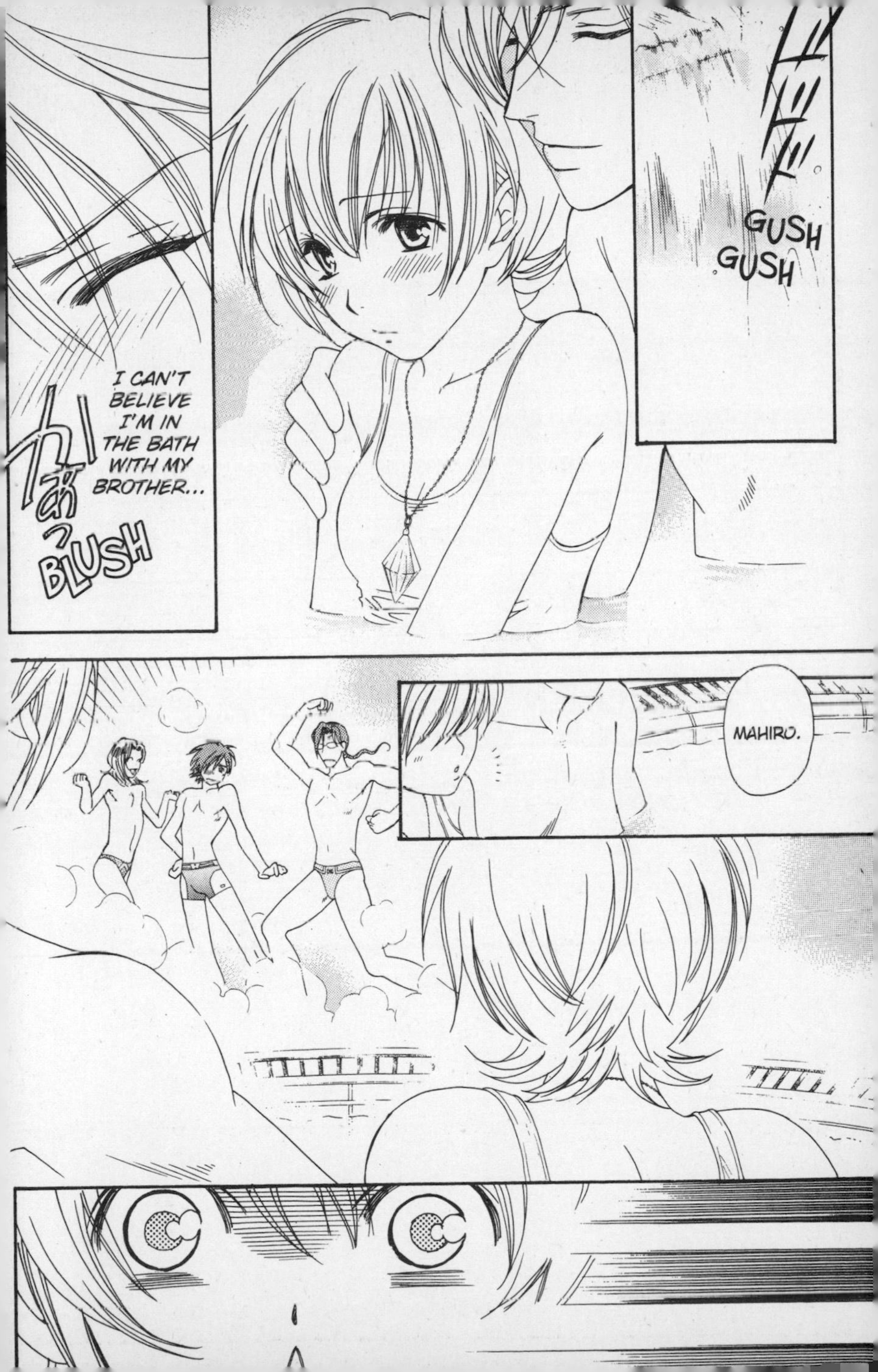
GUSH GUSH
I CAN'T BELIEVE I'M IN THE BATH WITH MY BROTHER...
BLUSH
MAHIRO.

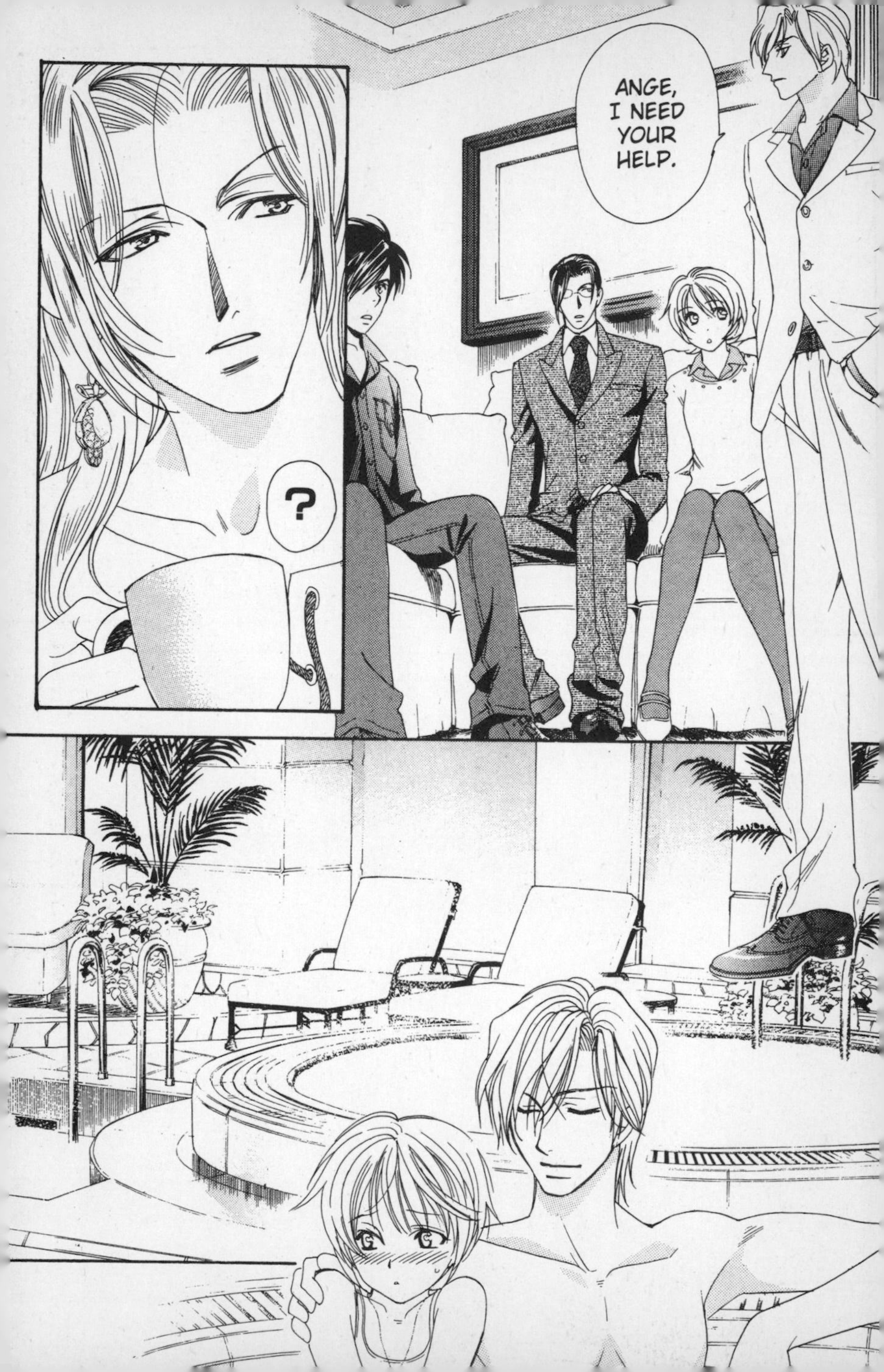
ANGE, I NEED YOUR HELP.
?

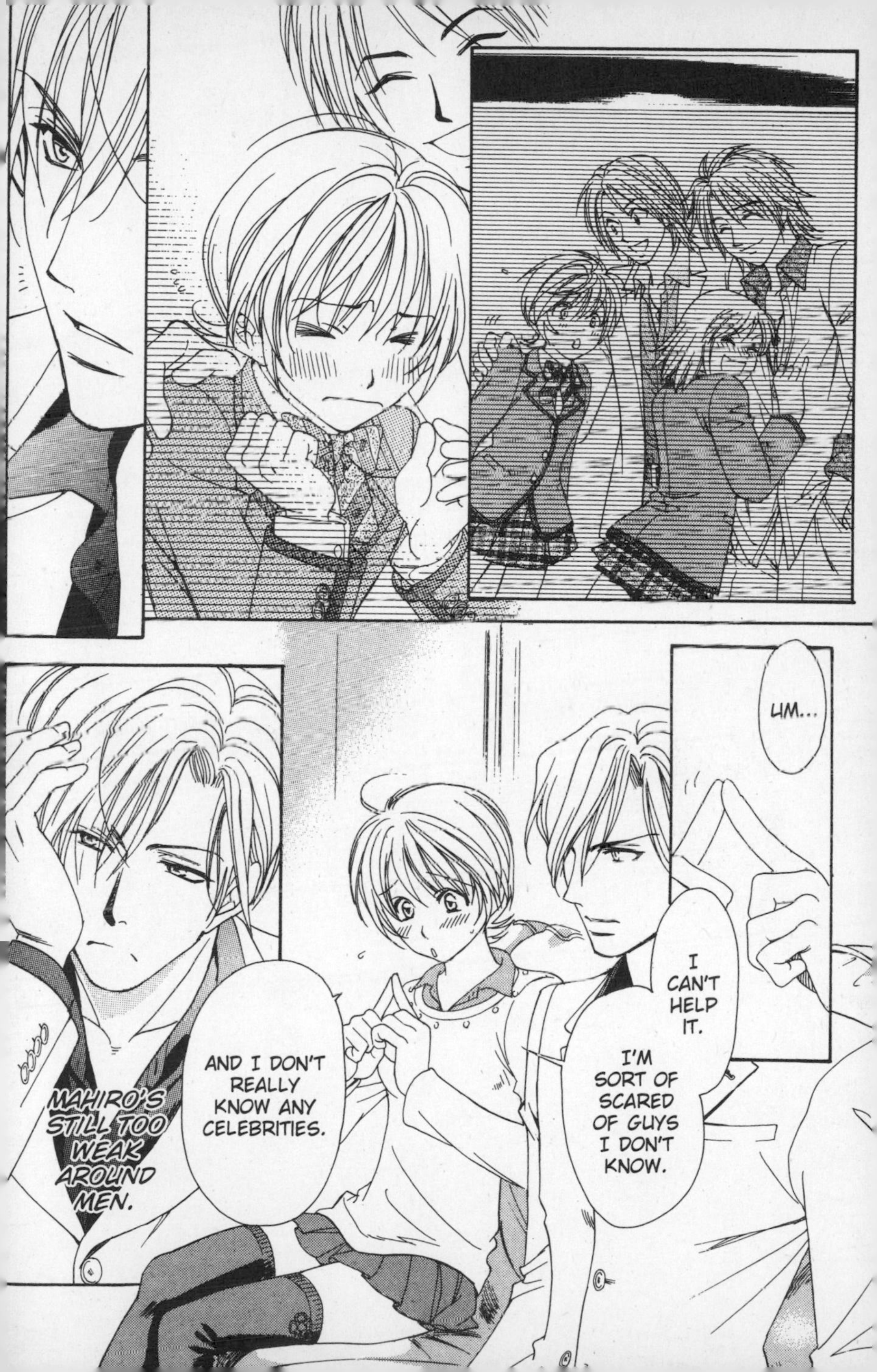
UM...
I CAN'T HELP IT.
I'M SORT OF SCARED OF GUYS I DON'T KNOW.
AND I DON'T REALLY KNOW ANY CELEBRITIES.
MAHIRO'S STILL TOO WEAK AROUND MEN.

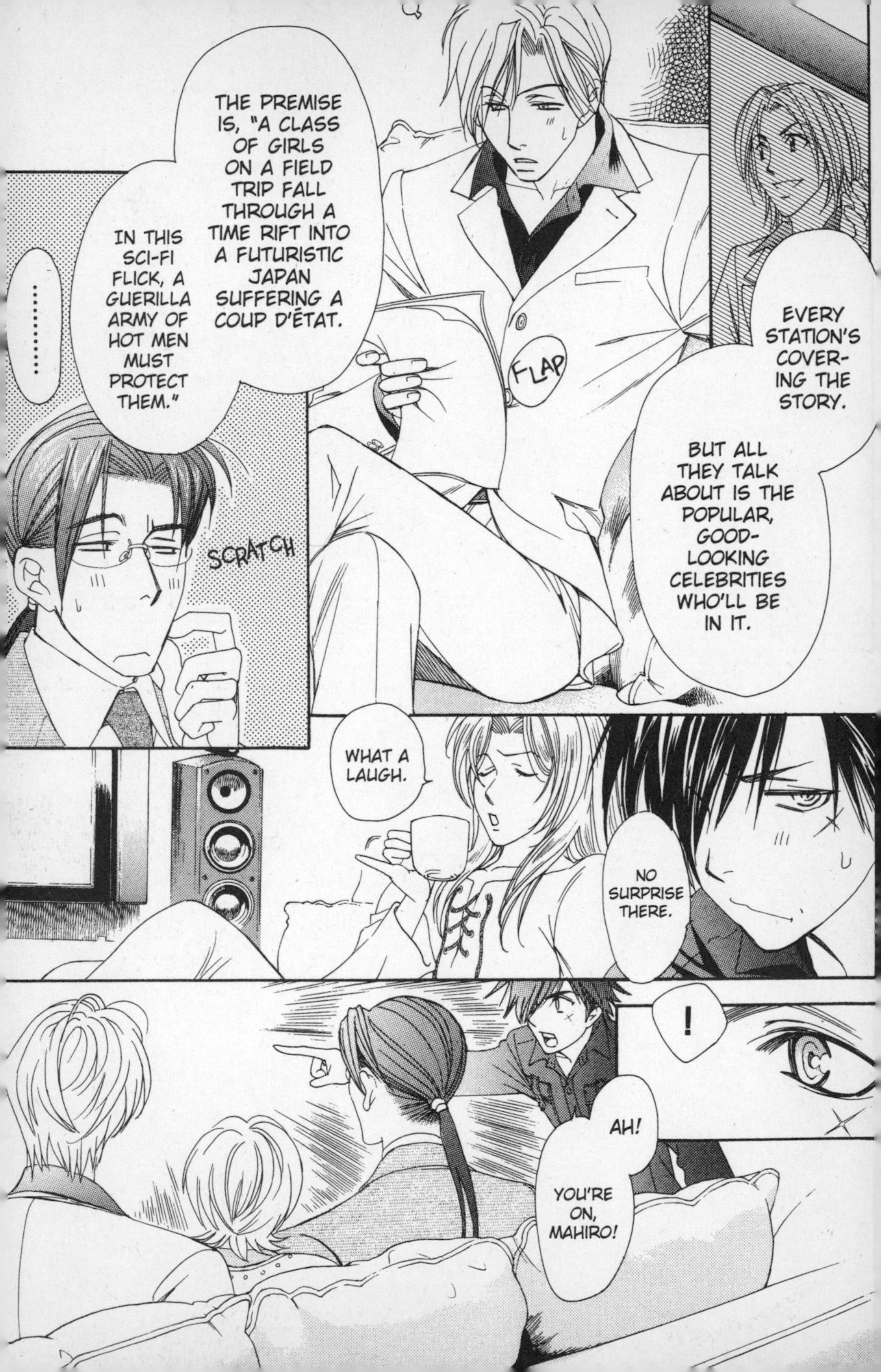
EVERY STATION'S COVERING THE STORY.
BUT ALL THEY TALK ABOUT IS THE POPULAR, GOOD-LOOKING CELEBRITIES WHO'LL BE IN IT.
FLAP
THE PREMISE IS, "A CLASS OF GIRLS ON A FIELD TRIP FALL THROUGH A TIME RIFT INTO A FUTURISTIC JAPAN SUFFERING A COUP D'ÉTAT.
IN THIS SCI-FI FLICK, A GUERILLA ARMY OF HOT MEN MUST PROTECT THEM."
......
SCRATCH
NO SURPRISE THERE.
WHAT A LAUGH.
!
AH!
YOU'RE ON, MAHIRO!

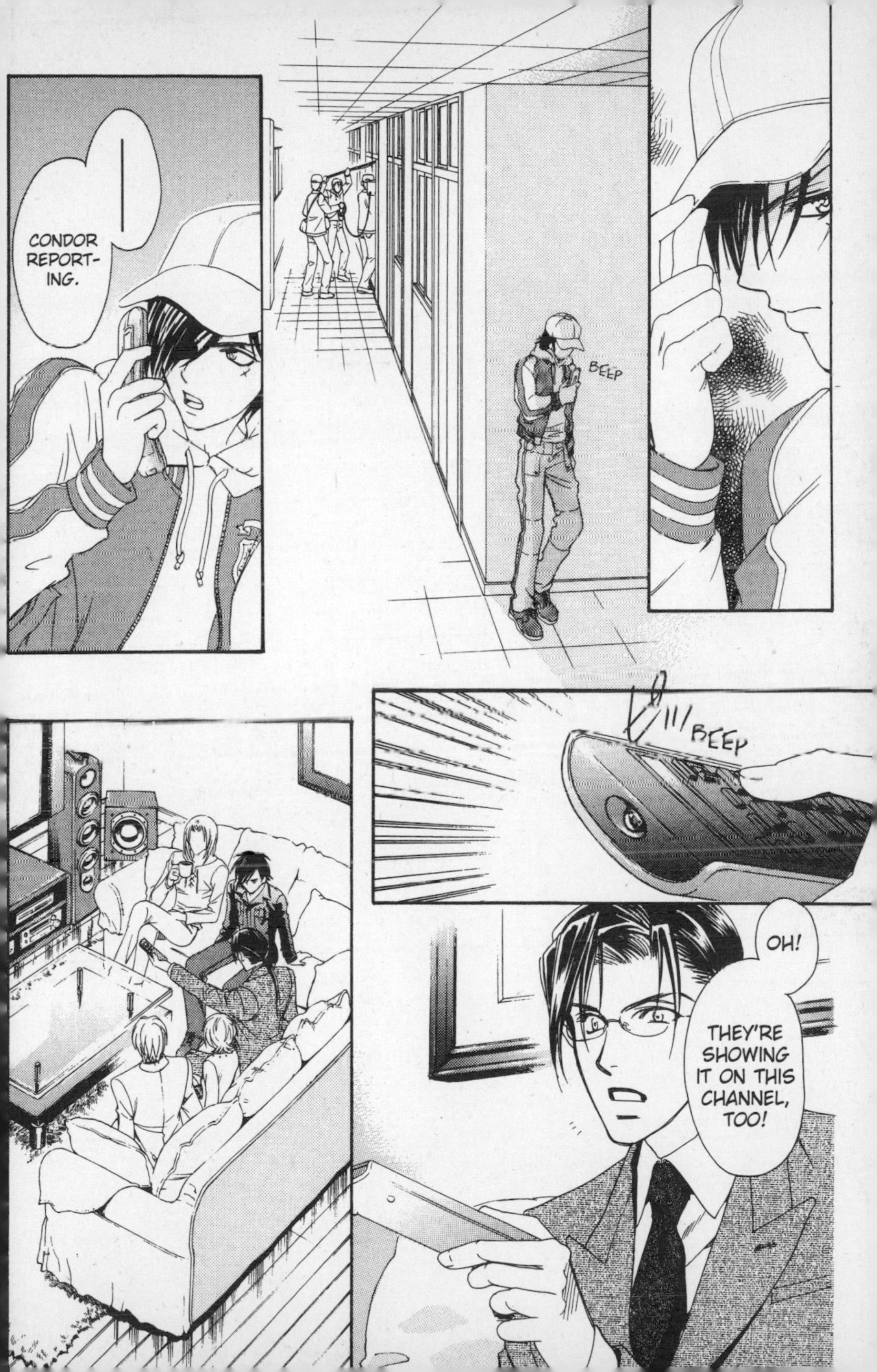

—
CONDOR REPORTING.
BEEP
BEEP
OH!
THEY'RE SHOWING IT ON THIS CHANNEL, TOO!

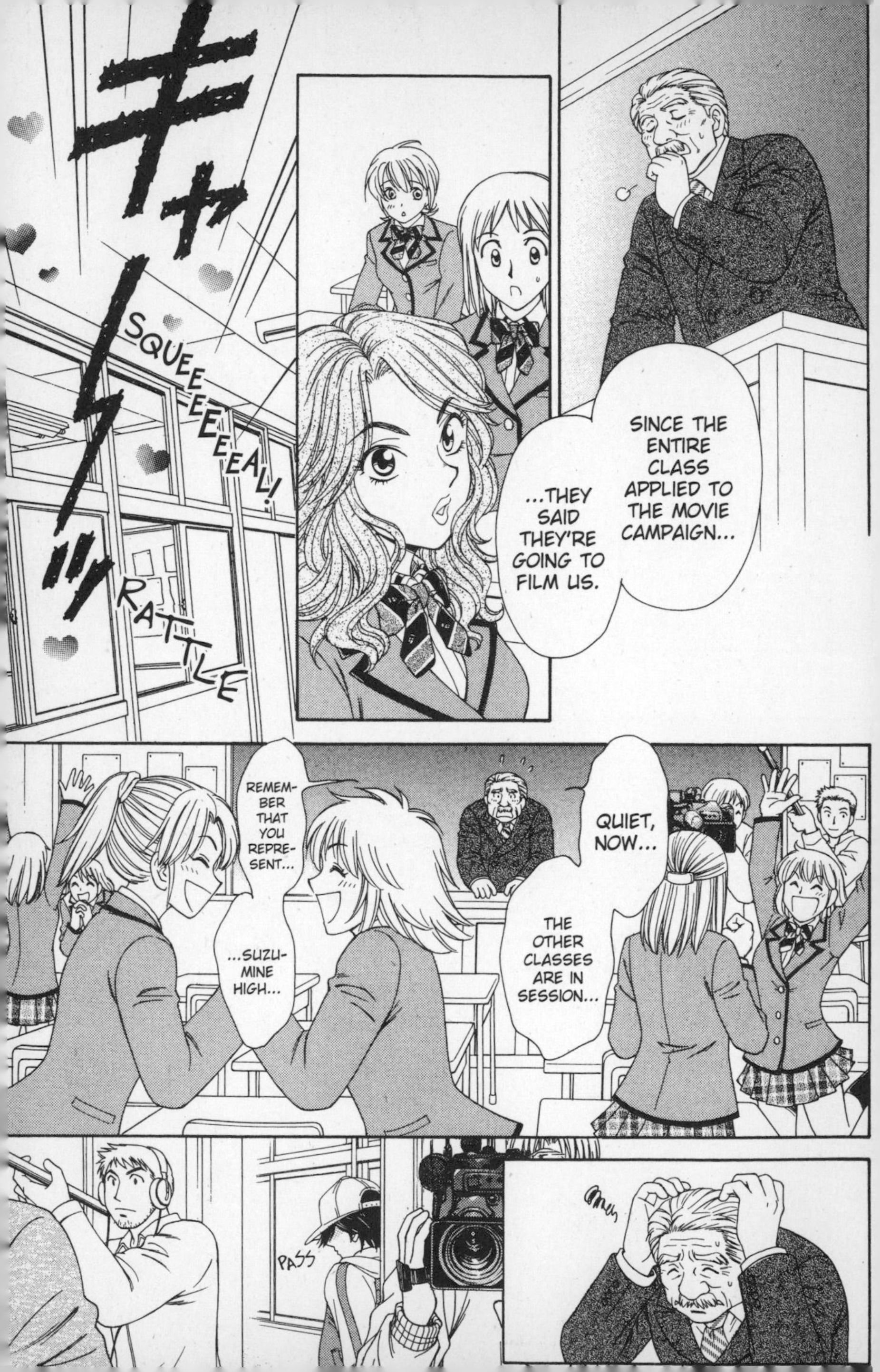

キャーッ
SQUEEEEEEEEAL!
RATTLE
SINCE THE ENTIRE CLASS APPLIED TO THE MOVIE CAMPAIGN...
...THEY SAID THEY'RE GOING TO FILM US.
QUIET, NOW...
THE OTHER CLASSES ARE IN SESSION...
REMEMBER THAT YOU REPRESENT...
...SUZUMINE HIGH...
PASS

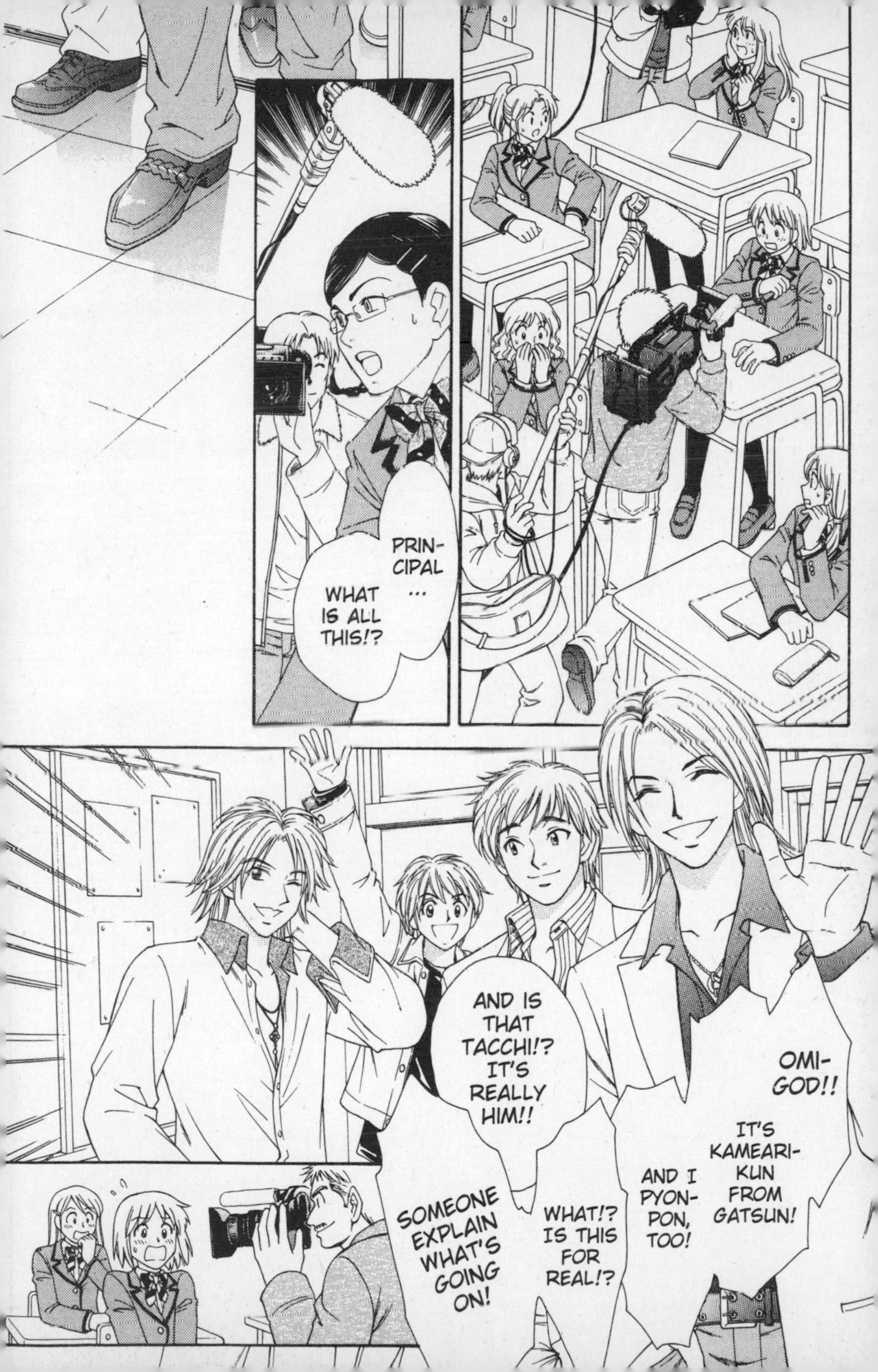
PRINCIPAL ...
WHAT IS ALL THIS!?
OMIGOD!!
IT'S KAMEARI-KUN FROM GATSUN!
AND IS THAT TACCHI!? IT'S REALLY HIM!!
AND I PYON-PON, TOO!
WHAT!? IS THIS FOR REAL!?
SOMEONE EXPLAIN WHAT'S GOING ON!

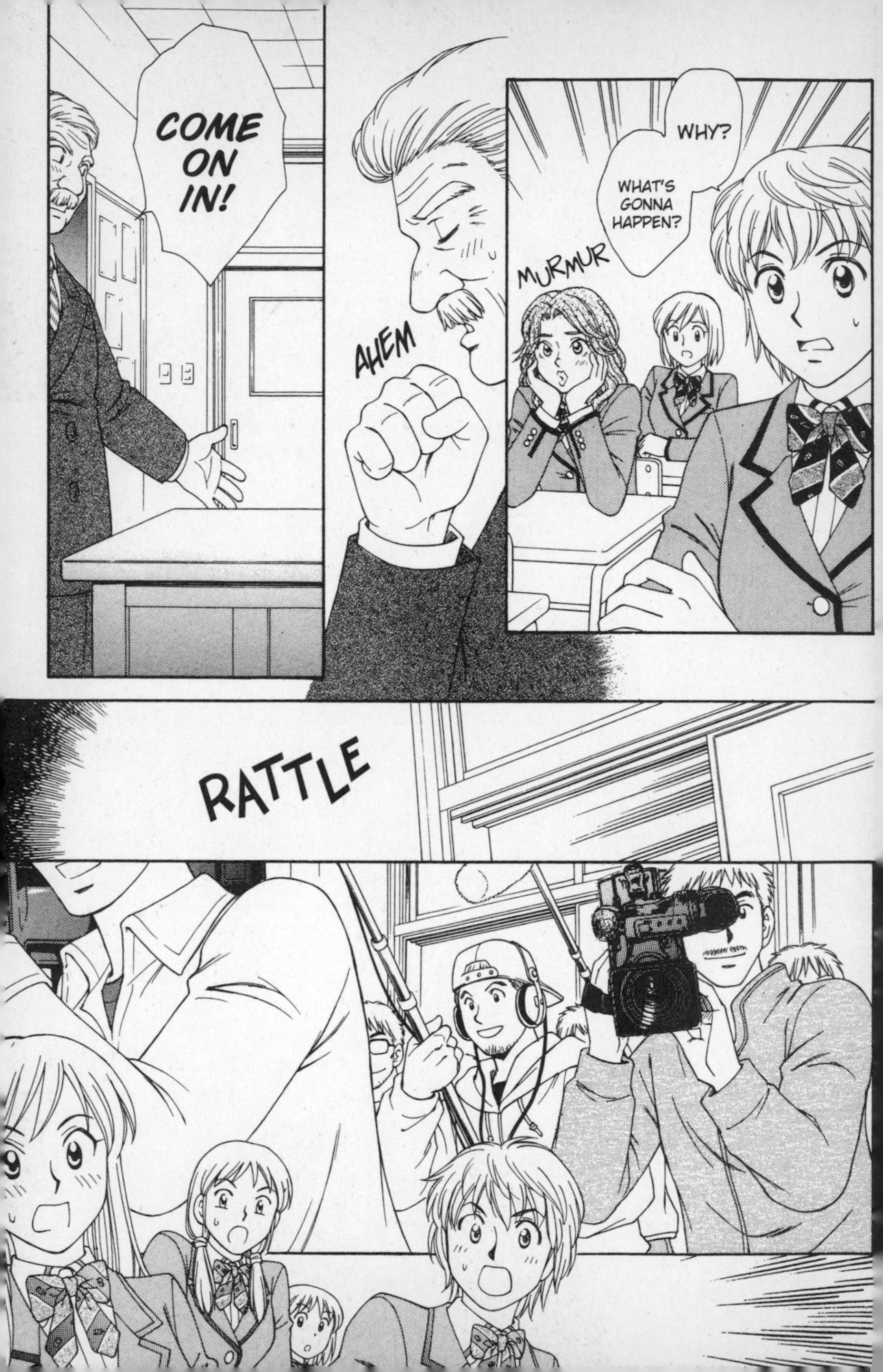
COME ON IN!
AHEM
WHY?
WHAT'S GONNA HAPPEN?
MURMUR
RATTLE

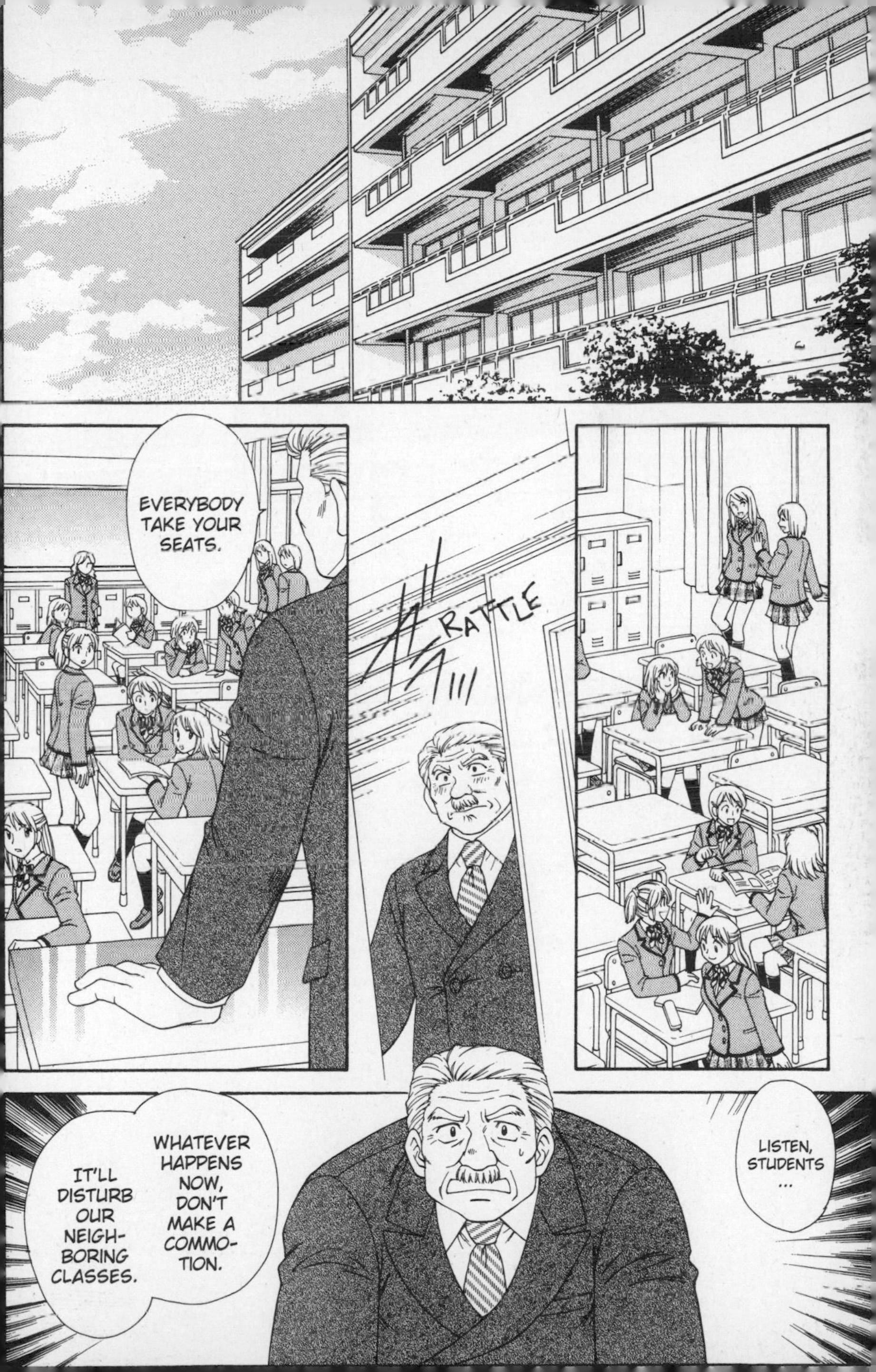
EVERYBODY TAKE YOUR SEATS.
RATTLE
LISTEN, STUDENTS ...
WHATEVER HAPPENS NOW, DON'T MAKE A COMMO-TION.
IT'LL DISTURB OUR NEIGH-BORING CLASSES.

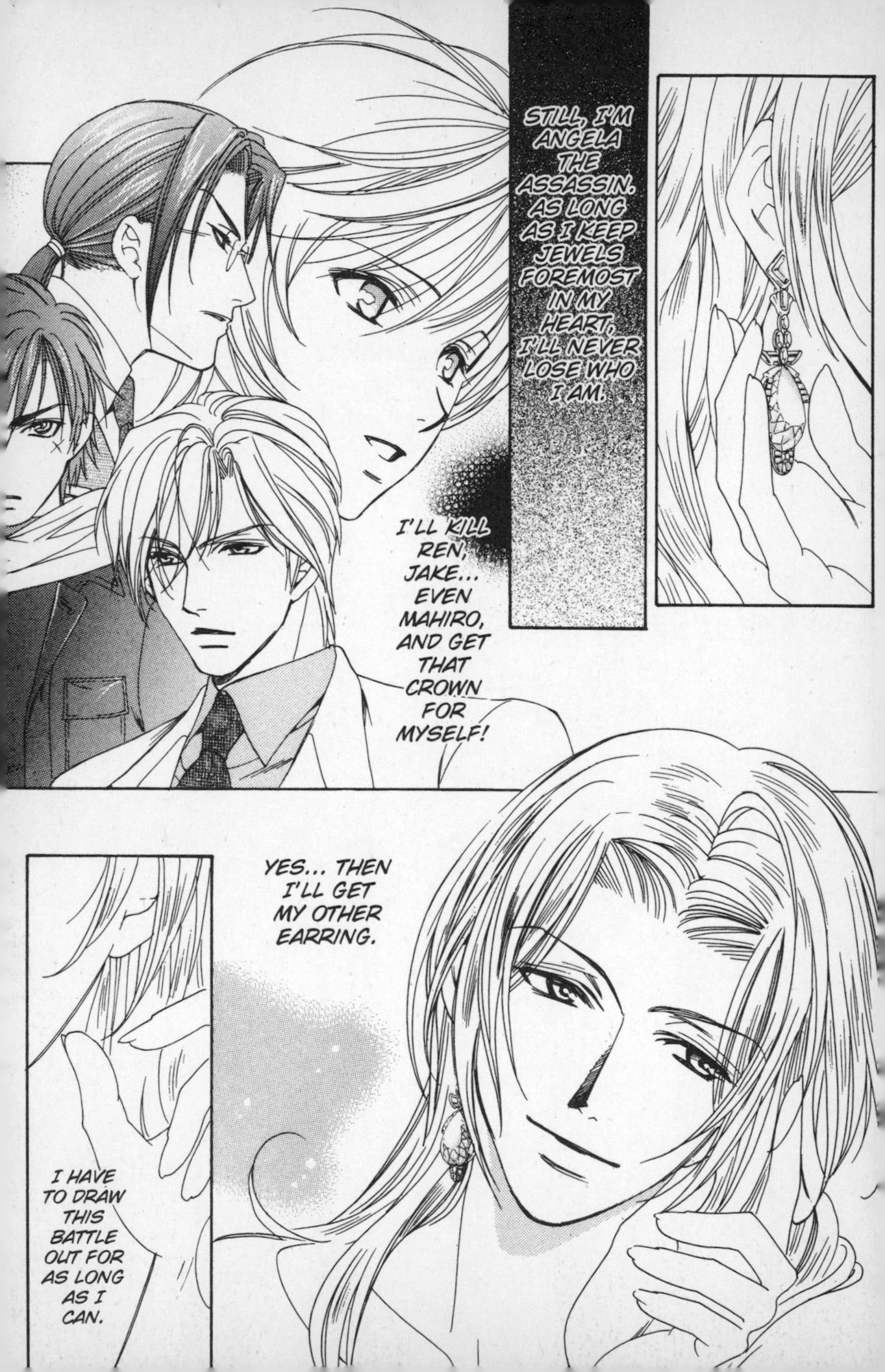
STILL, I'M ANGELA THE ASSASSIN. AS LONG AS I KEEP JEWELS FOREMOST IN MY HEART, I'LL NEVER LOSE WHO I AM.
I'LL KILL REN, JAKE... EVEN MAHIRO, AND GET THAT CROWN FOR MYSELF!
YES... THEN I'LL GET MY OTHER EARRING.
I HAVE TO DRAW THIS BATTLE OUT FOR AS LONG AS I CAN.

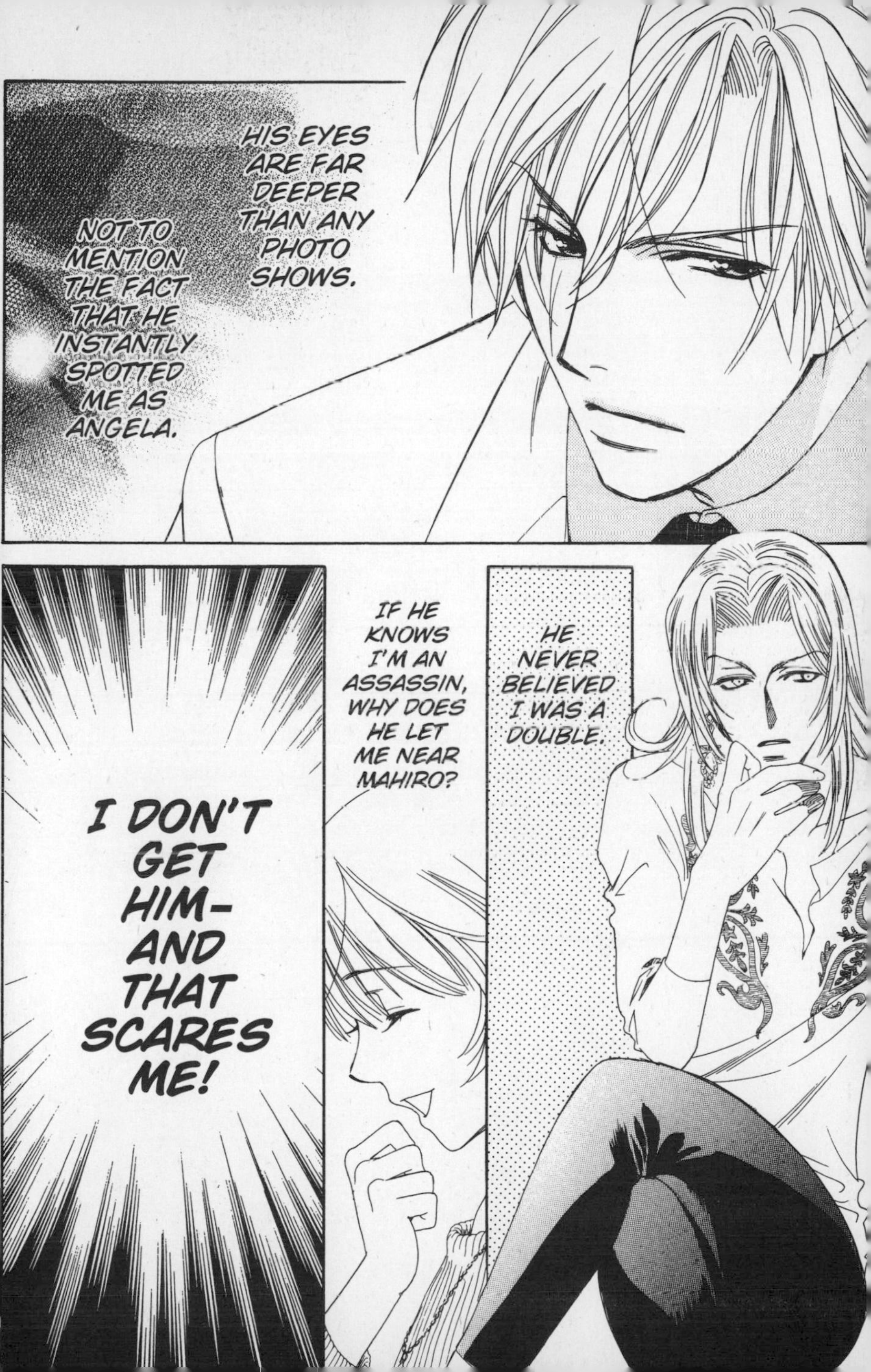
HIS EYES ARE FAR DEEPER THAN ANY PHOTO SHOWS.
NOT TO MENTION THE FACT THAT HE INSTANTLY SPOTTED ME AS ANGELA.
HE NEVER BELIEVED I WAS A DOUBLE.
IF HE KNOWS I'M AN ASSASSIN, WHY DOES HE LET ME NEAR MAHIRO?
I DON'T GET HIM-AND THAT SCARES ME!

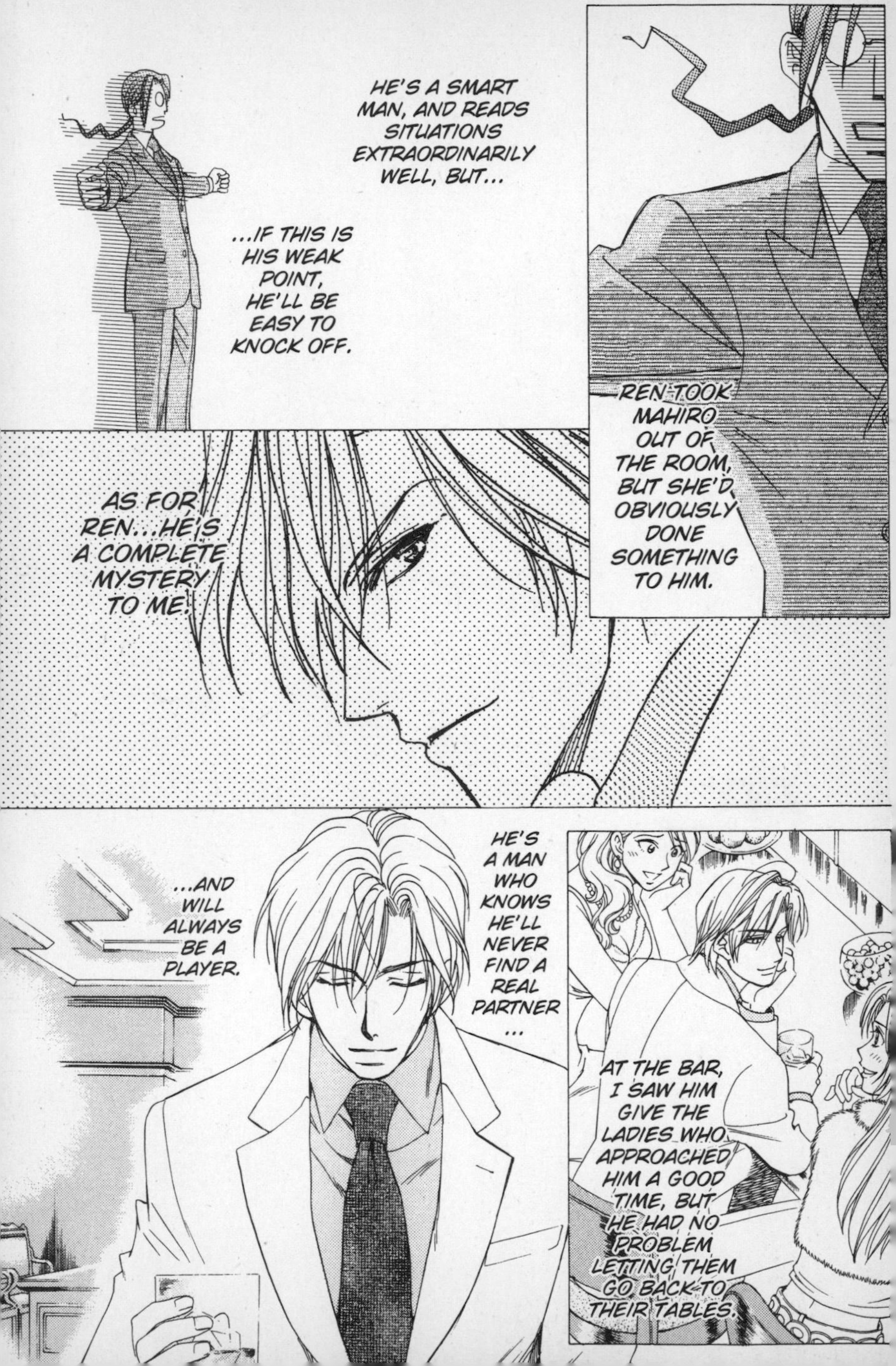
REN TOOK MAHIRO OUT OF THE ROOM, BUT SHE'D OBVIOUSLY DONE SOMETHING TO HIM.
HE'S A SMART MAN, AND READS SITUATIONS EXTRAORDINARILY WELL, BUT...
...IF THIS IS HIS WEAK POINT, HE'LL BE EASY TO KNOCK OFF.
AS FOR REN...HE'S A COMPLETE MYSTERY TO ME.
AT THE BAR, I SAW HIM GIVE THE LADIES WHO APPROACHED HIM A GOOD TIME, BUT HE HAD NO PROBLEM LETTING THEM GO BACK TO THEIR TABLES.
HE'S A MAN WHO KNOWS HE'LL NEVER FIND A REAL PARTNER...
...AND WILL ALWAYS BE A PLAYER.

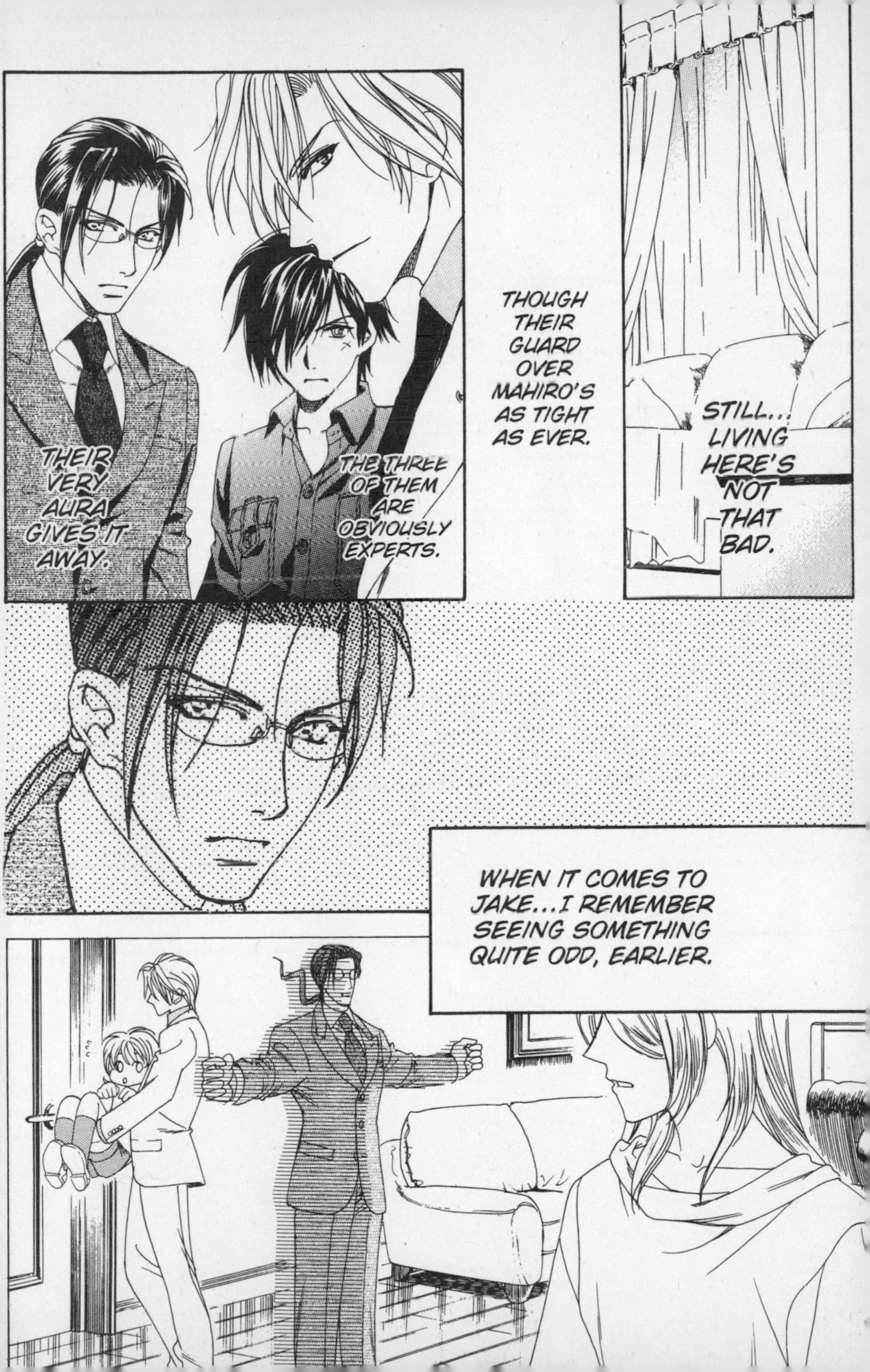
STILL... LIVING HERE'S NOT THAT BAD.
THOUGH THEIR GUARD OVER MAHIRO'S AS TIGHT AS EVER.
THE THREE OF THEM ARE OBVIOUSLY EXPERTS.
THEIR VERY AURA GIVES IT AWAY.
WHEN IT COMES TO JAKE...I REMEMBER SEEING SOMETHING QUITE ODD, EARLIER.

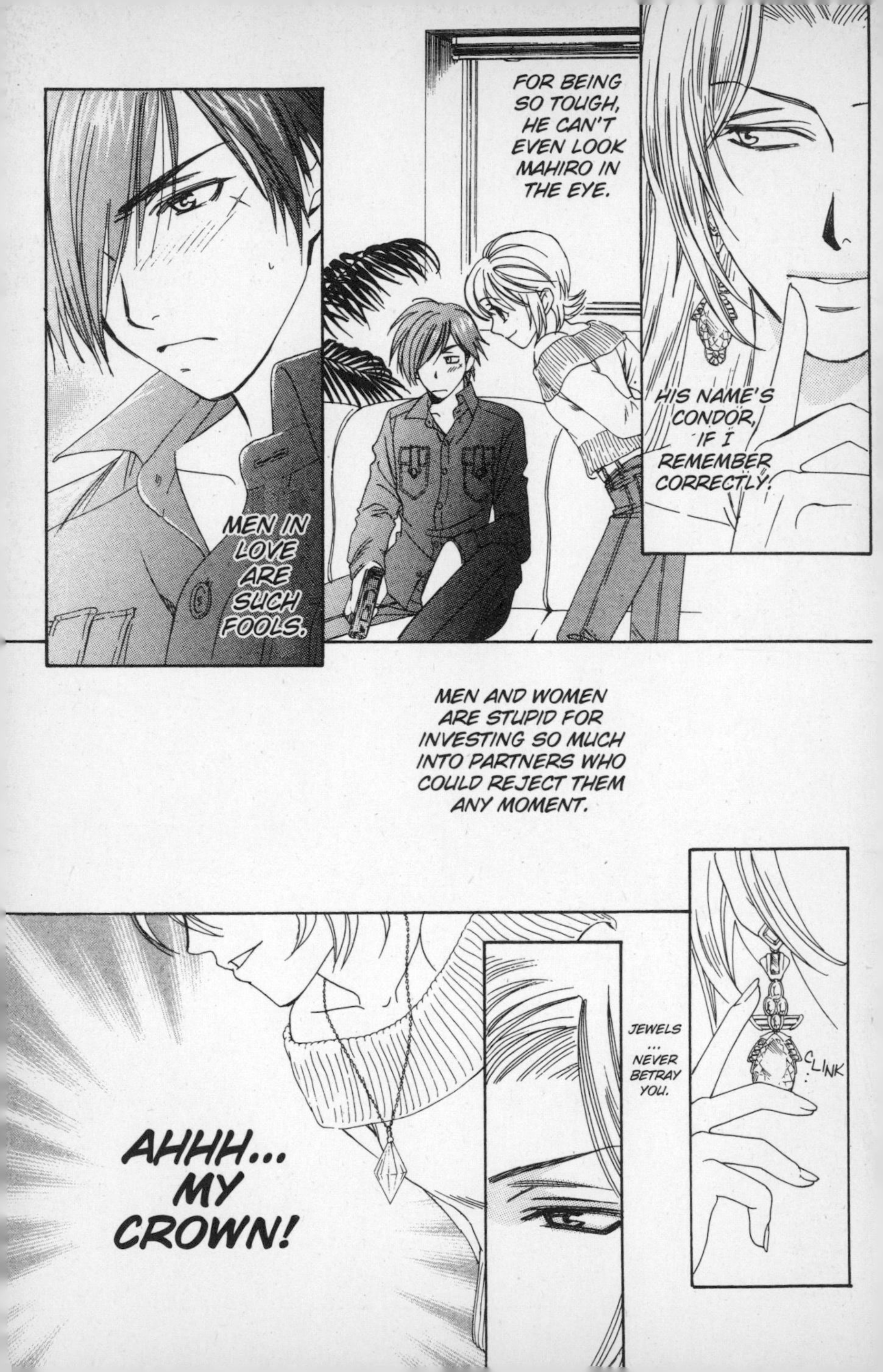
FOR BEING SO TOUGH, HE CAN'T EVEN LOOK MAHIRO IN THE EYE.
HIS NAME'S CONDOR, IF I REMEMBER CORRECTLY.
MEN IN LOVE ARE SUCH FOOLS.
MEN AND WOMEN ARE STUPID FOR INVESTING SO MUCH INTO PARTNERS WHO COULD REJECT THEM ANY MOMENT.
CLINK
JEWELS ... NEVER BETRAY YOU.
AHHH... MY CROWN!

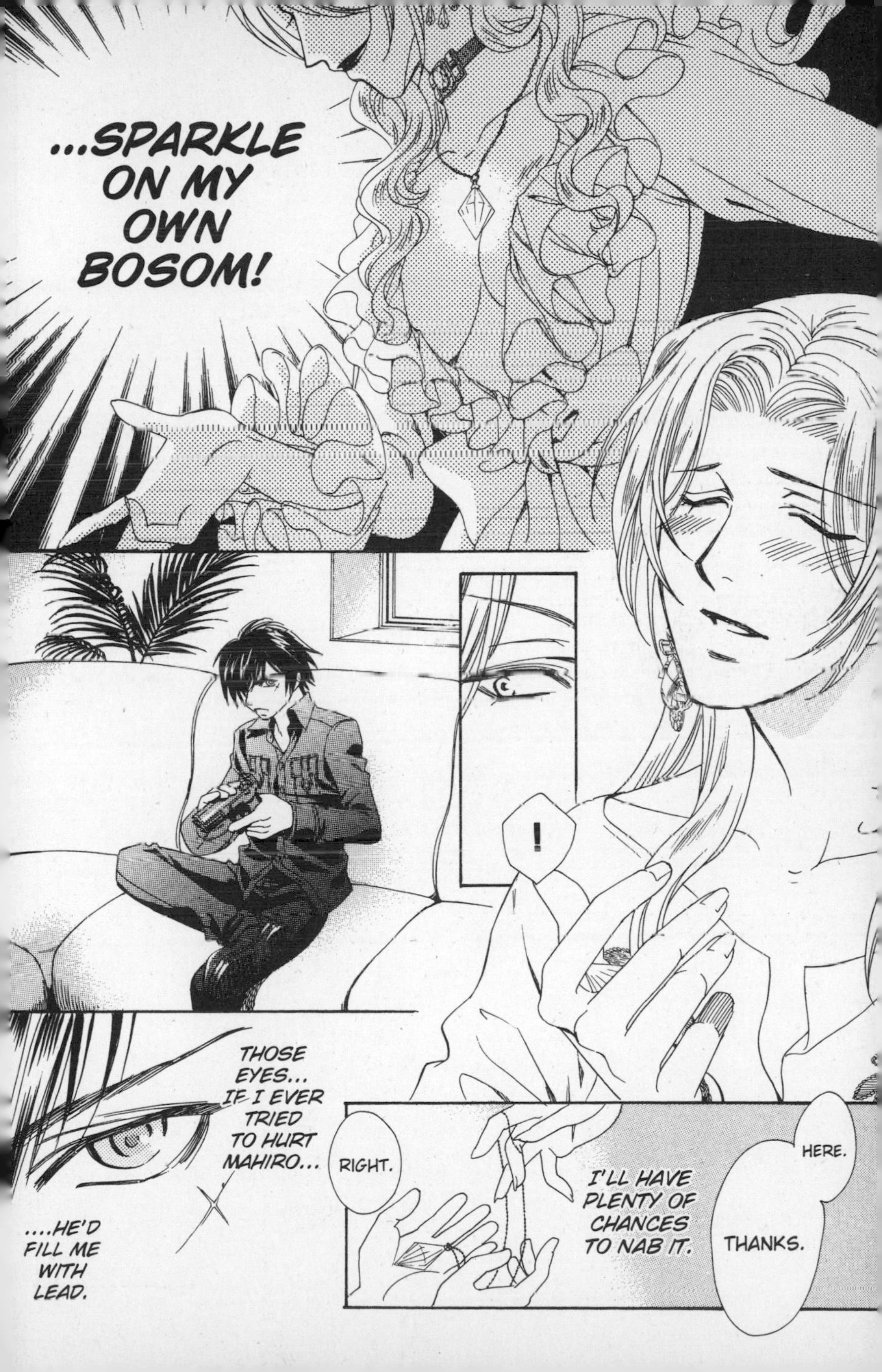
...SPARKLE ON MY OWN BOSOM!
!
HERE.
THANKS.
I'LL HAVE PLENTY OF CHANCES TO NAB IT.
RIGHT.
THOSE EYES... IF I EVER TRIED TO HURT MAHIRO...
....HE'D FILL ME WITH LEAD.

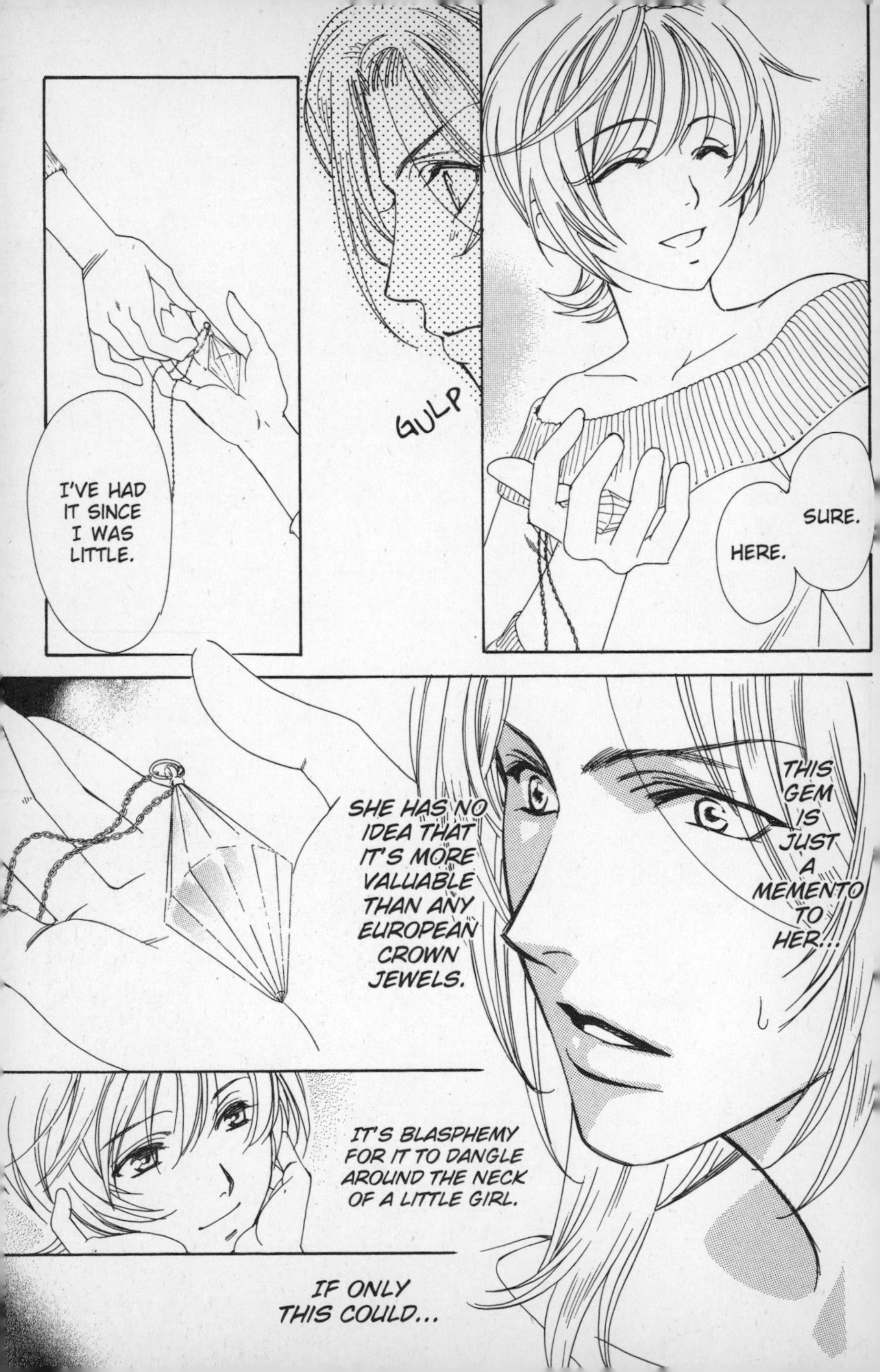
SURE.
HERE.
GULP
I'VE HAD IT SINCE I WAS LITTLE.
THIS GEM IS JUST A MEMENTO TO HER...
SHE HAS NO IDEA THAT IT'S MORE VALUABLE THAN ANY EUROPEAN CROWN JEWELS.
IT'S BLASPHEMY FOR IT TO DANGLE AROUND THE NECK OF A LITTLE GIRL.
IF ONLY THIS COULD...

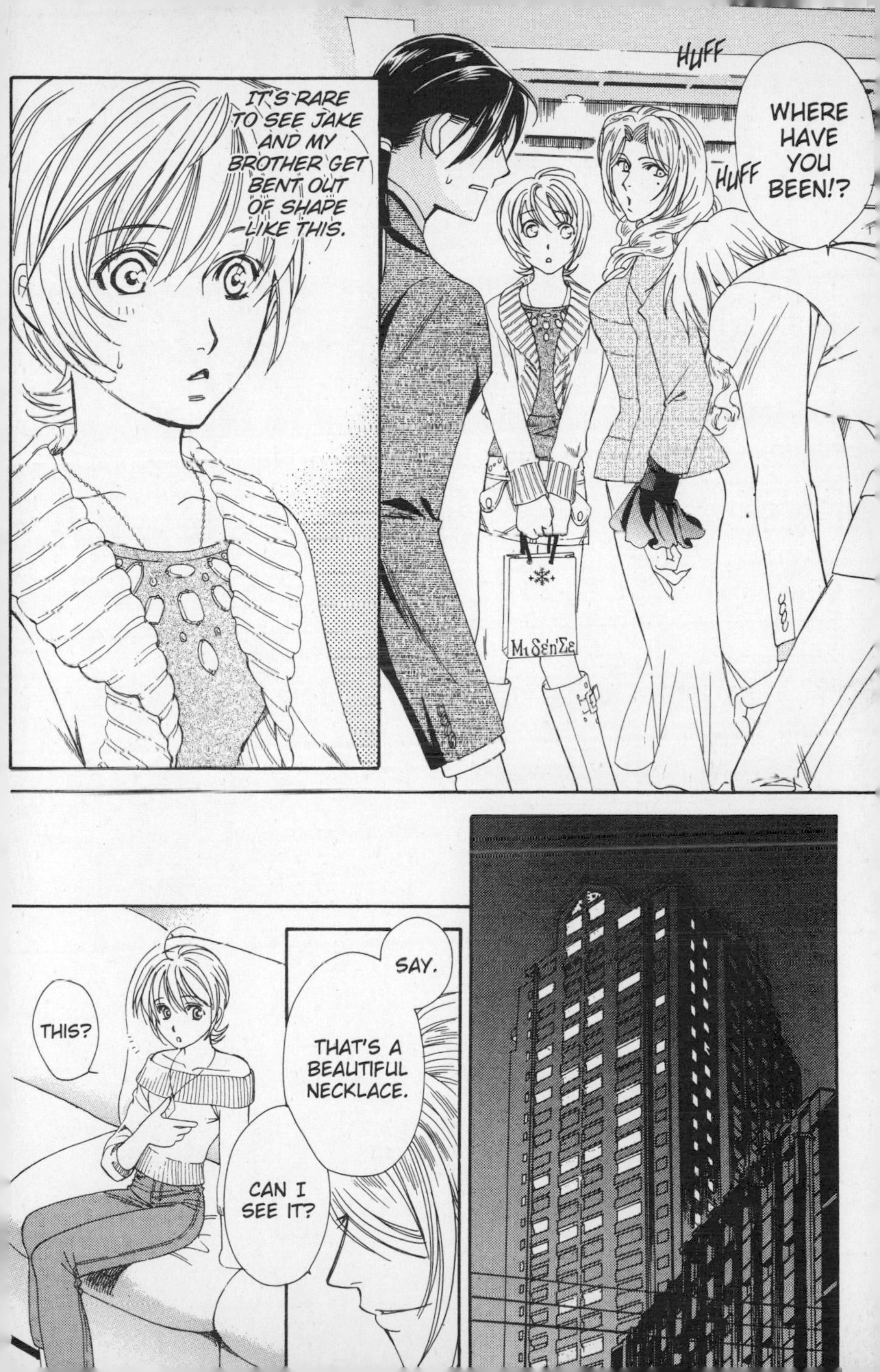
HUFF
WHERE HAVE YOU BEEN!?
HUFF
IT'S RARE TO SEE JAKE AND MY BROTHER GET BENT OUT OF SHAPE LIKE THIS.
SAY.
THAT'S A BEAUTIFUL NECKLACE.
THIS?
CAN I SEE IT?

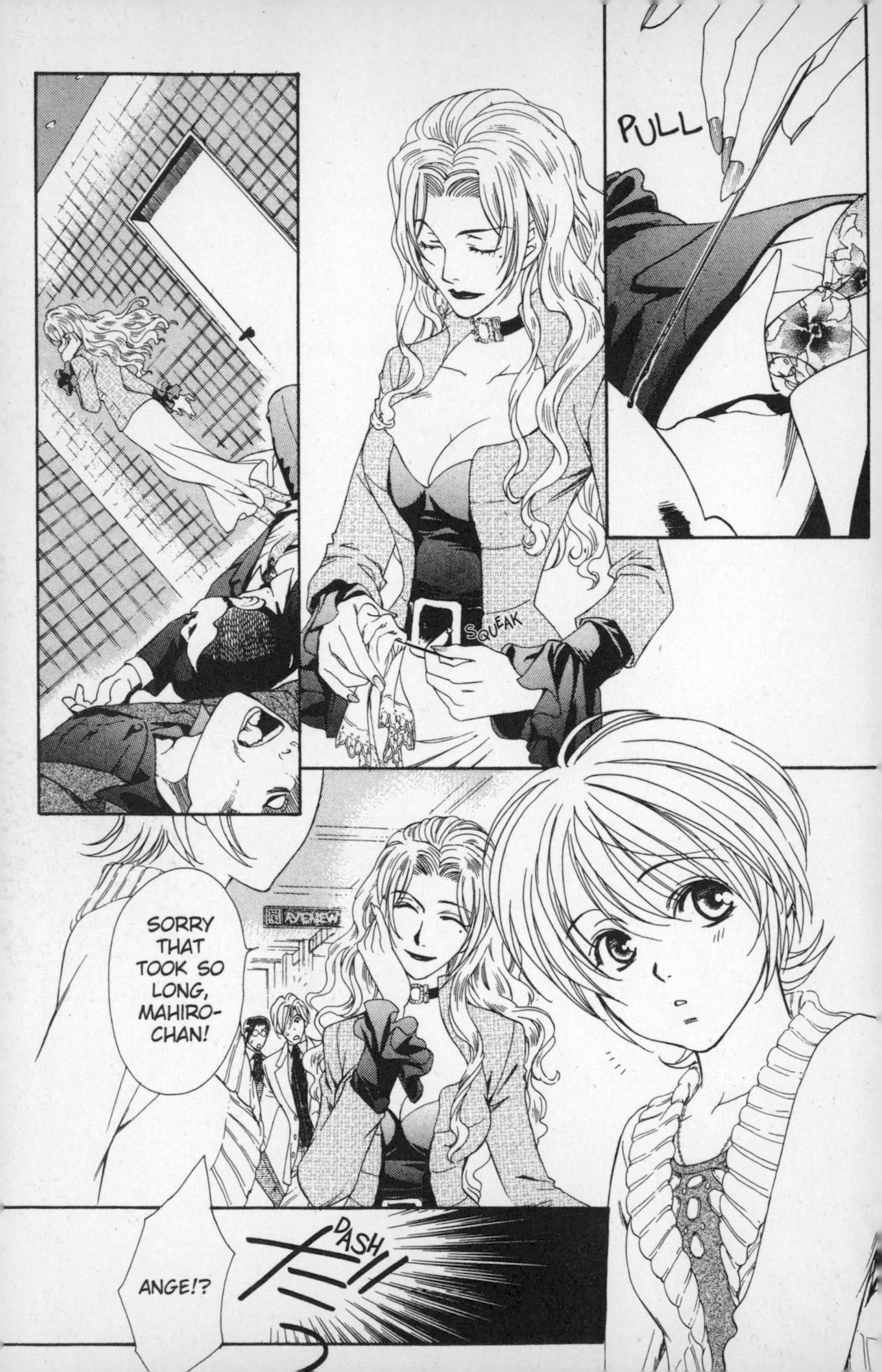
PULL
SQUEAK
SORRY THAT TOOK SO LONG, MAHIRO-CHAN!
DASH
ANGE!?

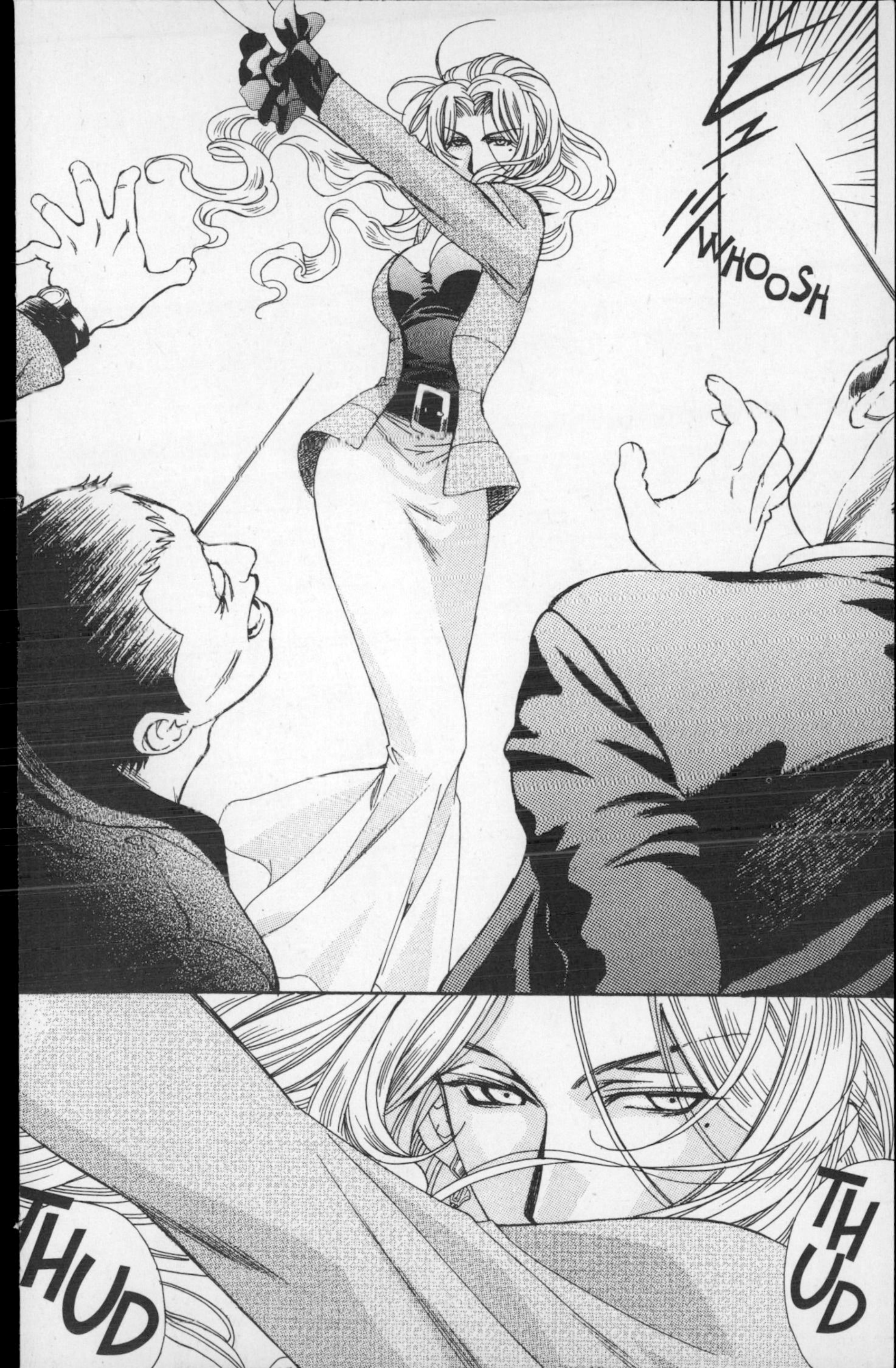
WHOOSH
THUD
THUD

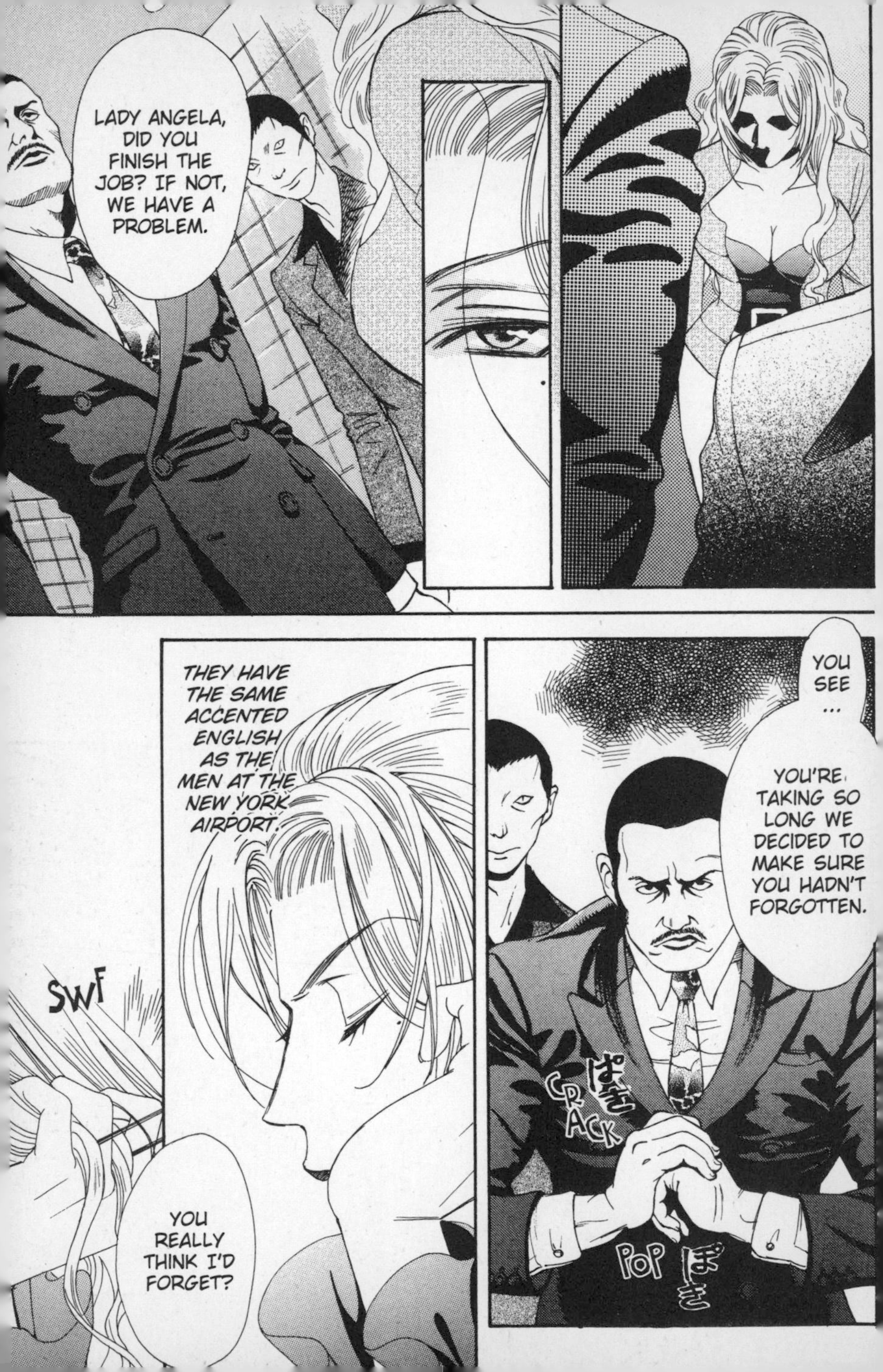
LADY ANGELA, DID YOU FINISH THE JOB? IF NOT, WE HAVE A PROBLEM.
YOU SEE ...
YOU'RE TAKING SO LONG WE DECIDED TO MAKE SURE YOU HADN'T FORGOTTEN.
ぱき CRACK
POP ぽき
THEY HAVE THE SAME ACCENTED ENGLISH AS THE MEN AT THE NEW YORK AIRPORT.
SWF
YOU REALLY THINK I'D FORGET?

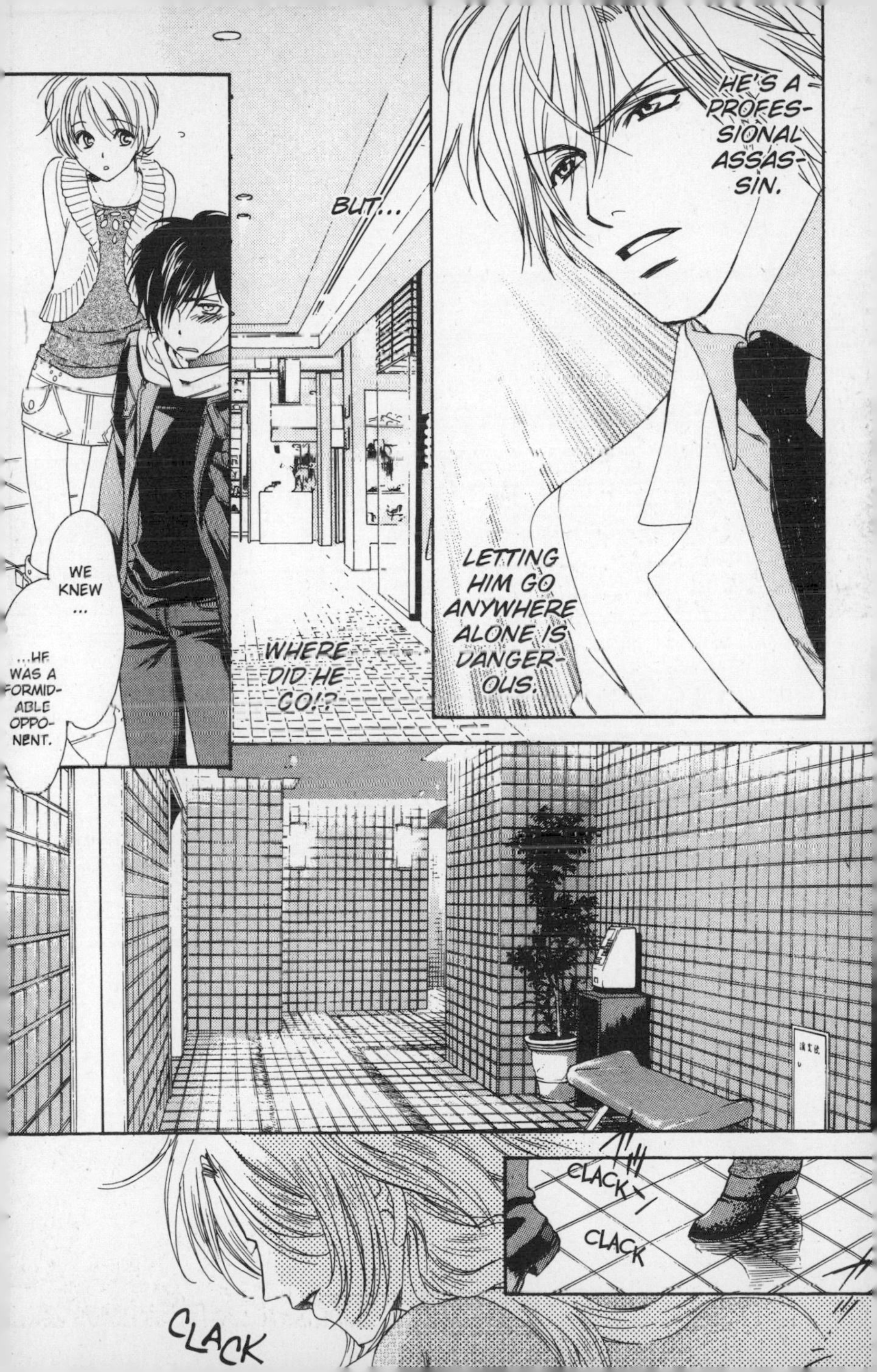
HE'S A PROFES-SIONAL ASSAS-SIN.
LETTING HIM GO ANYWHERE ALONE IS DANGER-OUS.
BUT...
WHERE DID HE GO!?
WE KNEW ...
...HE WAS A FORMID-ABLE OPPO-NENT.
CLACK
CLACK
CLACK

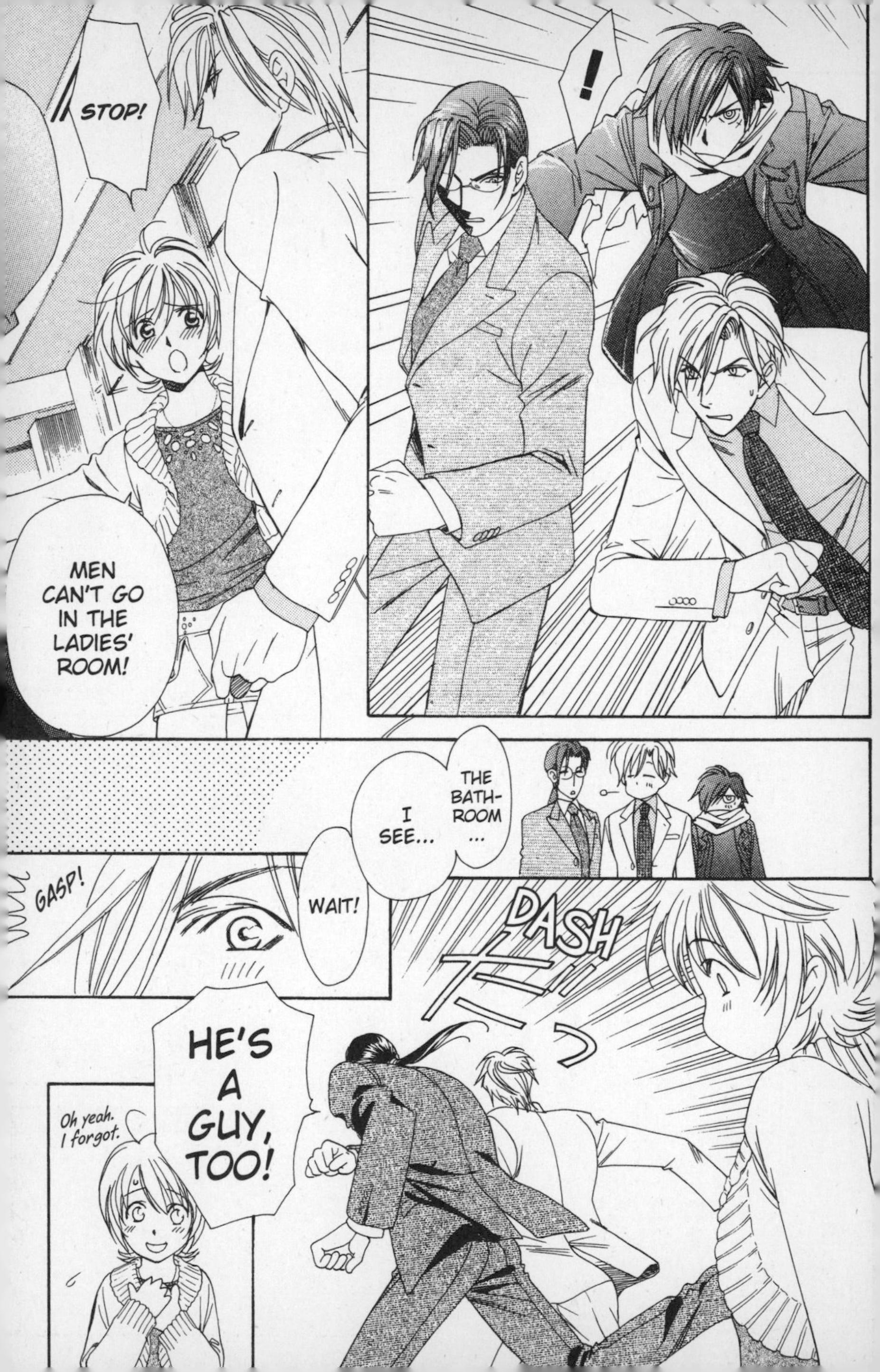
!
STOP!
MEN CAN'T GO IN THE LADIES' ROOM!
THE BATH-ROOM ...
I SEE...
WAIT!
GASP!
DASH
HE'S A GUY, TOO!
Oh yeah. I forgot.

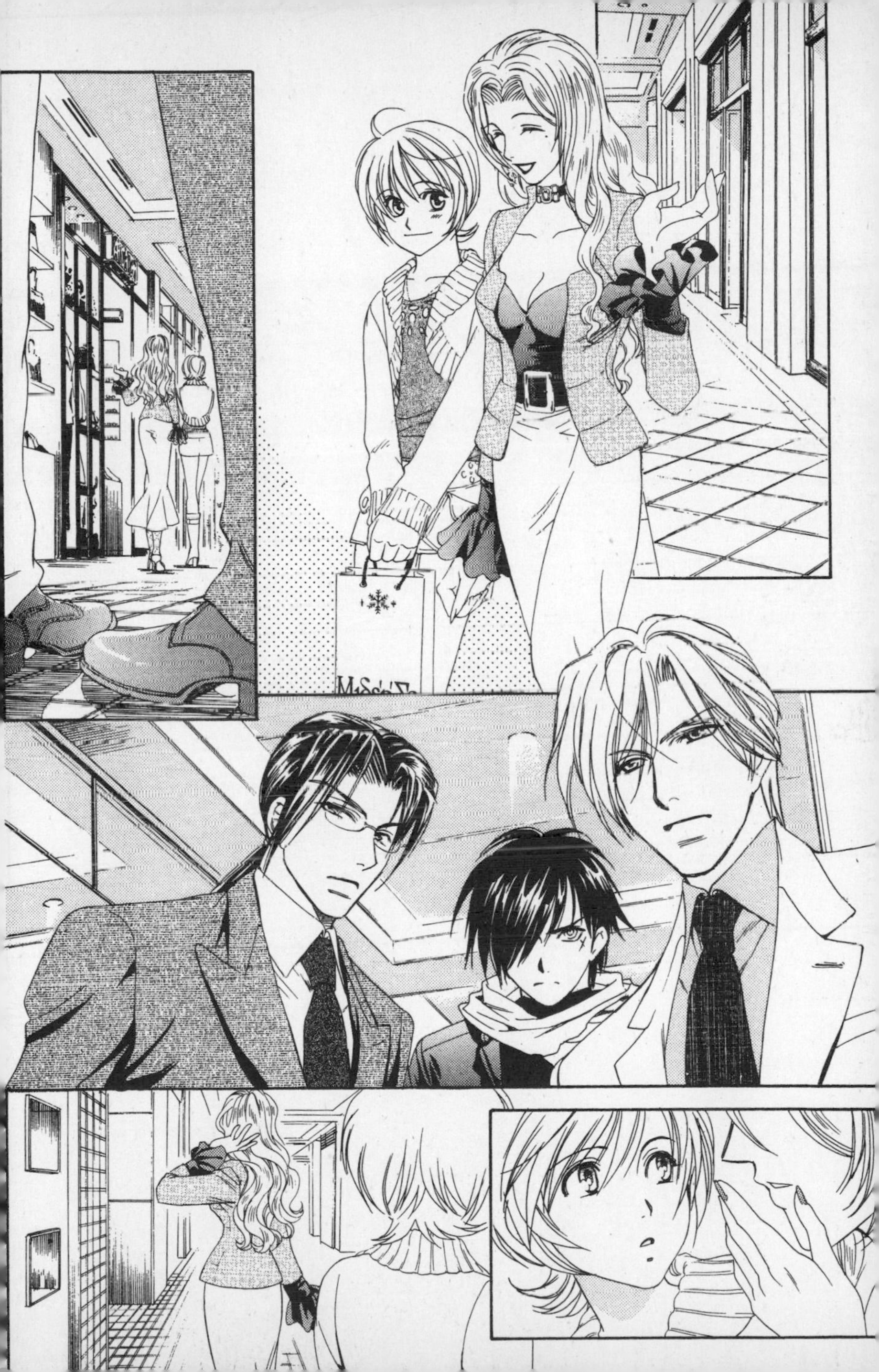

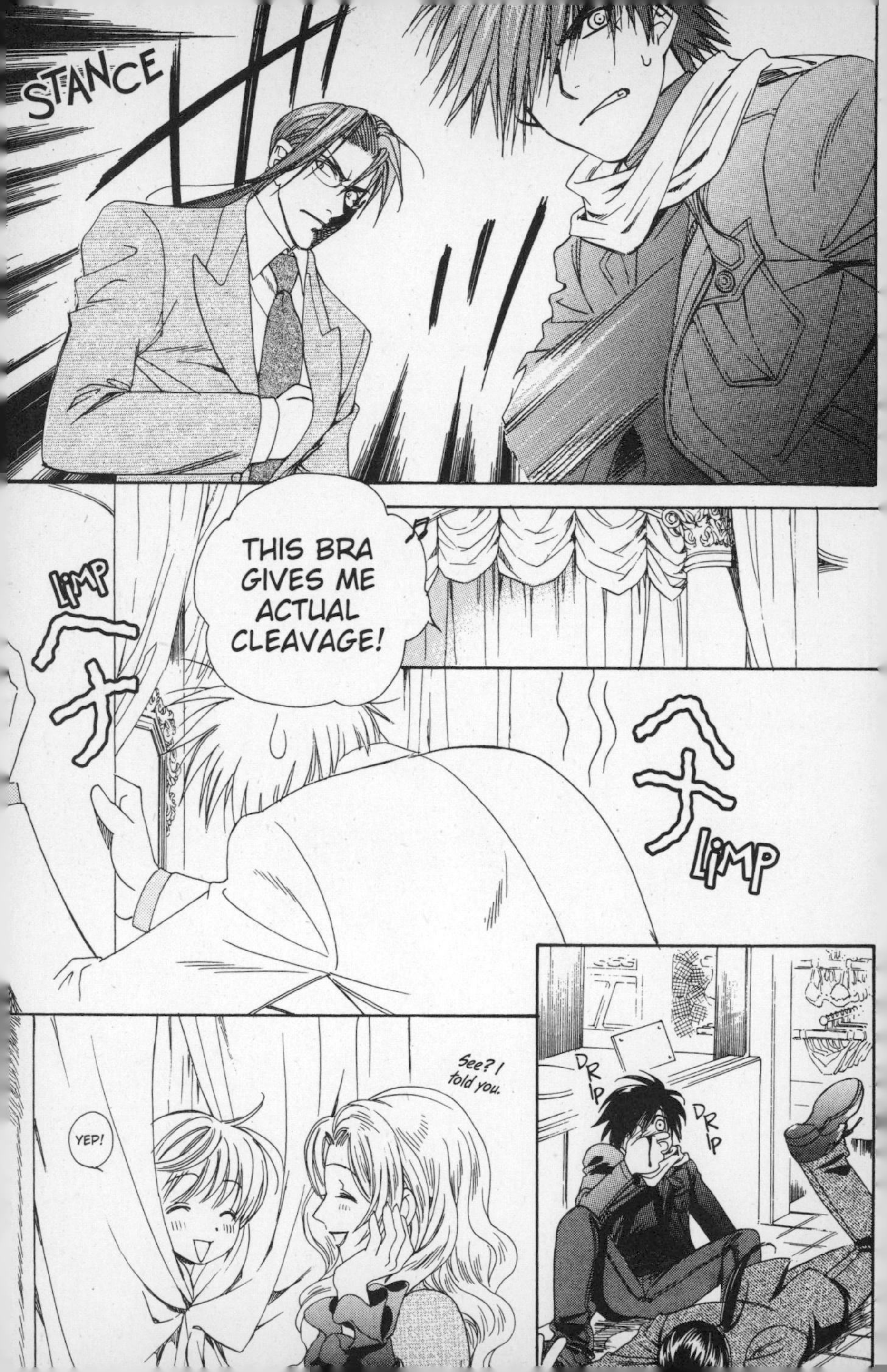
STANCE
THIS BRA GIVES ME ACTUAL CLEAVAGE!
LIMP
LIMP
See? I told you.
YEP!
DRIP
DRIP

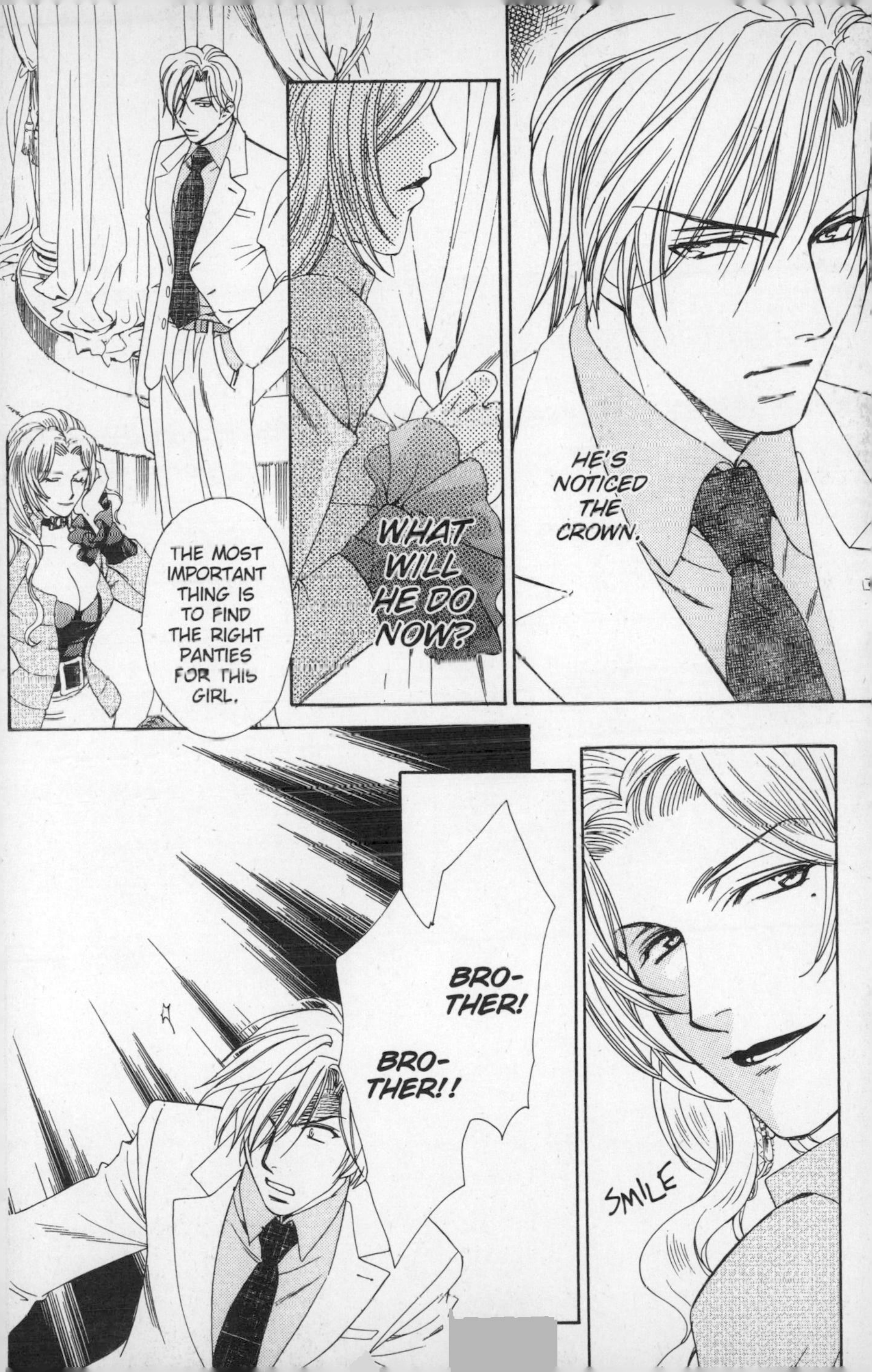
HE'S NOTICED THE CROWN.
WHAT WILL HE DO NOW?
THE MOST IMPORTANT THING IS TO FIND THE RIGHT PANTIES FOR THIS GIRL.
SMILE
BRO-THER!
BRO-THER!!

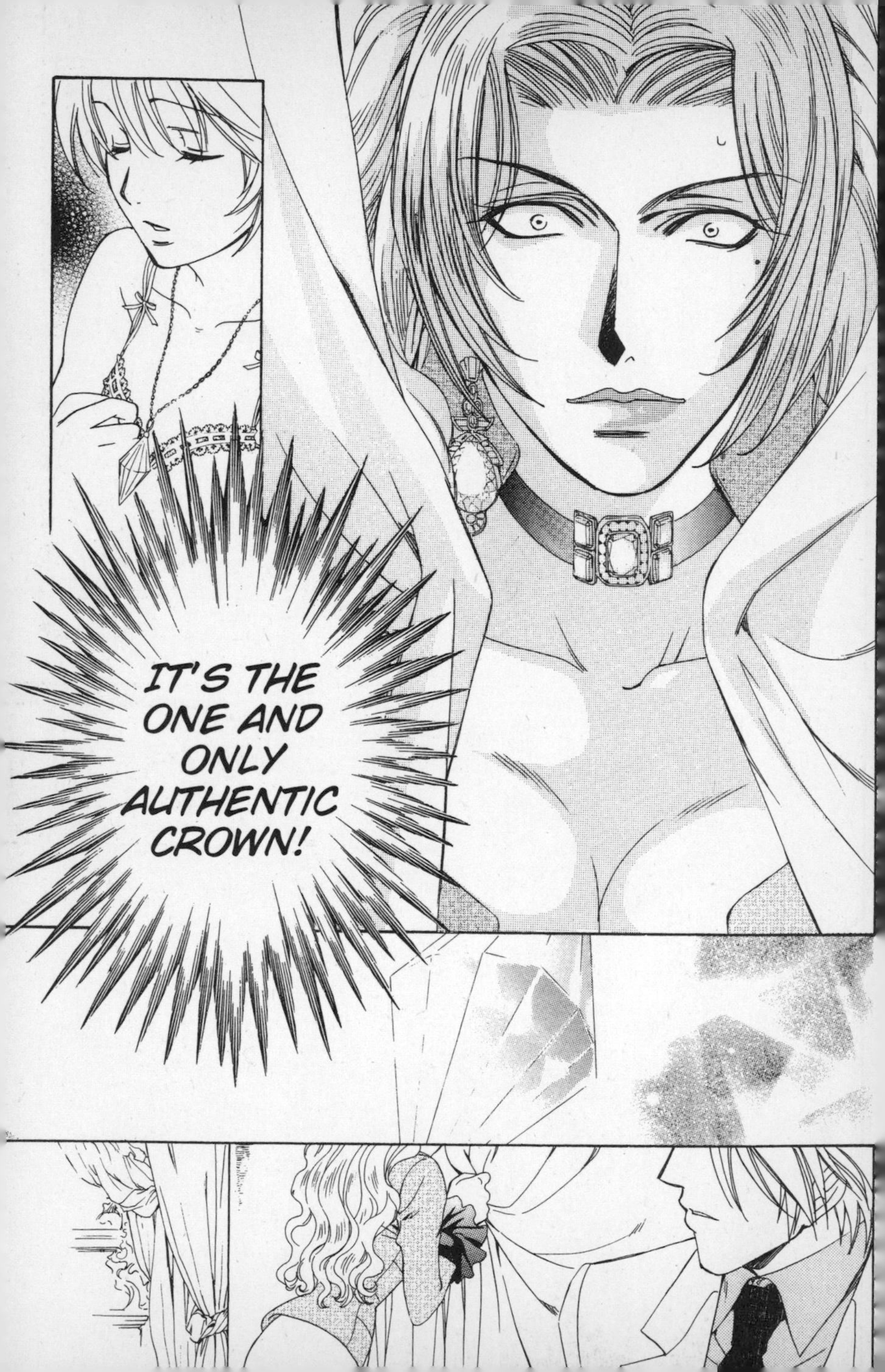
IT'S THE ONE AND ONLY AUTHENTIC CROWN!

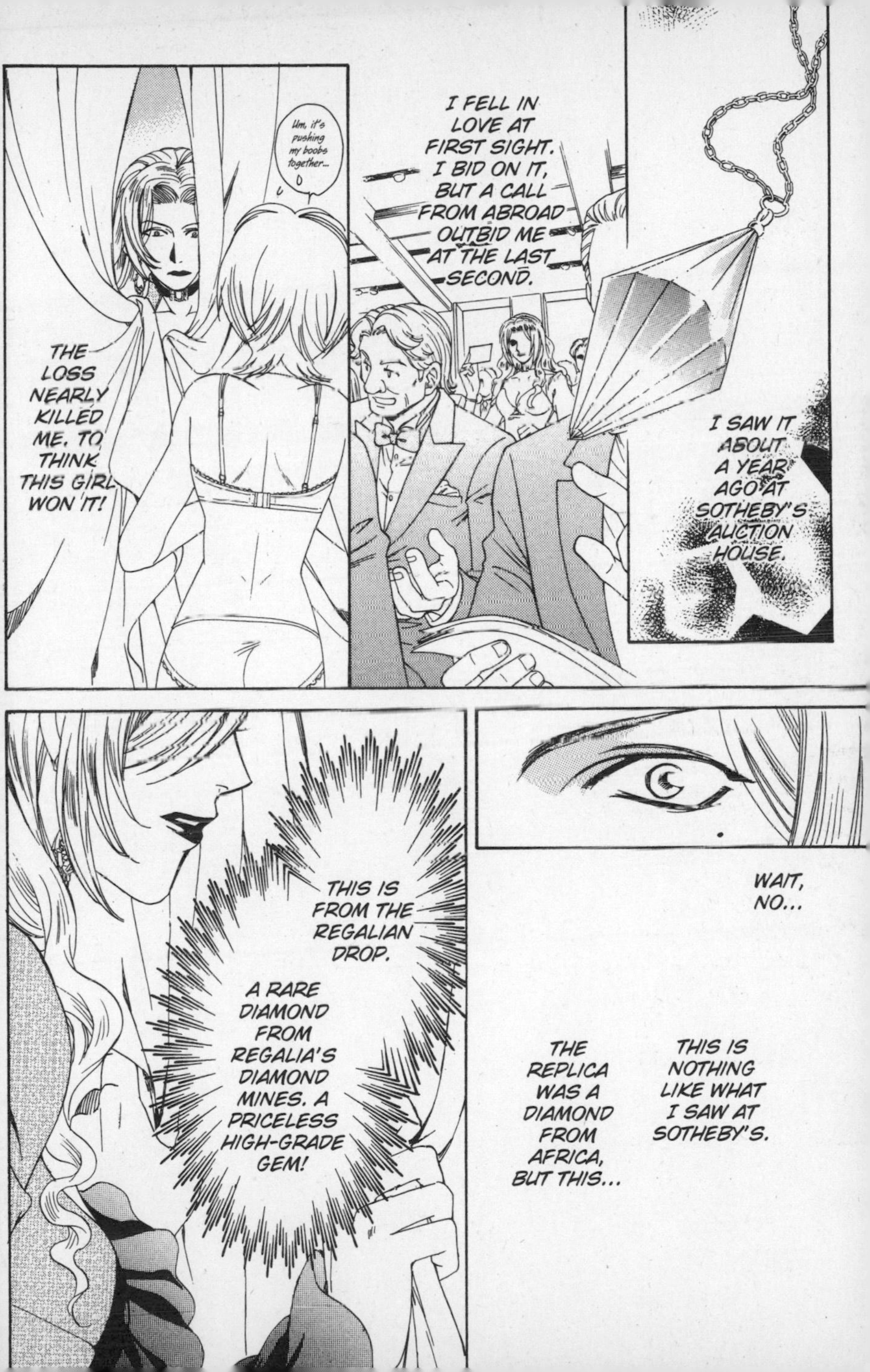
I SAW IT ABOUT A YEAR AGO AT SOTHEBY'S AUCTION HOUSE.
I FELL IN LOVE AT FIRST SIGHT. I BID ON IT, BUT A CALL FROM ABROAD OUTBID ME AT THE LAST SECOND.
Um, it's pushing my boobs together...
THE LOSS NEARLY KILLED ME. TO THINK THIS GIRL WON IT!
WAIT, NO...
THIS IS NOTHING LIKE WHAT I SAW AT SOTHEBY'S.
THE REPLICA WAS A DIAMOND FROM AFRICA, BUT THIS...
THIS IS FROM THE REGALIAN DROP.
A RARE DIAMOND FROM REGALIA'S DIAMOND MINES. A PRICELESS HIGH-GRADE GEM!

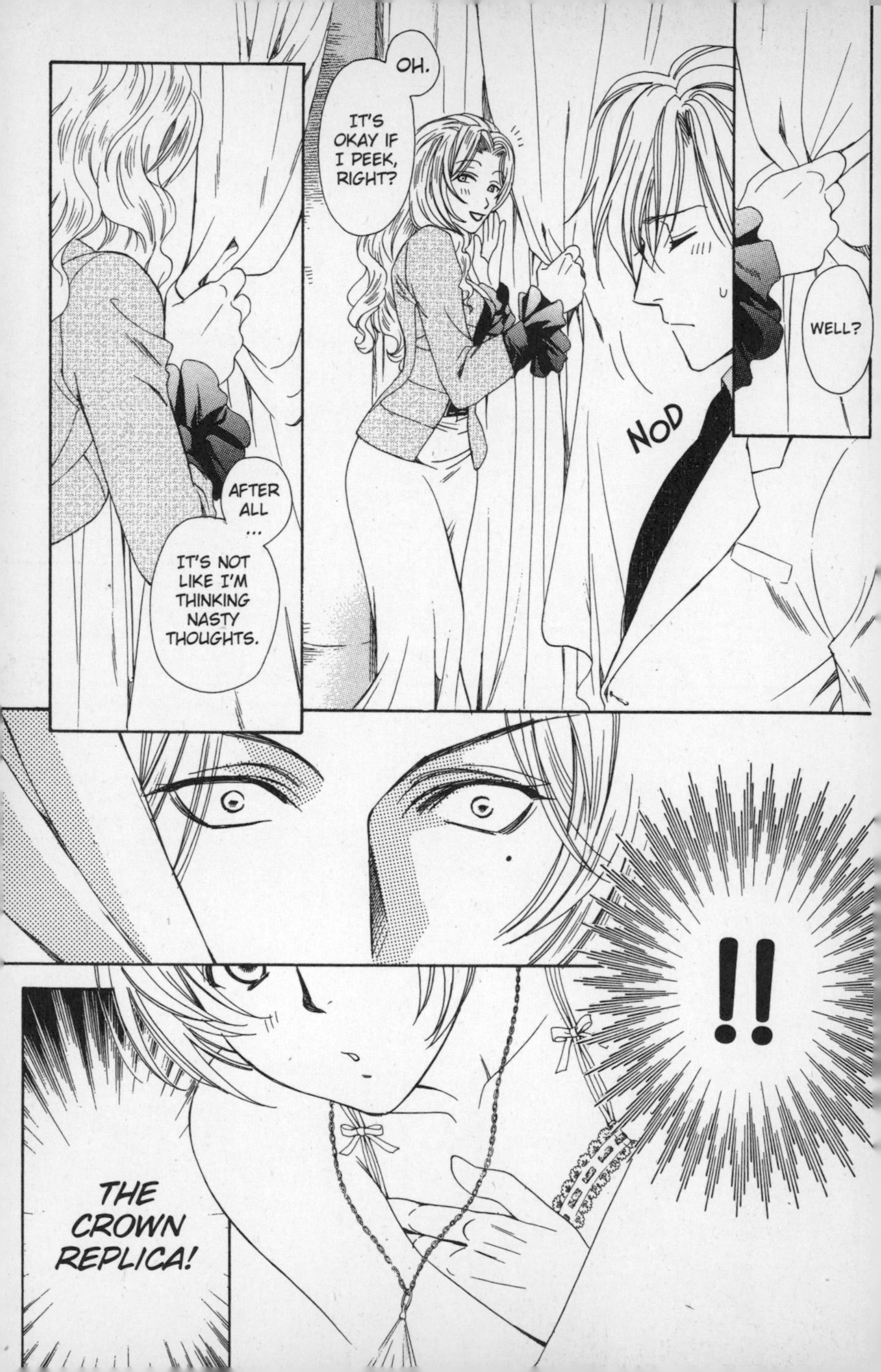
WELL?
OH.
IT'S OKAY IF I PEEK, RIGHT?
NOD
AFTER ALL ...
IT'S NOT LIKE I'M THINKING NASTY THOUGHTS.
!!
THE CROWN REPLICA!

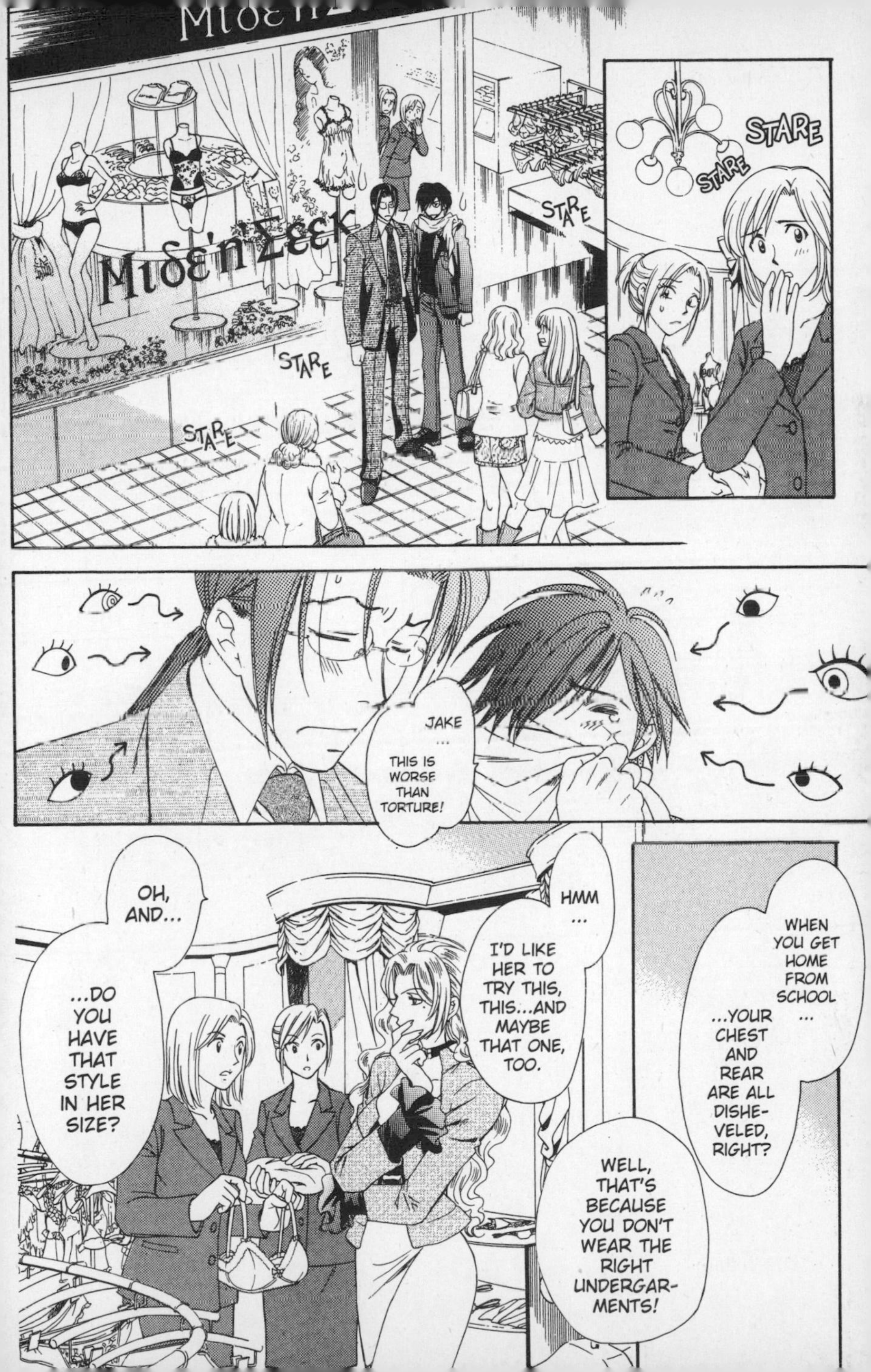
STARE
STARE
STARE
STARE
STARE
JAKE ... THIS IS WORSE THAN TORTURE!
WHEN YOU GET HOME FROM SCHOOL ...
...YOUR CHEST AND REAR ARE ALL DISHEVELED, RIGHT?
WELL, THAT'S BECAUSE YOU DON'T WEAR THE RIGHT UNDERGARMENTS!
HMM ...
I'D LIKE HER TO TRY THIS, THIS...AND MAYBE THAT ONE, TOO.
OH, AND...
...DO YOU HAVE THAT STYLE IN HER SIZE?

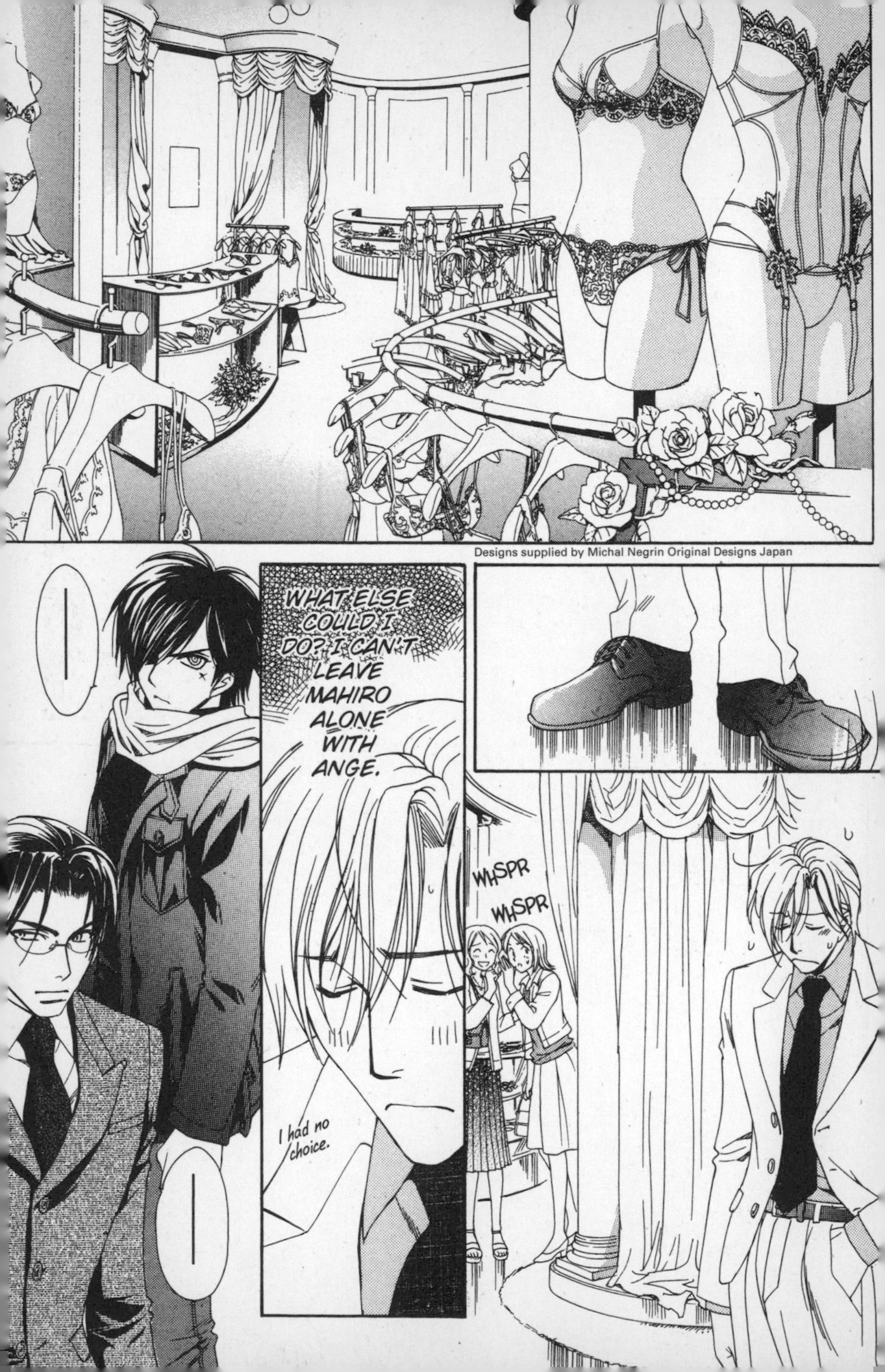
Designs supplied by Michal Negrin Original Designs Japan
WHAT ELSE COULD I DO? I CAN'T LEAVE MAHIRO ALONE WITH ANGE.
WHSPR
WHSPR
I had no choice.

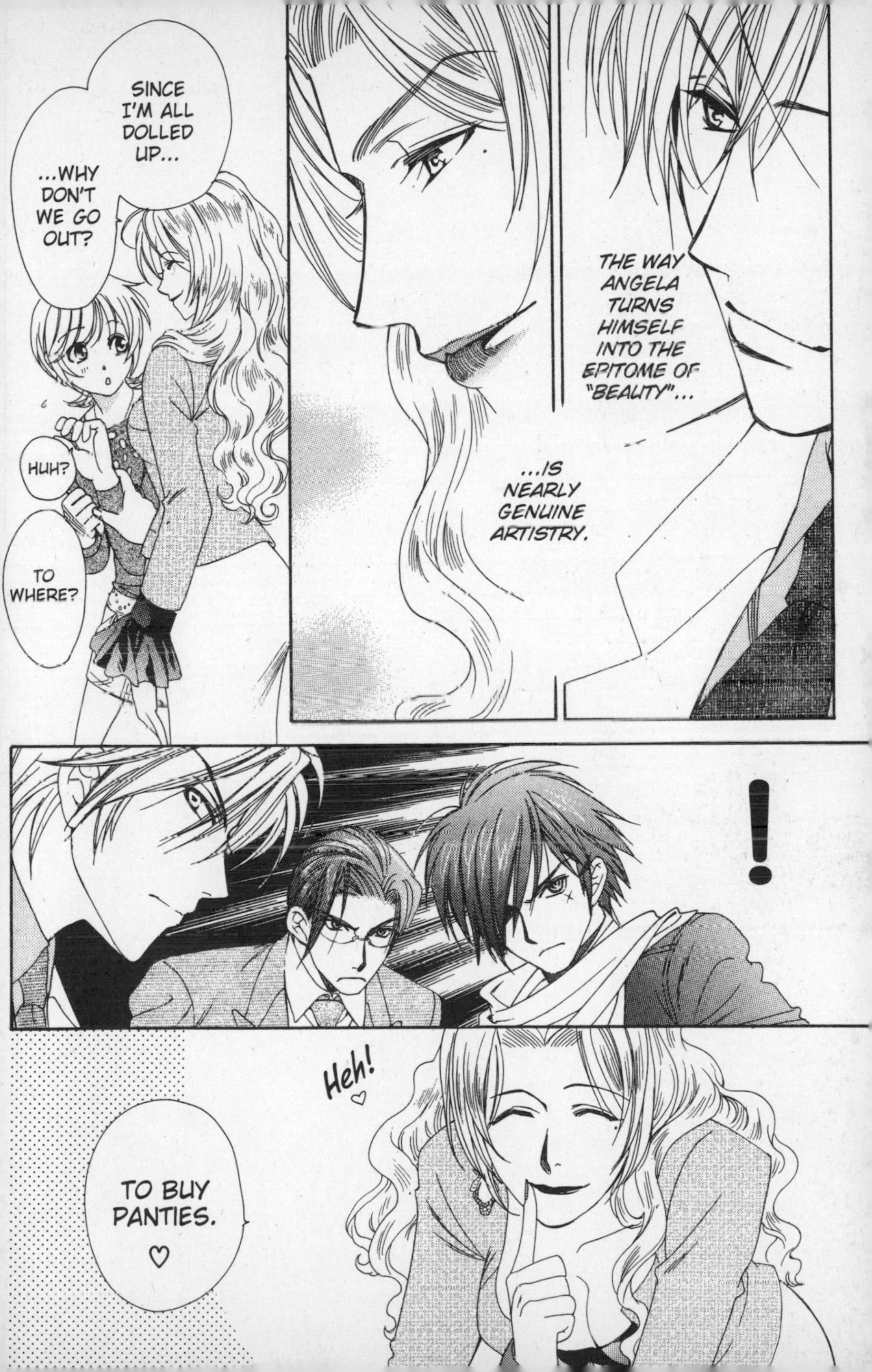
THE WAY ANGELA TURNS HIMSELF INTO THE EPITOME OF "BEAUTY"...
...IS NEARLY GENUINE ARTISTRY.
SINCE I'M ALL DOLLED UP...
...WHY DON'T WE GO OUT?
HUH?
TO WHERE?
!
Heh! ♡
TO BUY PANTIES. ♡

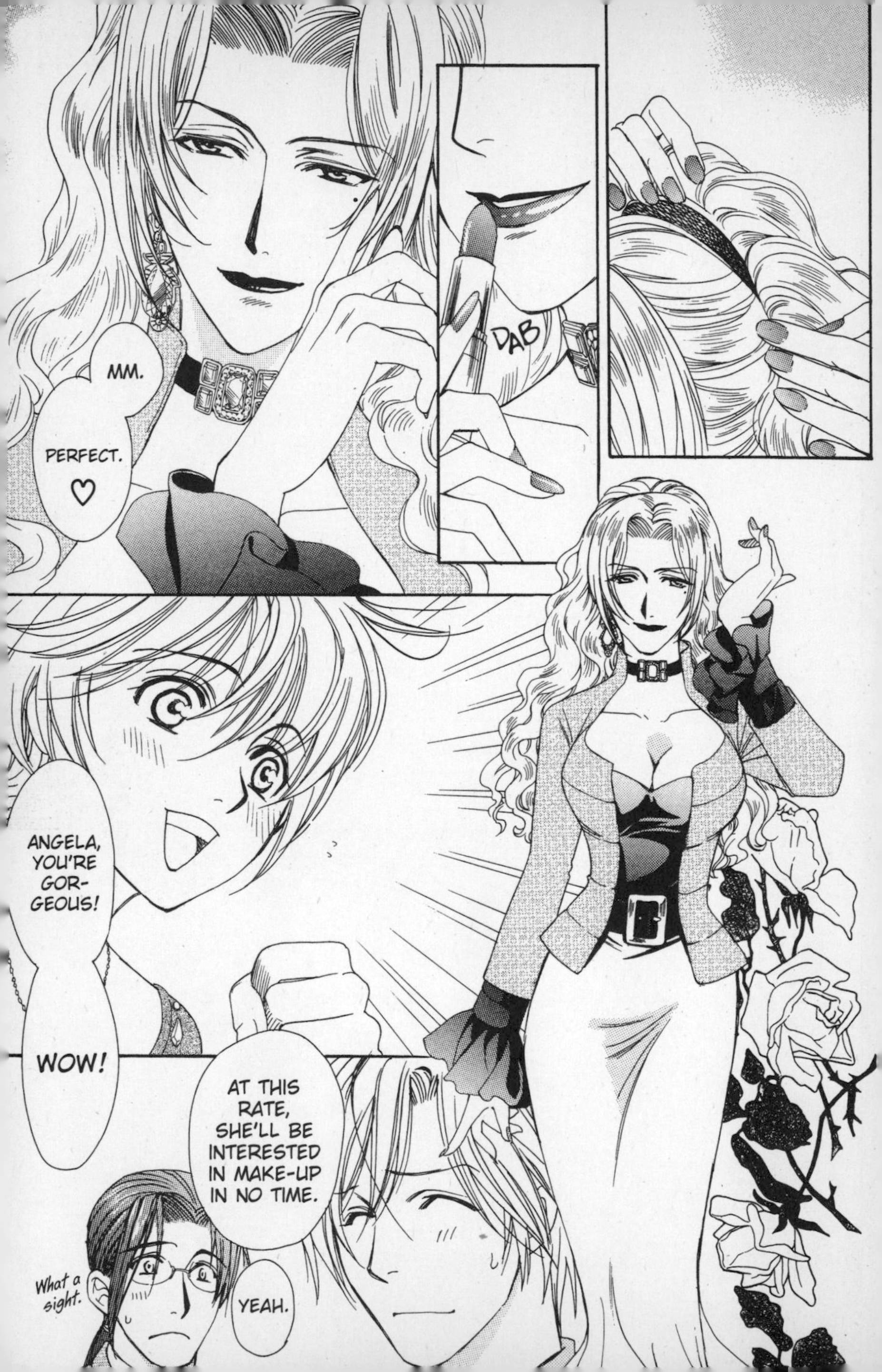

MM.
PERFECT. ♡
DAB
ANGELA, YOU'RE GOR- GEOUS!
WOW!
AT THIS RATE, SHE'LL BE INTERESTED IN MAKE-UP IN NO TIME.
YEAH.
What a sight.

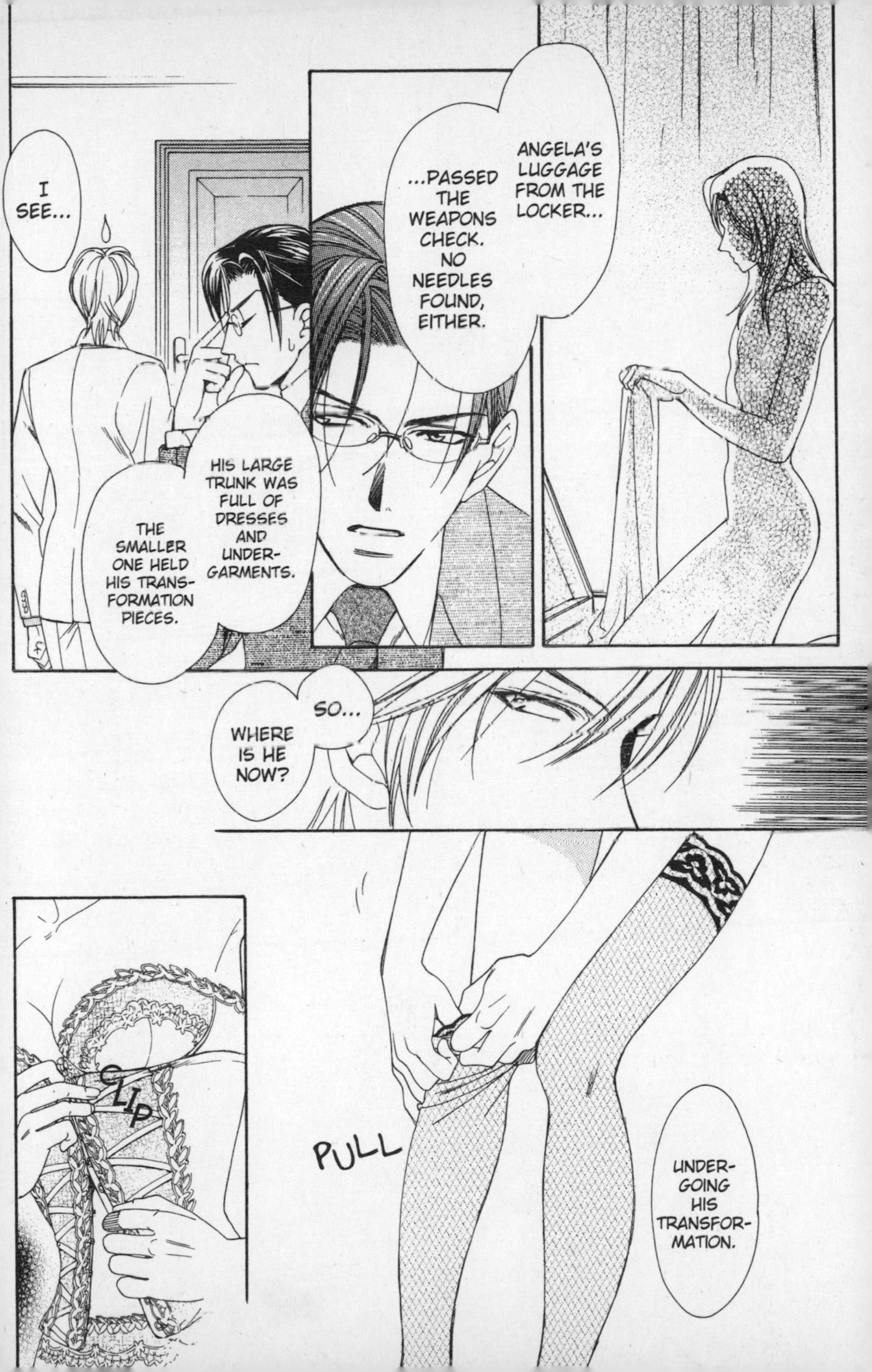
ANGELA'S LUGGAGE FROM THE LOCKER...
...PASSED THE WEAPONS CHECK. NO NEEDLES FOUND, EITHER.
I SEE...
HIS LARGE TRUNK WAS FULL OF DRESSES AND UNDER-GARMENTS.
THE SMALLER ONE HELD HIS TRANS-FORMATION PIECES.
SO...
WHERE IS HE NOW?
UNDER-GOING HIS TRANSFOR-MATION.
PULL
CLIP

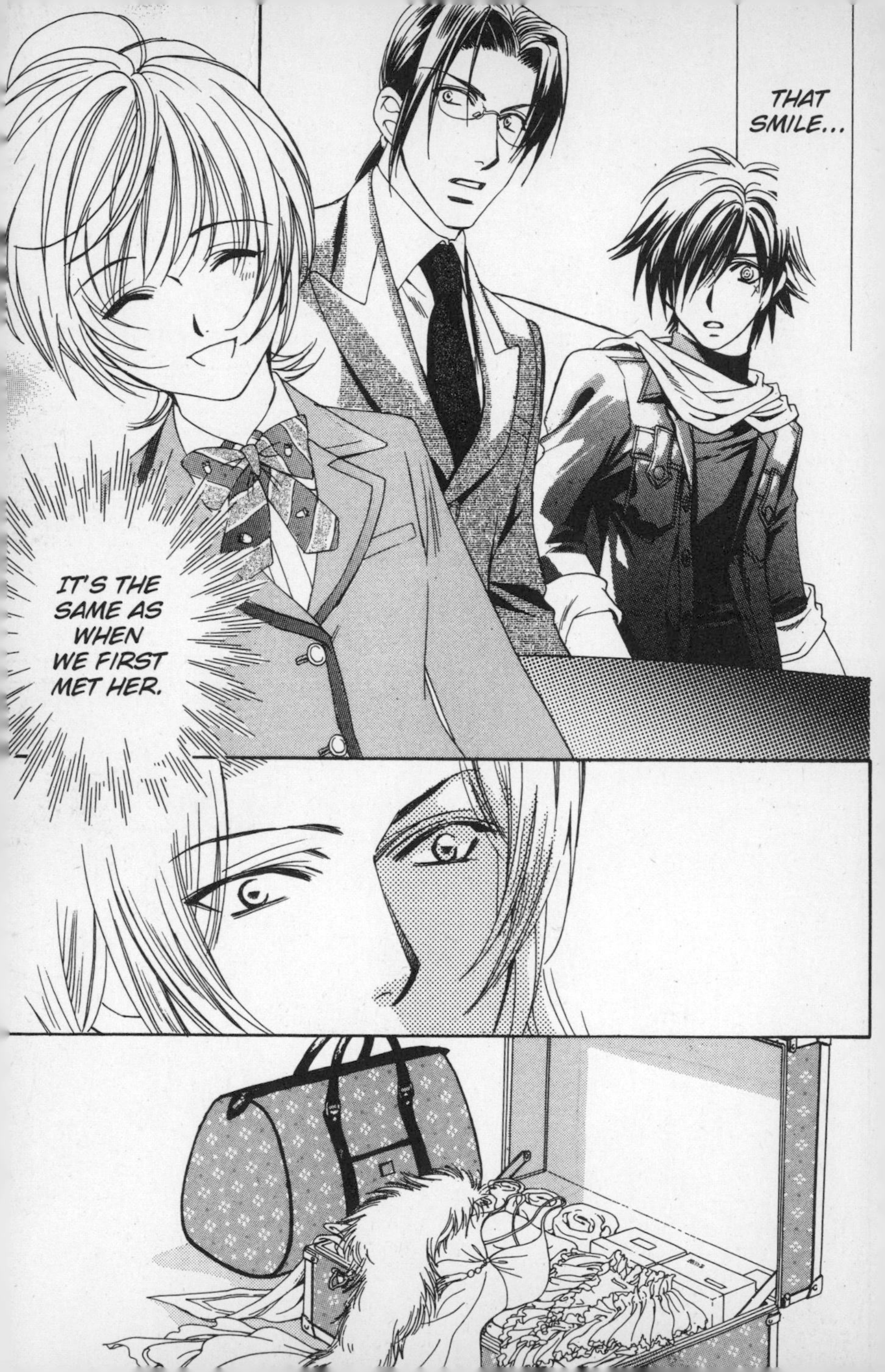
THAT SMILE...
IT'S THE SAME AS WHEN WE FIRST MET HER.

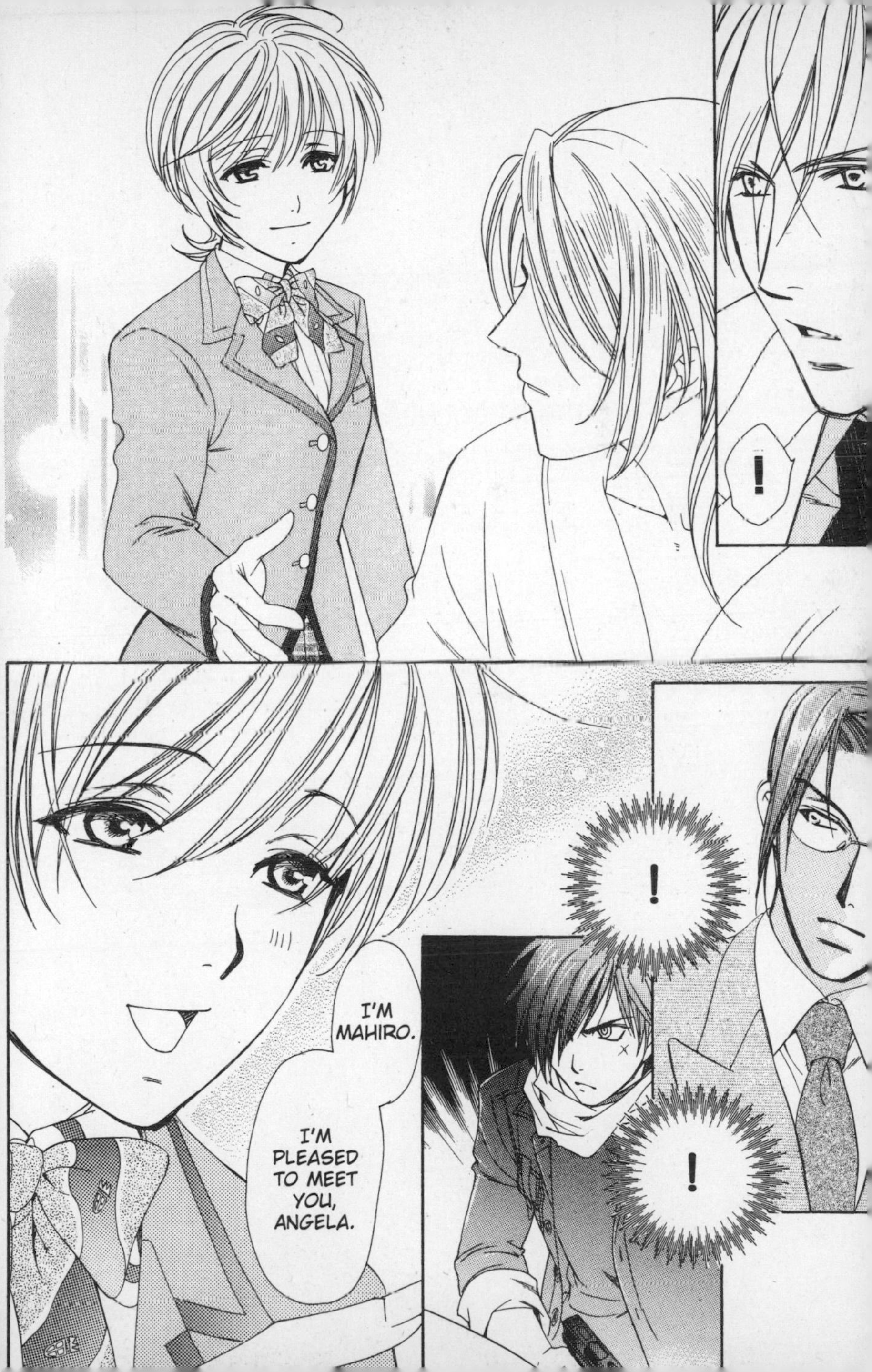
!
!
!
I'M MAHIRO.
I'M PLEASED TO MEET YOU, ANGELA.

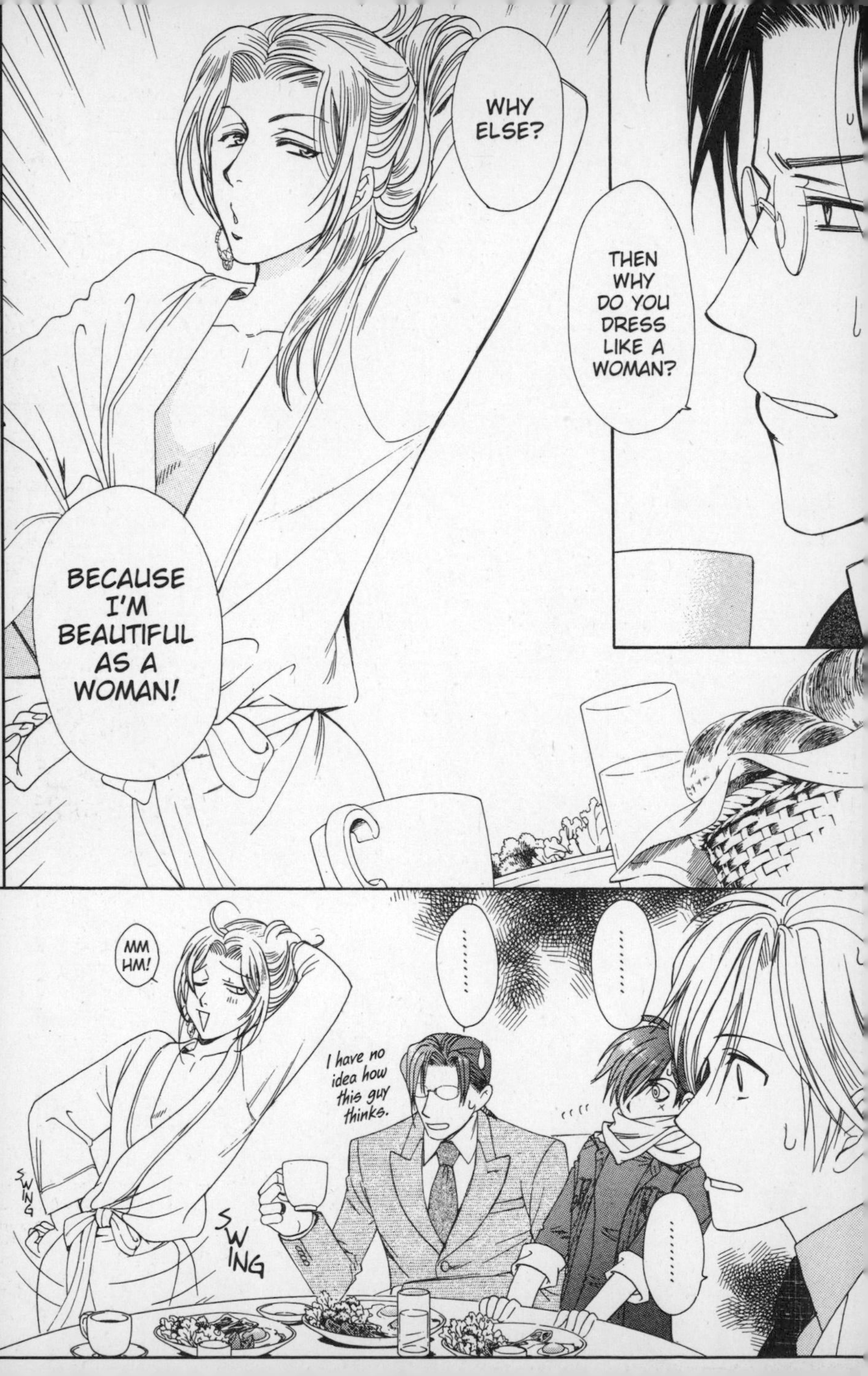
WHY ELSE?
THEN WHY DO YOU DRESS LIKE A WOMAN?
BECAUSE I'M BEAUTIFUL AS A WOMAN!
......
......
......
I have no idea how this guy thinks.
MM HM!
SWING
SWING

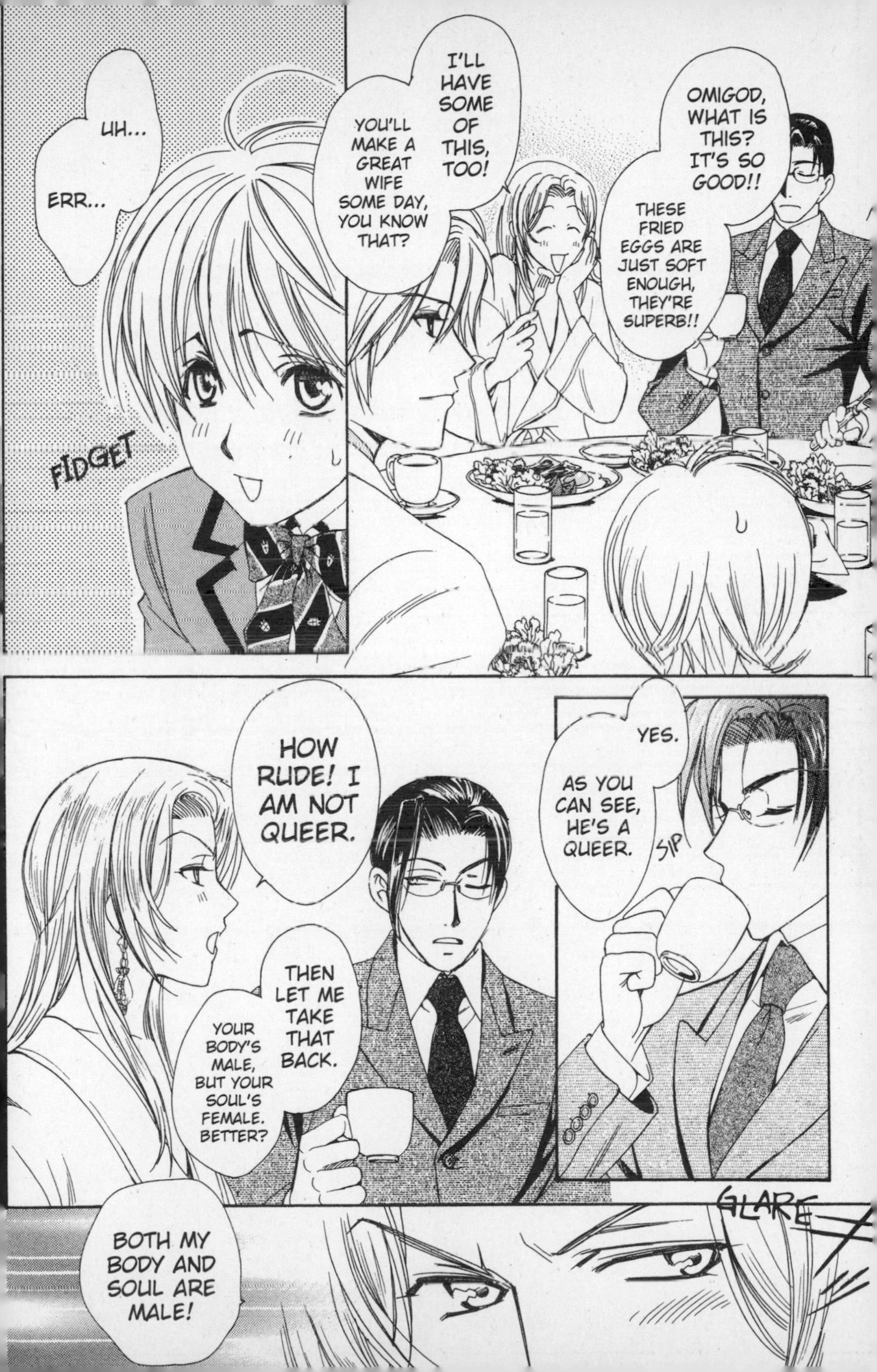
OMIGOD, WHAT IS THIS? IT'S SO GOOD!!
THESE FRIED EGGS ARE JUST SOFT ENOUGH, THEY'RE SUPERB!!
I'LL HAVE SOME OF THIS, TOO!
YOU'LL MAKE A GREAT WIFE SOME DAY, YOU KNOW THAT?
UH...
ERR...
FIDGET
YES.
AS YOU CAN SEE, HE'S A QUEER.
SIP
HOW RUDE! I AM NOT QUEER.
THEN LET ME TAKE THAT BACK.
YOUR BODY'S MALE, BUT YOUR SOUL'S FEMALE. BETTER?
GLARE
BOTH MY BODY AND SOUL ARE MALE!

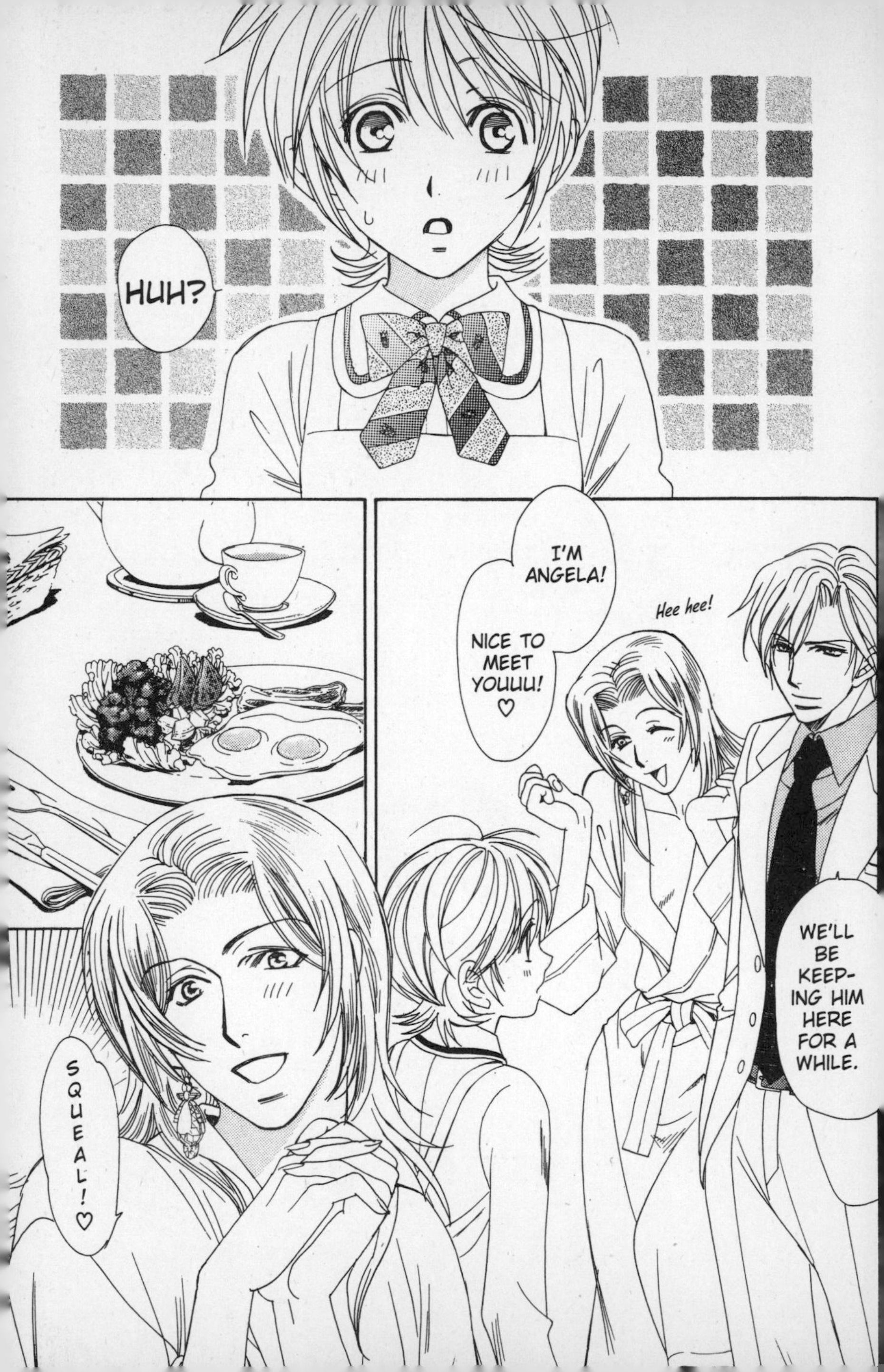
HUH?
I'M ANGELA!
NICE TO MEET YOUUU! ♡
Hee hee!
WE'LL BE KEEPING HIM HERE FOR A WHILE.
SQUEAL! ♡

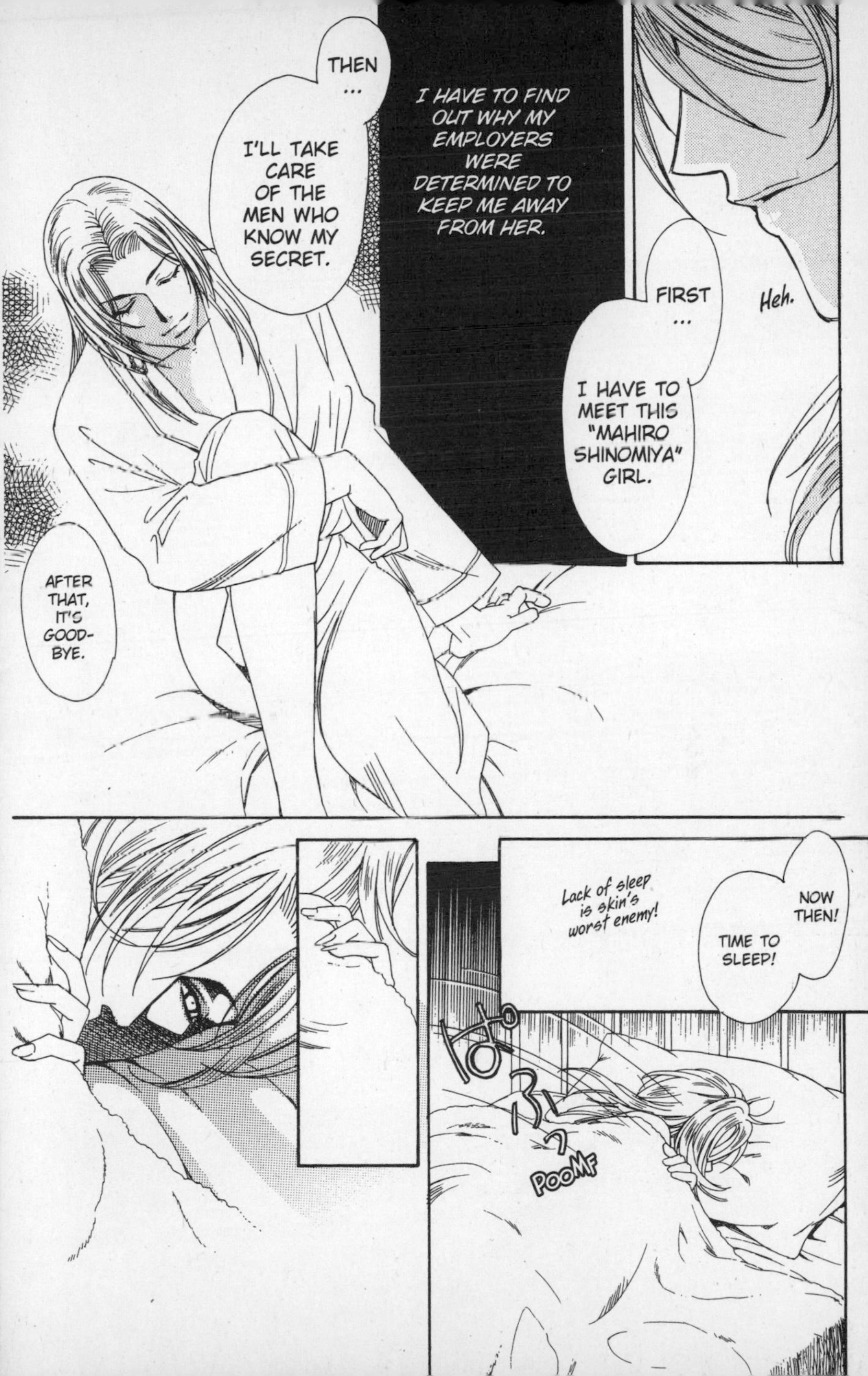
Heh.
FIRST ...
I HAVE TO MEET THIS "MAHIRO SHINOMIYA" GIRL.
I HAVE TO FIND OUT WHY MY EMPLOYERS WERE DETERMINED TO KEEP ME AWAY FROM HER.
THEN ...
I'LL TAKE CARE OF THE MEN WHO KNOW MY SECRET.
AFTER THAT, IT'S GOOD-BYE.
NOW THEN!
TIME TO SLEEP!
Lack of sleep is skin's worst enemy!
POOMF

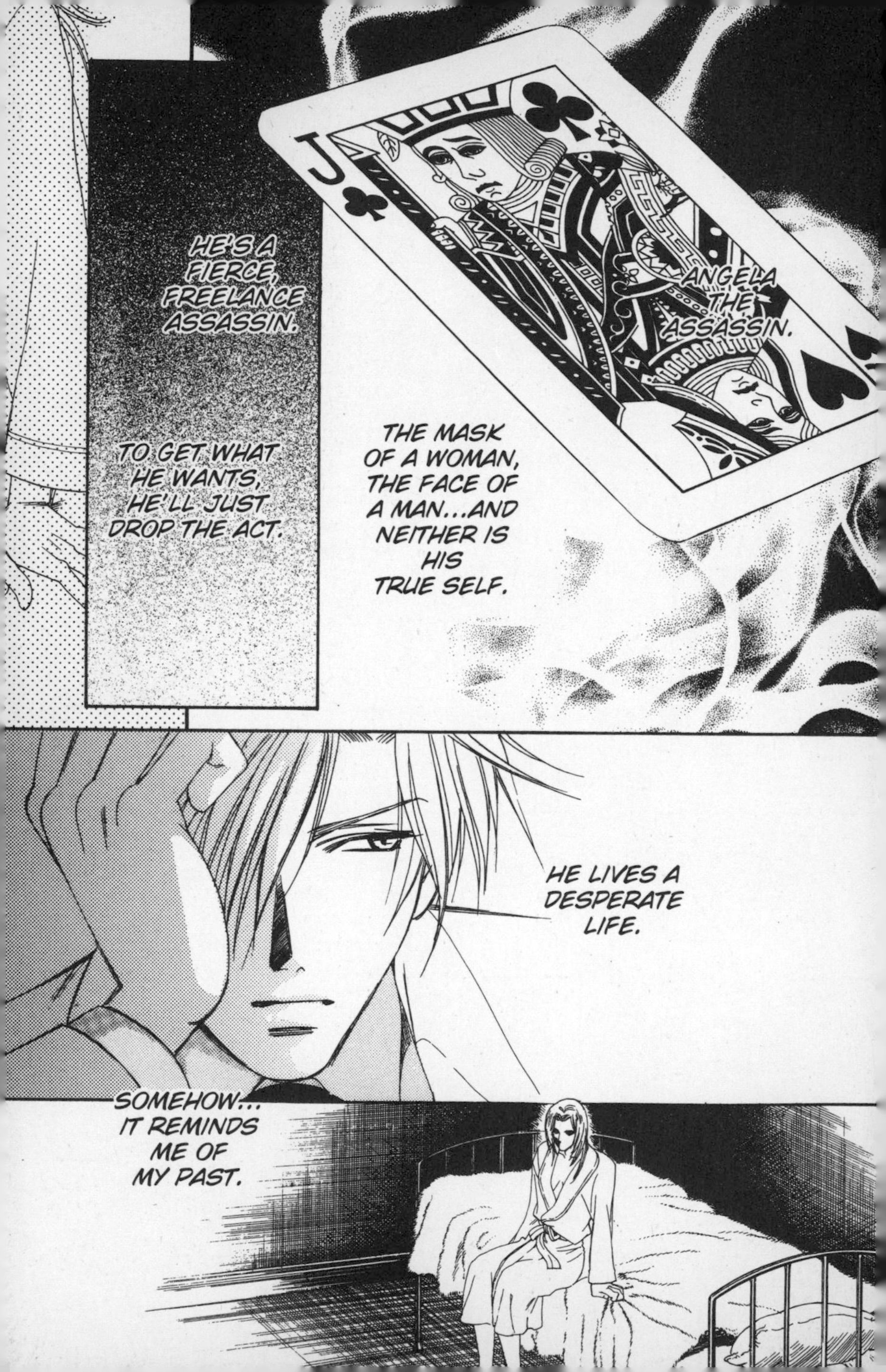
ANGELA THE ASSASSIN.
HE'S A FIERCE, FREELANCE ASSASSIN.
THE MASK OF A WOMAN, THE FACE OF A MAN...AND NEITHER IS HIS TRUE SELF.
TO GET WHAT HE WANTS, HE'LL JUST DROP THE ACT.
HE LIVES A DESPERATE LIFE.
SOMEHOW... IT REMINDS ME OF MY PAST.

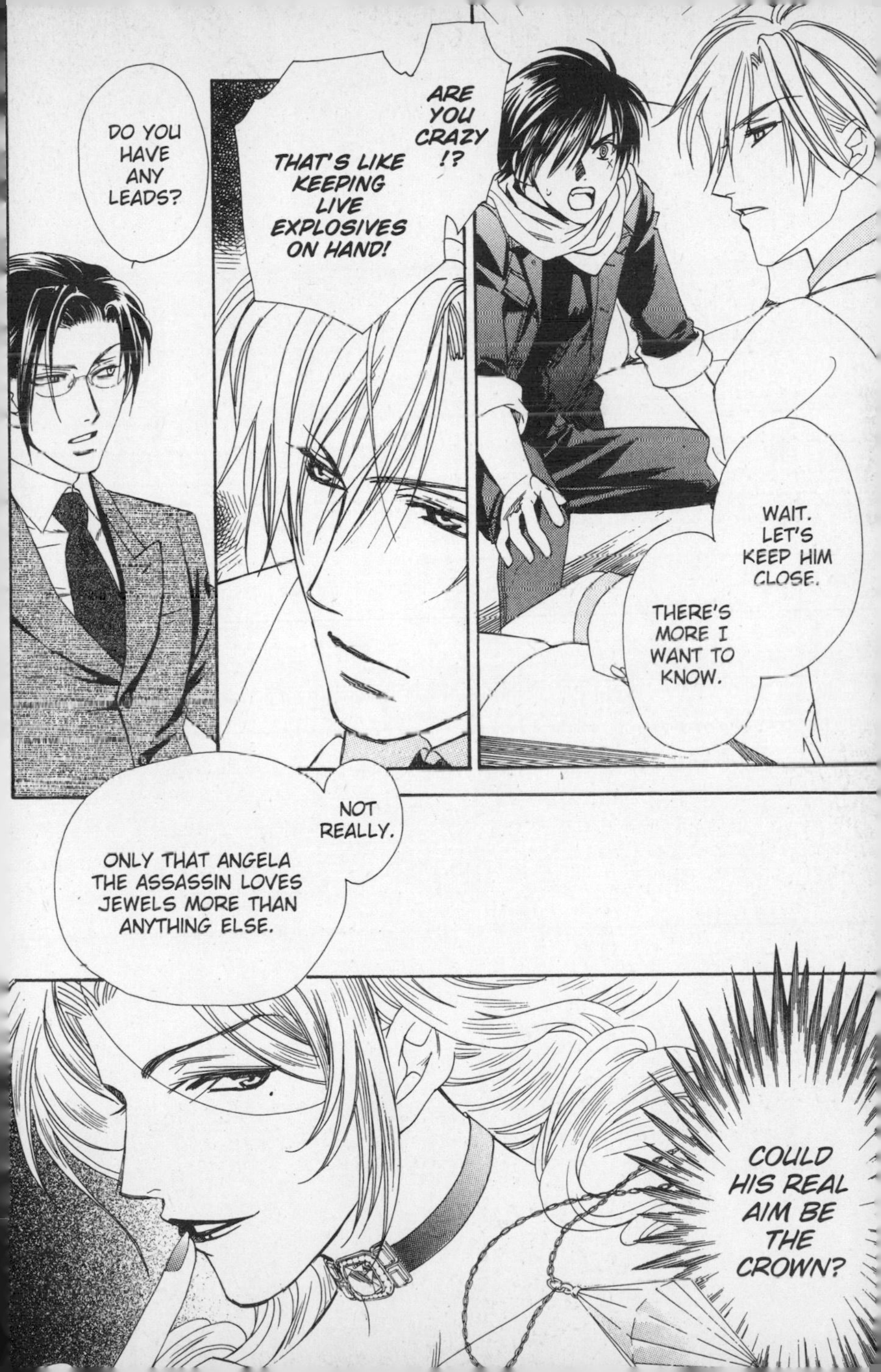
ARE YOU CRAZY !?
THAT'S LIKE KEEPING LIVE EXPLOSIVES ON HAND!
WAIT. LET'S KEEP HIM CLOSE.
THERE'S MORE I WANT TO KNOW.
DO YOU HAVE ANY LEADS?
NOT REALLY.
ONLY THAT ANGELA THE ASSASSIN LOVES JEWELS MORE THAN ANYTHING ELSE.
COULD HIS REAL AIM BE THE CROWN?

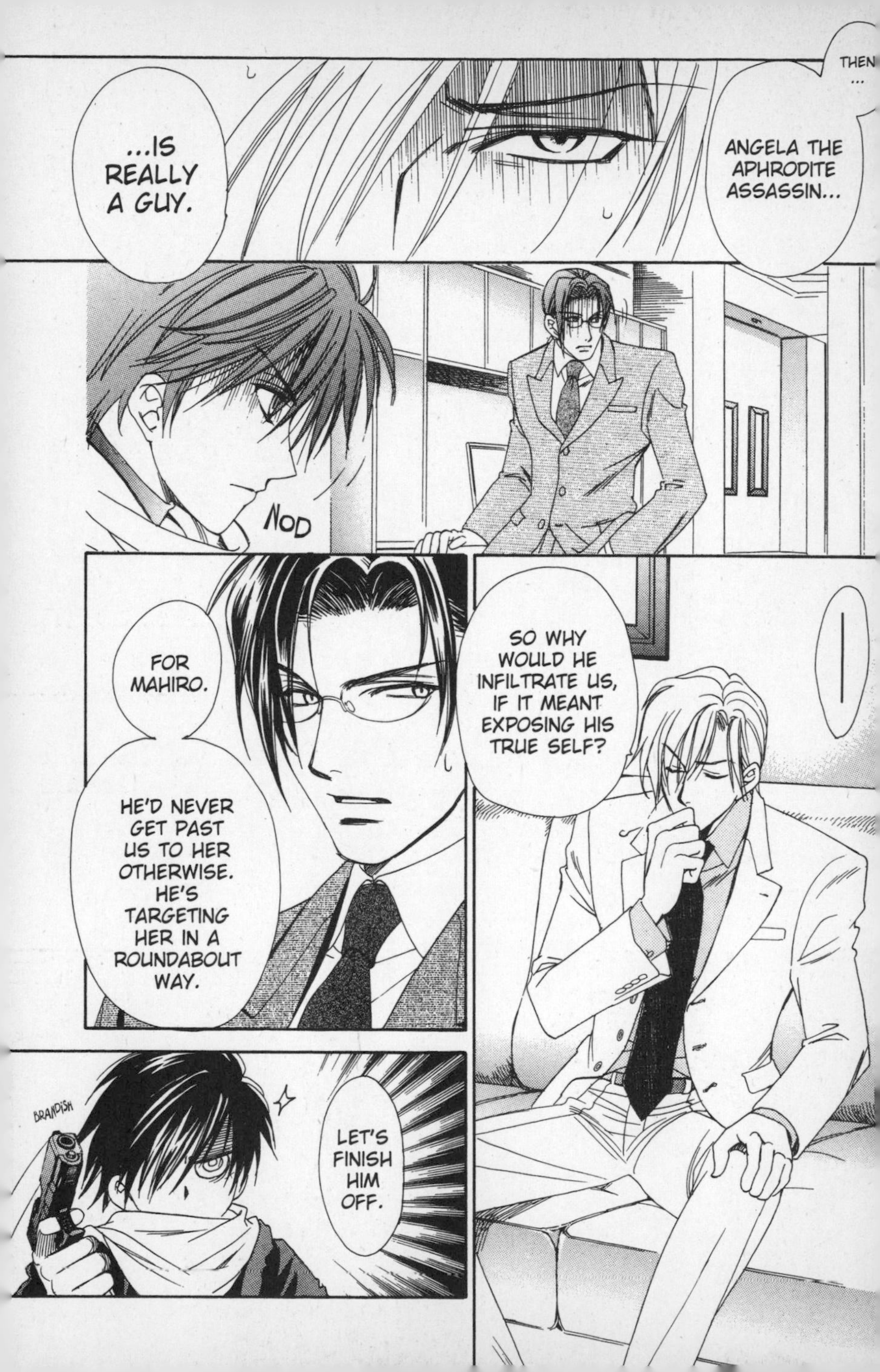
THEN ...
ANGELA THE APHRODITE ASSASSIN...
...IS REALLY A GUY.
NOD
SO WHY WOULD HE INFILTRATE US, IF IT MEANT EXPOSING HIS TRUE SELF?
FOR MAHIRO.
HE'D NEVER GET PAST US TO HER OTHERWISE. HE'S TARGETING HER IN A ROUNDABOUT WAY.
BRANDISH
LET'S FINISH HIM OFF.

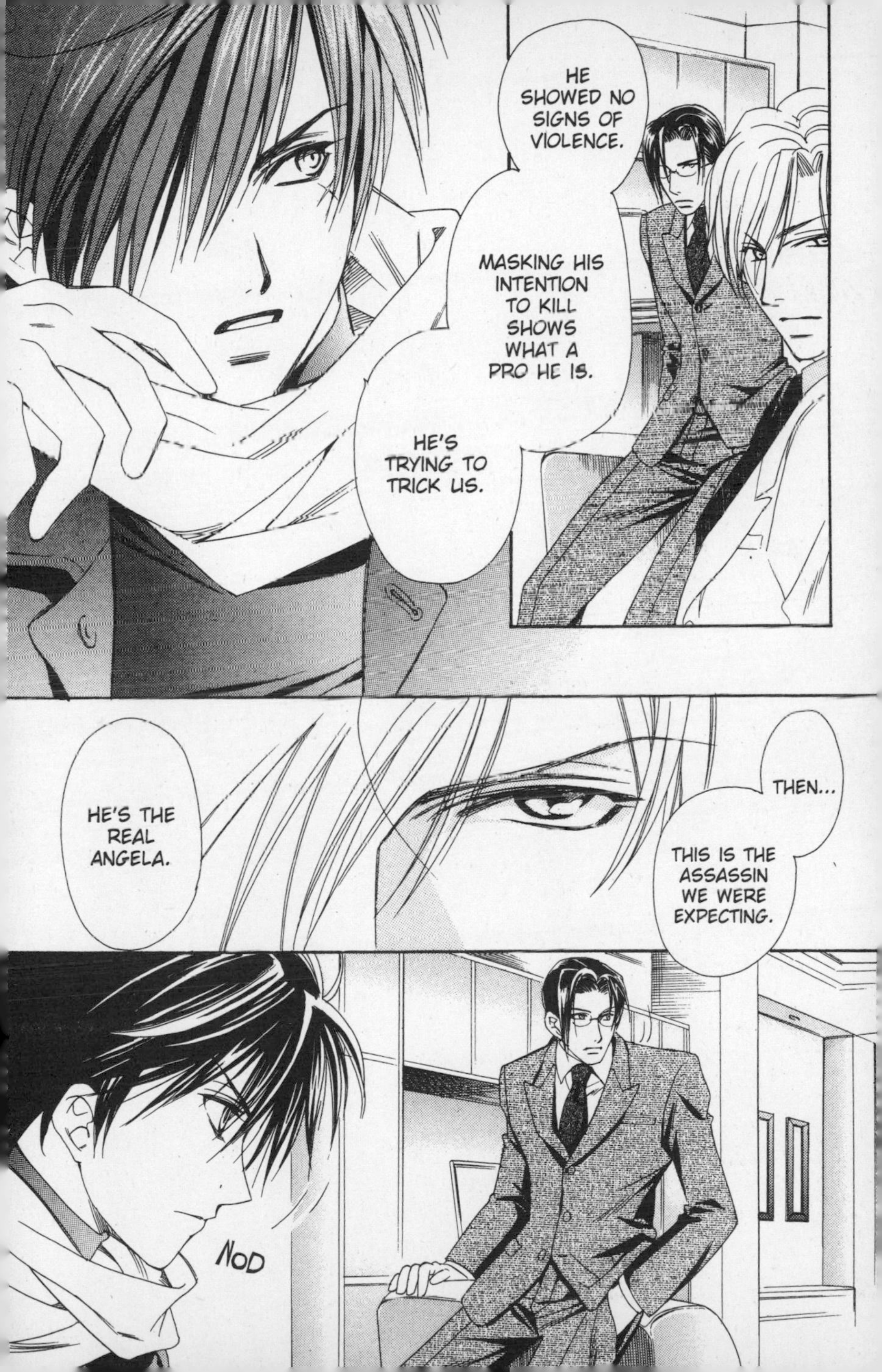
HE SHOWED NO SIGNS OF VIOLENCE.
MASKING HIS INTENTION TO KILL SHOWS WHAT A PRO HE IS.
HE'S TRYING TO TRICK US.
THEN...
THIS IS THE ASSASSIN WE WERE EXPECTING.
HE'S THE REAL ANGELA.
NOD

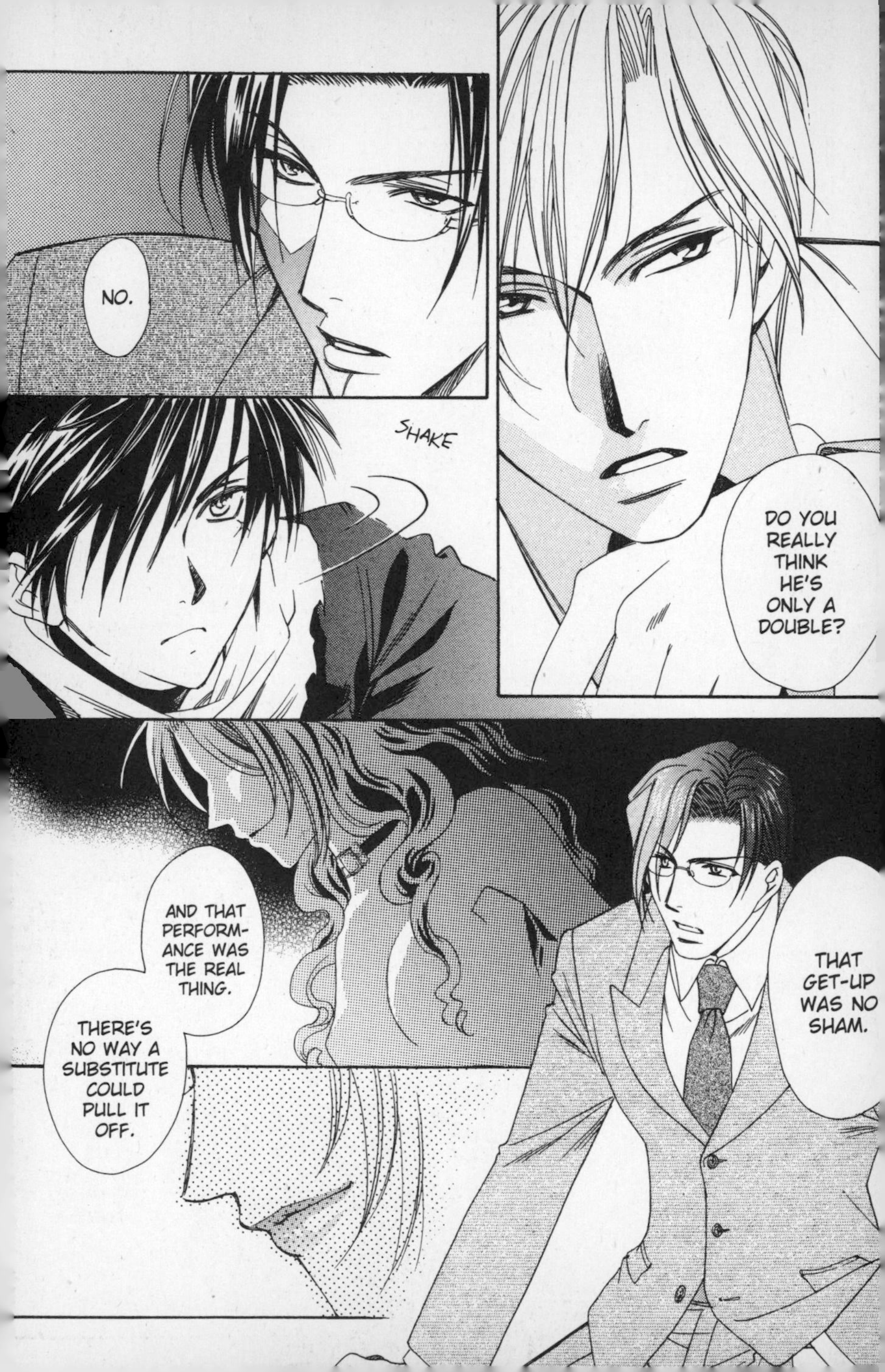

DO YOU REALLY THINK HE'S ONLY A DOUBLE?
NO.
SHAKE
THAT GET-UP WAS NO SHAM.
AND THAT PERFORM-ANCE WAS THE REAL THING.
THERE'S NO WAY A SUBSTITUTE COULD PULL IT OFF.

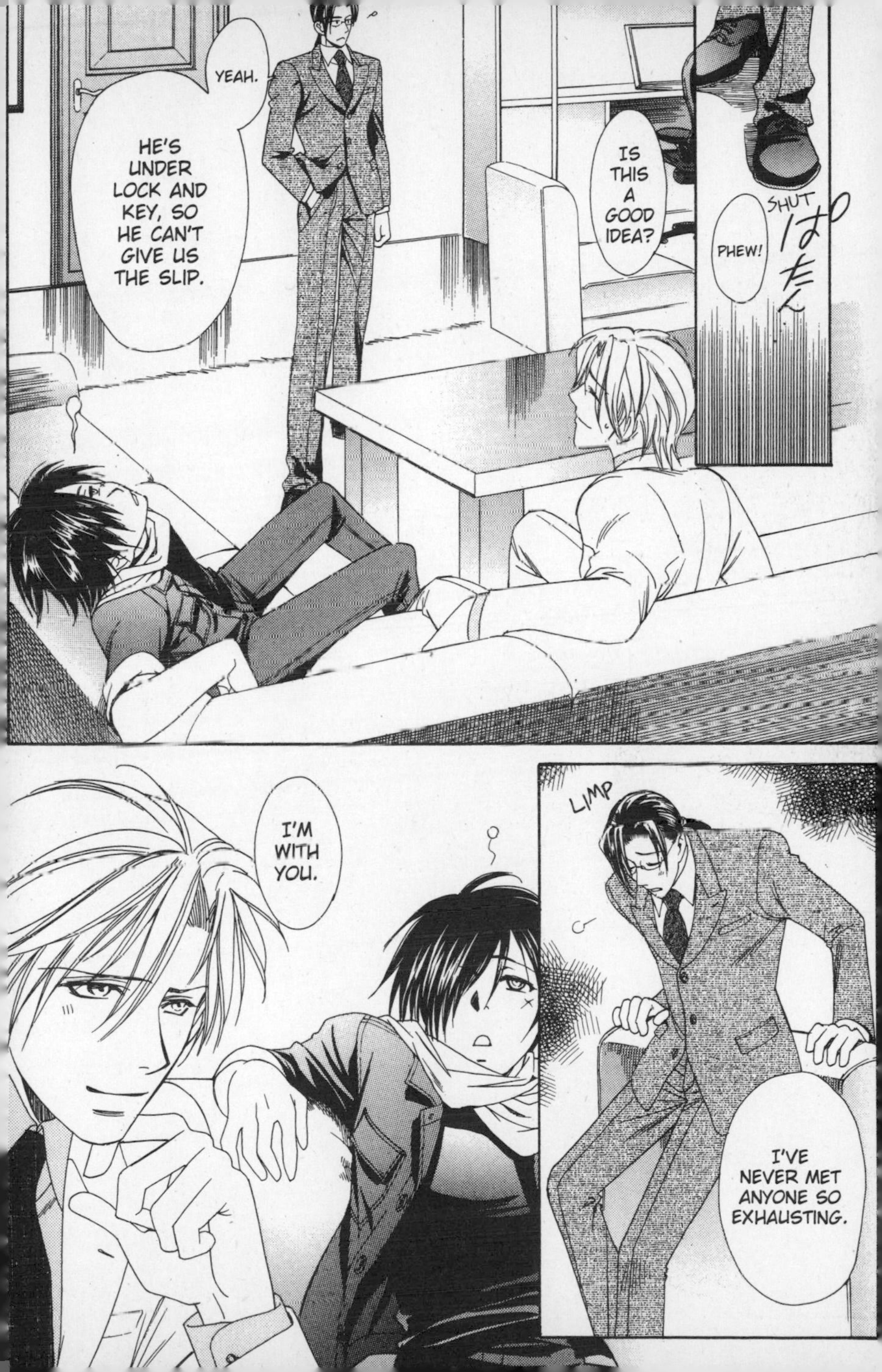
SHUT
ぱたん
PHEW!
IS THIS A GOOD IDEA?
YEAH.
HE'S UNDER LOCK AND KEY, SO HE CAN'T GIVE US THE SLIP.
LIMP
I'VE NEVER MET ANYONE SO EXHAUSTING.
I'M WITH YOU.

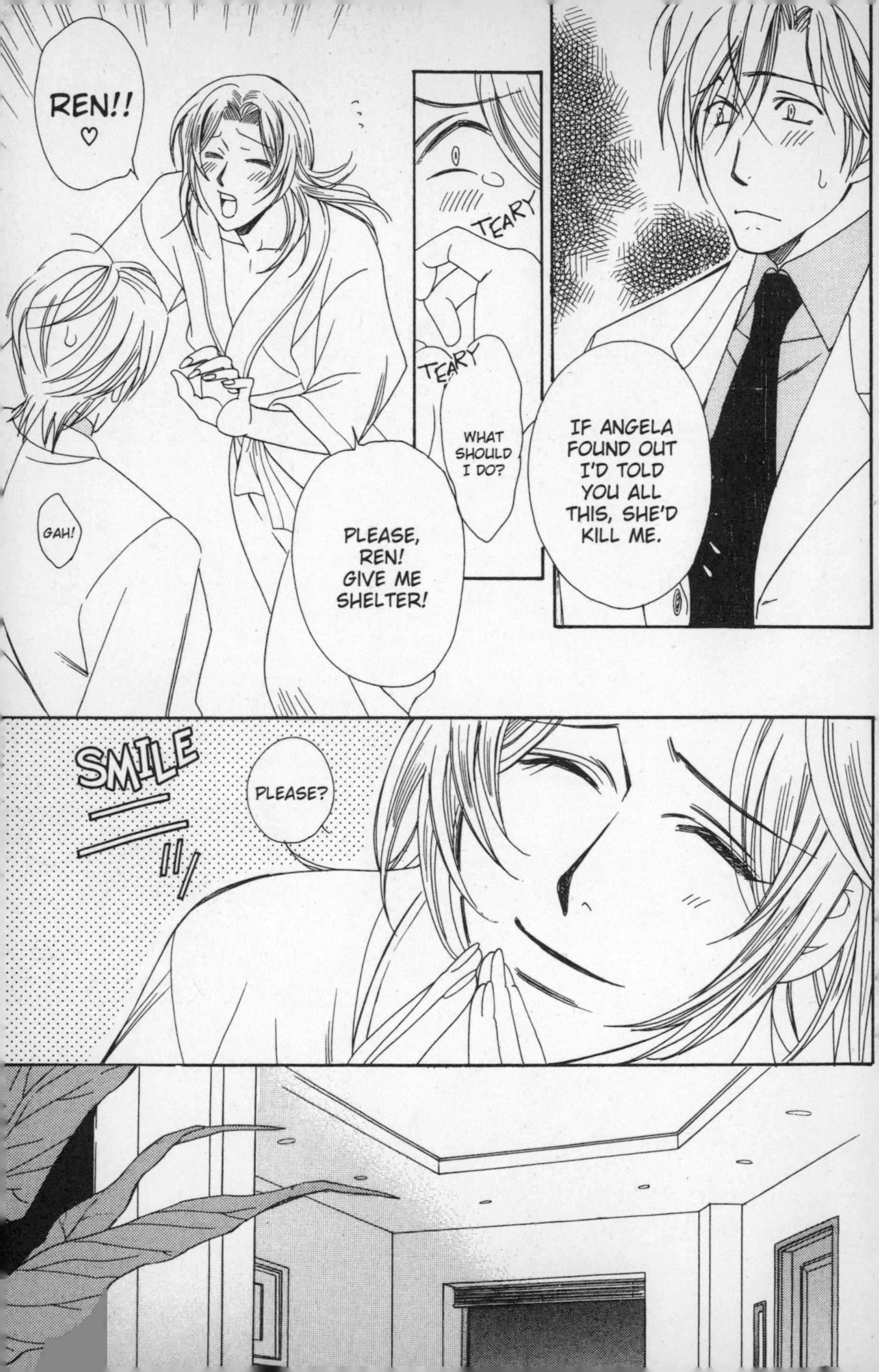

IF ANGELA FOUND OUT I'D TOLD YOU ALL THIS, SHE'D KILL ME.
TEARY
TEARY
WHAT SHOULD I DO?
REN!! ♡
GAH!
PLEASE, REN! GIVE ME SHELTER!
SMILE
PLEASE?

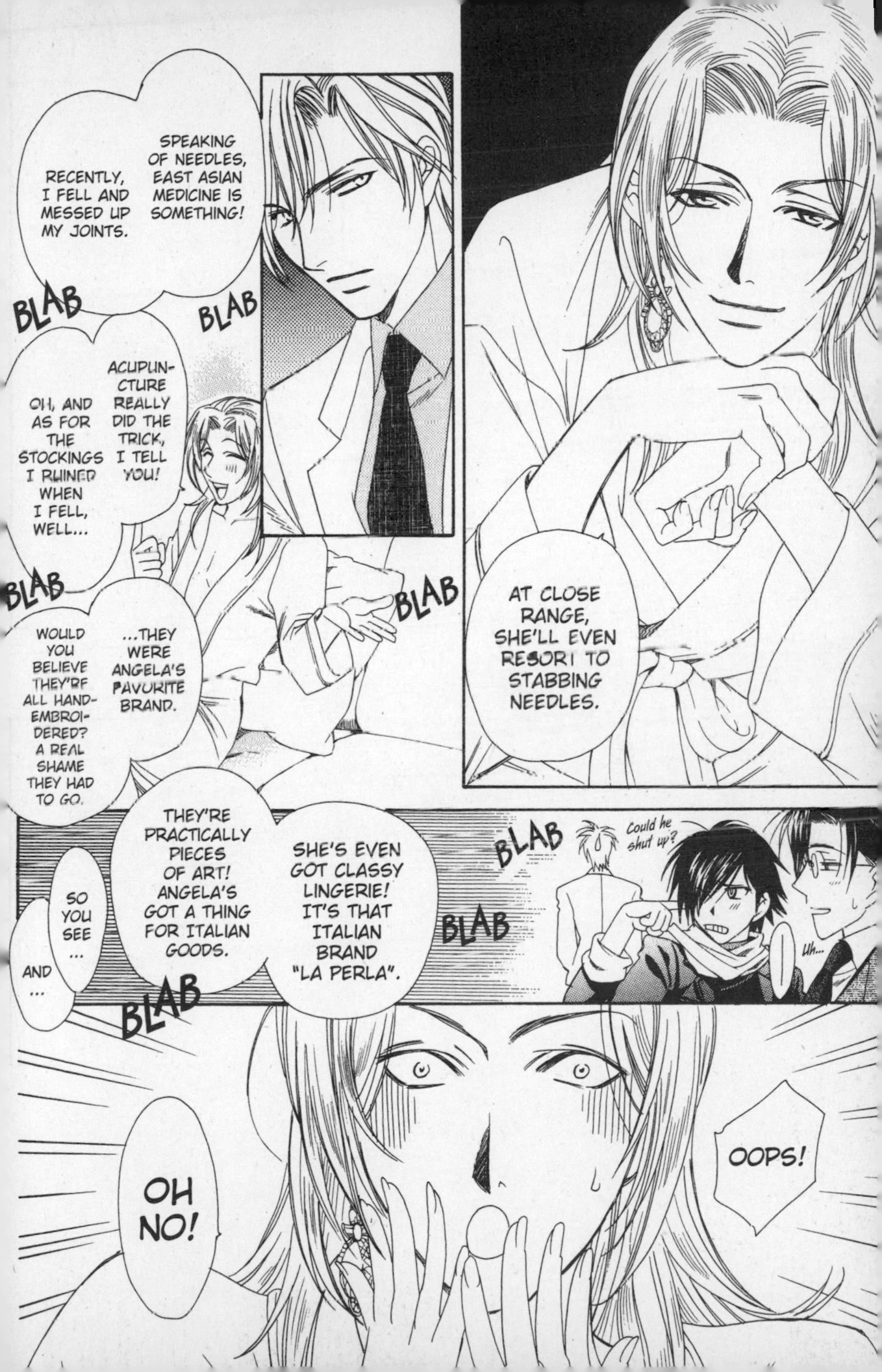

SPEAKING OF NEEDLES, EAST ASIAN MEDICINE IS SOMETHING!
RECENTLY, I FELL AND MESSED UP MY JOINTS.
BLAB
BLAB
ACUPUNCTURE REALLY DID THE TRICK, I TELL YOU!
OH, AND AS FOR THE STOCKINGS I RUINED WHEN I FELL, WELL...
AT CLOSE RANGE, SHE'LL EVEN RESORT TO STABBING NEEDLES.
BLAB
BLAB
...THEY WERE ANGELA'S FAVORITE BRAND.
WOULD YOU BELIEVE THEY'RE ALL HAND-EMBROIDERED? A REAL SHAME THEY HAD TO GO.
Could he shut up?
BLAB
Uh...
BLAB
SHE'S EVEN GOT CLASSY LINGERIE! IT'S THAT ITALIAN BRAND "LA PERLA".
THEY'RE PRACTICALLY PIECES OF ART! ANGELA'S GOT A THING FOR ITALIAN GOODS.
BLAB
SO YOU SEE ...
AND ...
OOPS!
OH NO!

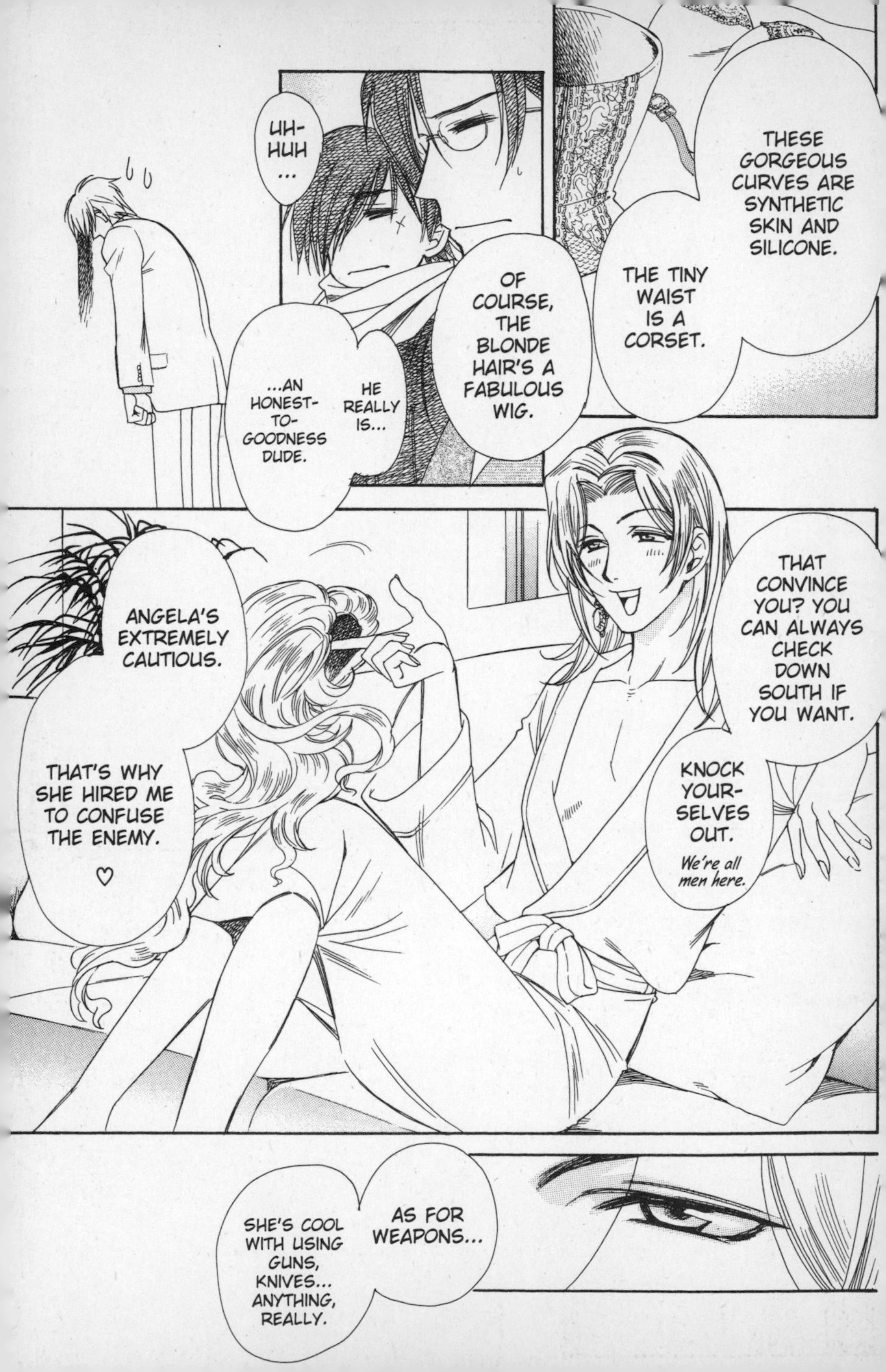
THESE GORGEOUS CURVES ARE SYNTHETIC SKIN AND SILICONE.
THE TINY WAIST IS A CORSET.
OF COURSE, THE BLONDE HAIR'S A FABULOUS WIG.
UH-HUH...
HE REALLY IS...
...AN HONEST-TO-GOODNESS DUDE.
THAT CONVINCE YOU? YOU CAN ALWAYS CHECK DOWN SOUTH IF YOU WANT.
KNOCK YOURSELVES OUT.
We're all men here.
ANGELA'S EXTREMELY CAUTIOUS.
THAT'S WHY SHE HIRED ME TO CONFUSE THE ENEMY. ♡
AS FOR WEAPONS...
SHE'S COOL WITH USING GUNS, KNIVES... ANYTHING, REALLY.

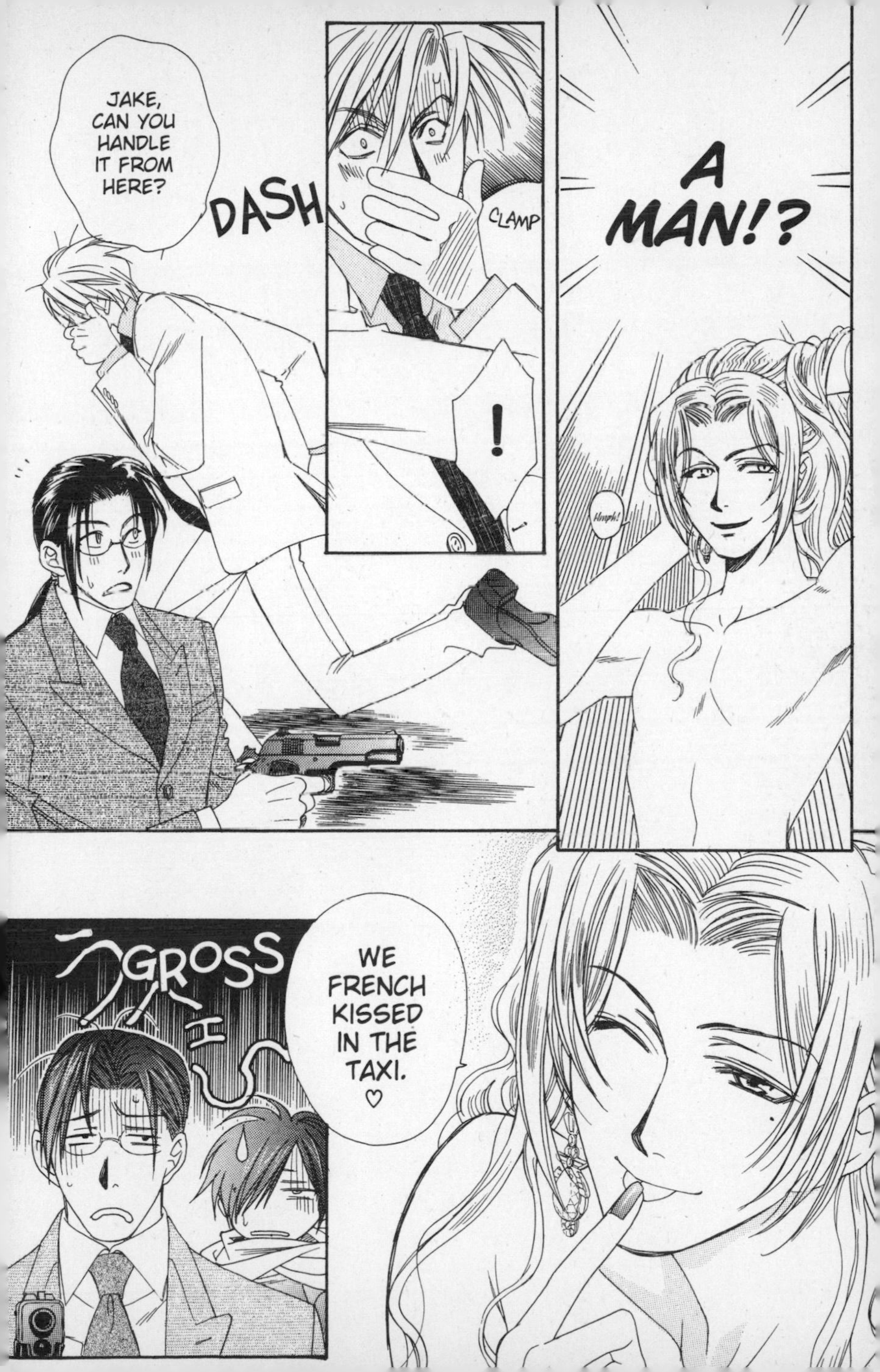
A MAN!?
Hmph!
CLAMP
!
JAKE, CAN YOU HANDLE IT FROM HERE?
DASH
WE FRENCH KISSED IN THE TAXI. ♡
GROSS

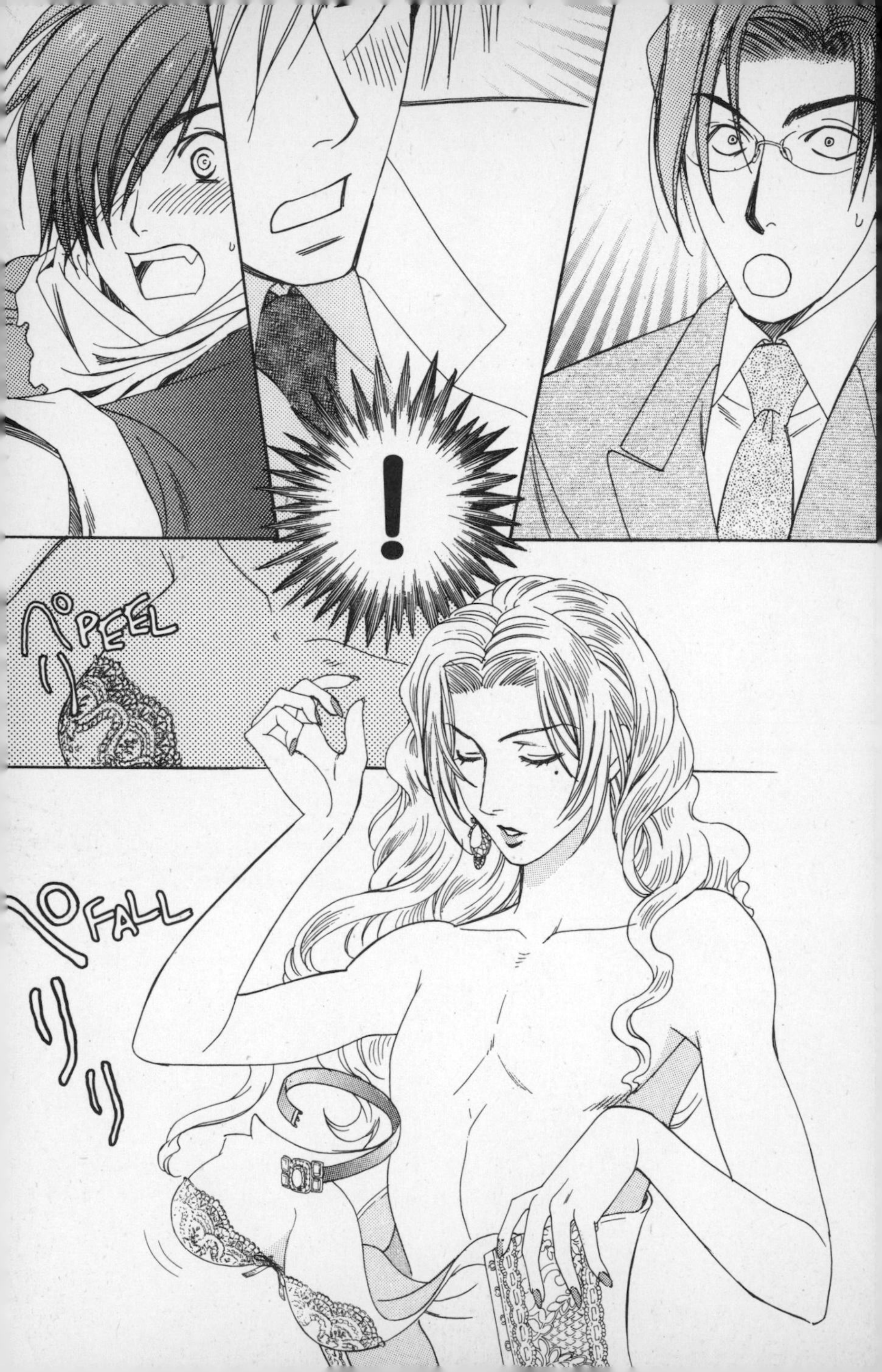
!
PEEL
FALL

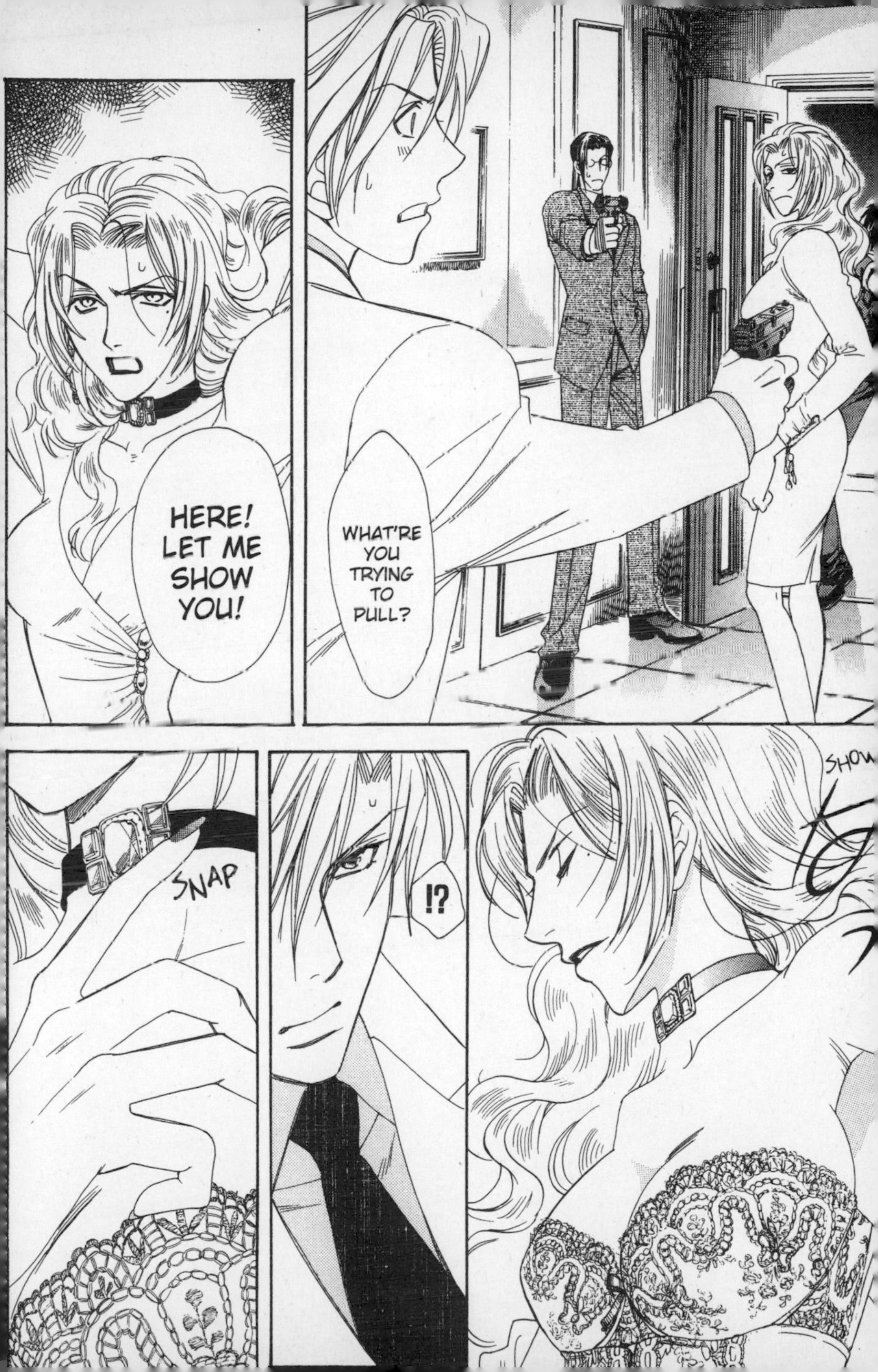
WHAT'RE YOU TRYING TO PULL?
HERE! LET ME SHOW YOU!
SHOW
!?
SNAP

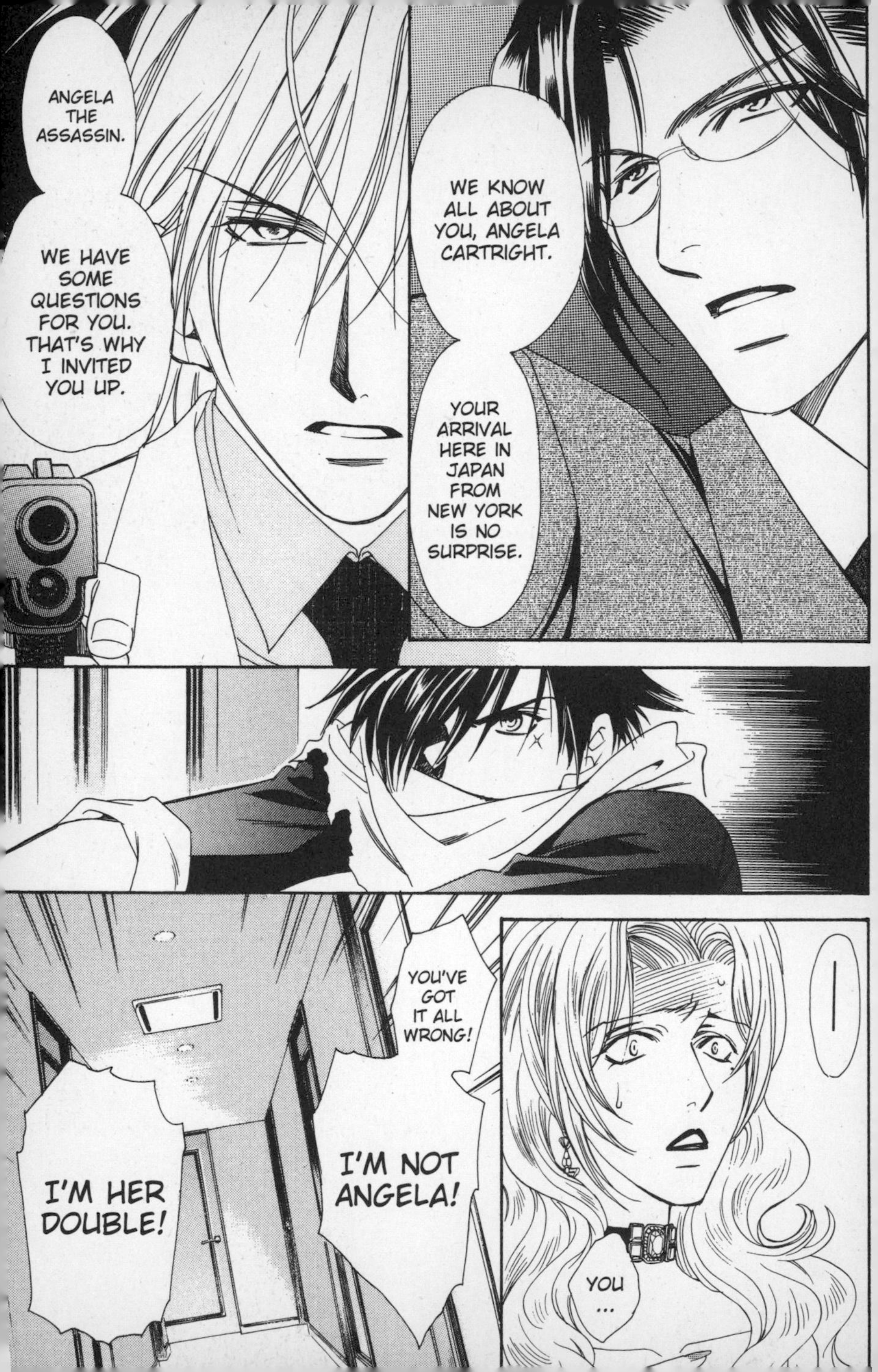

WE KNOW ALL ABOUT YOU, ANGELA CARTRIGHT.
YOUR ARRIVAL HERE IN JAPAN FROM NEW YORK IS NO SURPRISE.
ANGELA THE ASSASSIN.
WE HAVE SOME QUESTIONS FOR YOU. THAT'S WHY I INVITED YOU UP.
!
YOU ...
YOU'VE GOT IT ALL WRONG!
I'M NOT ANGELA!
I'M HER DOUBLE!

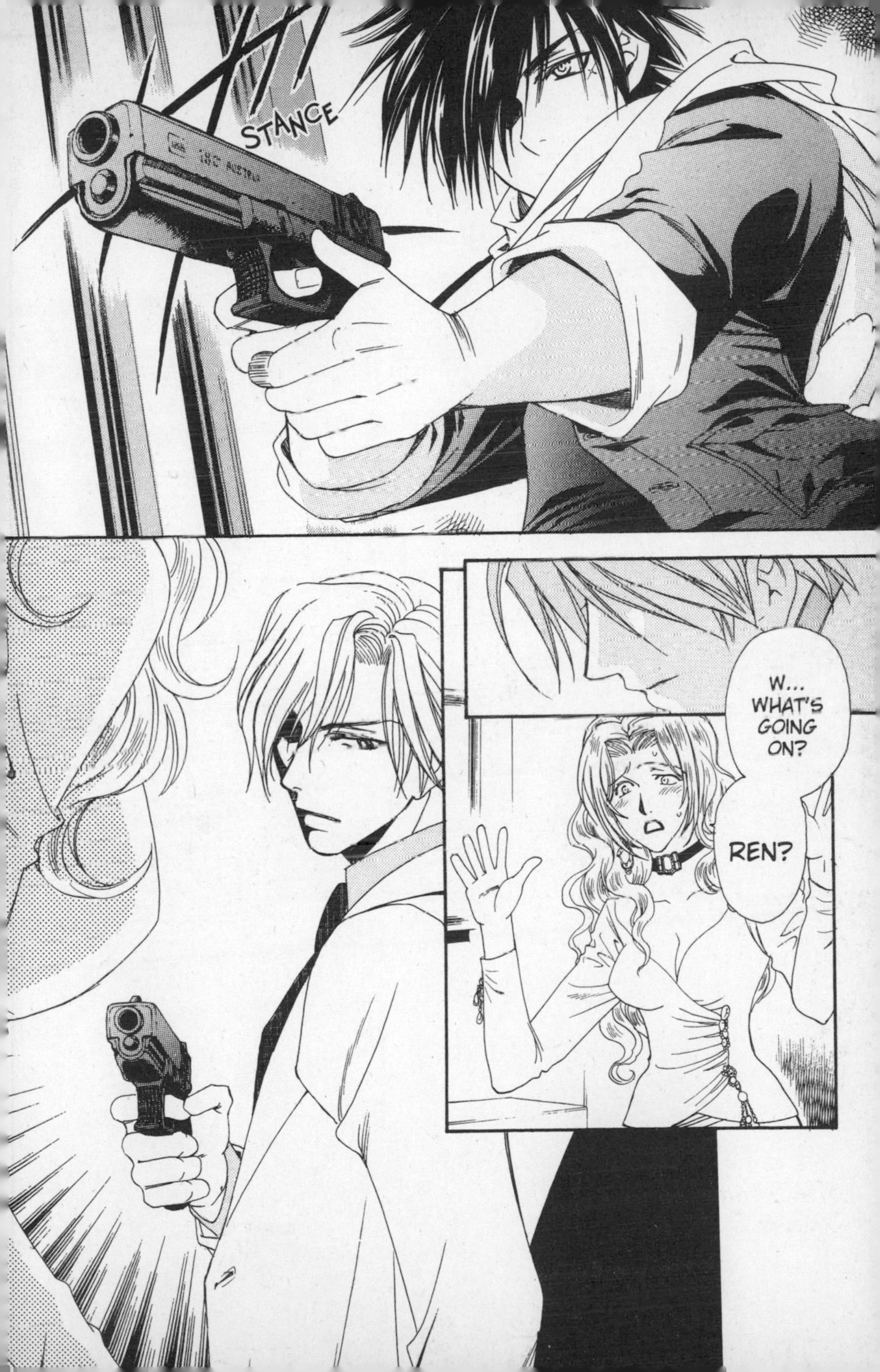
STANCE
W... WHAT'S GOING ON?
REN?

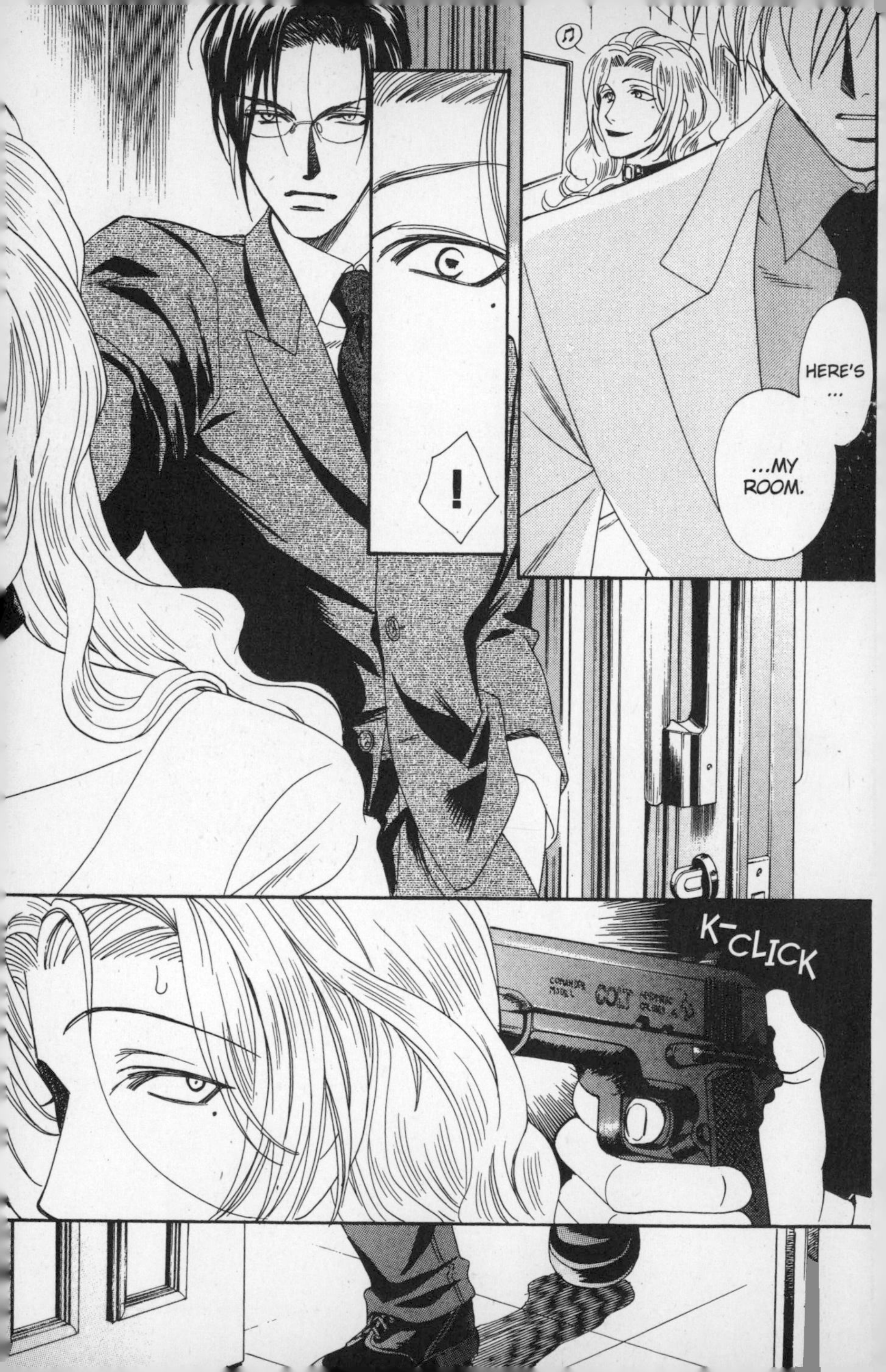
HERE'S ...
...MY ROOM.
!
K-CLICK
COLT

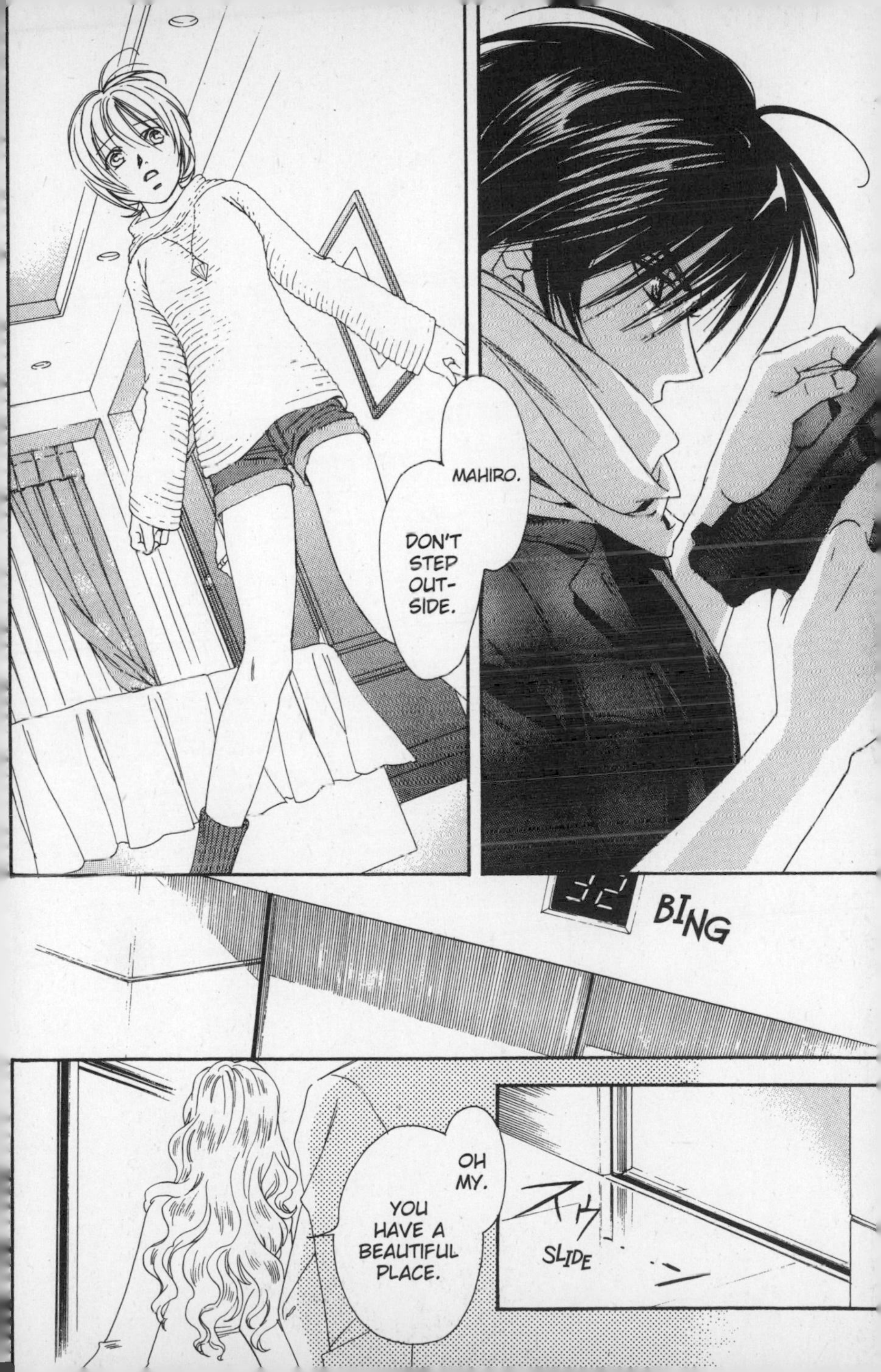
MAHIRO.
DON'T STEP OUT-SIDE.
BING
SLIDE
OH MY.
YOU HAVE A BEAUTIFUL PLACE.

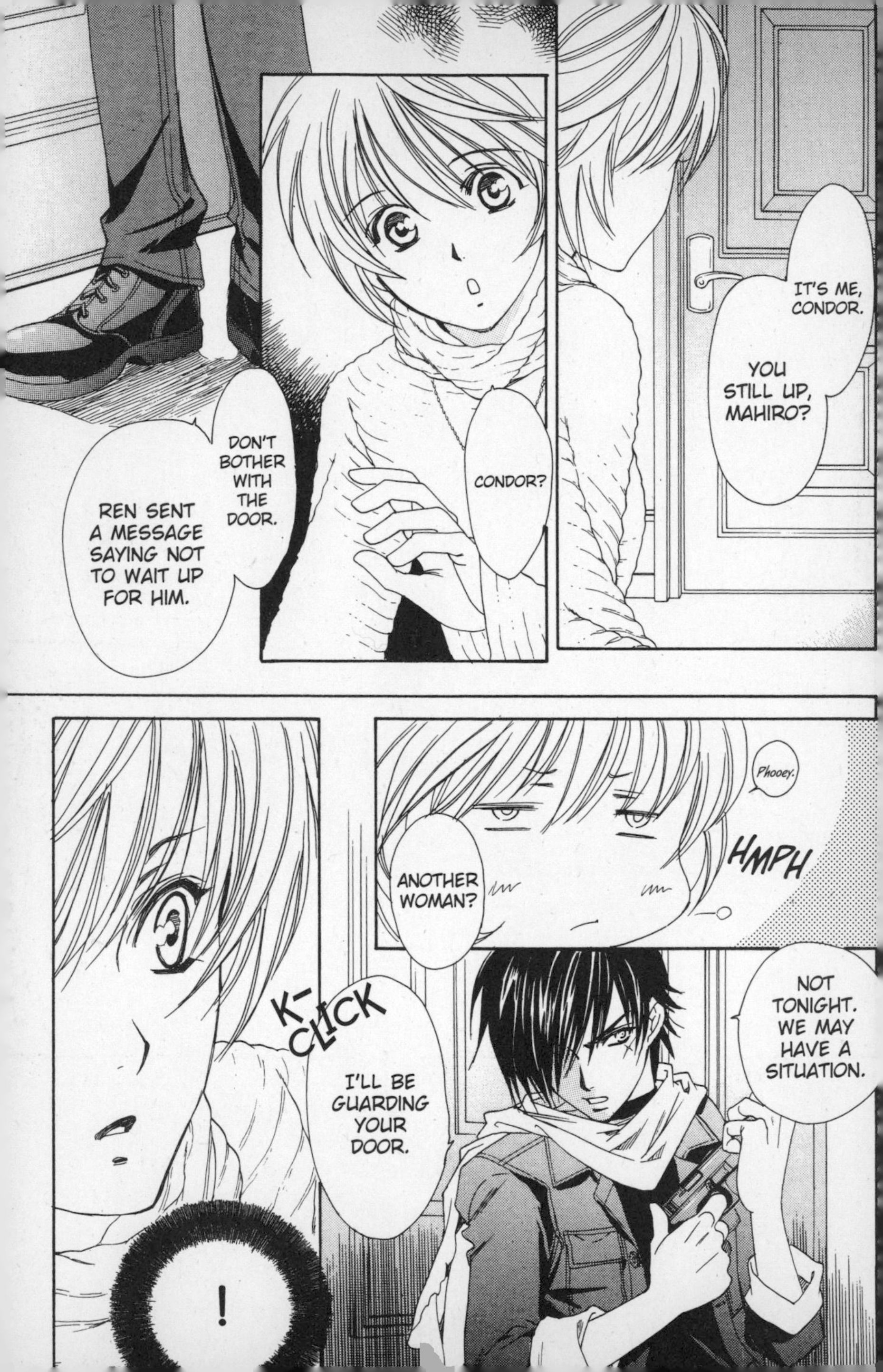
IT'S ME, CONDOR.
YOU STILL UP, MAHIRO?
CONDOR?
DON'T BOTHER WITH THE DOOR.
REN SENT A MESSAGE SAYING NOT TO WAIT UP FOR HIM.
Phooey.
HMPH
ANOTHER WOMAN?
NOT TONIGHT. WE MAY HAVE A SITUATION.
K-CLICK
I'LL BE GUARDING YOUR DOOR.
!

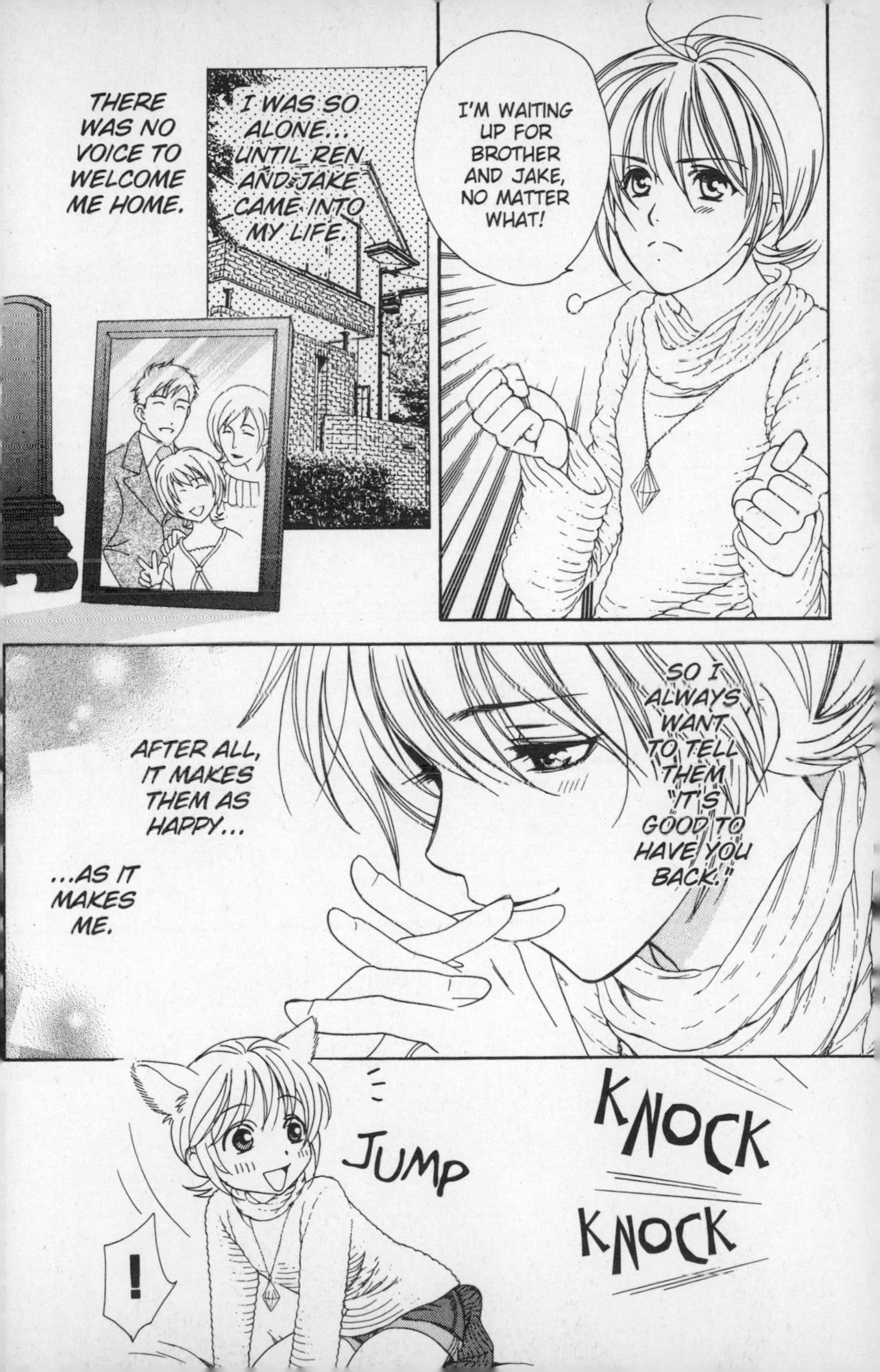
I'M WAITING UP FOR BROTHER AND JAKE, NO MATTER WHAT!
I WAS SO ALONE... UNTIL REN AND JAKE CAME INTO MY LIFE.
THERE WAS NO VOICE TO WELCOME ME HOME.
SO I ALWAYS WANT TO TELL THEM "IT'S GOOD TO HAVE YOU BACK."
AFTER ALL, IT MAKES THEM AS HAPPY...
...AS IT MAKES ME.
KNOCK
KNOCK
JUMP
!

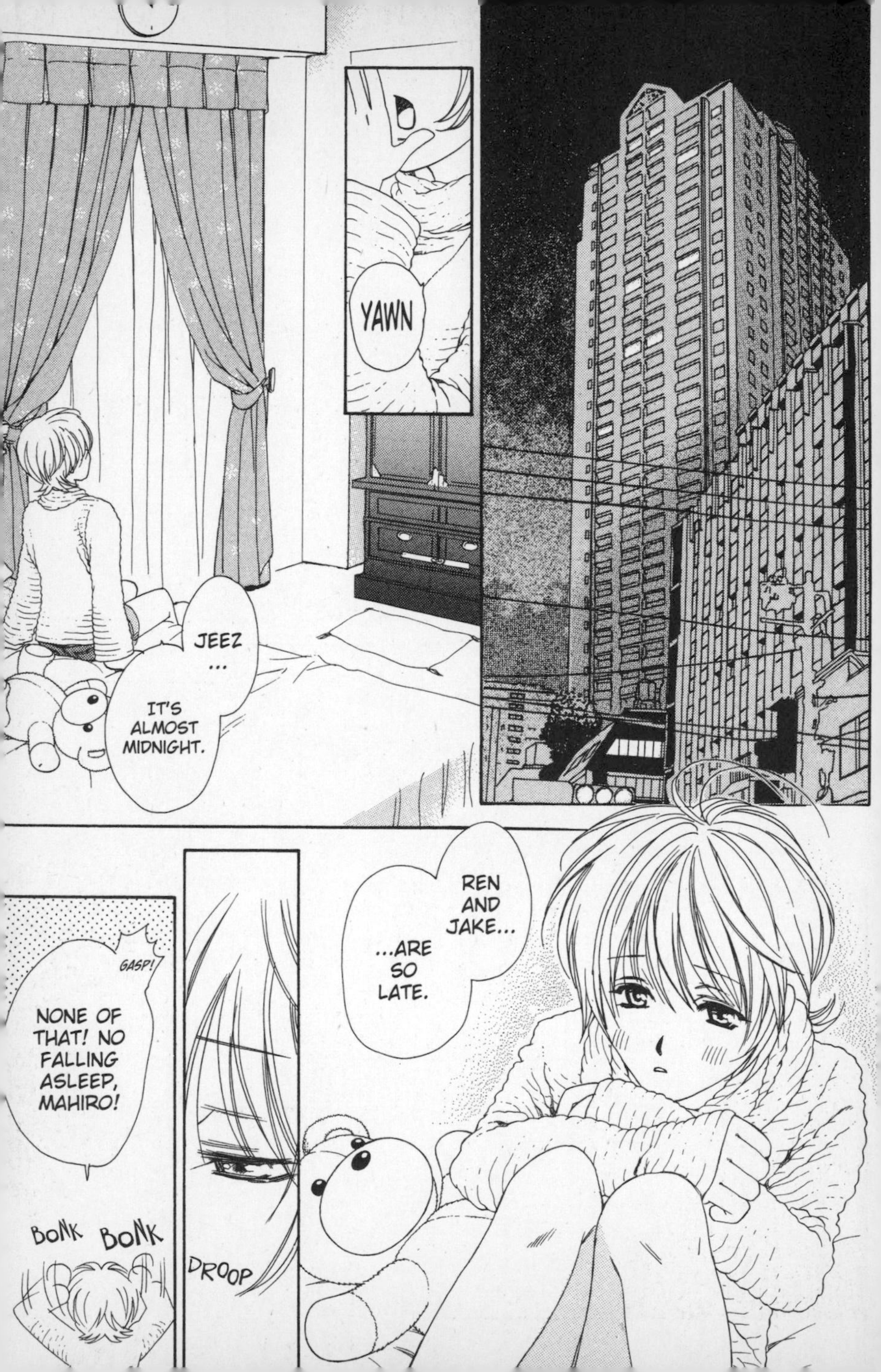
YAWN
JEEZ ...
IT'S ALMOST MIDNIGHT.
REN AND JAKE...
...ARE SO LATE.
DROOP
GASP!
NONE OF THAT! NO FALLING ASLEEP, MAHIRO!
BONK BONK

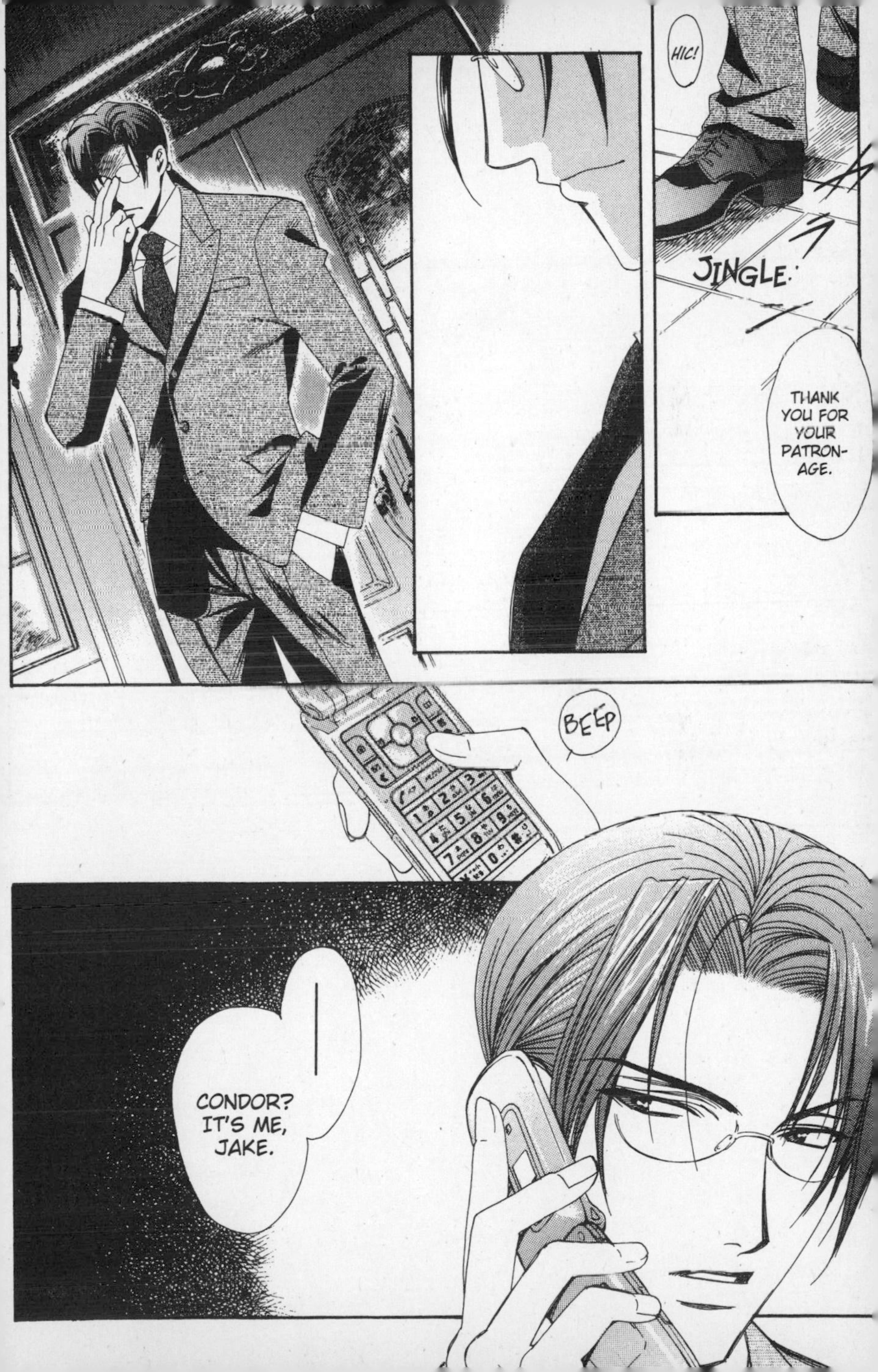
HIC!
JINGLE
THANK YOU FOR YOUR PATRON-AGE.
BEEP
CONDOR? IT'S ME, JAKE.

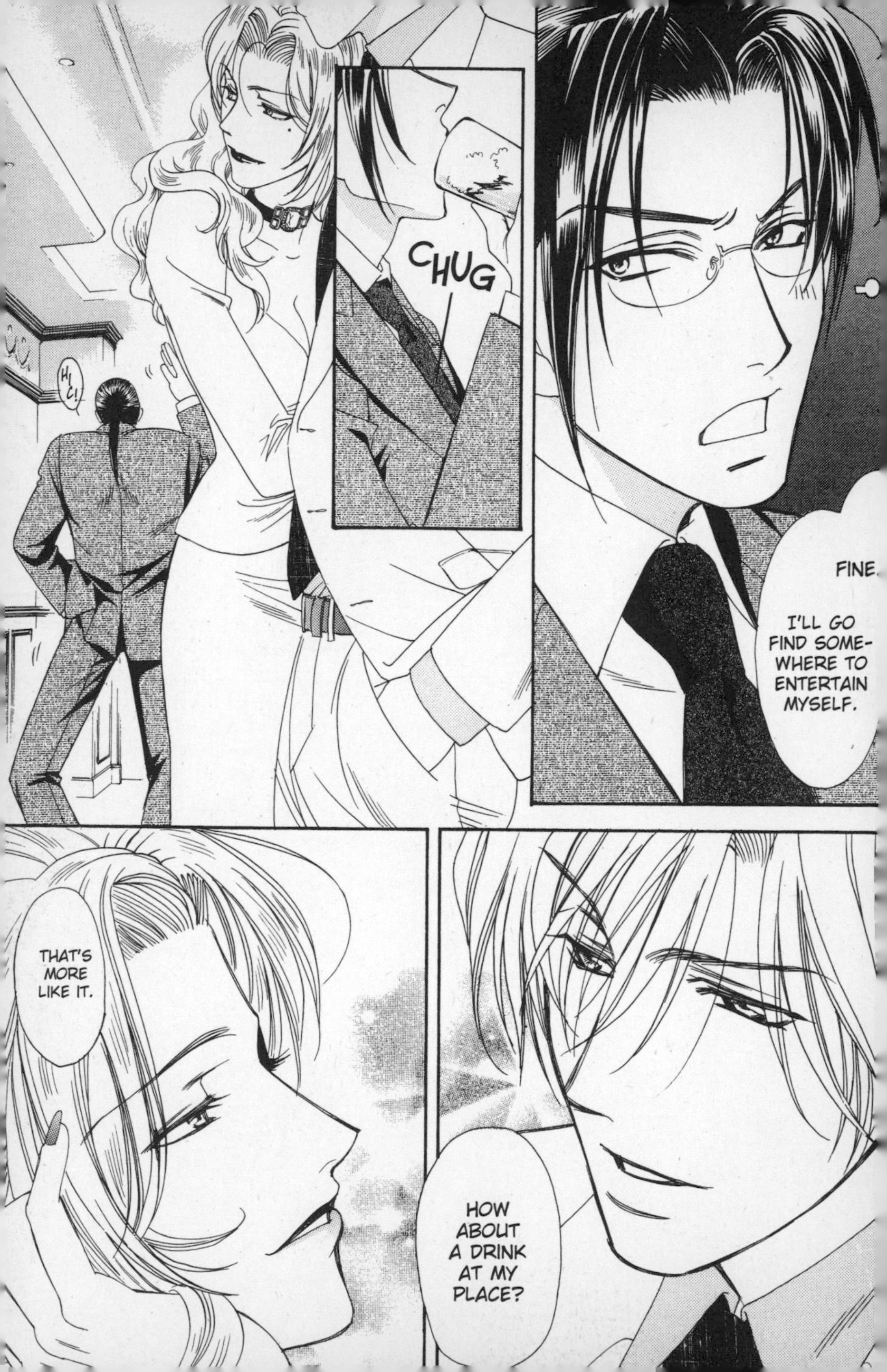
FINE.
I'LL GO FIND SOME-WHERE TO ENTERTAIN MYSELF.
CHUG
HI C!
HOW ABOUT A DRINK AT MY PLACE?
THAT'S MORE LIKE IT.

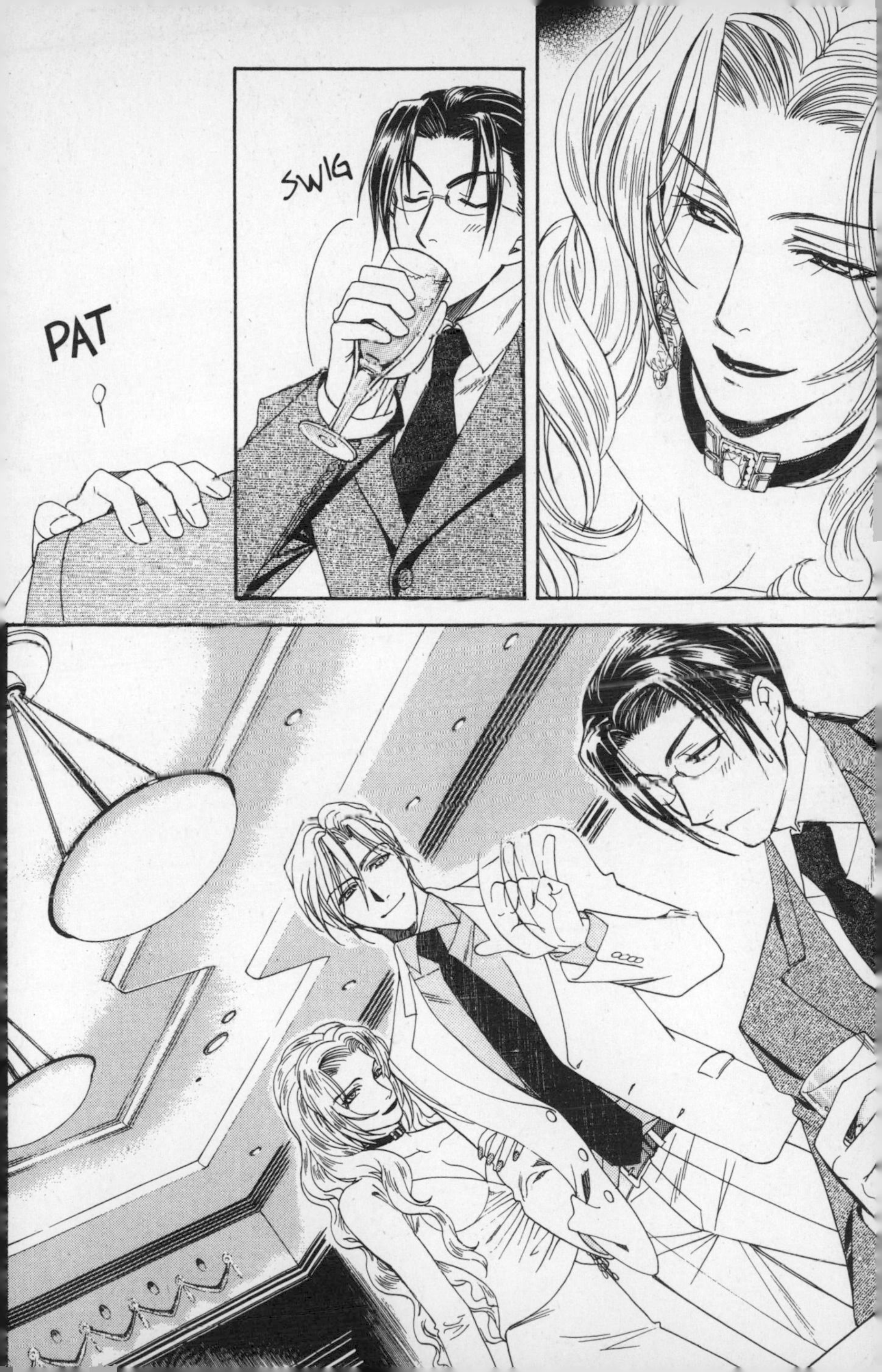
SWIG
PAT

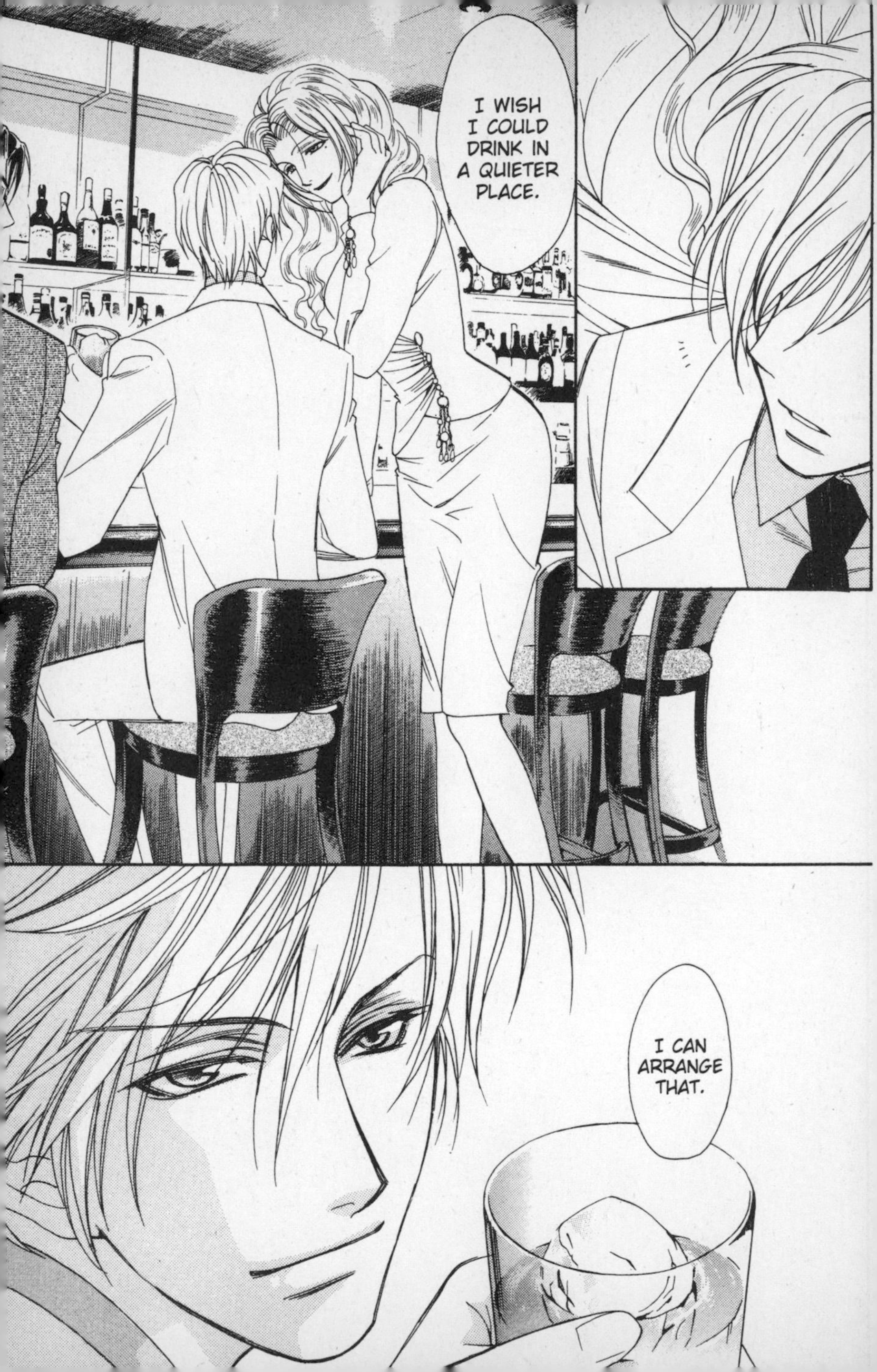
I WISH I COULD DRINK IN A QUIETER PLACE.
I CAN ARRANGE THAT.

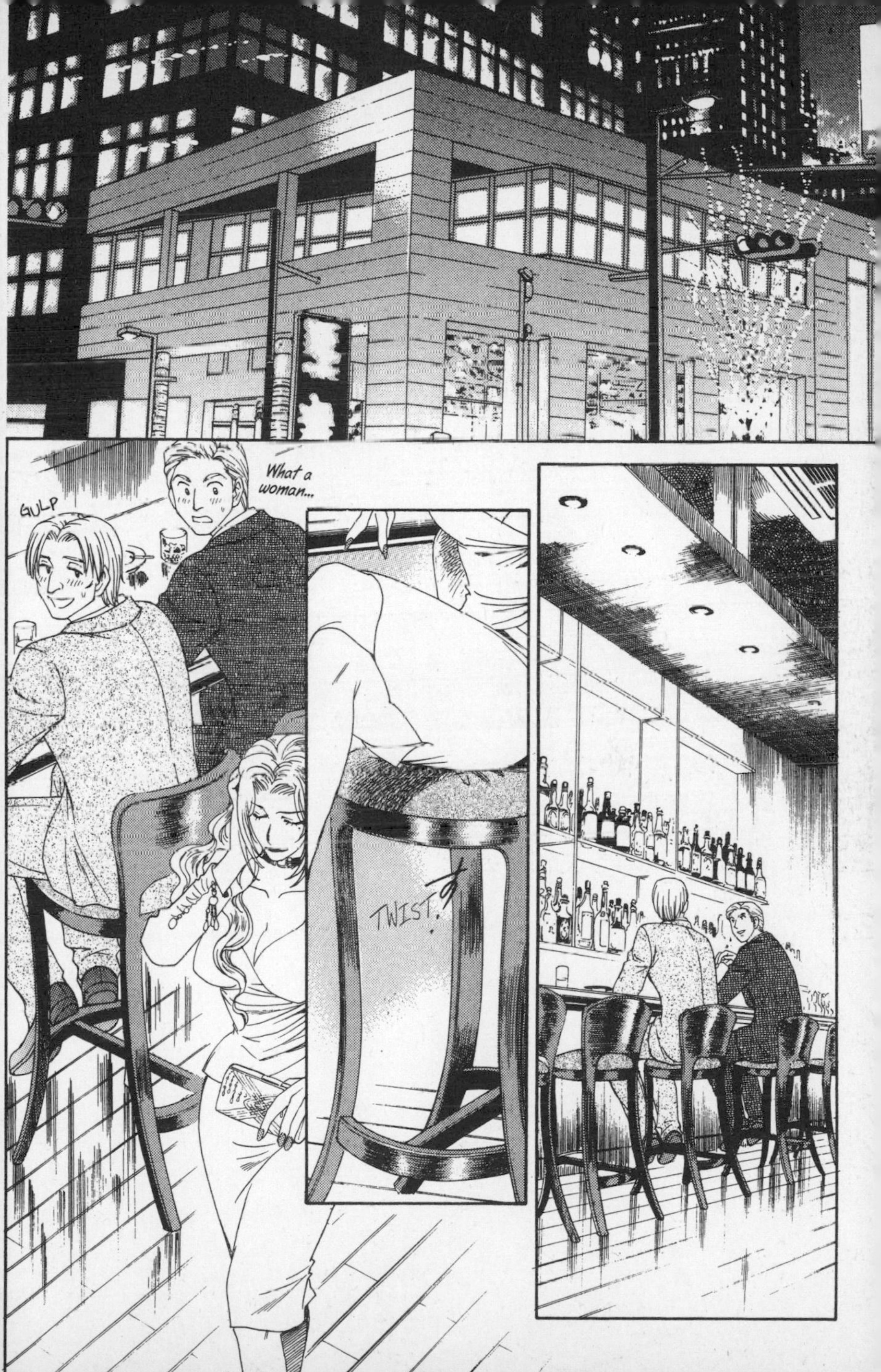

What a woman...
GULP
TWIST

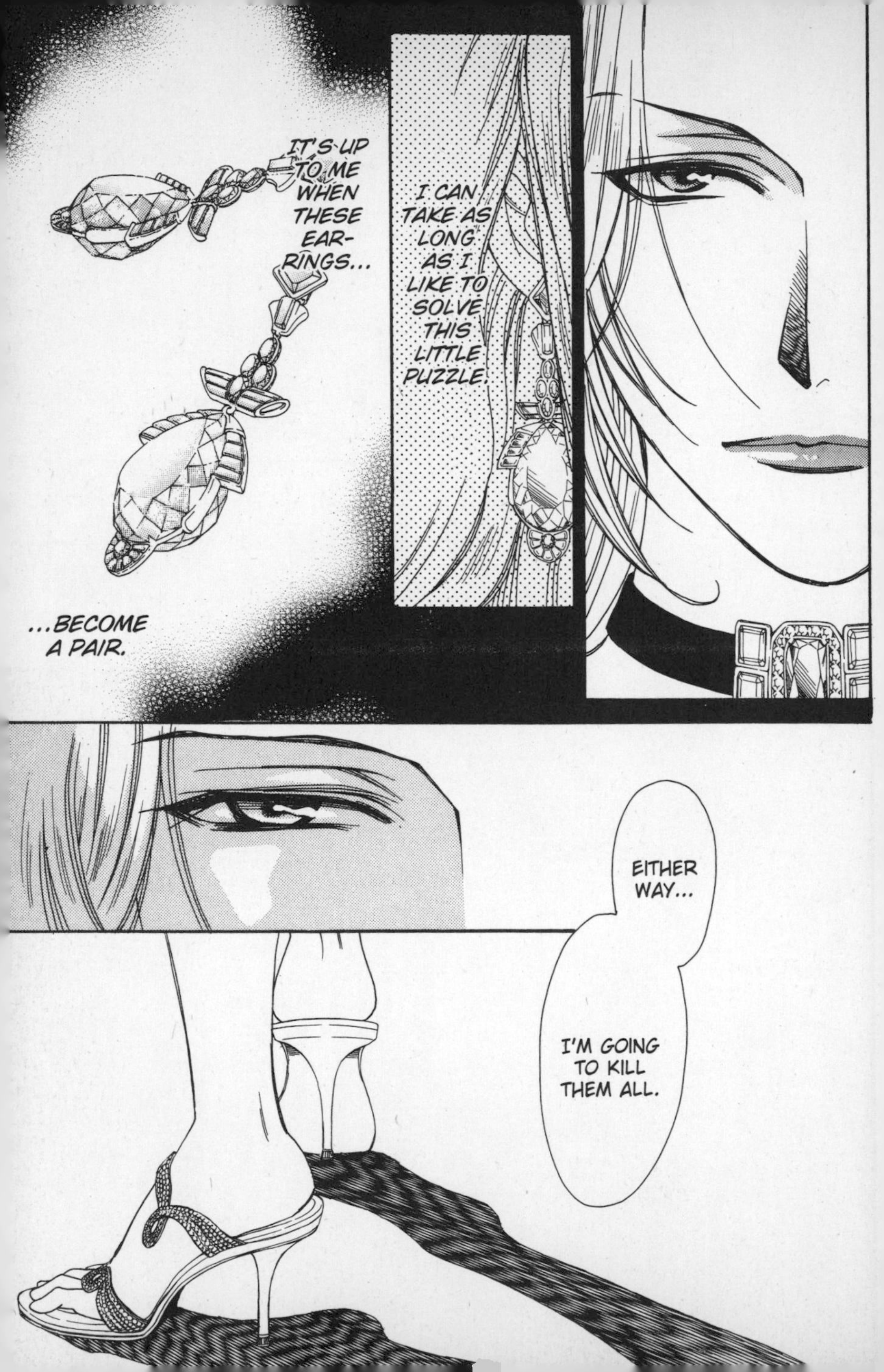
I CAN TAKE AS LONG AS I LIKE TO SOLVE THIS LITTLE PUZZLE.
IT'S UP TO ME WHEN THESE EAR-RINGS...
...BECOME A PAIR.
EITHER WAY...
I'M GOING TO KILL THEM ALL.

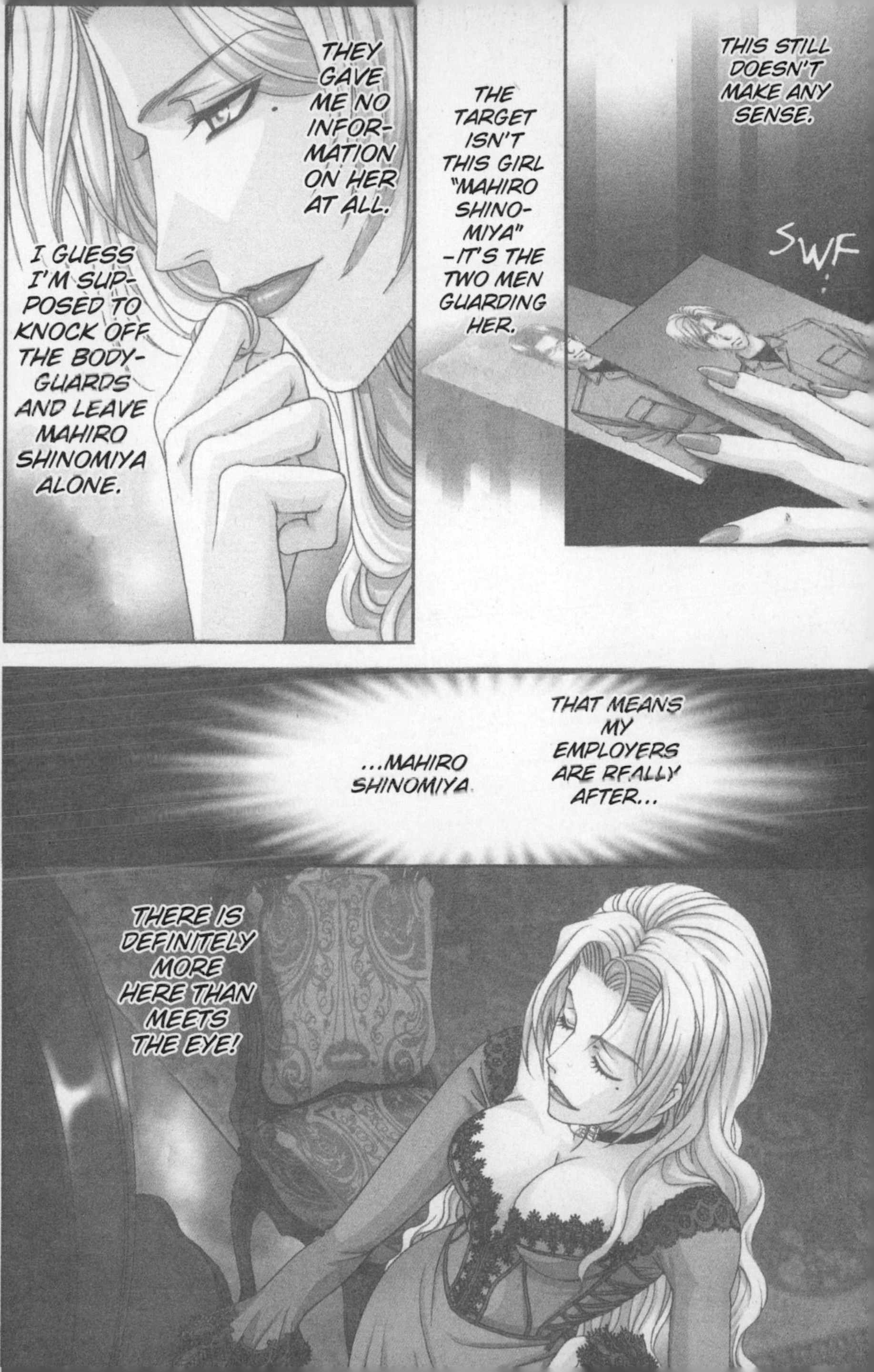
THIS STILL DOESN'T MAKE ANY SENSE.
SWF
THE TARGET ISN'T THIS GIRL "MAHIRO SHINO-MIYA" -IT'S THE TWO MEN GUARDING HER.
THEY GAVE ME NO INFOR-MATION ON HER AT ALL.
I GUESS I'M SUP-POSED TO KNOCK OFF THE BODY-GUARDS AND LEAVE MAHIRO SHINOMIYA ALONE.
THAT MEANS MY EMPLOYERS ARE REALLY AFTER...
...MAHIRO SHINOMIYA.
THERE IS DEFINITELY MORE HERE THAN MEETS THE EYE!

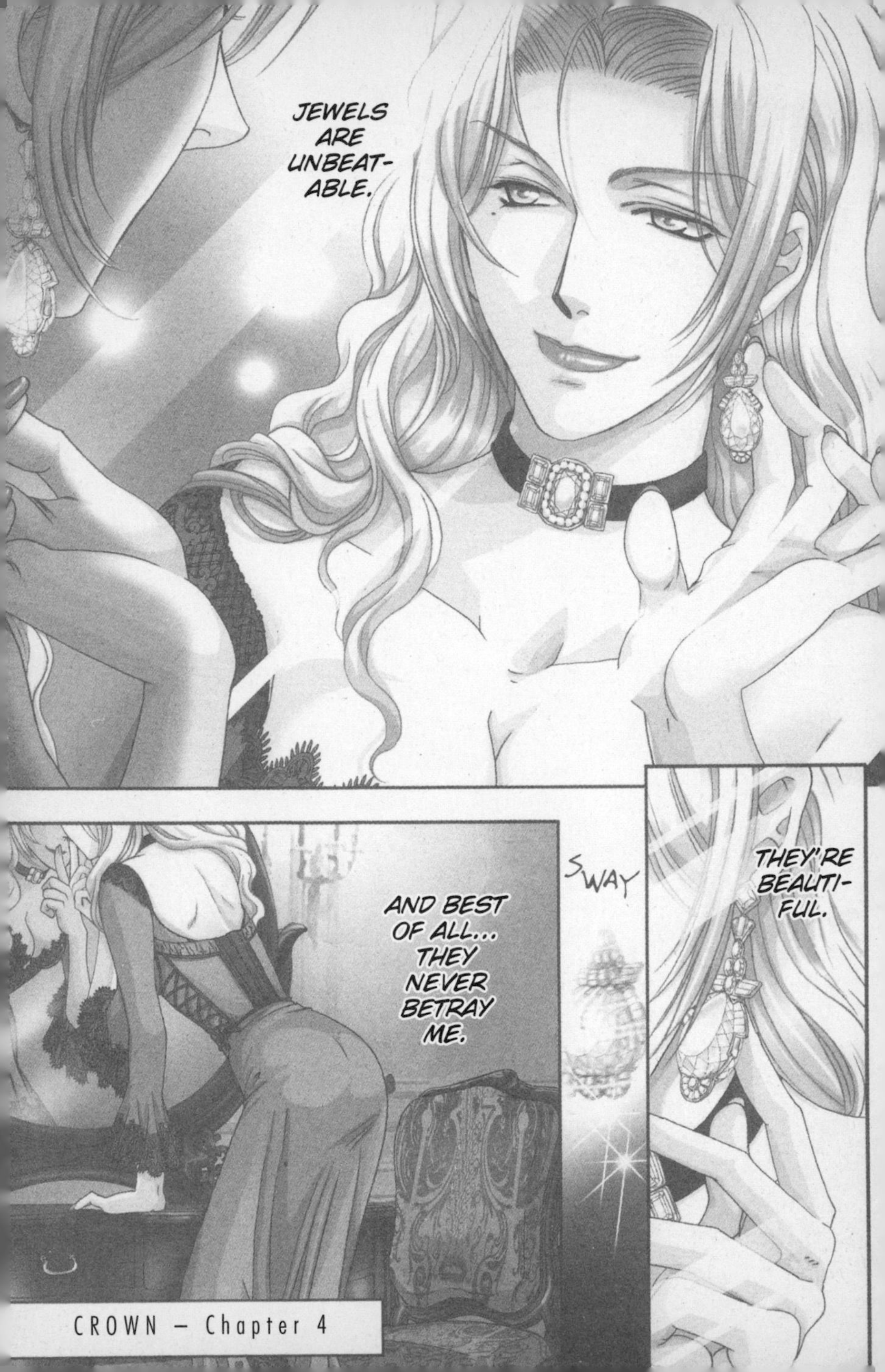
JEWELS ARE UNBEAT-ABLE.
THEY'RE BEAUTI-FUL.
SWAY
AND BEST OF ALL... THEY NEVER BETRAY ME.
CROWN – Chapter 4

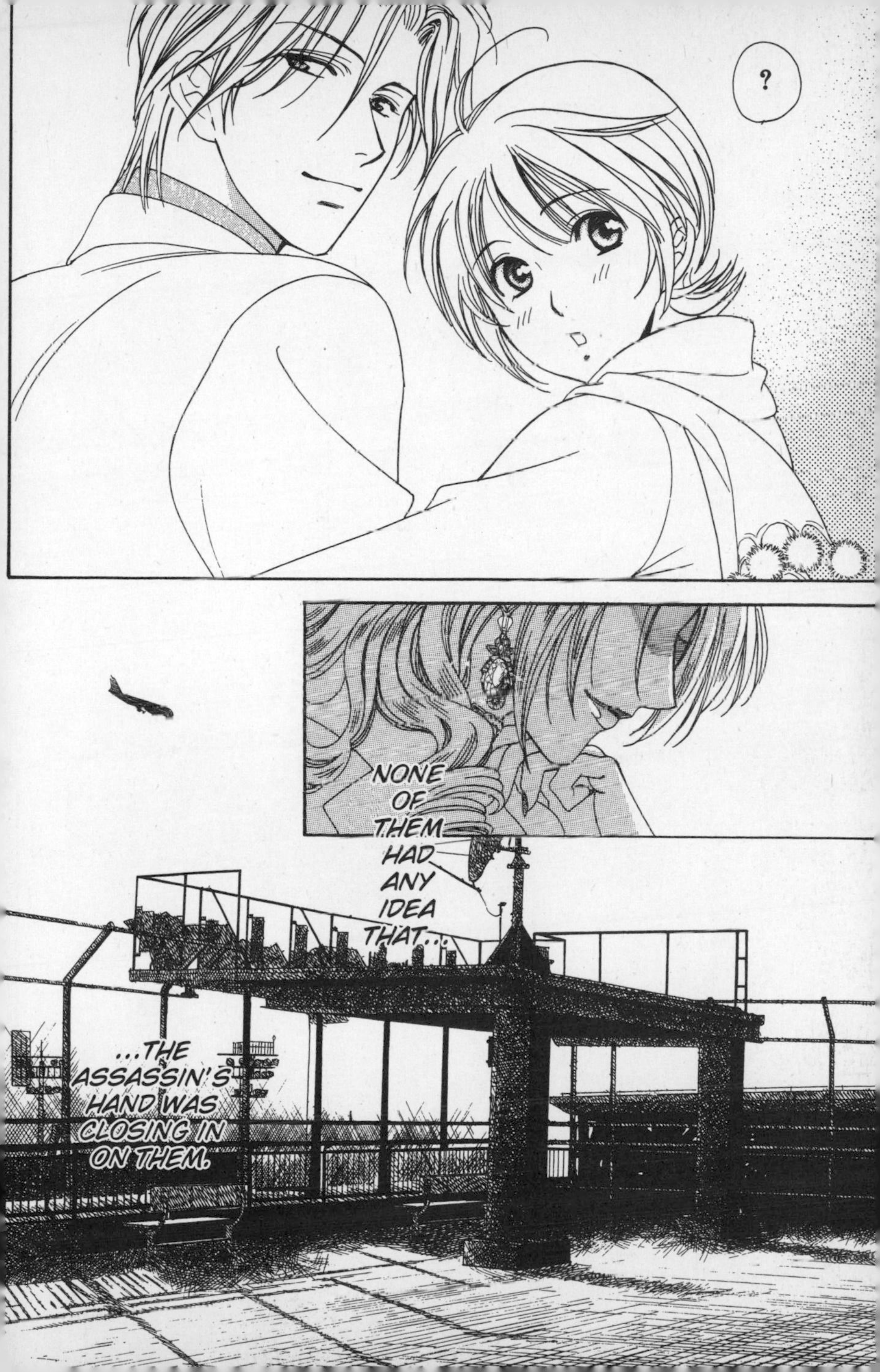
?
NONE OF THEM HAD ANY IDEA THAT...
...THE ASSASSIN'S HAND WAS CLOSING IN ON THEM.

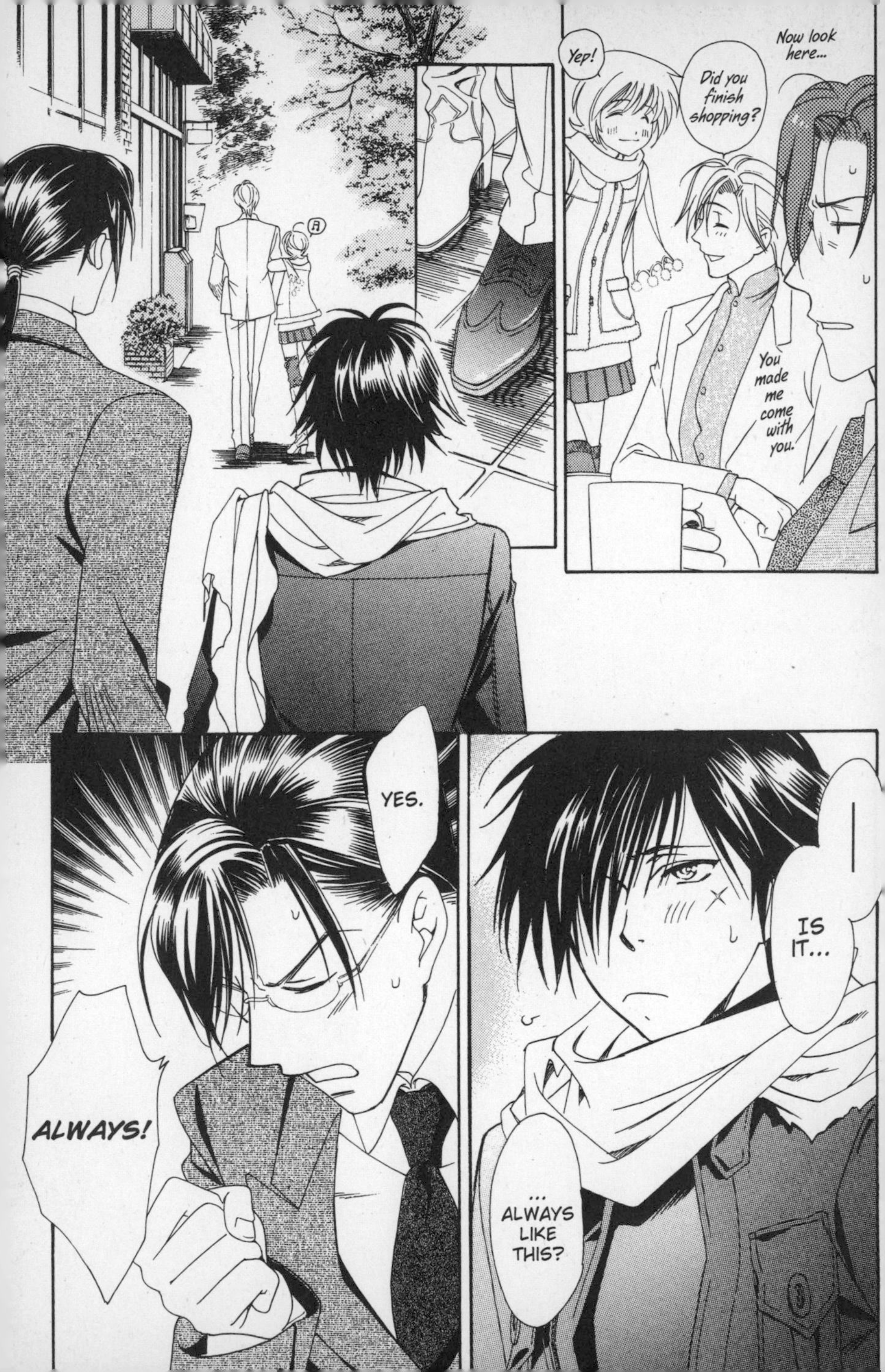
Now look here...
Did you finish shopping?
Yep!
You made me come with you.
IS IT...
... ALWAYS LIKE THIS?
YES.
ALWAYS!

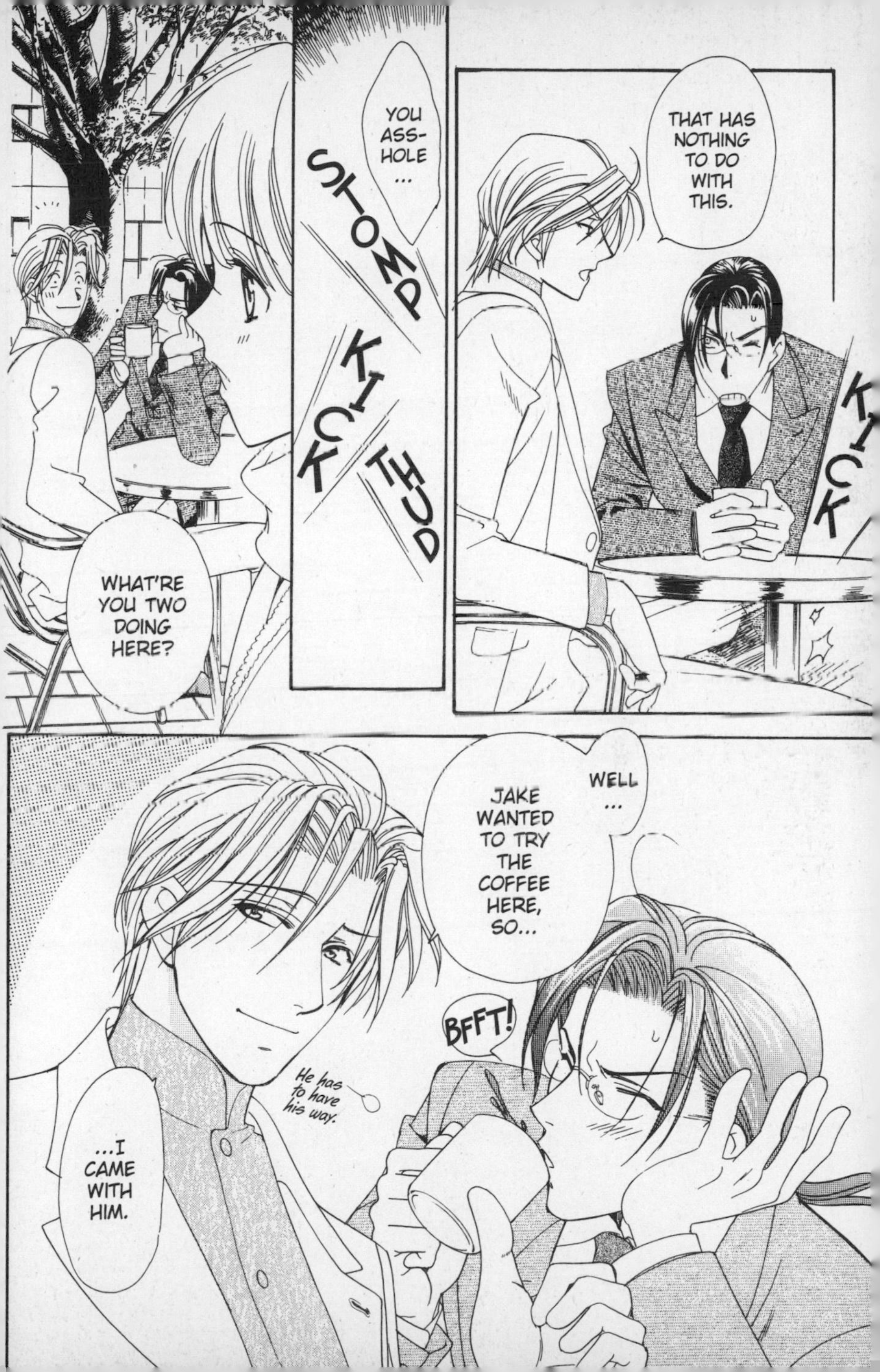
THAT HAS NOTHING TO DO WITH THIS.
KICK
YOU ASS-HOLE ...
STOMP
KICK
THUD
WHAT'RE YOU TWO DOING HERE?
WELL ...
JAKE WANTED TO TRY THE COFFEE HERE, SO...
BFFT!
He has to have his way.
...I CAME WITH HIM.

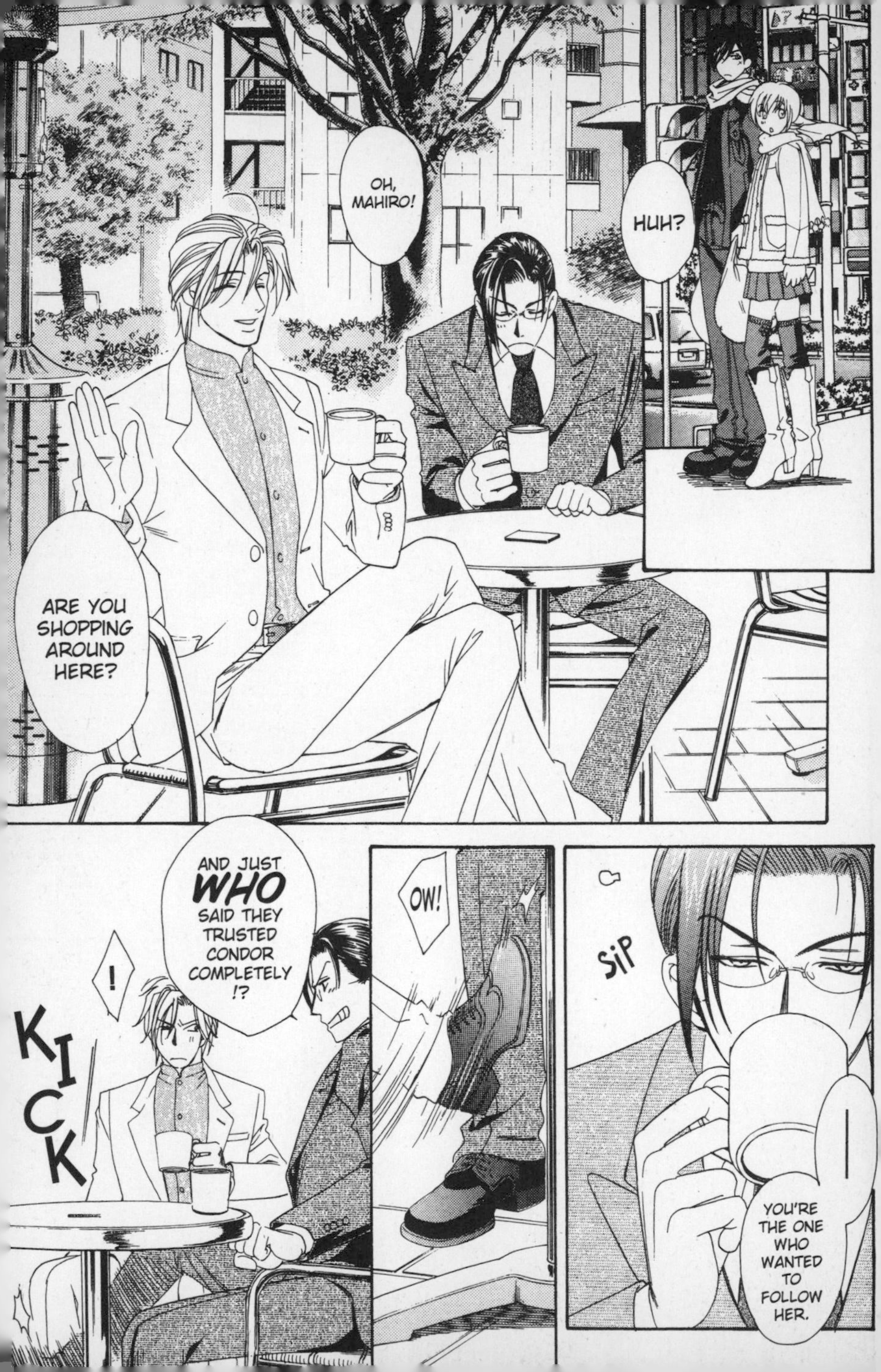
OH, MAHIRO!
HUH?
ARE YOU SHOPPING AROUND HERE?
SIP
YOU'RE THE ONE WHO WANTED TO FOLLOW HER.
OW!
KICK
!
AND JUST WHO SAID THEY TRUSTED CONDOR COMPLETELY !?

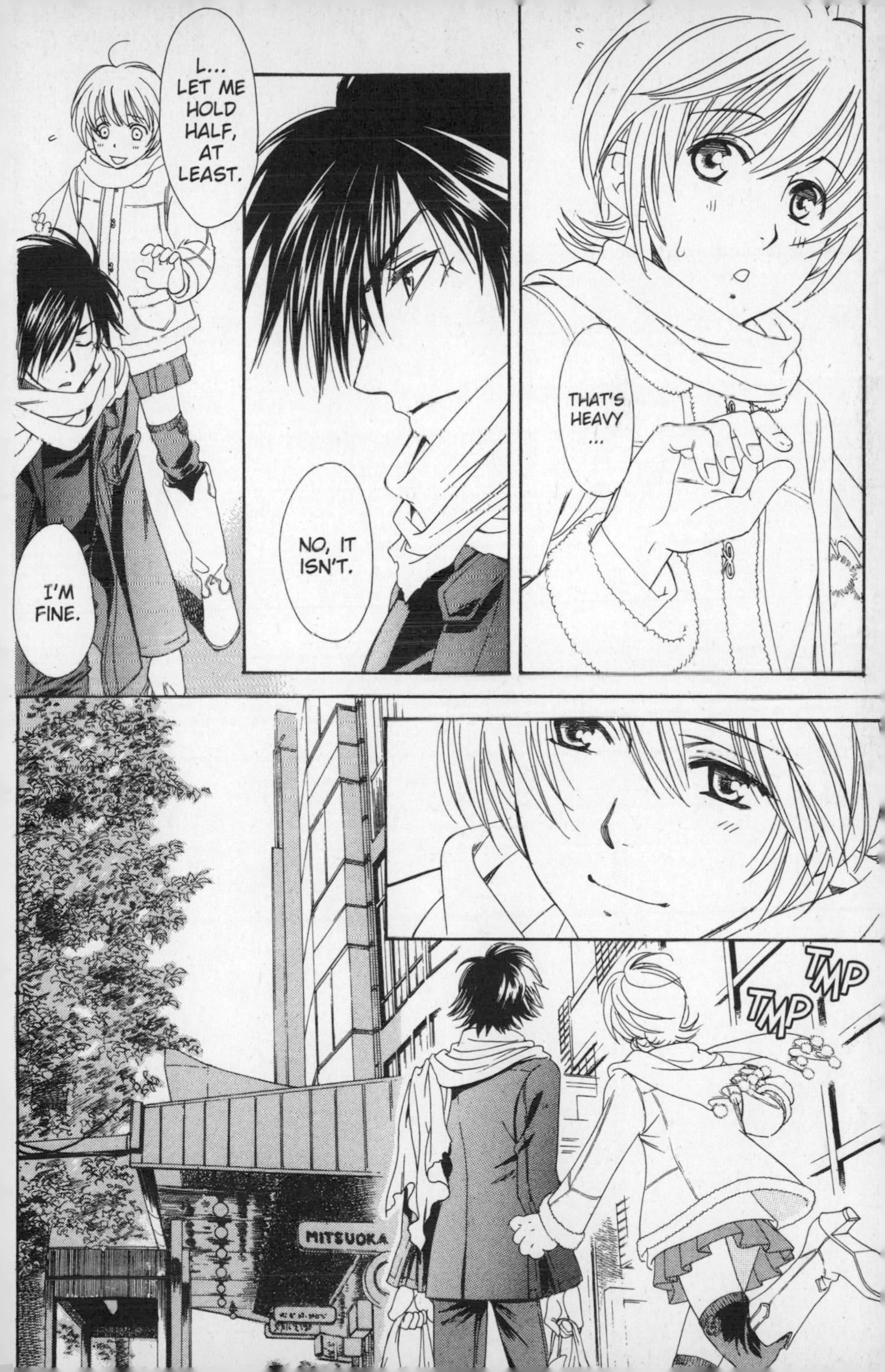
THAT'S HEAVY ...
NO, IT ISN'T.
L... LET ME HOLD HALF, AT LEAST.
I'M FINE.
TMP TMP
MITSUOKA

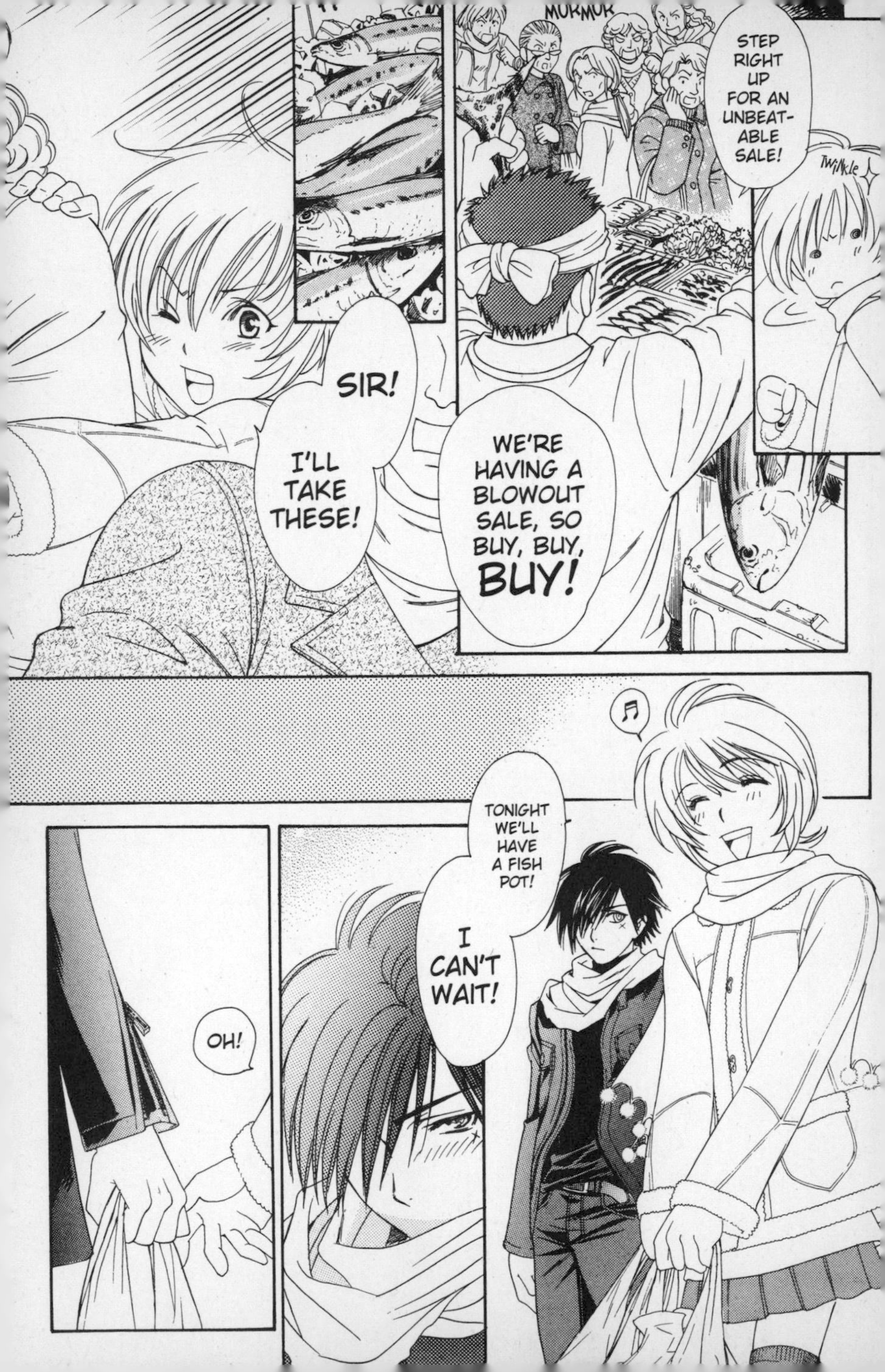
MURMUR
STEP RIGHT UP FOR AN UNBEAT-ABLE SALE!
TWINKLE
WE'RE HAVING A BLOWOUT SALE, SO BUY, BUY, BUY!
SIR!
I'LL TAKE THESE!
TONIGHT WE'LL HAVE A FISH POT!
I CAN'T WAIT!
OH!

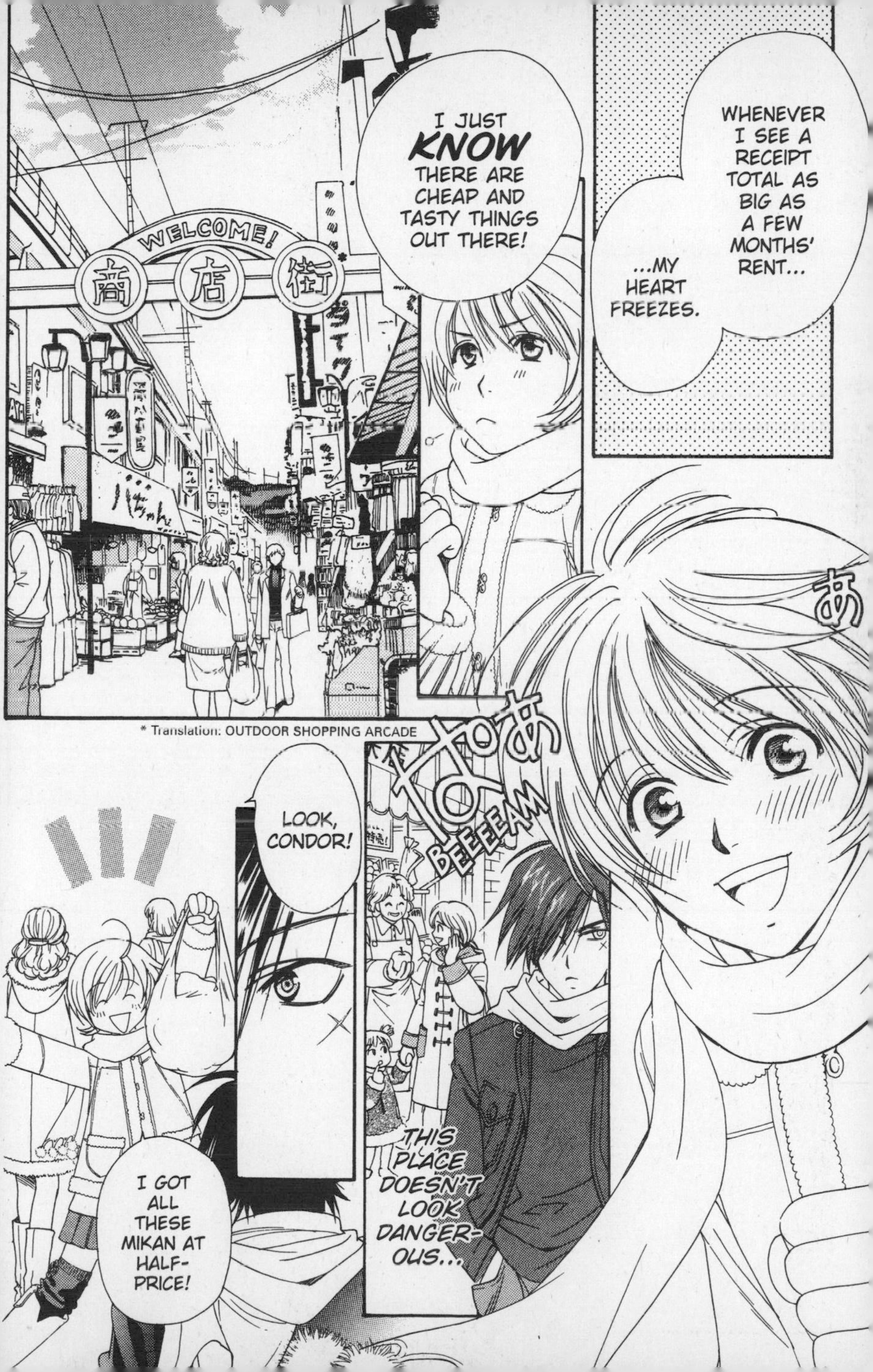
WHENEVER I SEE A RECEIPT TOTAL AS BIG AS A FEW MONTHS' RENT...
...MY HEART FREEZES.
I JUST KNOW THERE ARE CHEAP AND TASTY THINGS OUT THERE!
WELCOME!
商店街*
BEEEEAM
LOOK, CONDOR!
THIS PLACE DOESN'T LOOK DANGEROUS...
I GOT ALL THESE MIKAN AT HALF-PRICE!

* Translation: OUTDOOR SHOPPING ARCADE

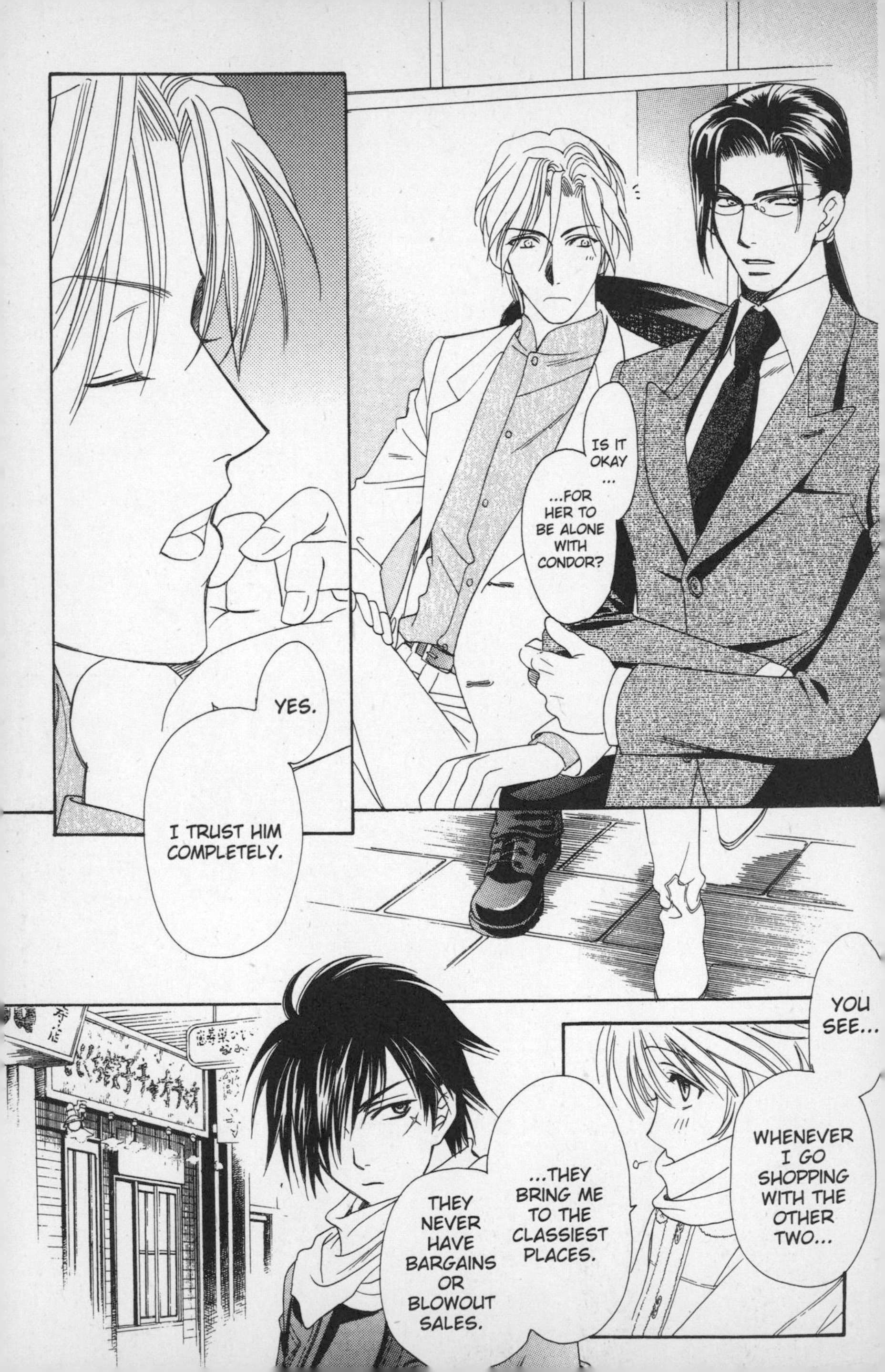
IS IT OKAY ...
...FOR HER TO BE ALONE WITH CONDOR?
YES.
I TRUST HIM COMPLETELY.
YOU SEE...
WHENEVER I GO SHOPPING WITH THE OTHER TWO...
...THEY BRING ME TO THE CLASSIEST PLACES.
THEY NEVER HAVE BARGAINS OR BLOWOUT SALES.

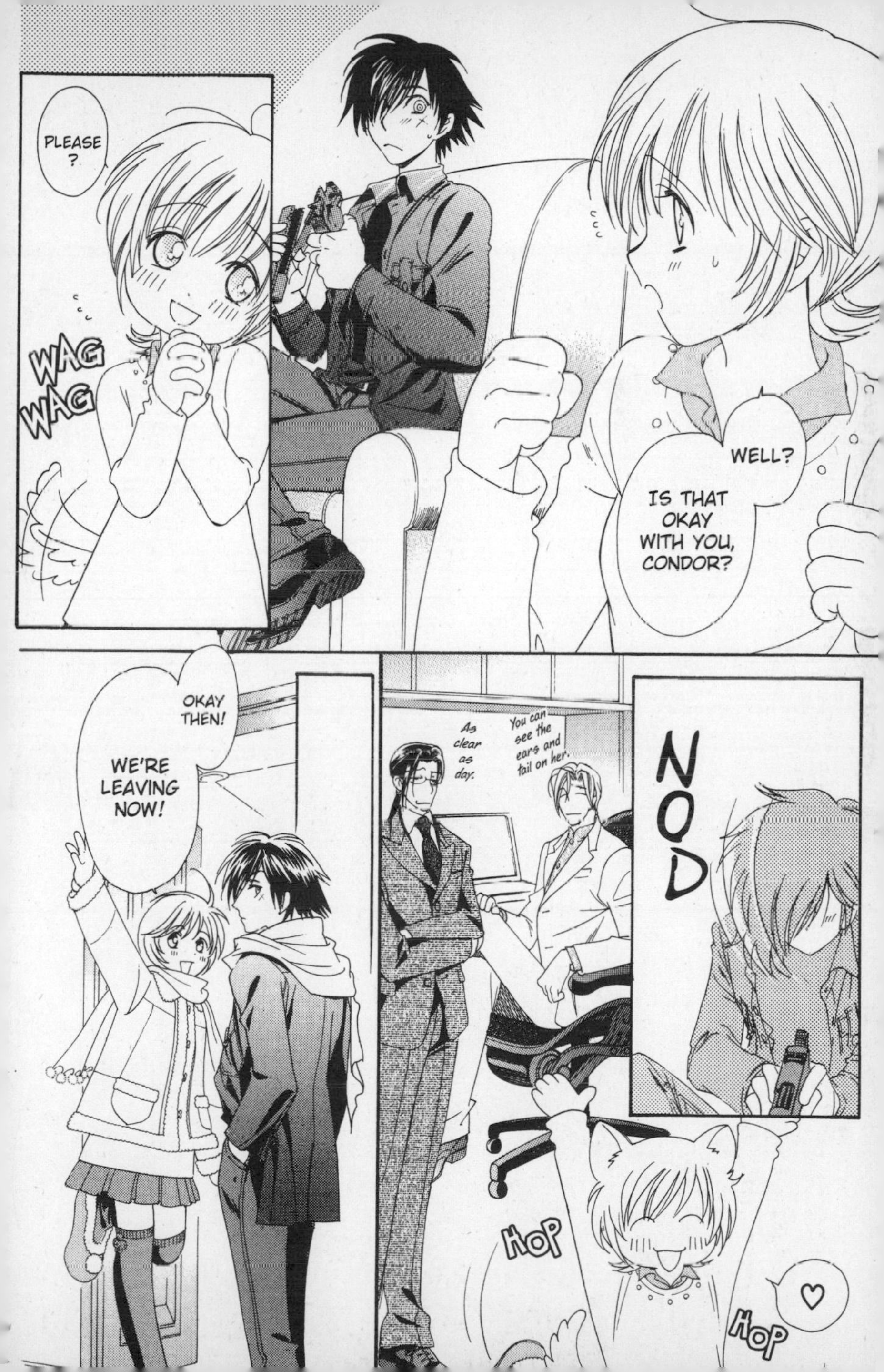
WELL?
IS THAT OKAY WITH YOU, CONDOR?
PLEASE?
WAG WAG
NOD
HOP
HOP
♥
You can see the ears and tail on her.
As clear as day.
OKAY THEN!
WE'RE LEAVING NOW!

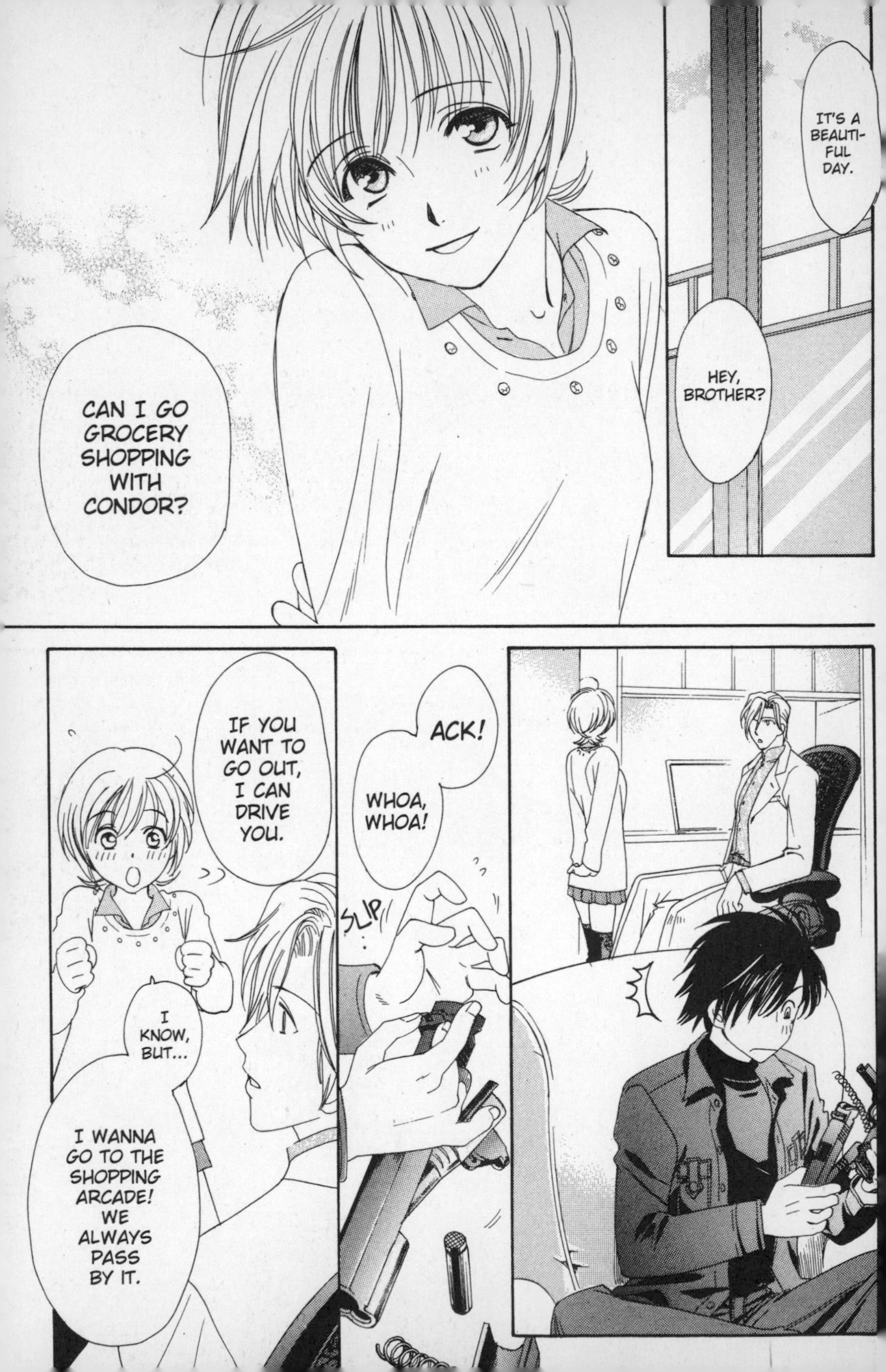
IT'S A BEAUTI-FUL DAY.
HEY, BROTHER?
CAN I GO GROCERY SHOPPING WITH CONDOR?
ACK!
WHOA, WHOA!
SLIP
IF YOU WANT TO GO OUT, I CAN DRIVE YOU.
I KNOW, BUT...
I WANNA GO TO THE SHOPPING ARCADE! WE ALWAYS PASS BY IT.

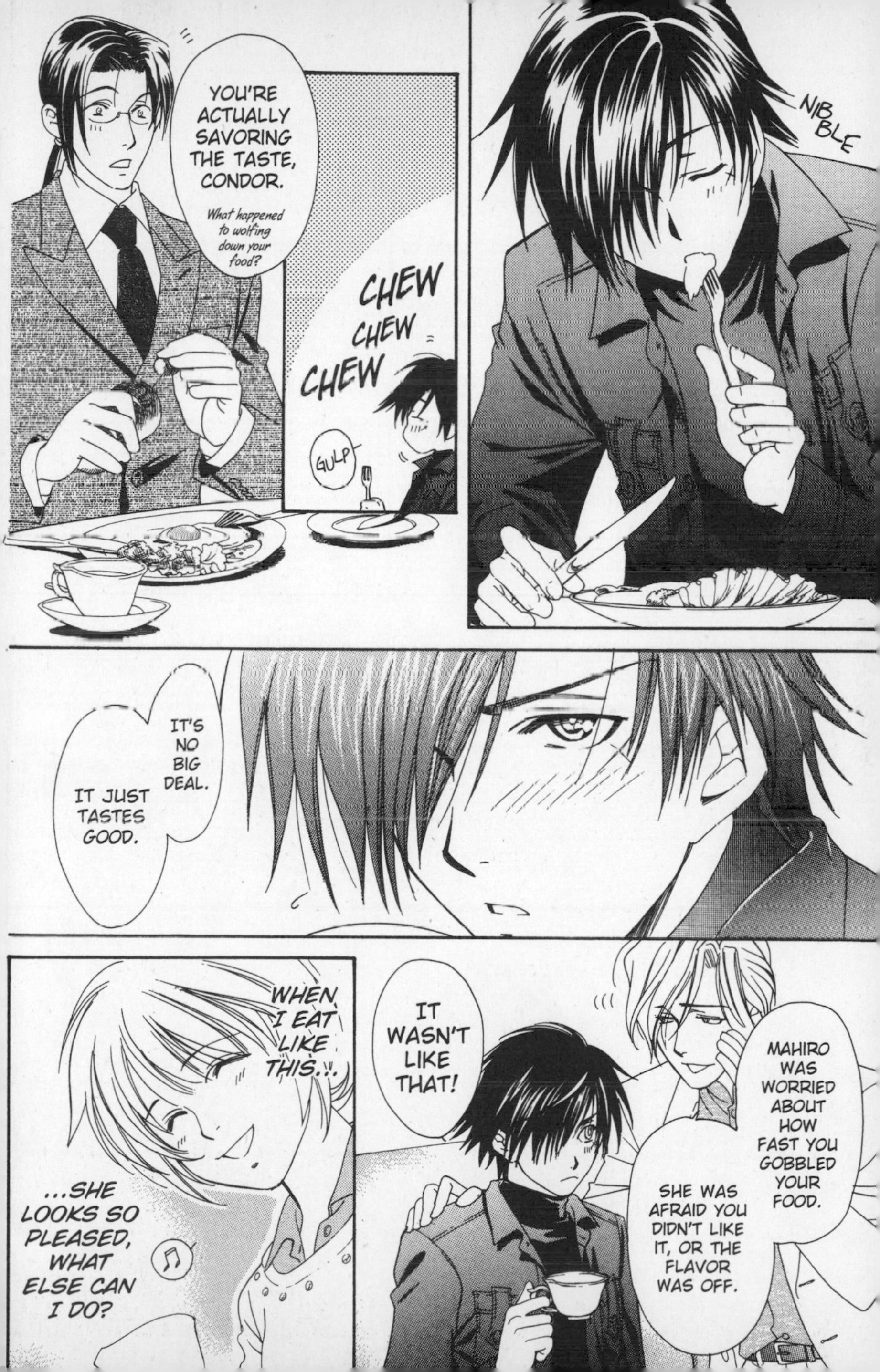
NIBBLE
YOU'RE ACTUALLY SAVORING THE TASTE, CONDOR.
What happened to wolfing down your food?
CHEW CHEW CHEW
GULP
IT'S NO BIG DEAL.
IT JUST TASTES GOOD.
MAHIRO WAS WORRIED ABOUT HOW FAST YOU GOBBLED YOUR FOOD.
SHE WAS AFRAID YOU DIDN'T LIKE IT, OR THE FLAVOR WAS OFF.
IT WASN'T LIKE THAT!
WHEN I EAT LIKE THIS...
...SHE LOOKS SO PLEASED, WHAT ELSE CAN I DO?

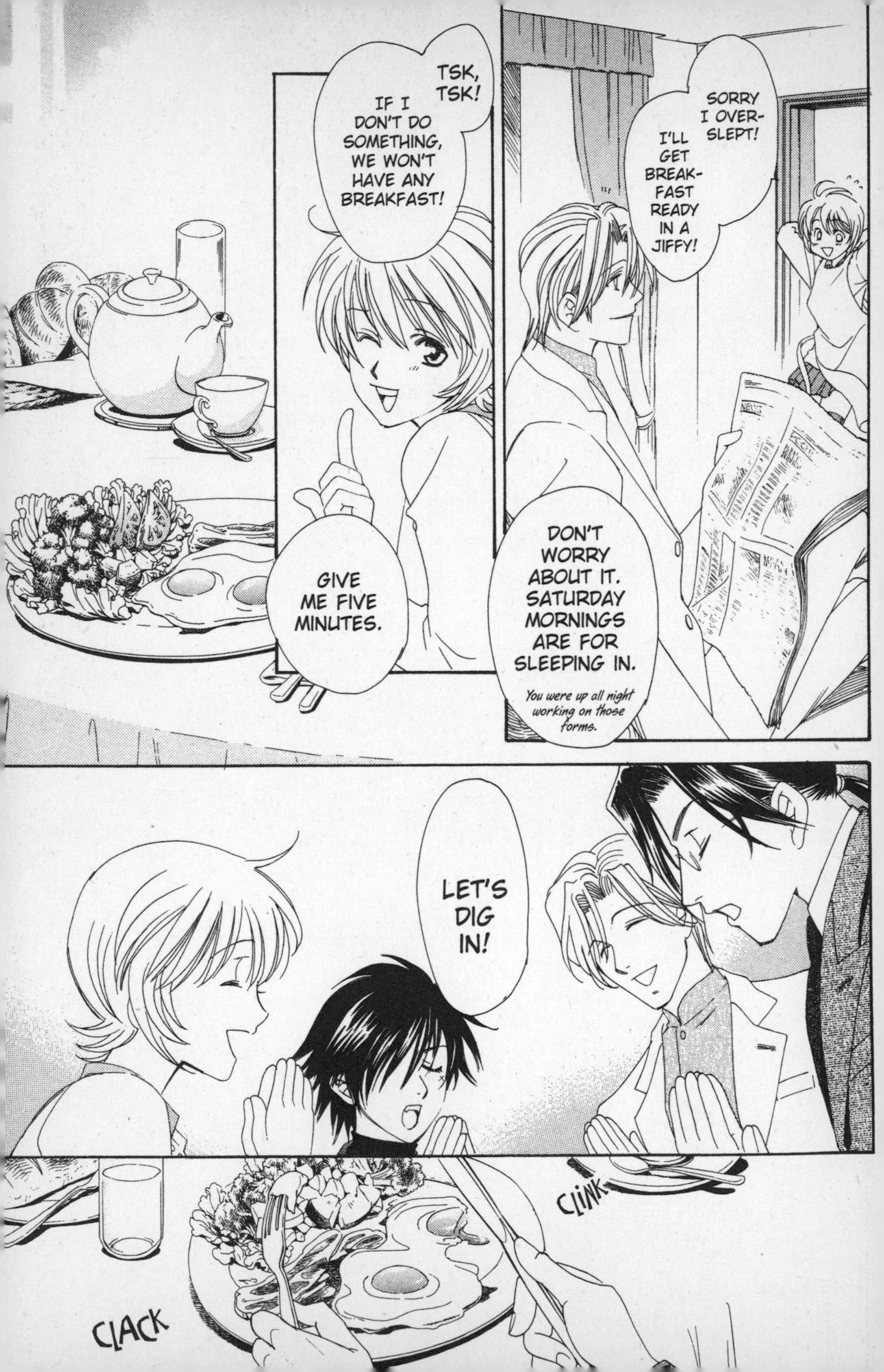
SORRY I OVER-SLEPT!
I'LL GET BREAK-FAST READY IN A JIFFY!
DON'T WORRY ABOUT IT. SATURDAY MORNINGS ARE FOR SLEEPING IN.
You were up all night working on those forms.
TSK, TSK!
IF I DON'T DO SOMETHING, WE WON'T HAVE ANY BREAKFAST!
GIVE ME FIVE MINUTES.
LET'S DIG IN!
CLINK
CLACK

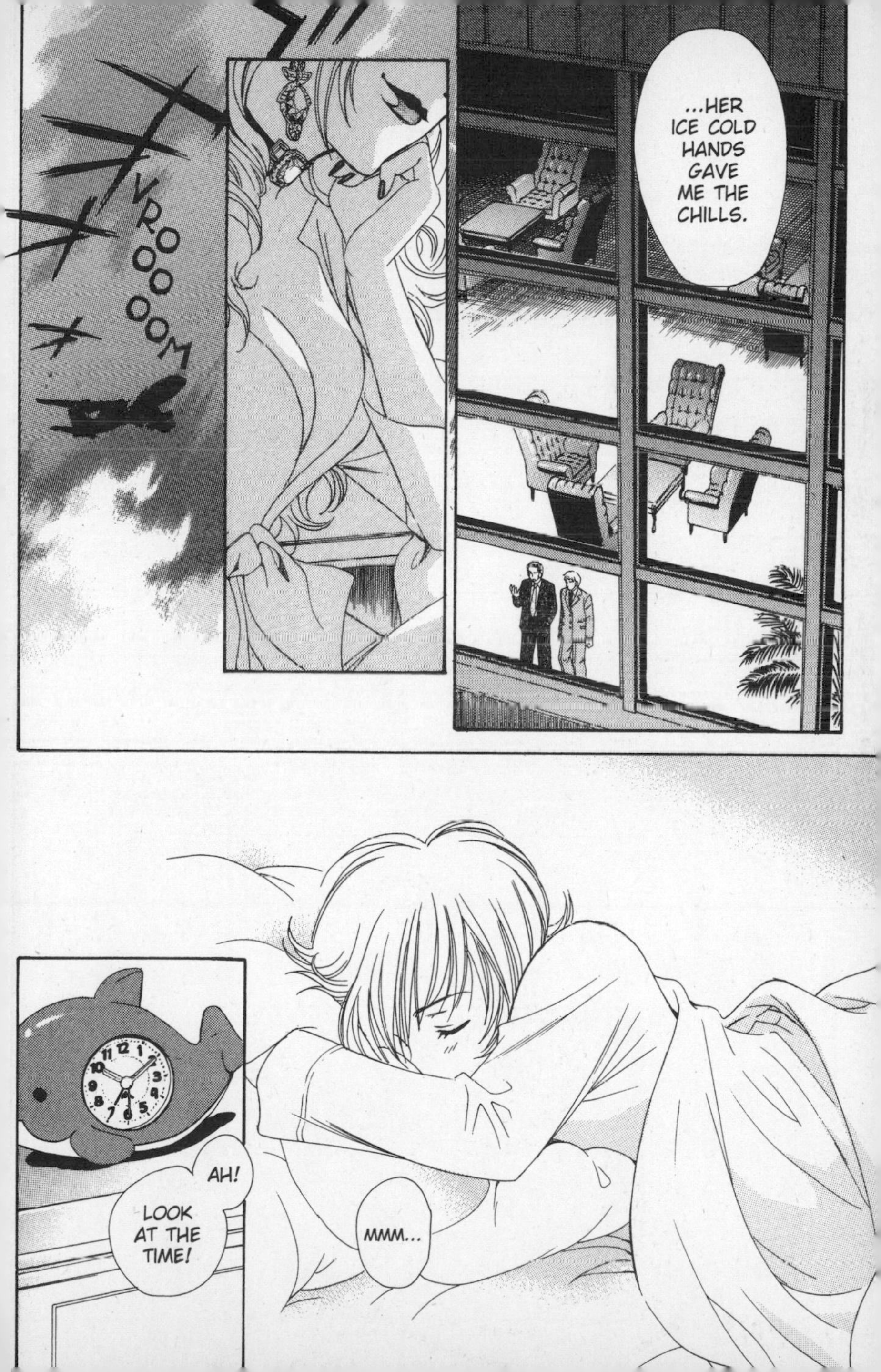
...HER ICE COLD HANDS GAVE ME THE CHILLS.
VROOOOOOOM
MMM...
AH!
LOOK AT THE TIME!

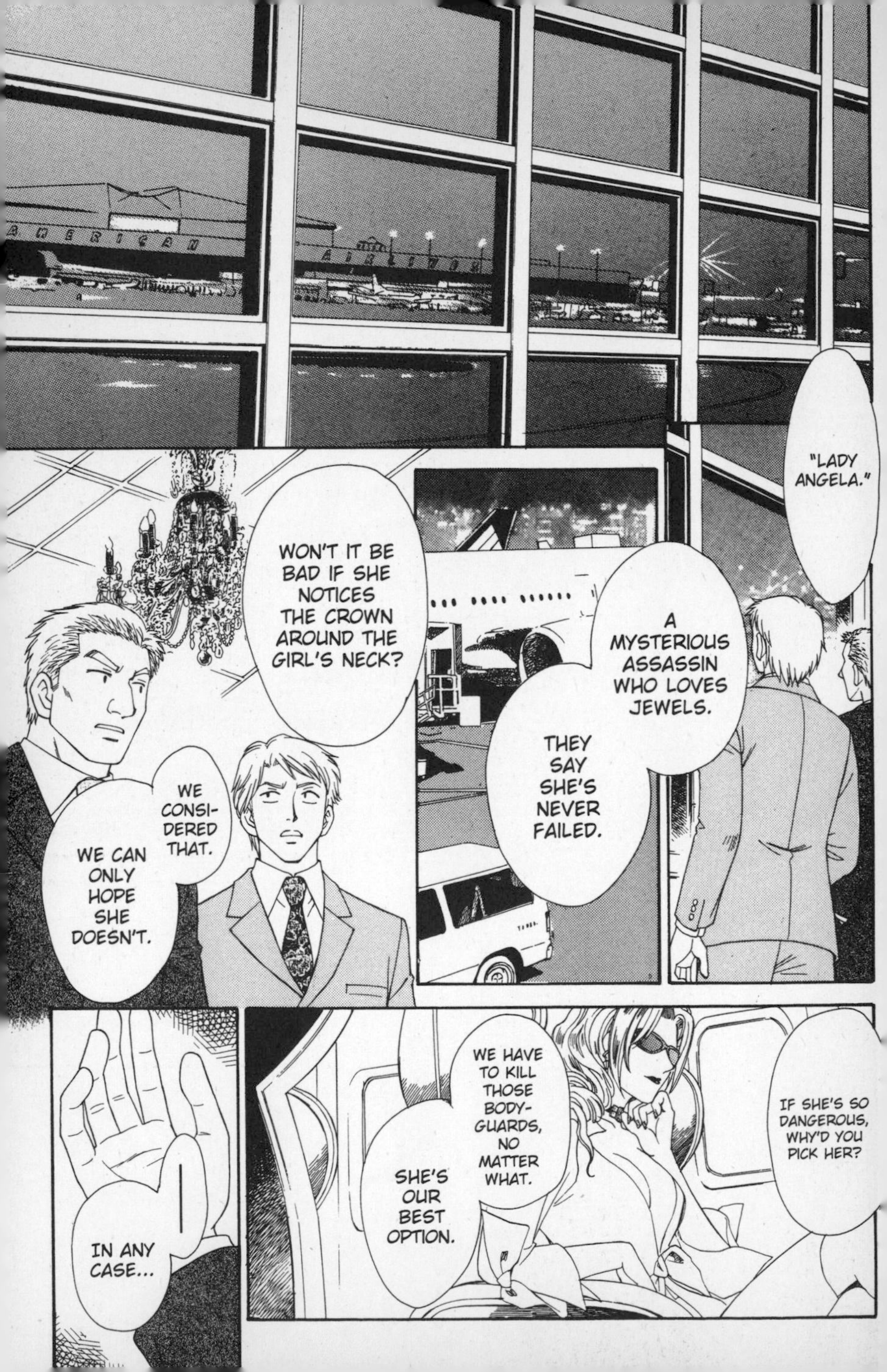
"LADY ANGELA."
A MYSTERIOUS ASSASSIN WHO LOVES JEWELS.
THEY SAY SHE'S NEVER FAILED.
WON'T IT BE BAD IF SHE NOTICES THE CROWN AROUND THE GIRL'S NECK?
WE CONSIDERED THAT.
WE CAN ONLY HOPE SHE DOESN'T.
IF SHE'S SO DANGEROUS, WHY'D YOU PICK HER?
WE HAVE TO KILL THOSE BODYGUARDS, NO MATTER WHAT.
SHE'S OUR BEST OPTION.
IN ANY CASE...

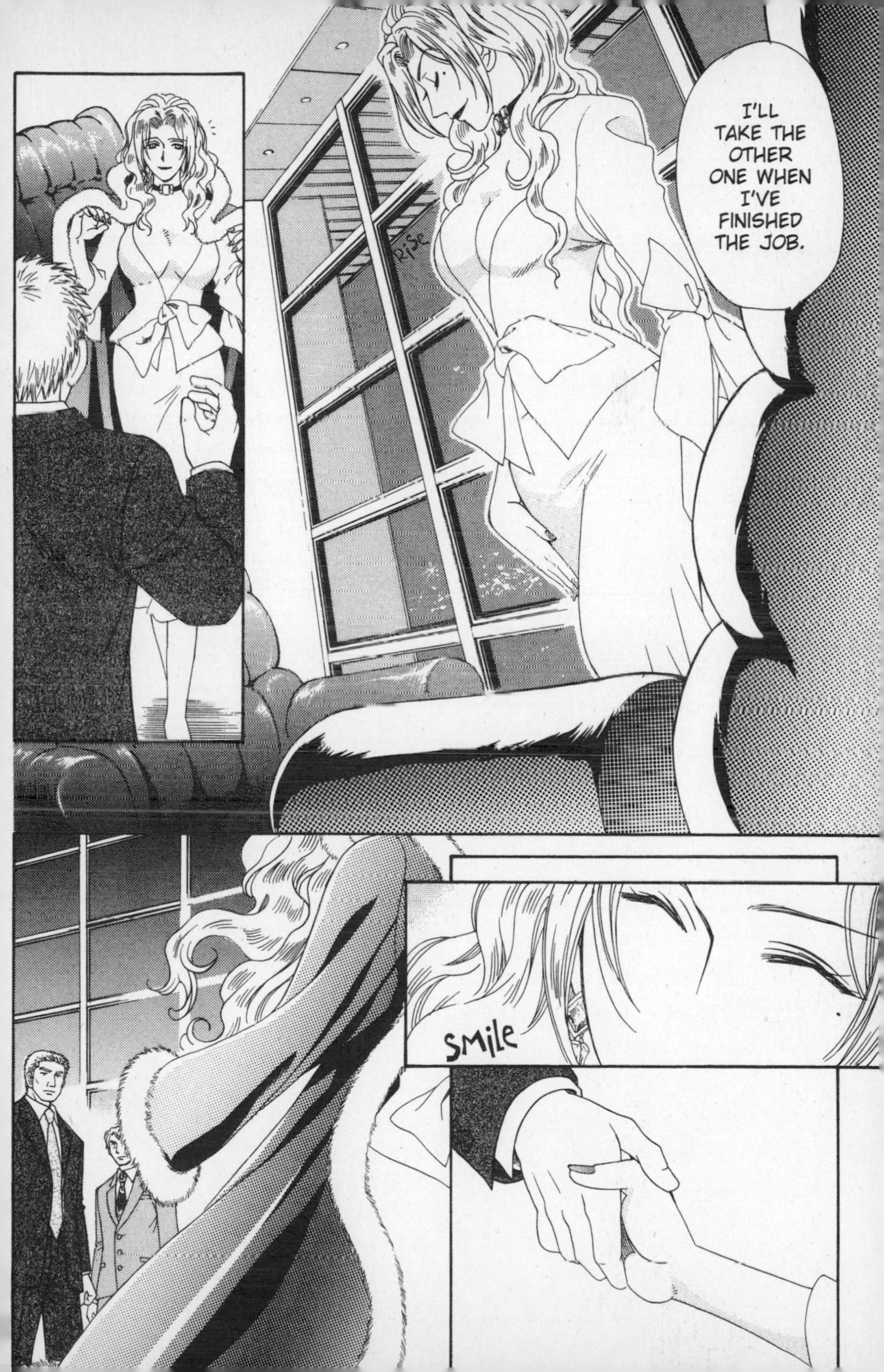
RISE
I'LL TAKE THE OTHER ONE WHEN I'VE FINISHED THE JOB.
SMILE

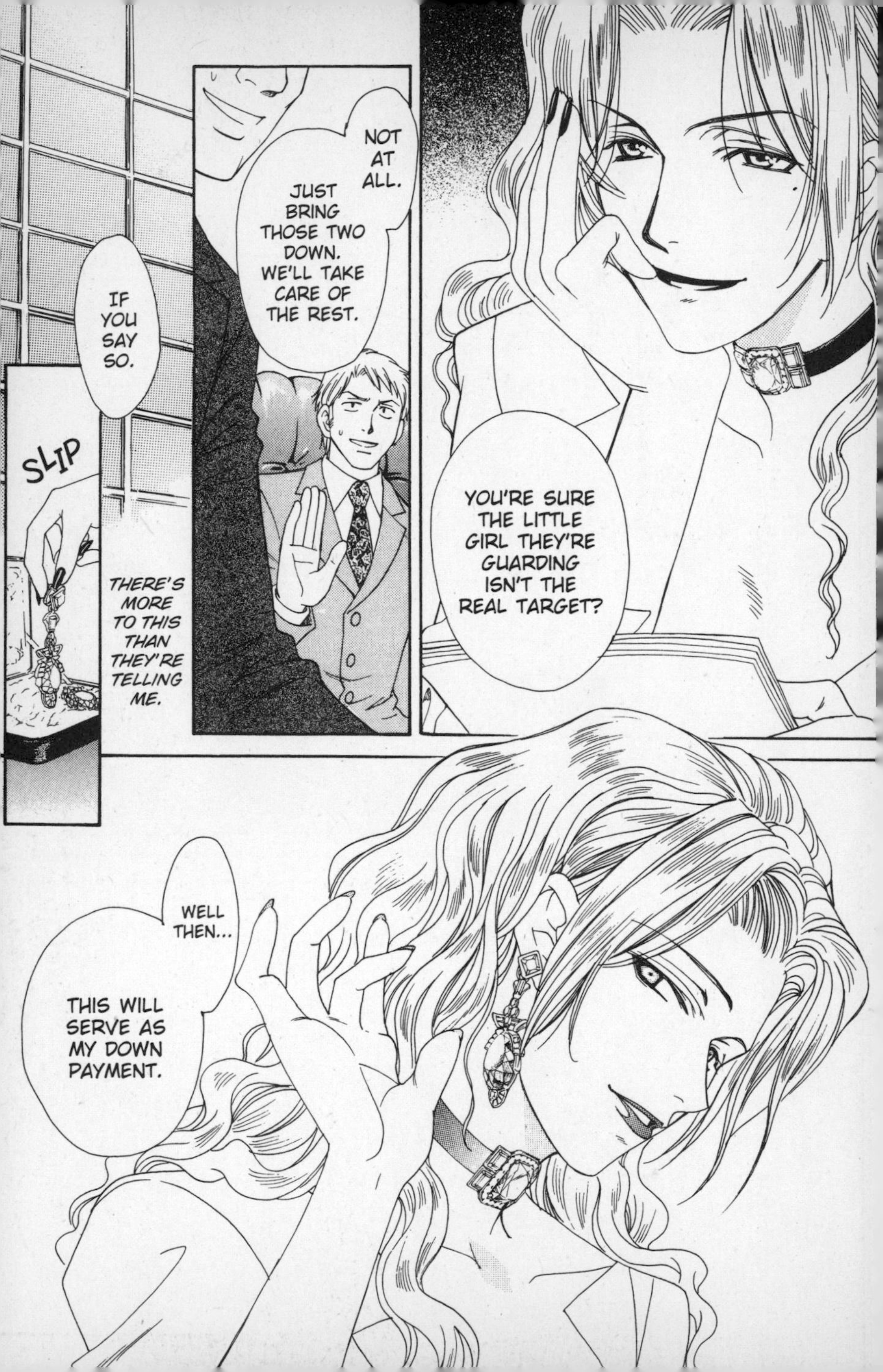
YOU'RE SURE THE LITTLE GIRL THEY'RE GUARDING ISN'T THE REAL TARGET?
NOT AT ALL.
JUST BRING THOSE TWO DOWN. WE'LL TAKE CARE OF THE REST.
IF YOU SAY SO.
SLIP
THERE'S MORE TO THIS THAN THEY'RE TELLING ME.
WELL THEN...
THIS WILL SERVE AS MY DOWN PAYMENT.

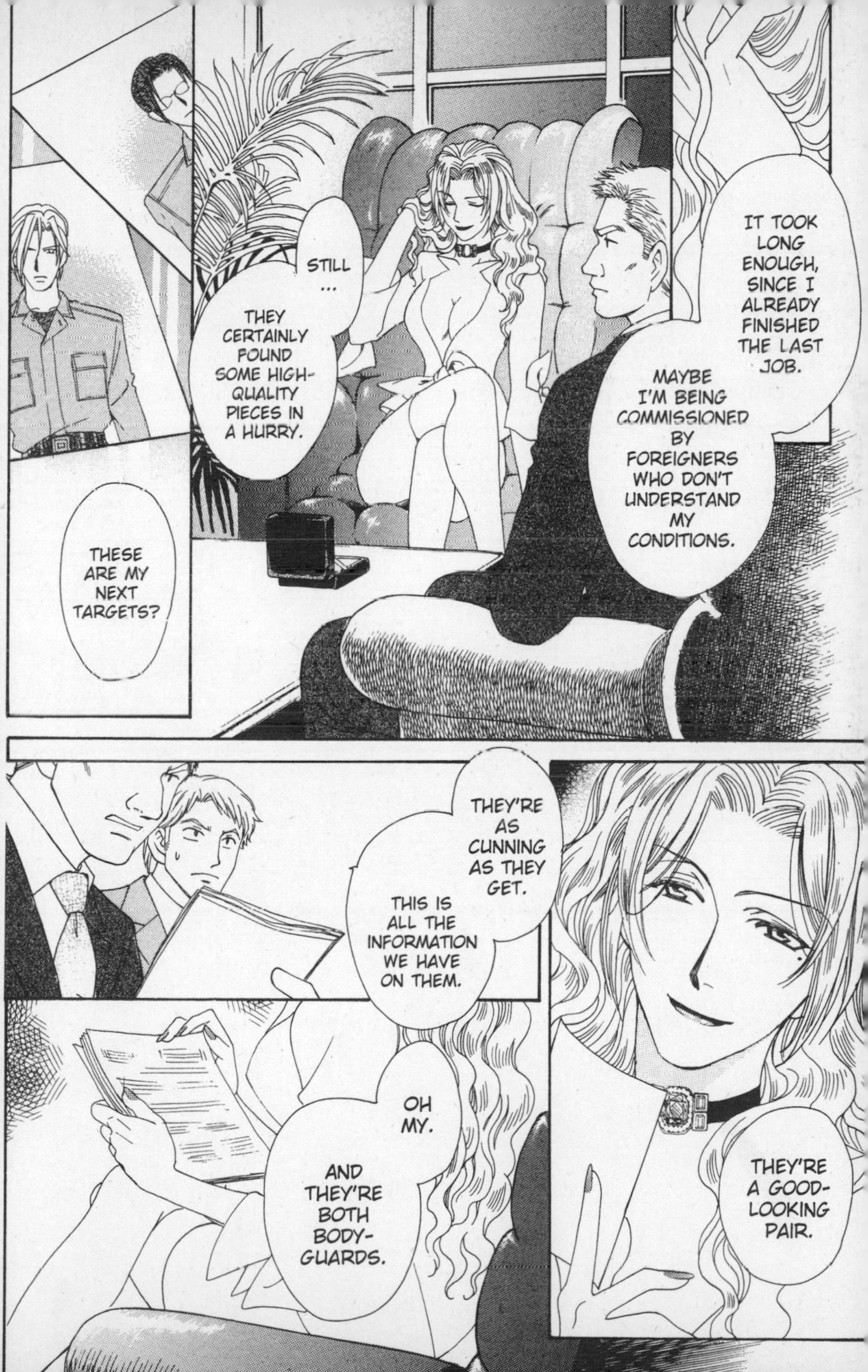
IT TOOK LONG ENOUGH, SINCE I ALREADY FINISHED THE LAST JOB.
MAYBE I'M BEING COMMISSIONED BY FOREIGNERS WHO DON'T UNDERSTAND MY CONDITIONS.
STILL ...
THEY CERTAINLY FOUND SOME HIGH-QUALITY PIECES IN A HURRY.
THESE ARE MY NEXT TARGETS?
THEY'RE AS CUNNING AS THEY GET.
THIS IS ALL THE INFORMATION WE HAVE ON THEM.
THEY'RE A GOOD-LOOKING PAIR.
OH MY.
AND THEY'RE BOTH BODY-GUARDS.

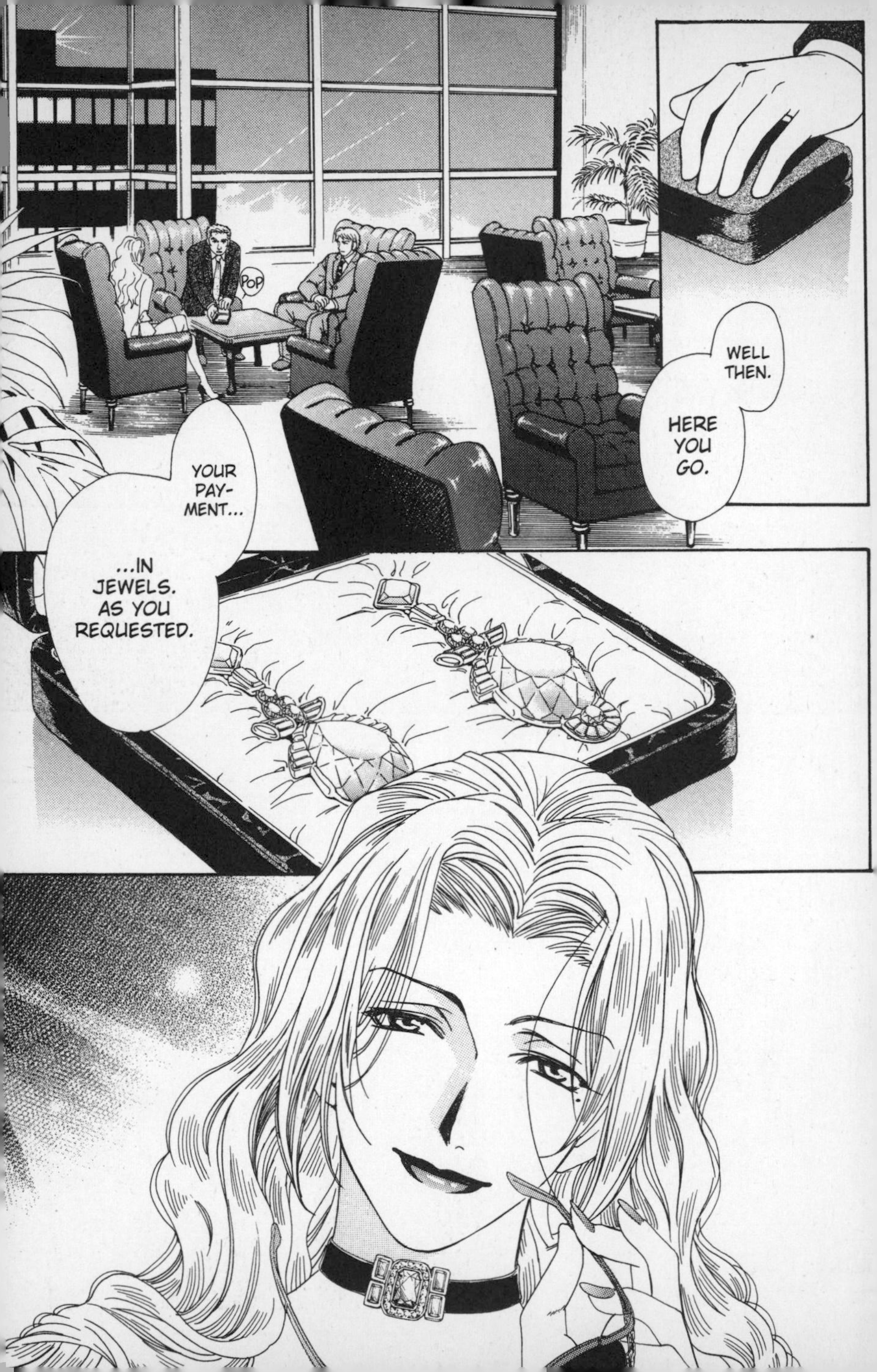
POP
WELL THEN.
HERE YOU GO.
YOUR PAY-MENT...
...IN JEWELS. AS YOU REQUESTED.

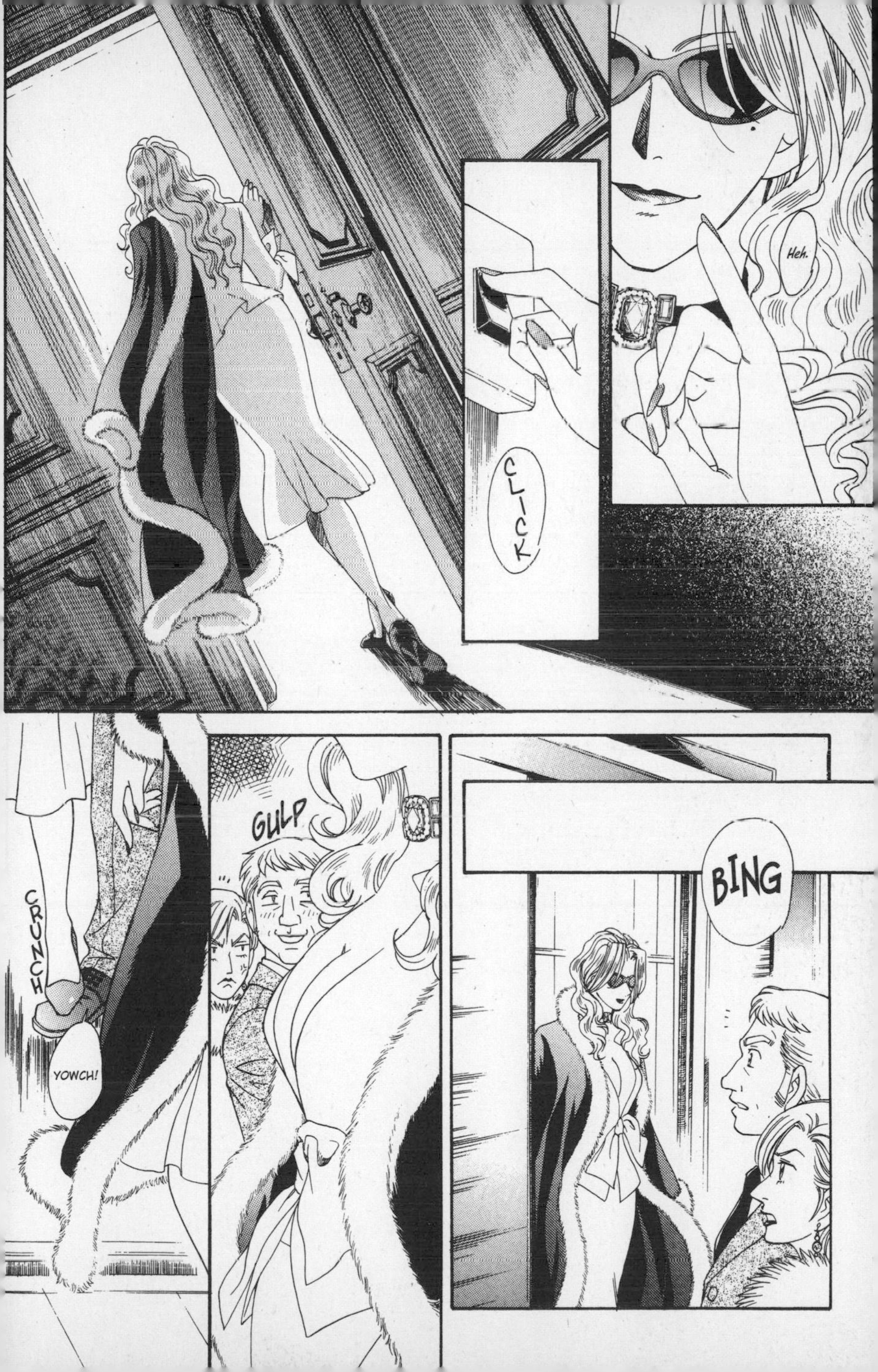

Heh.
CLICK
BING
GULP
CRUNCH
YOWCH!

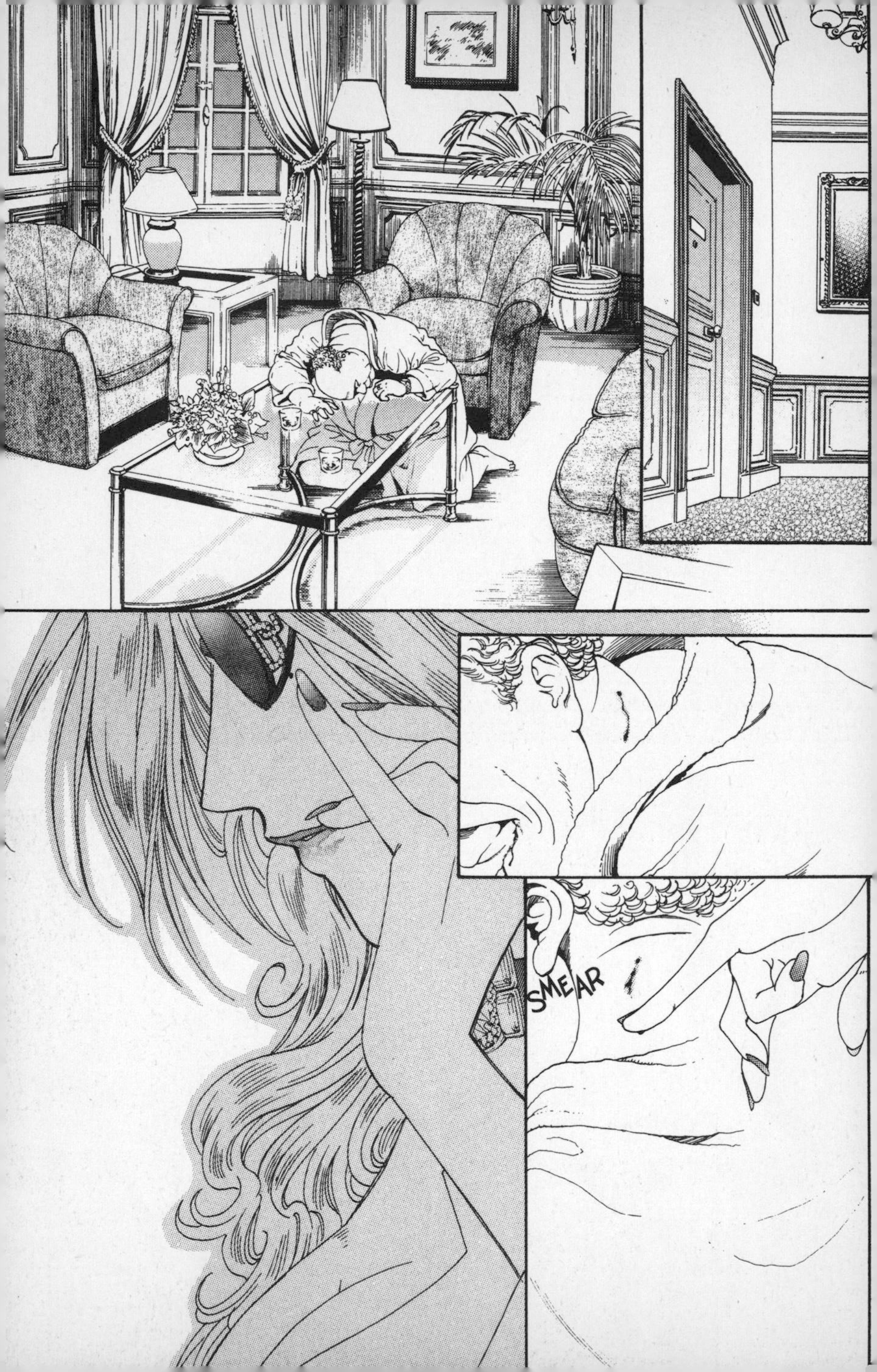
SMEAR

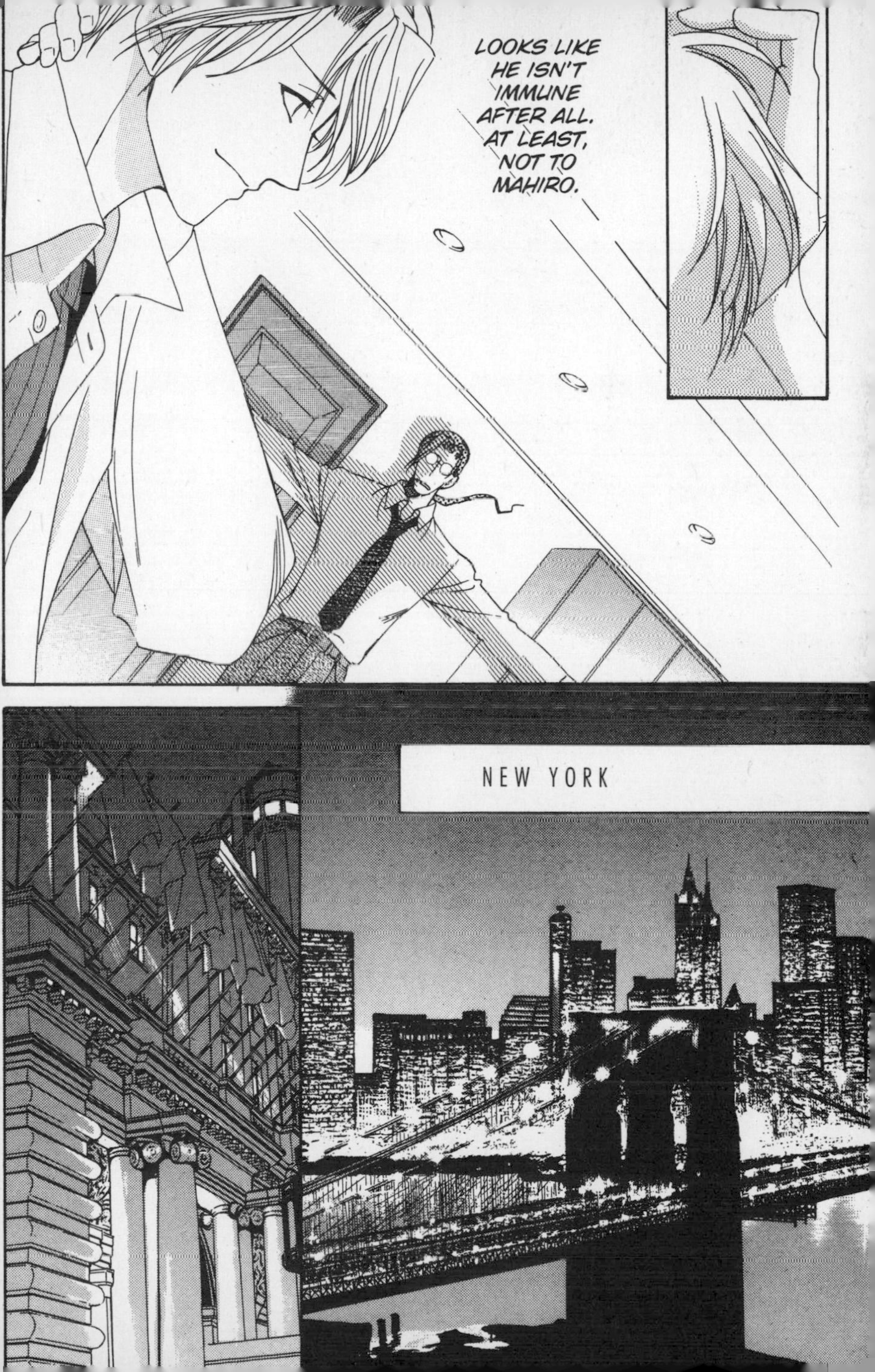
LOOKS LIKE HE ISN'T IMMUNE AFTER ALL. AT LEAST, NOT TO MAHIRO.
NEW YORK

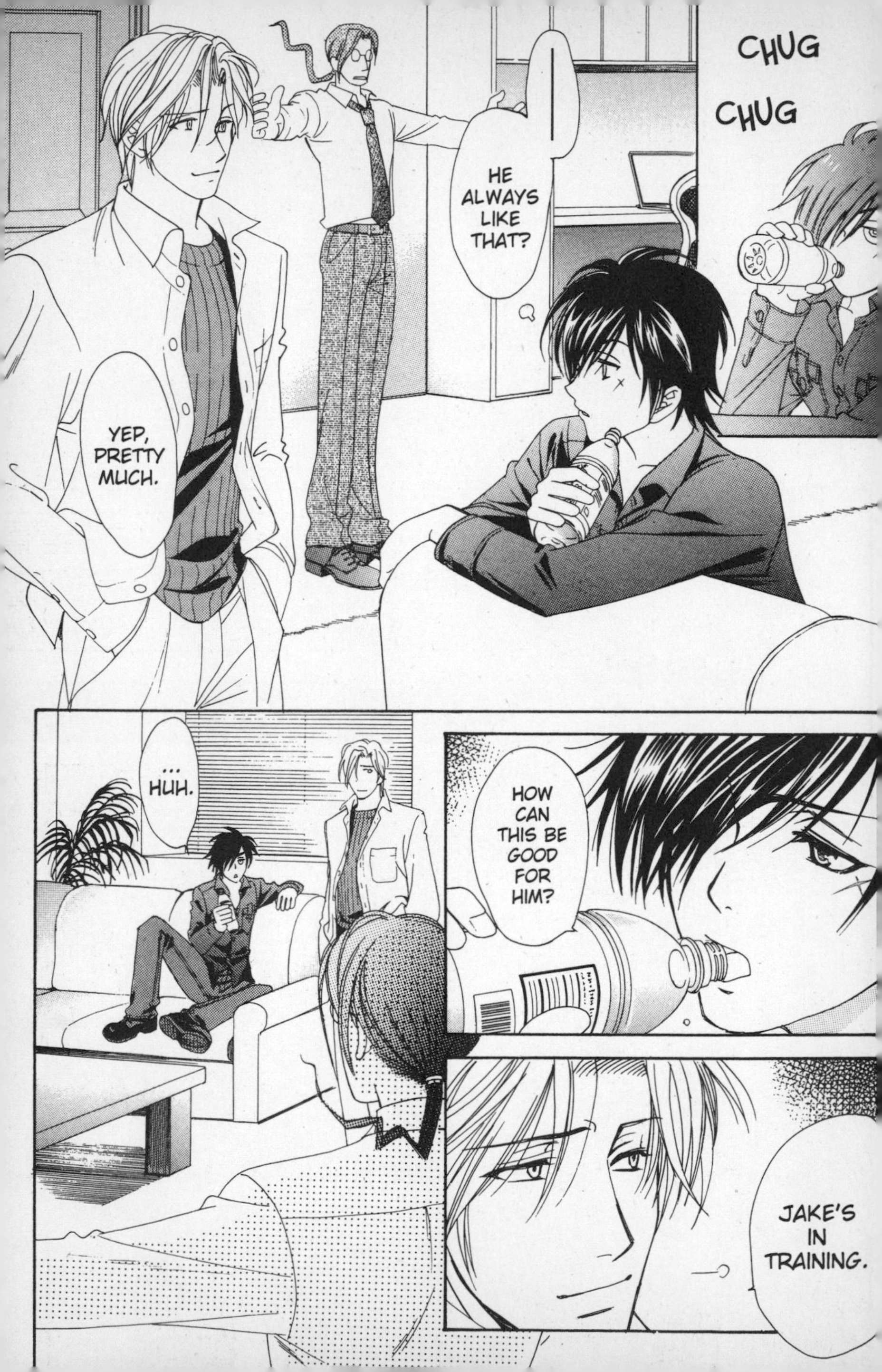
CHUG
CHUG
HE ALWAYS LIKE THAT?
YEP, PRETTY MUCH.
HOW CAN THIS BE GOOD FOR HIM?
... HUH.
JAKE'S IN TRAINING.

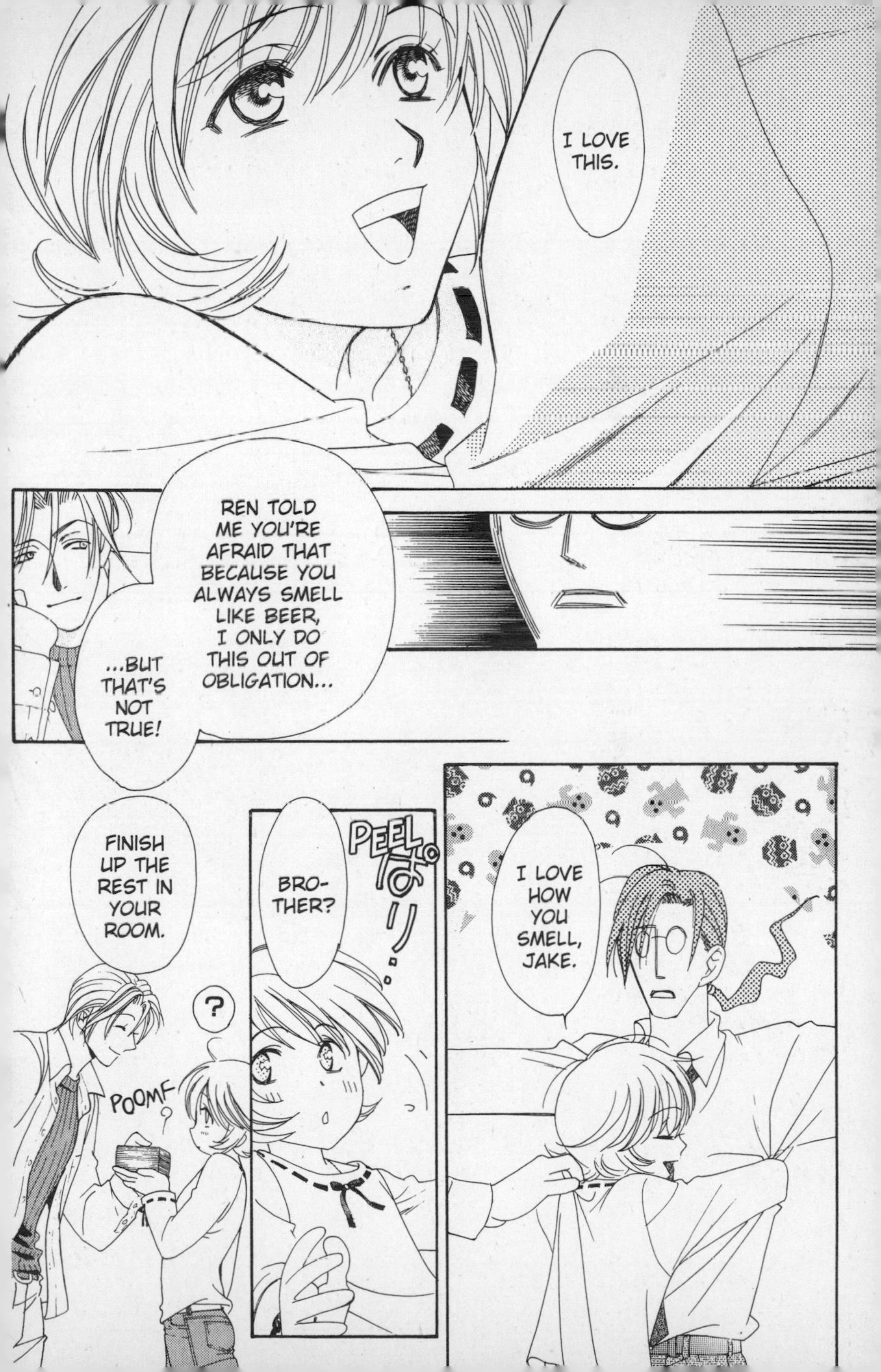
I LOVE THIS.
REN TOLD ME YOU'RE AFRAID THAT BECAUSE YOU ALWAYS SMELL LIKE BEER, I ONLY DO THIS OUT OF OBLIGATION...
...BUT THAT'S NOT TRUE!
I LOVE HOW YOU SMELL, JAKE.
PEEL
BRO-THER?
FINISH UP THE REST IN YOUR ROOM.
?
POOMF

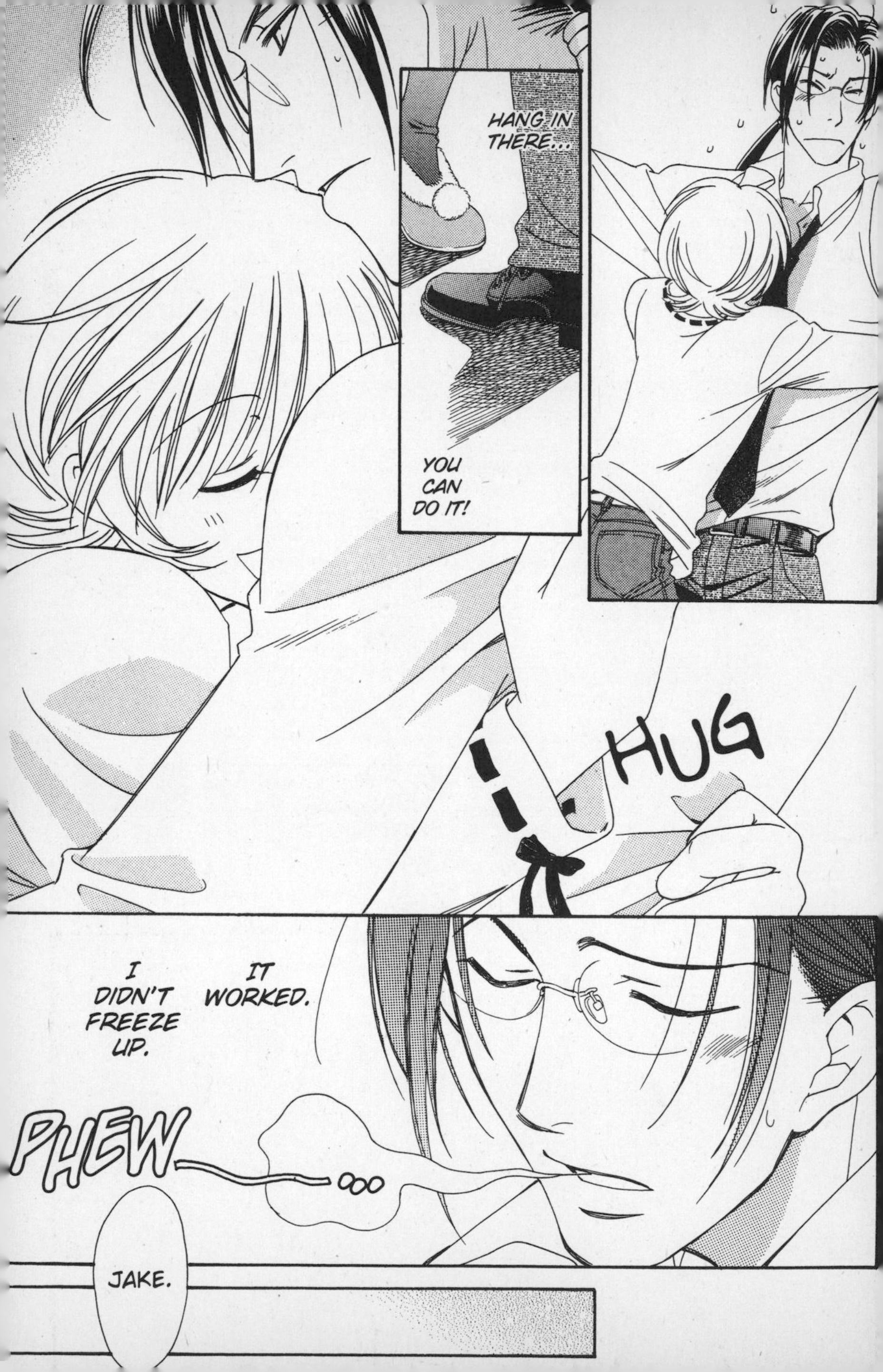
HANG IN THERE...
YOU CAN DO IT!
HUG
IT WORKED.
I DIDN'T FREEZE UP.
PHEW
JAKE.

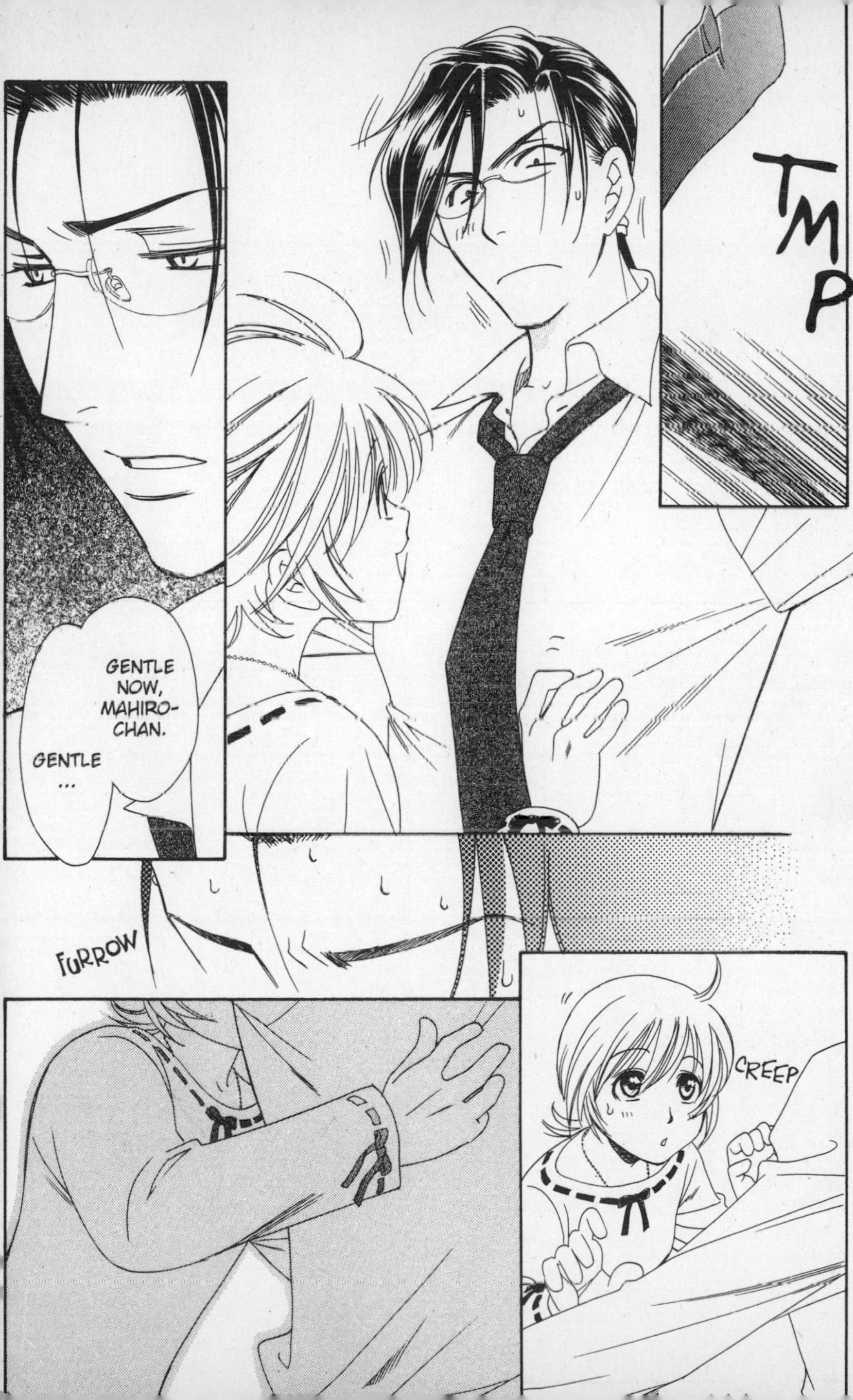
TMP
GENTLE NOW, MAHIRO-CHAN.
GENTLE ...
FURROW
CREEP

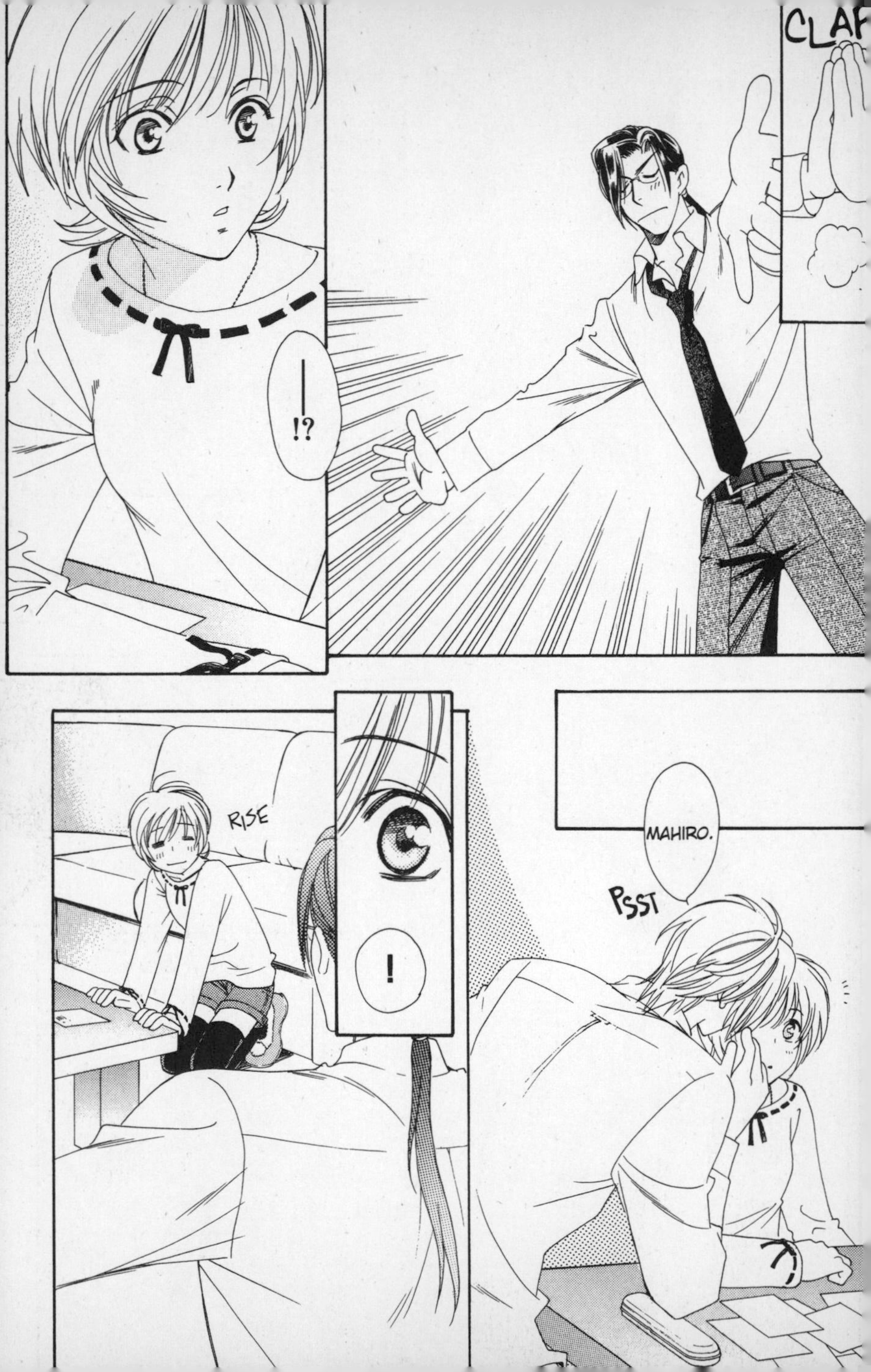
CLAP
―!?
MAHIRO.
PSST
!
RISE

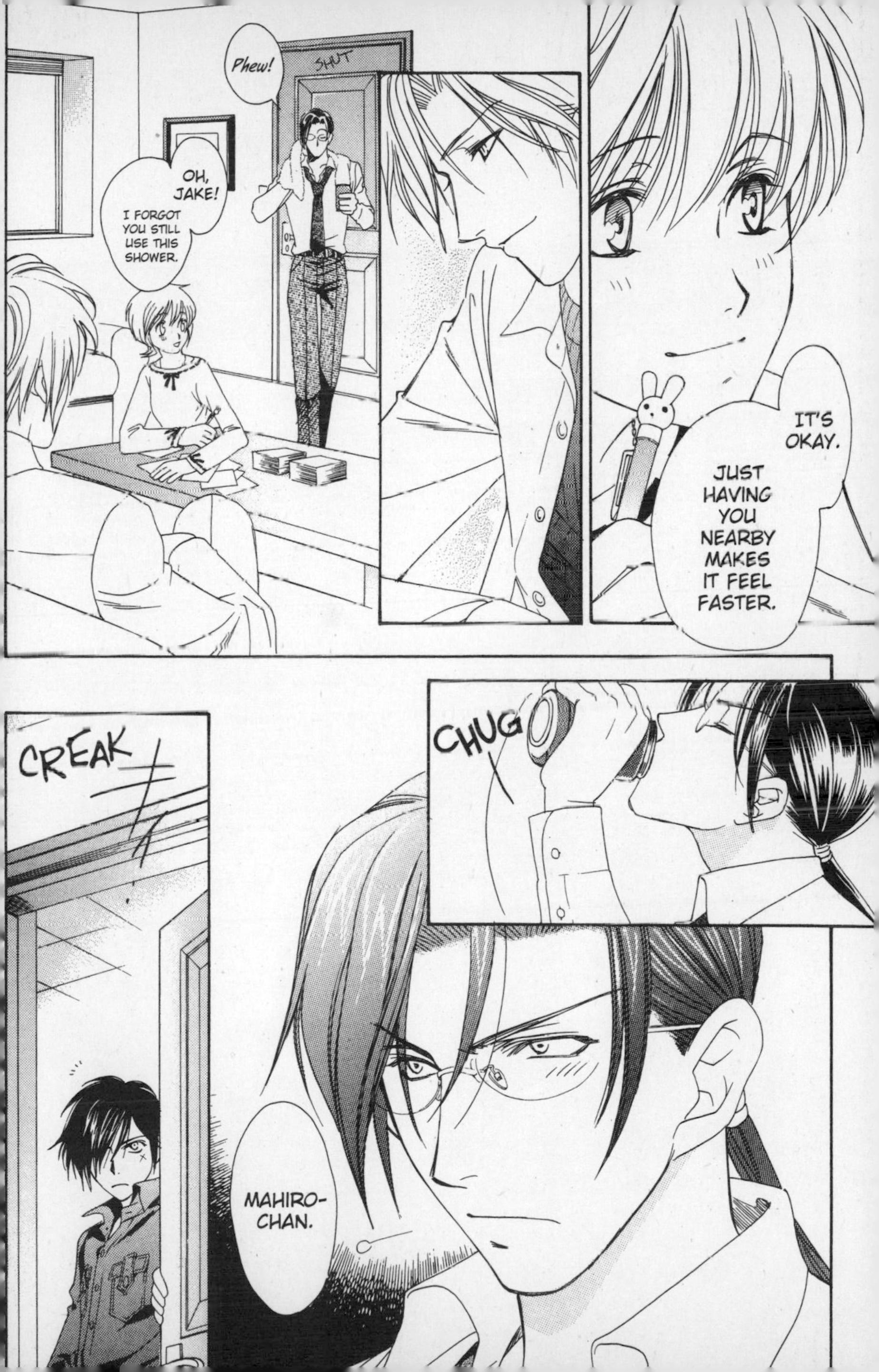
IT'S OKAY.
JUST HAVING YOU NEARBY MAKES IT FEEL FASTER.
Phew!
SHUT
OH, JAKE!
I FORGOT YOU STILL USE THIS SHOWER.
CHUG
MAHIRO-CHAN.
CREAK

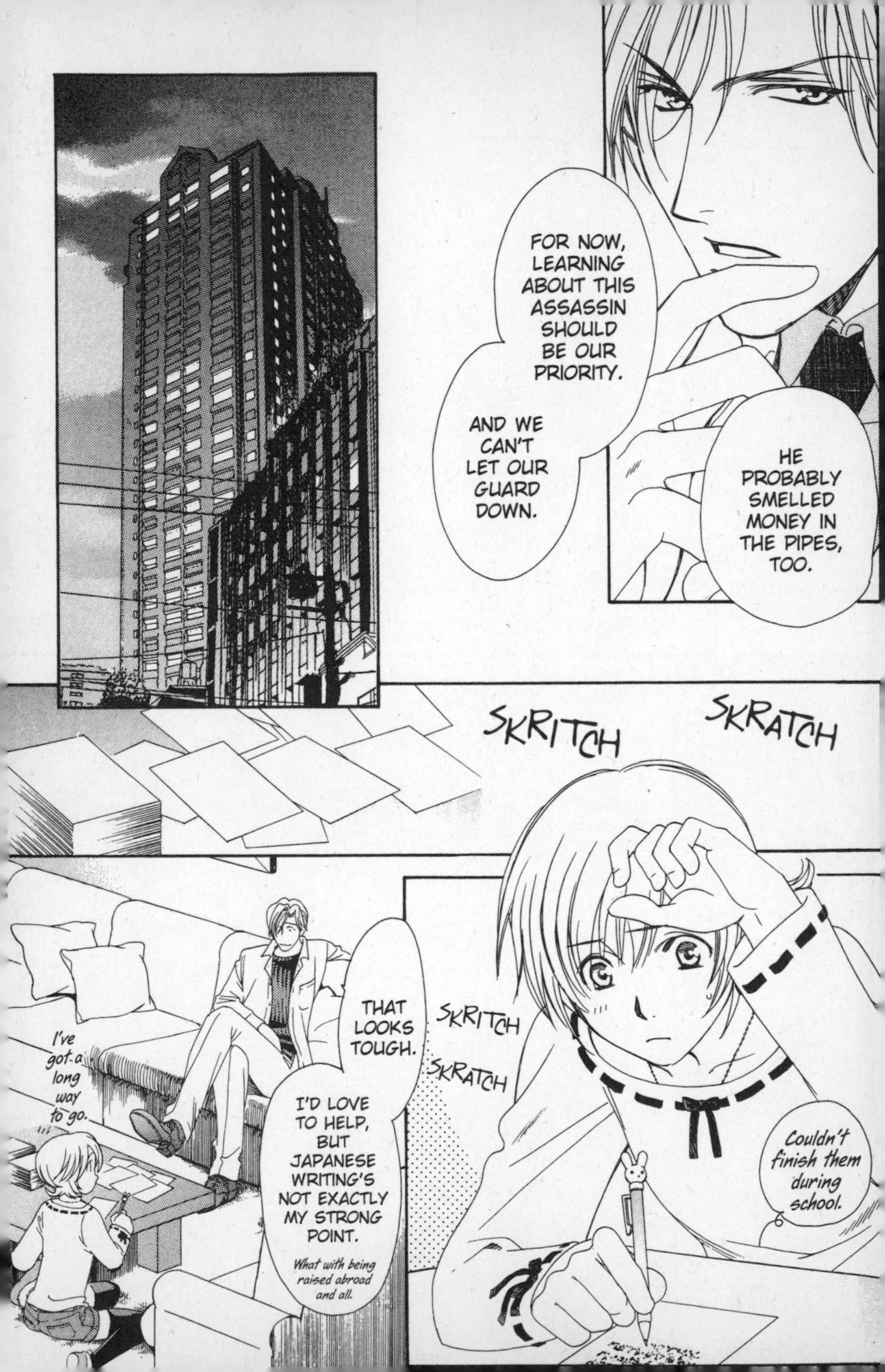
FOR NOW, LEARNING ABOUT THIS ASSASSIN SHOULD BE OUR PRIORITY.
HE PROBABLY SMELLED MONEY IN THE PIPES, TOO.
AND WE CAN'T LET OUR GUARD DOWN.
SKRATCH
SKRITCH
SKRITCH
SKRATCH
Couldn't finish them during school.
THAT LOOKS TOUGH.
I'D LOVE TO HELP, BUT JAPANESE WRITING'S NOT EXACTLY MY STRONG POINT.
What with being raised abroad and all.
I've got a long way to go.

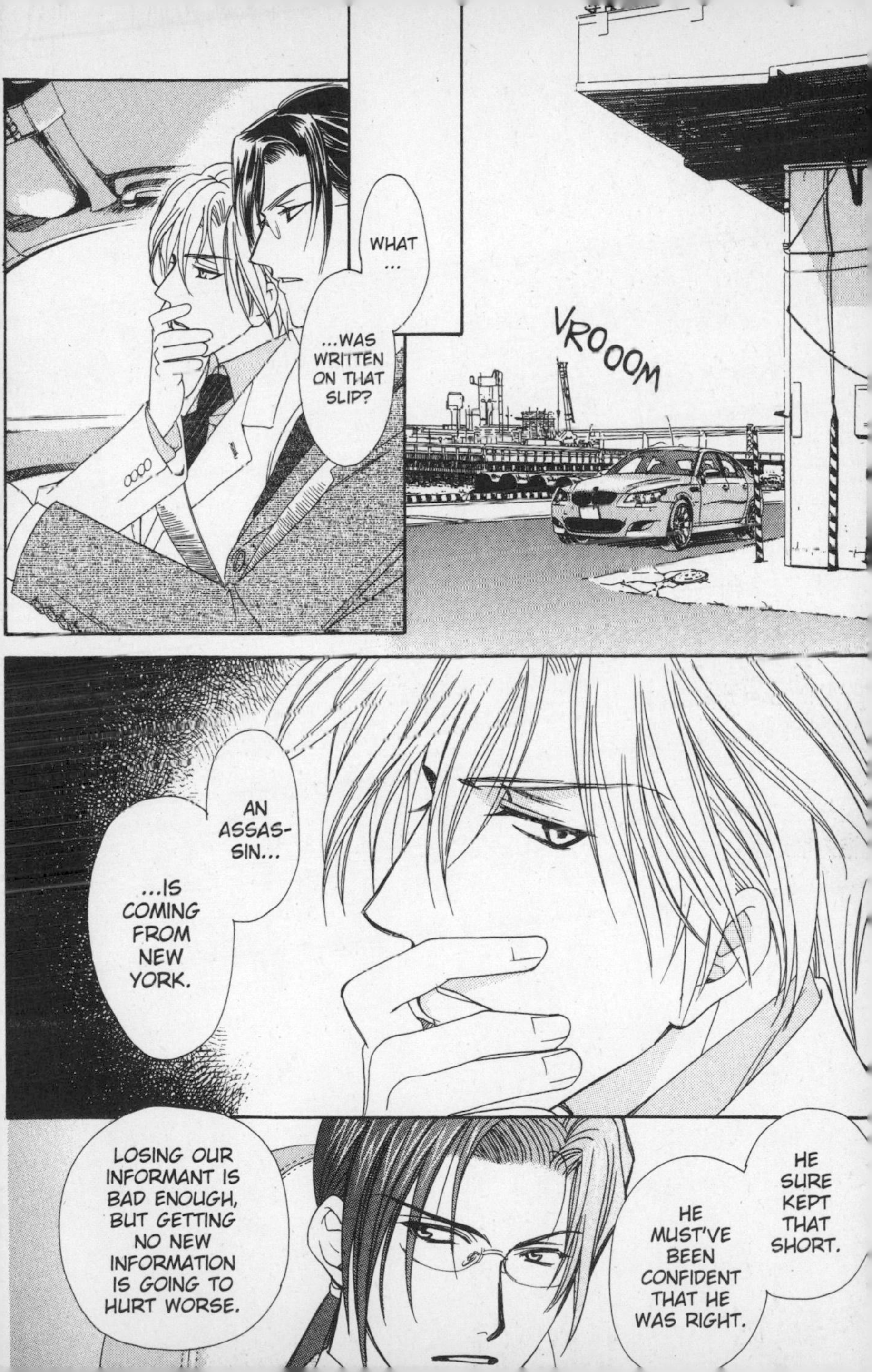
VROOOM
WHAT ...
...WAS WRITTEN ON THAT SLIP?
AN ASSAS-SIN...
...IS COMING FROM NEW YORK.
HE SURE KEPT THAT SHORT.
HE MUST'VE BEEN CONFIDENT THAT HE WAS RIGHT.
LOSING OUR INFORMANT IS BAD ENOUGH, BUT GETTING NO NEW INFORMATION IS GOING TO HURT WORSE.

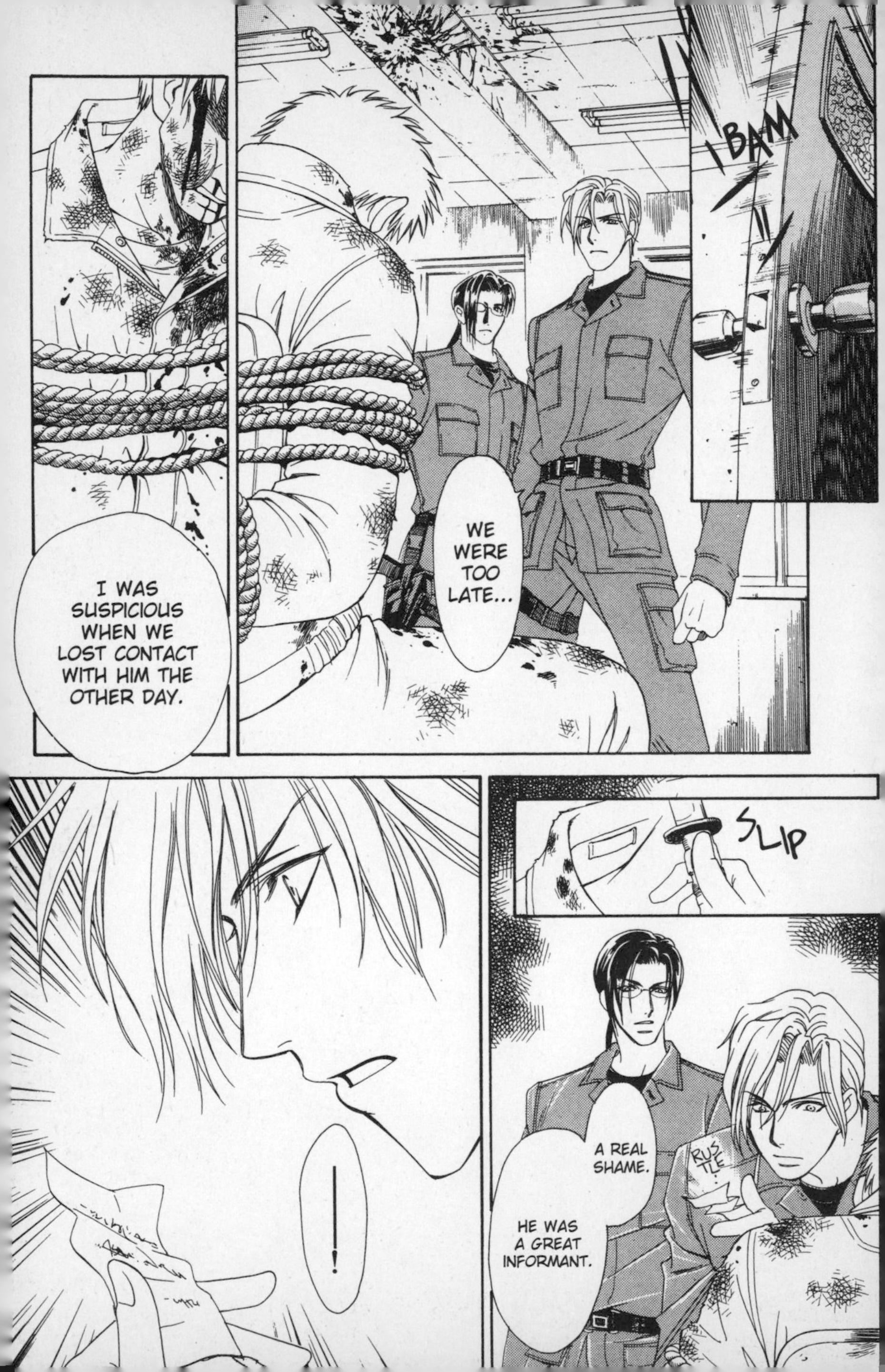
BAM
WE WERE TOO LATE...
I WAS SUSPICIOUS WHEN WE LOST CONTACT WITH HIM THE OTHER DAY.
SLIP
A REAL SHAME.
HE WAS A GREAT INFORMANT.
RUSTLE
!

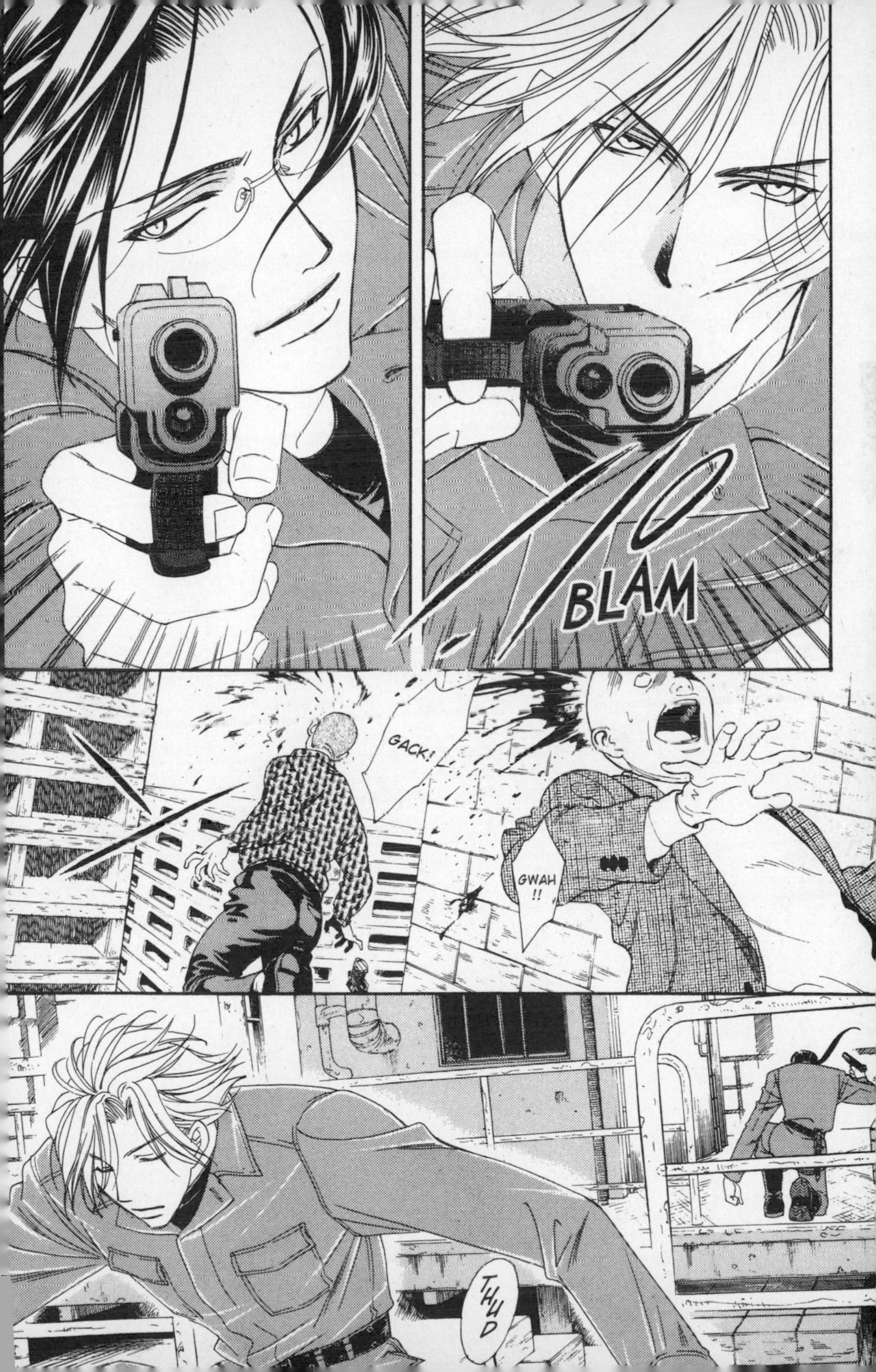
BLAM
GACK!
GWAH !!
THUD

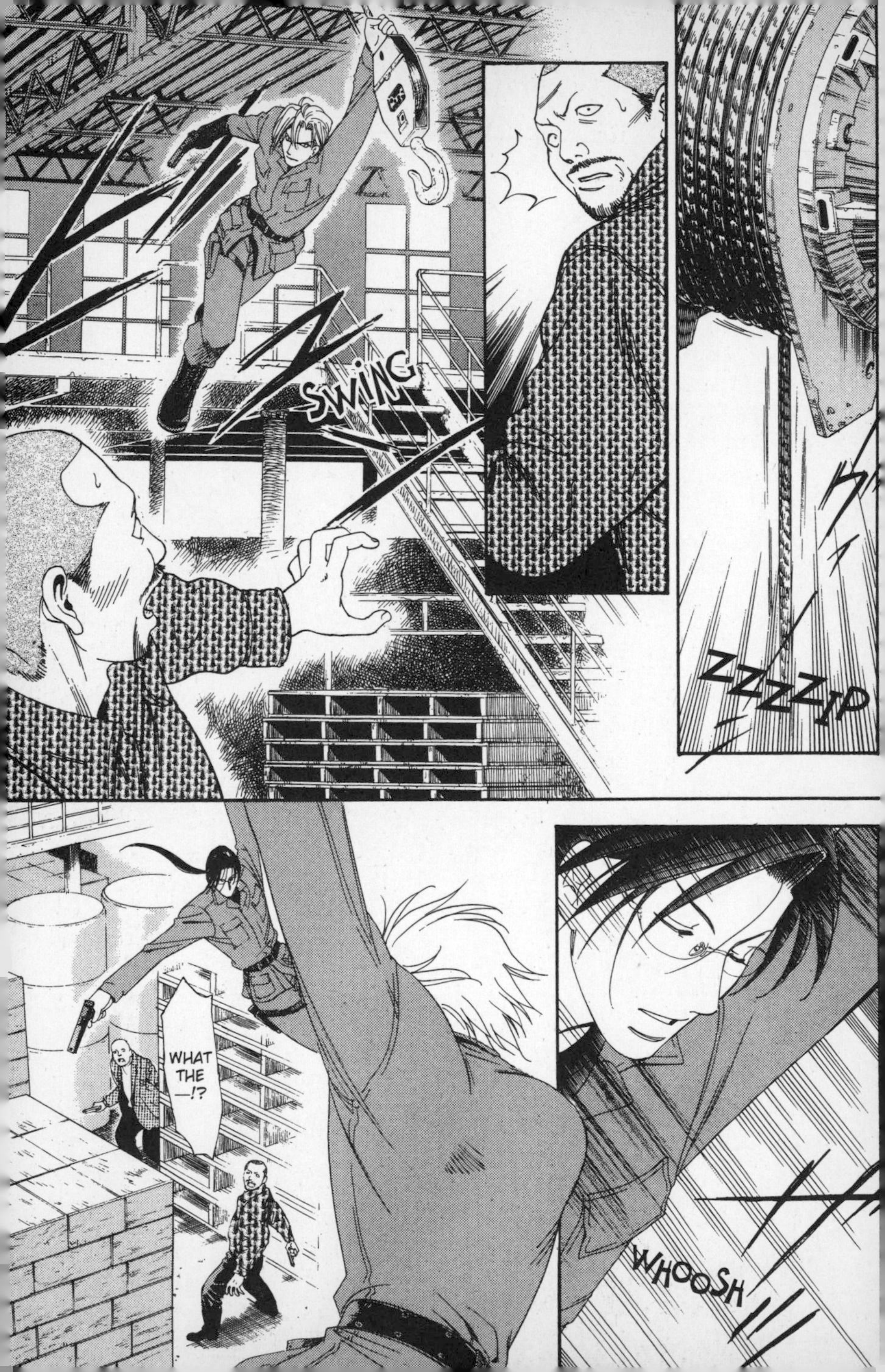

SWING
ZZZZIP
WHAT THE —!?
WHOOSH

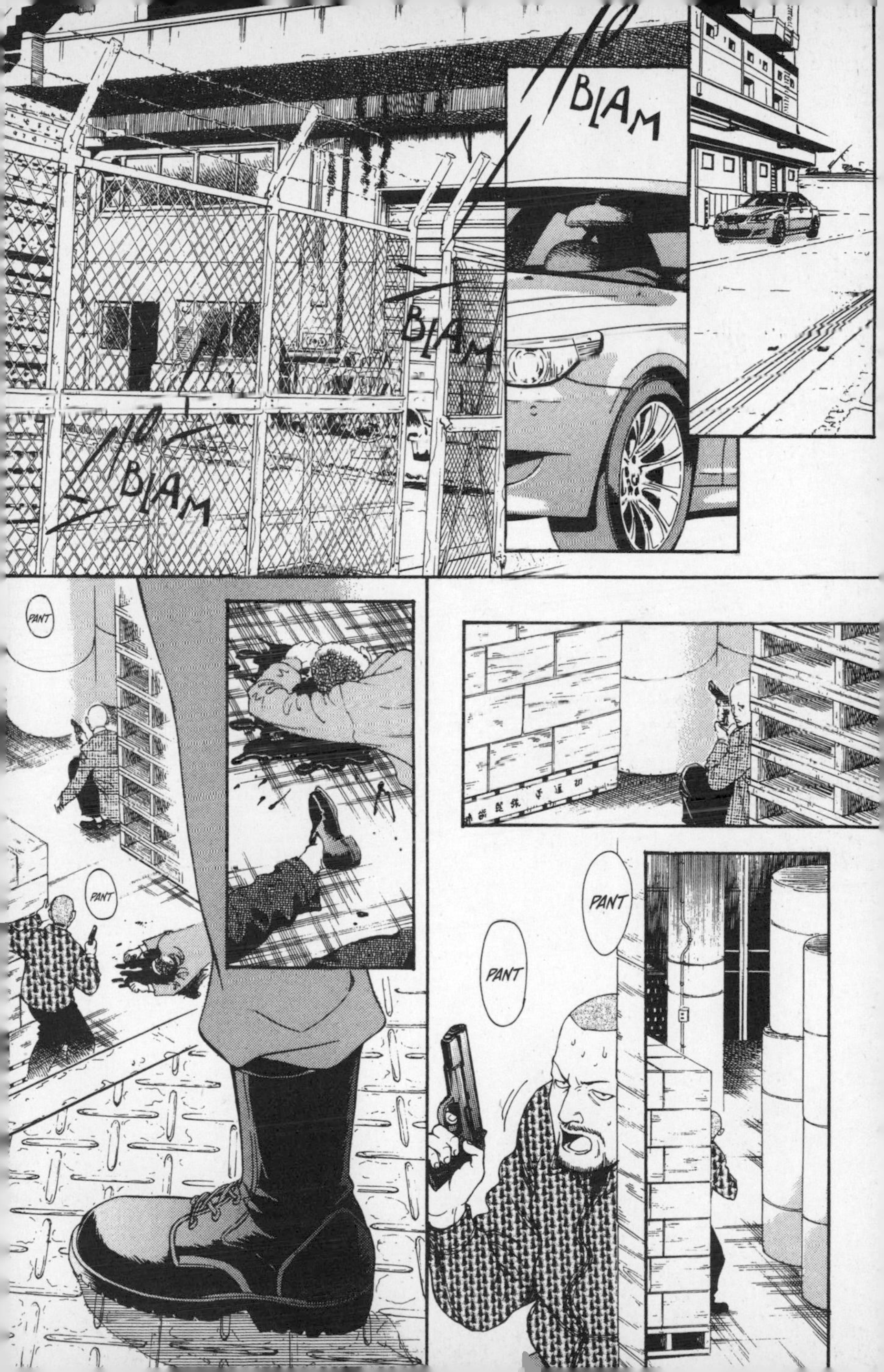

BLAM
BLAM
BLAM
PANT
PANT
PANT
PANT

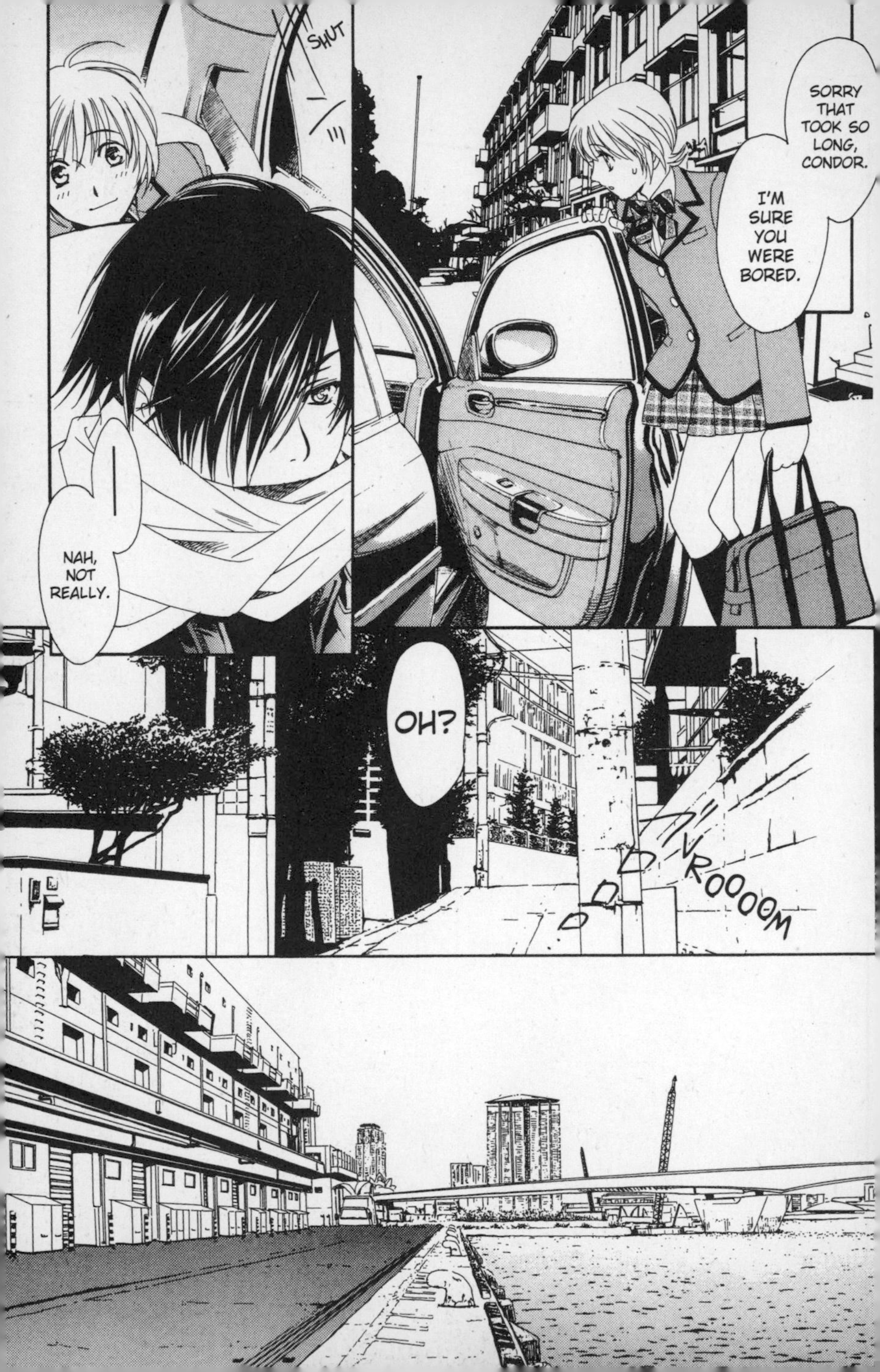
SORRY THAT TOOK SO LONG, CONDOR.
I'M SURE YOU WERE BORED.
SHUT
NAH, NOT REALLY.
VROOOOM
OH?

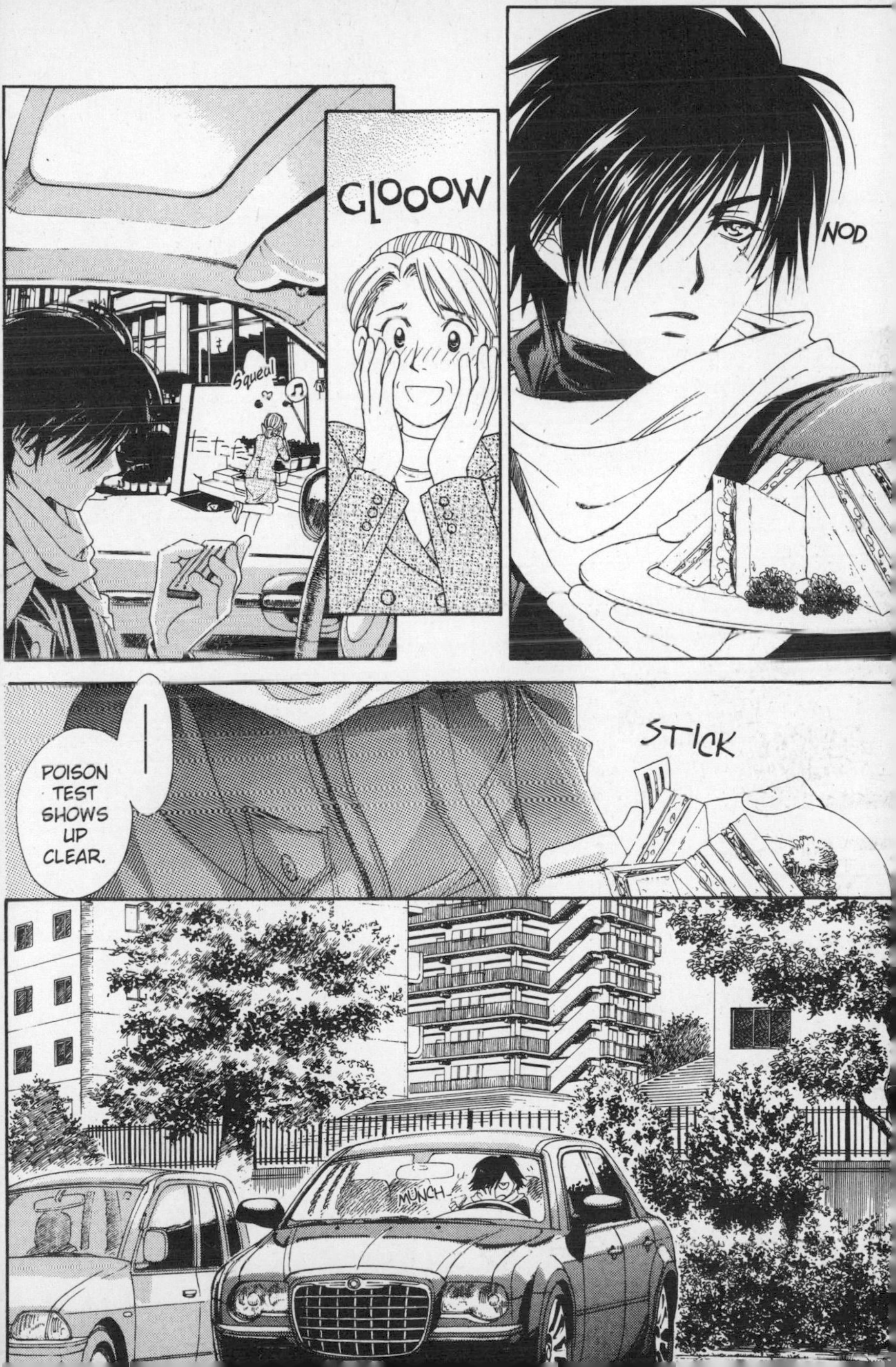

NOD
GLOOOW
Squeal
たたた
STICK
POISON TEST SHOWS UP CLEAR.
MUNCH

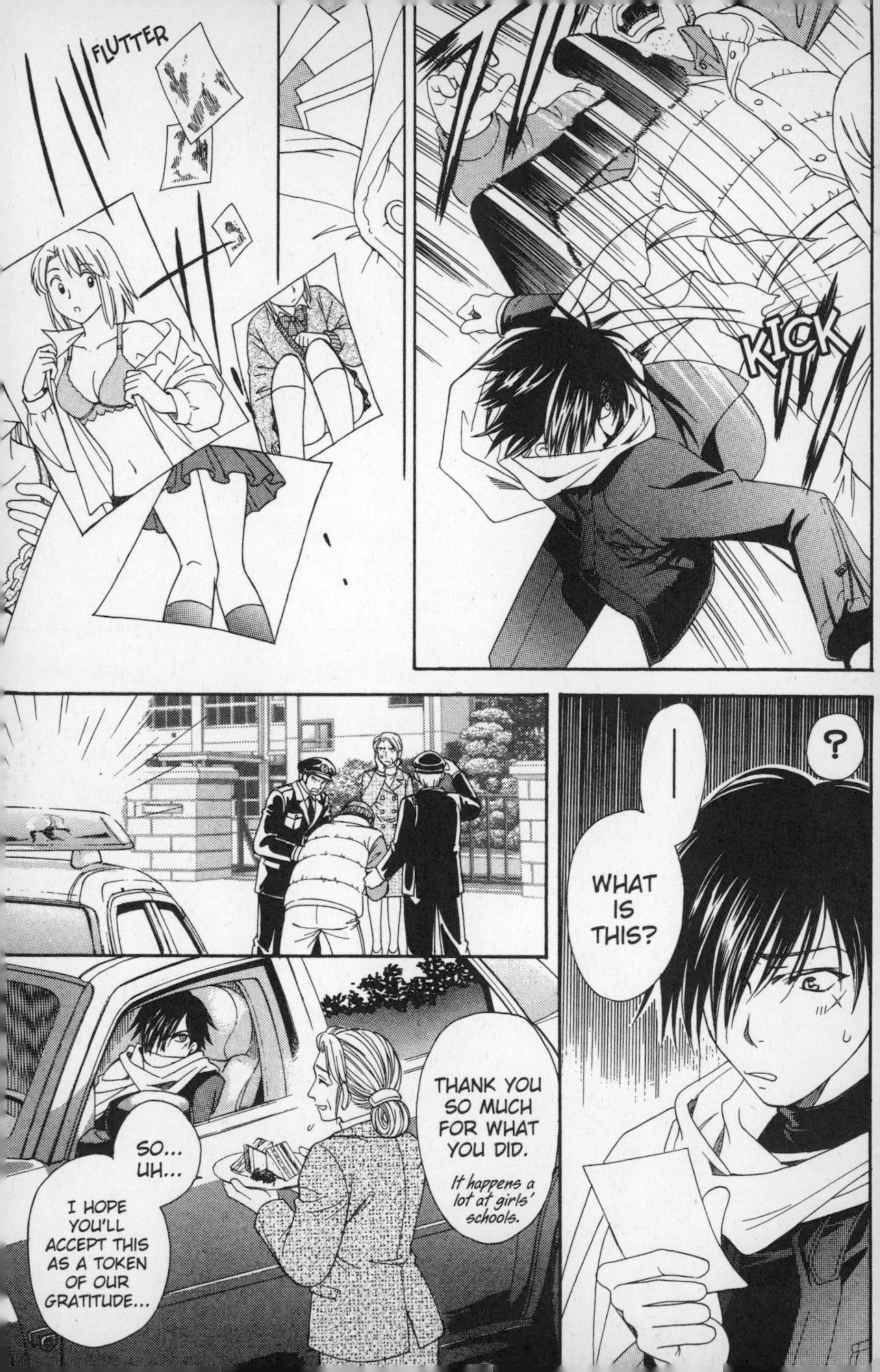
FLUTTER
KICK
?
WHAT IS THIS?
THANK YOU SO MUCH FOR WHAT YOU DID.
It happens a lot at girls' schools.
SO... UH...
I HOPE YOU'LL ACCEPT THIS AS A TOKEN OF OUR GRATITUDE...

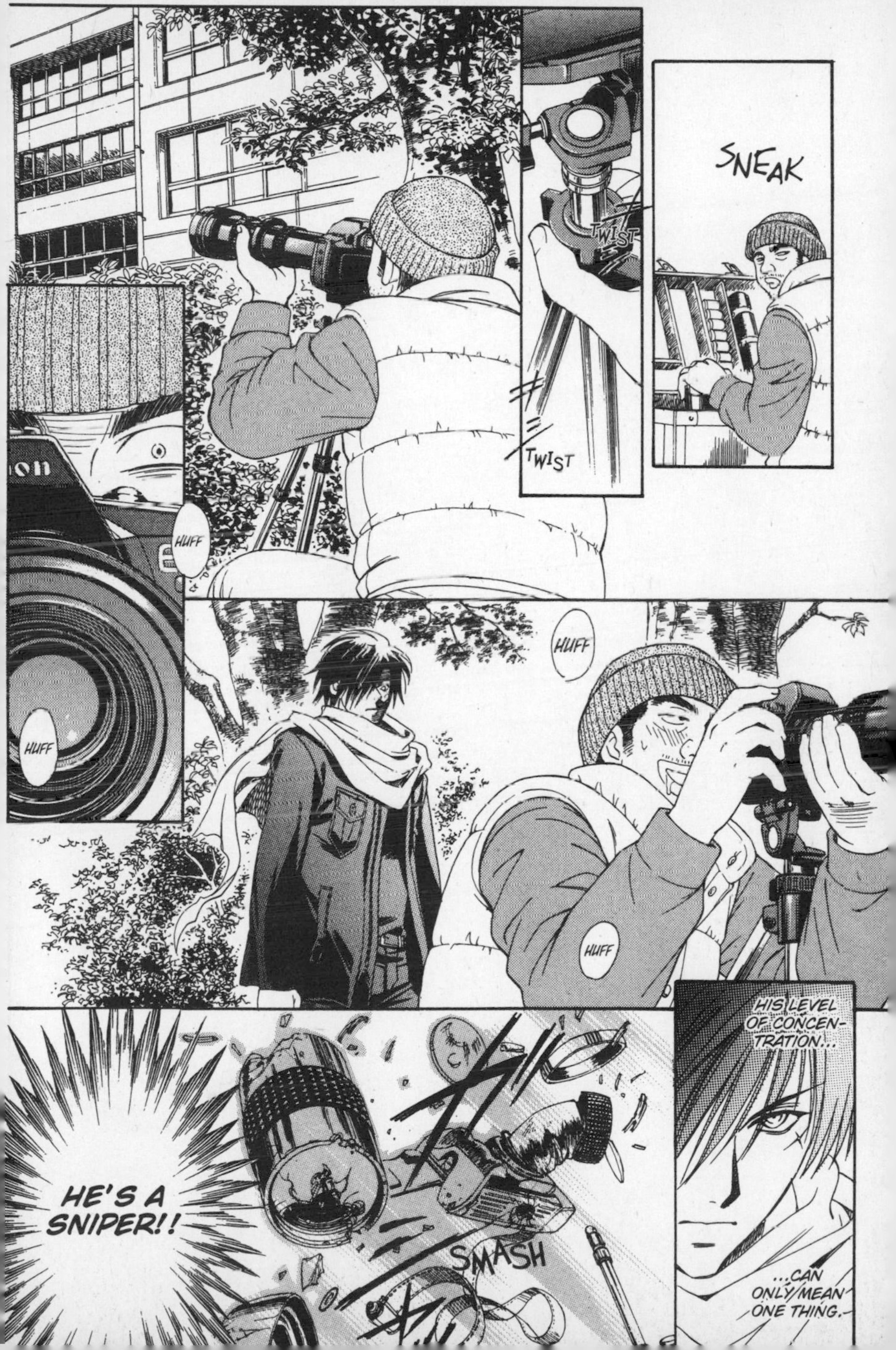

SNEAK
TWIST
TWIST
HUFF
HUFF
HUFF
HUFF
HIS LEVEL OF CONCEN-TRATION...
...CAN ONLY MEAN ONE THING.
SMASH
HE'S A SNIPER!!

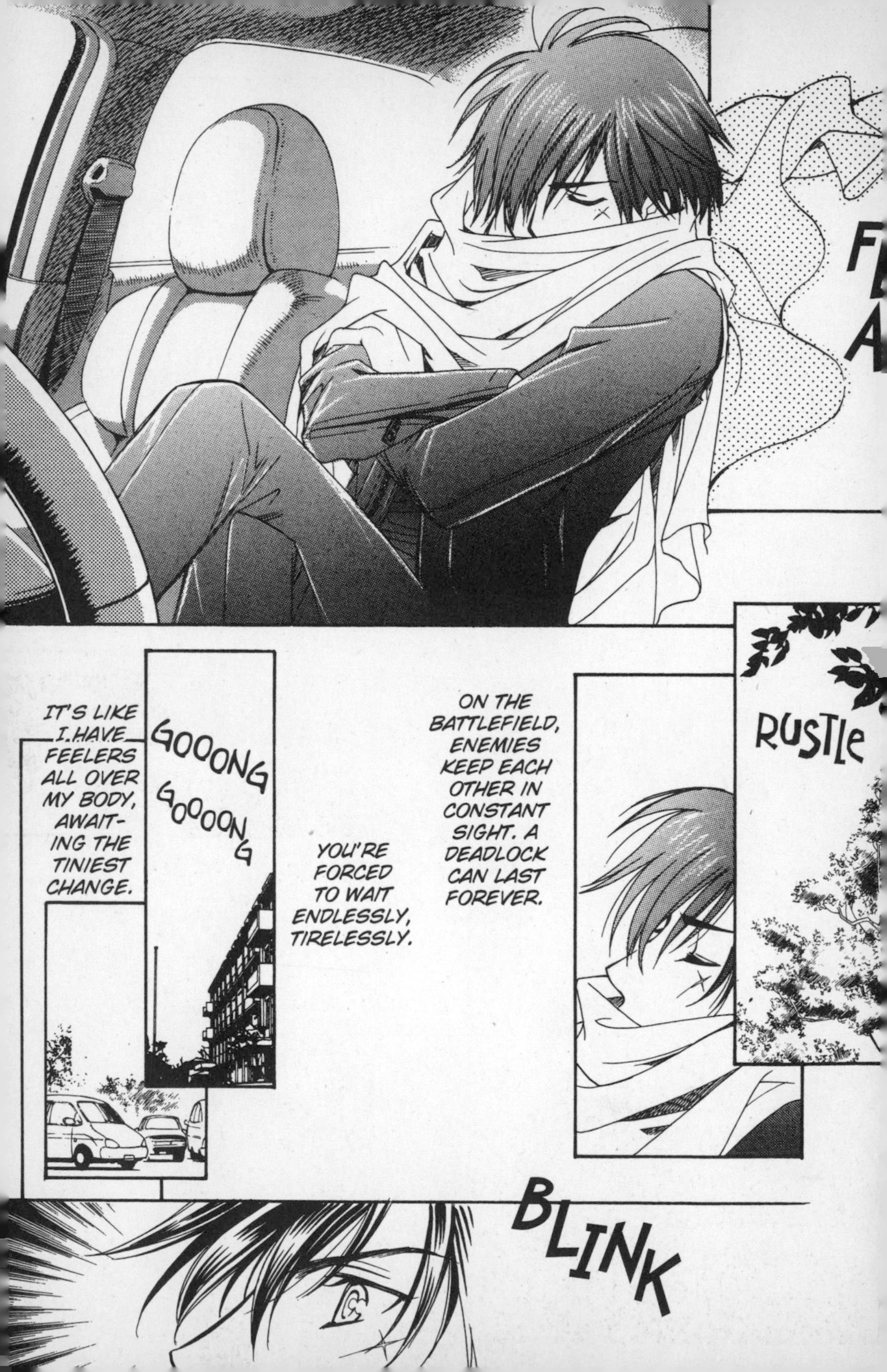
RUSTLE
ON THE BATTLEFIELD, ENEMIES KEEP EACH OTHER IN CONSTANT SIGHT. A DEADLOCK CAN LAST FOREVER.
YOU'RE FORCED TO WAIT ENDLESSLY, TIRELESSLY.
GOOONG
GOOOONG
IT'S LIKE I HAVE FEELERS ALL OVER MY BODY, AWAIT-ING THE TINIEST CHANGE.
BLINK

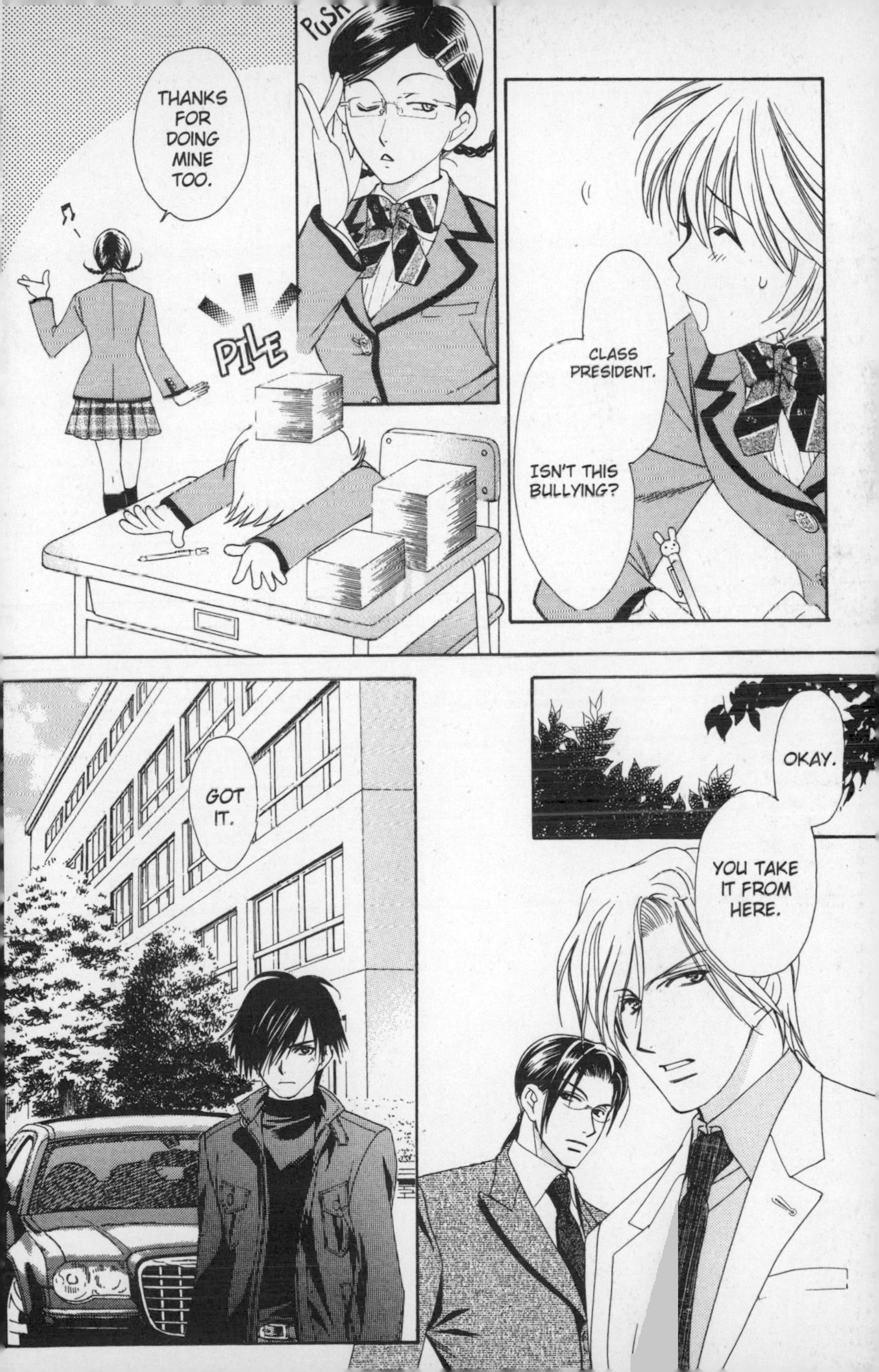
CLASS PRESIDENT.
ISN'T THIS BULLYING?
PUSH
THANKS FOR DOING MINE TOO.
PILE
OKAY.
YOU TAKE IT FROM HERE.
GOT IT.

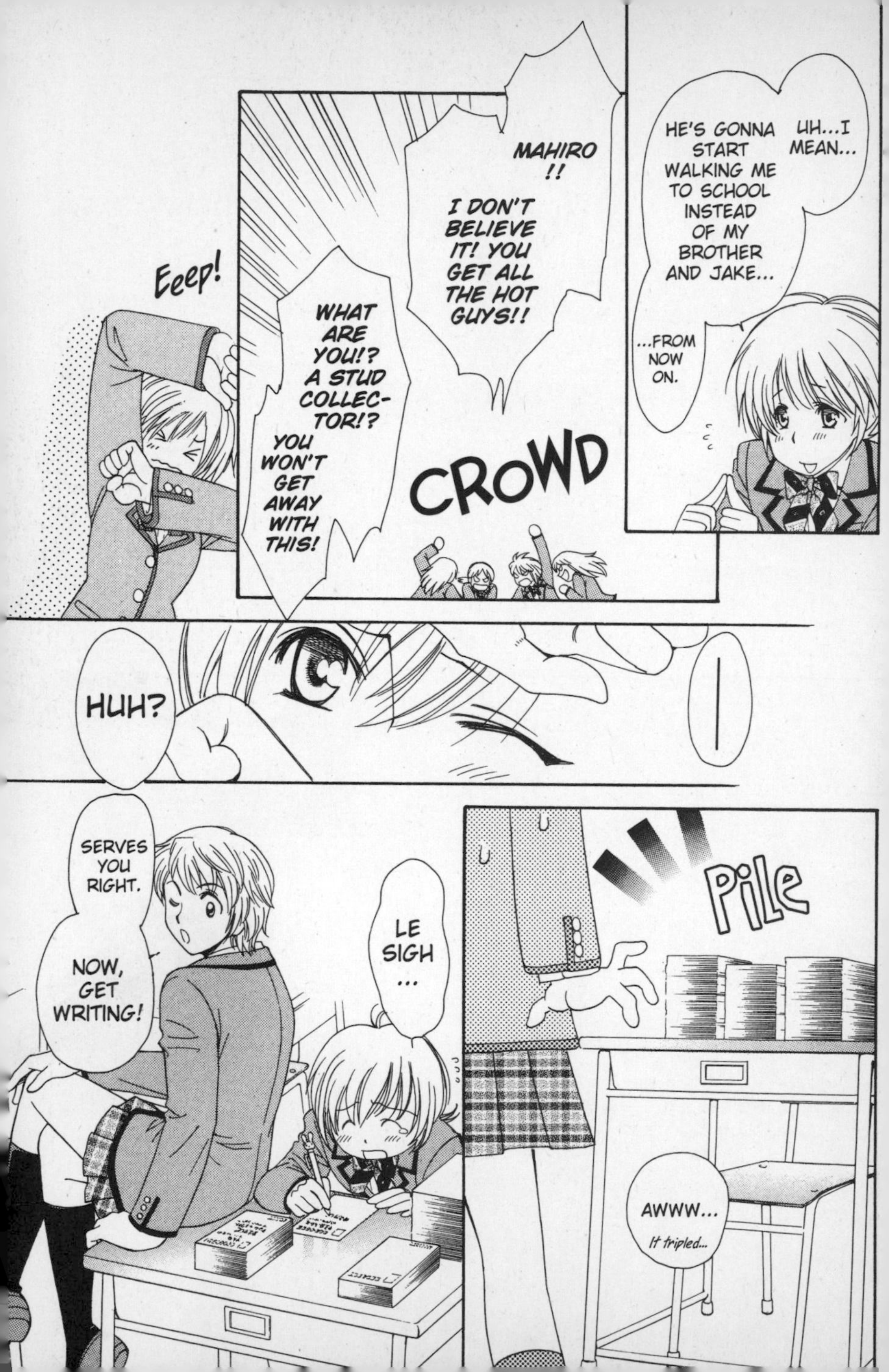
UH...I MEAN...
HE'S GONNA START WALKING ME TO SCHOOL INSTEAD OF MY BROTHER AND JAKE...
...FROM NOW ON.
MAHIRO !!
I DON'T BELIEVE IT! YOU GET ALL THE HOT GUYS!!
WHAT ARE YOU!? A STUD COLLECTOR!?
YOU WON'T GET AWAY WITH THIS!
CROWD
Eeep!
HUH?
Pile
AWWW...
It tripled...
LE SIGH ...
SERVES YOU RIGHT.
NOW, GET WRITING!

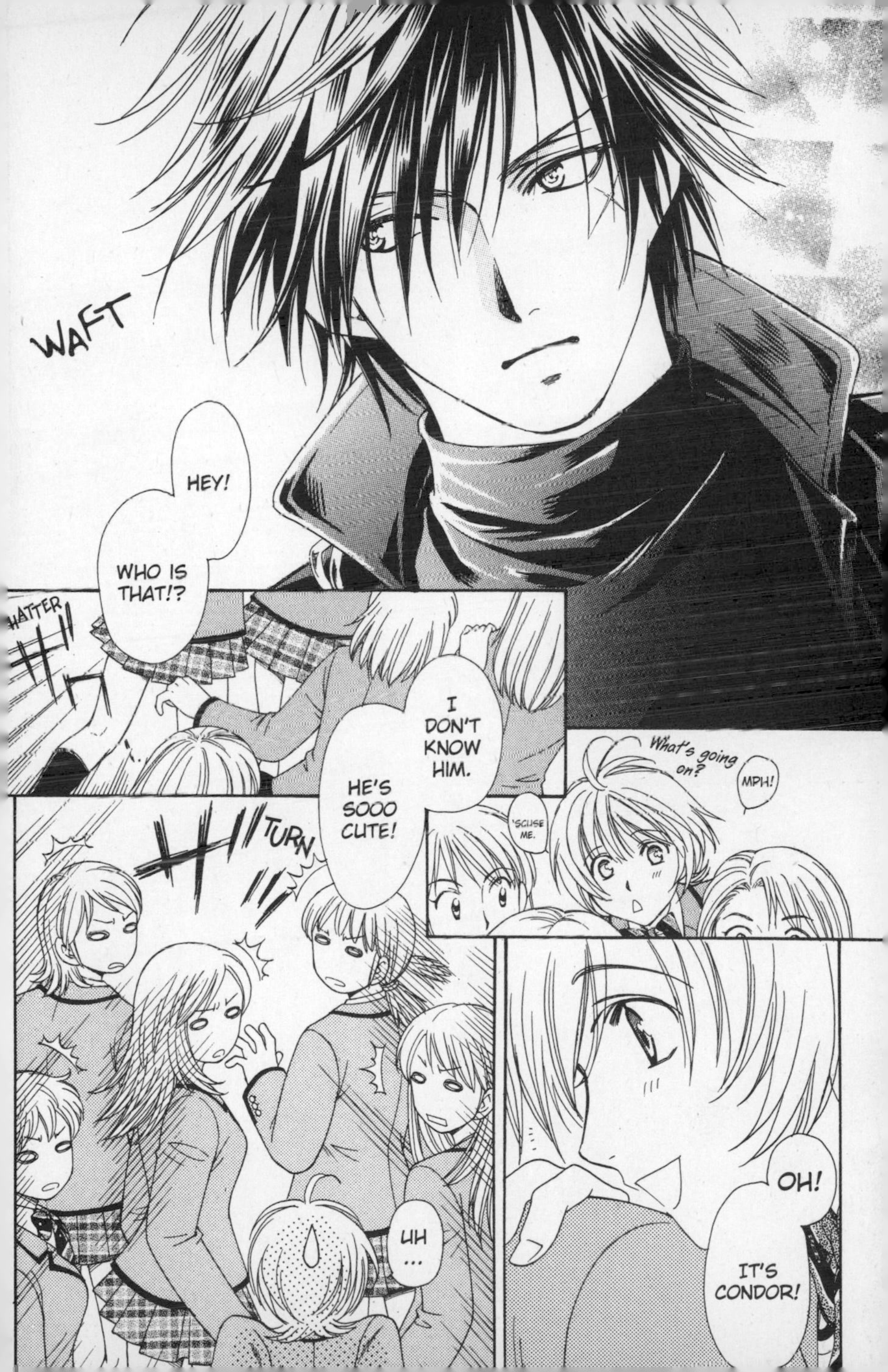
WAFT
HEY!
WHO IS THAT!?
HATTER
I DON'T KNOW HIM.
HE'S SOOO CUTE!
What's going on?
MPH!
'SCUSE ME.
OH!
IT'S CONDOR!
TURN
UH ...

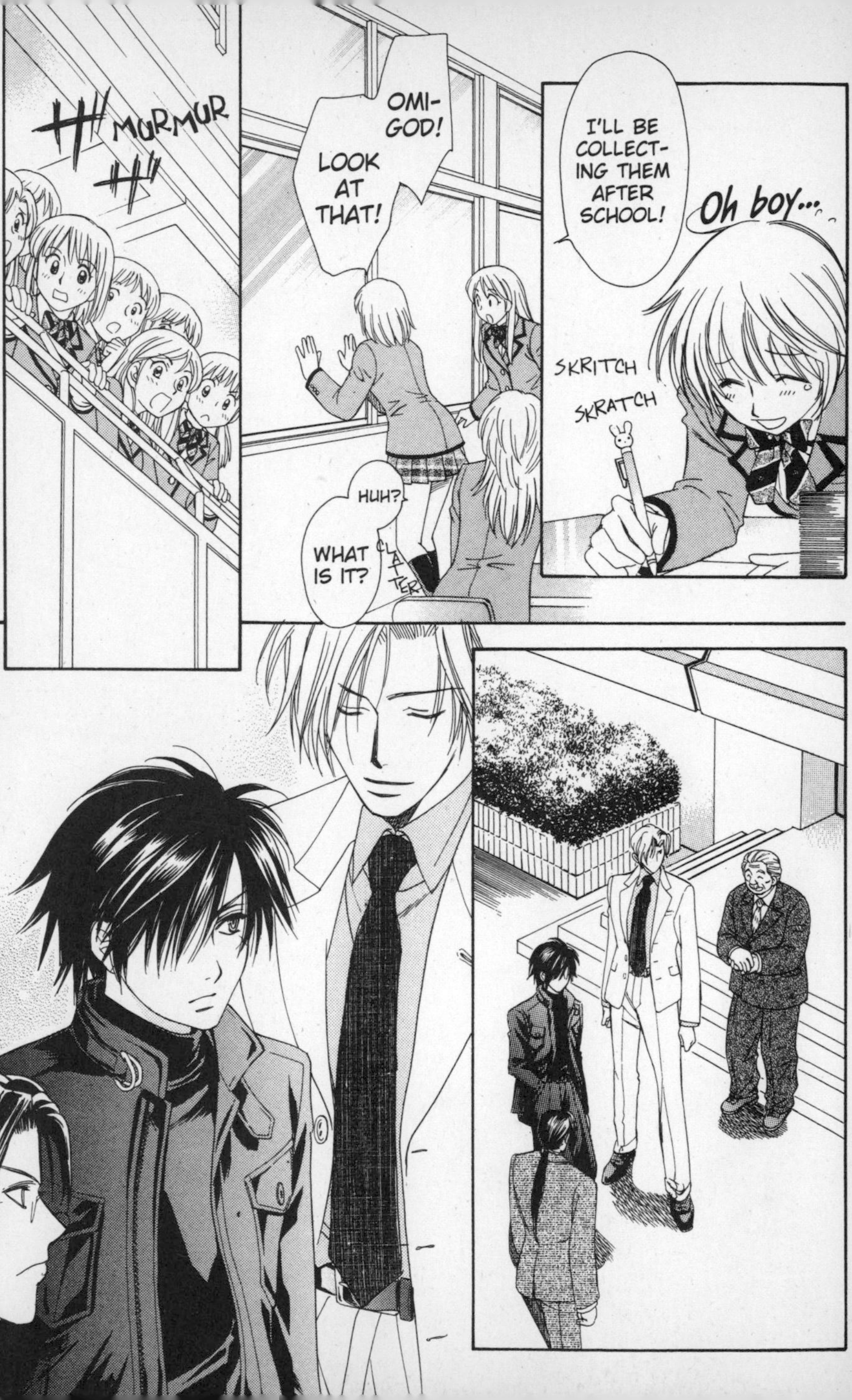
I'LL BE COLLECTING THEM AFTER SCHOOL!
Oh boy...
SKRITCH
SKRATCH
OMI-GOD!
LOOK AT THAT!
HUH?
WHAT IS IT?
CLATTER
MURMUR

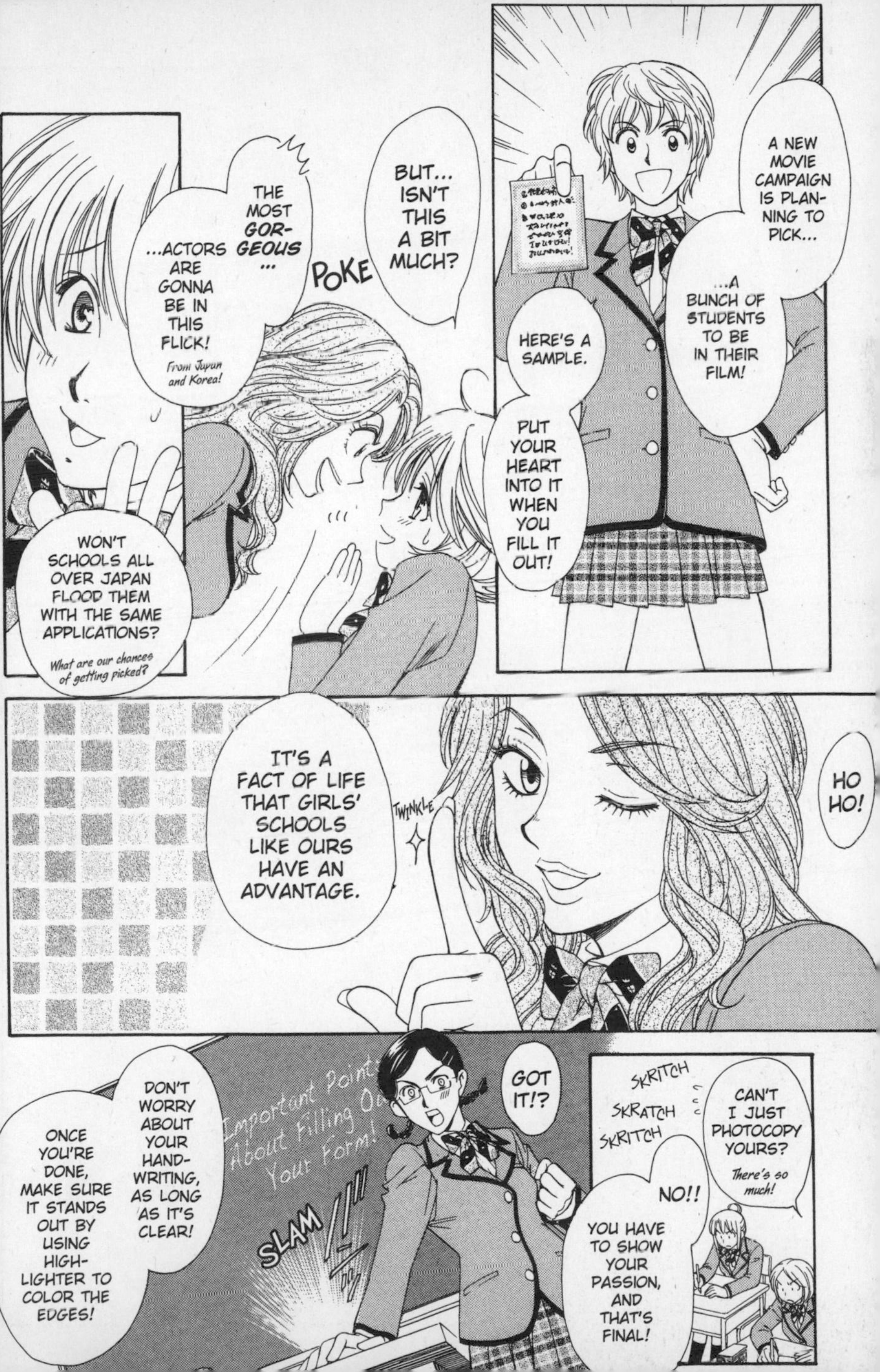
A NEW MOVIE CAMPAIGN IS PLAN-NING TO PICK...
...A BUNCH OF STUDENTS TO BE IN THEIR FILM!
HERE'S A SAMPLE.
PUT YOUR HEART INTO IT WHEN YOU FILL IT OUT!
BUT... ISN'T THIS A BIT MUCH?
POKE
THE MOST GOR-GEOUS ...
...ACTORS ARE GONNA BE IN THIS FLICK!
From Japan and Korea!
WON'T SCHOOLS ALL OVER JAPAN FLOOD THEM WITH THE SAME APPLICATIONS?
What are our chances of getting picked?
HO HO!
IT'S A FACT OF LIFE THAT GIRLS' SCHOOLS LIKE OURS HAVE AN ADVANTAGE.
TWINKLE
SKRITCH
SKRATCH
SKRITCH
CAN'T I JUST PHOTOCOPY YOURS?
There's so much!
NO!!
YOU HAVE TO SHOW YOUR PASSION, AND THAT'S FINAL!
GOT IT!?
Important Points About Filling Out Your Form!
SLAM
DON'T WORRY ABOUT YOUR HAND-WRITING, AS LONG AS IT'S CLEAR!
ONCE YOU'RE DONE, MAKE SURE IT STANDS OUT BY USING HIGH-LIGHTER TO COLOR THE EDGES!

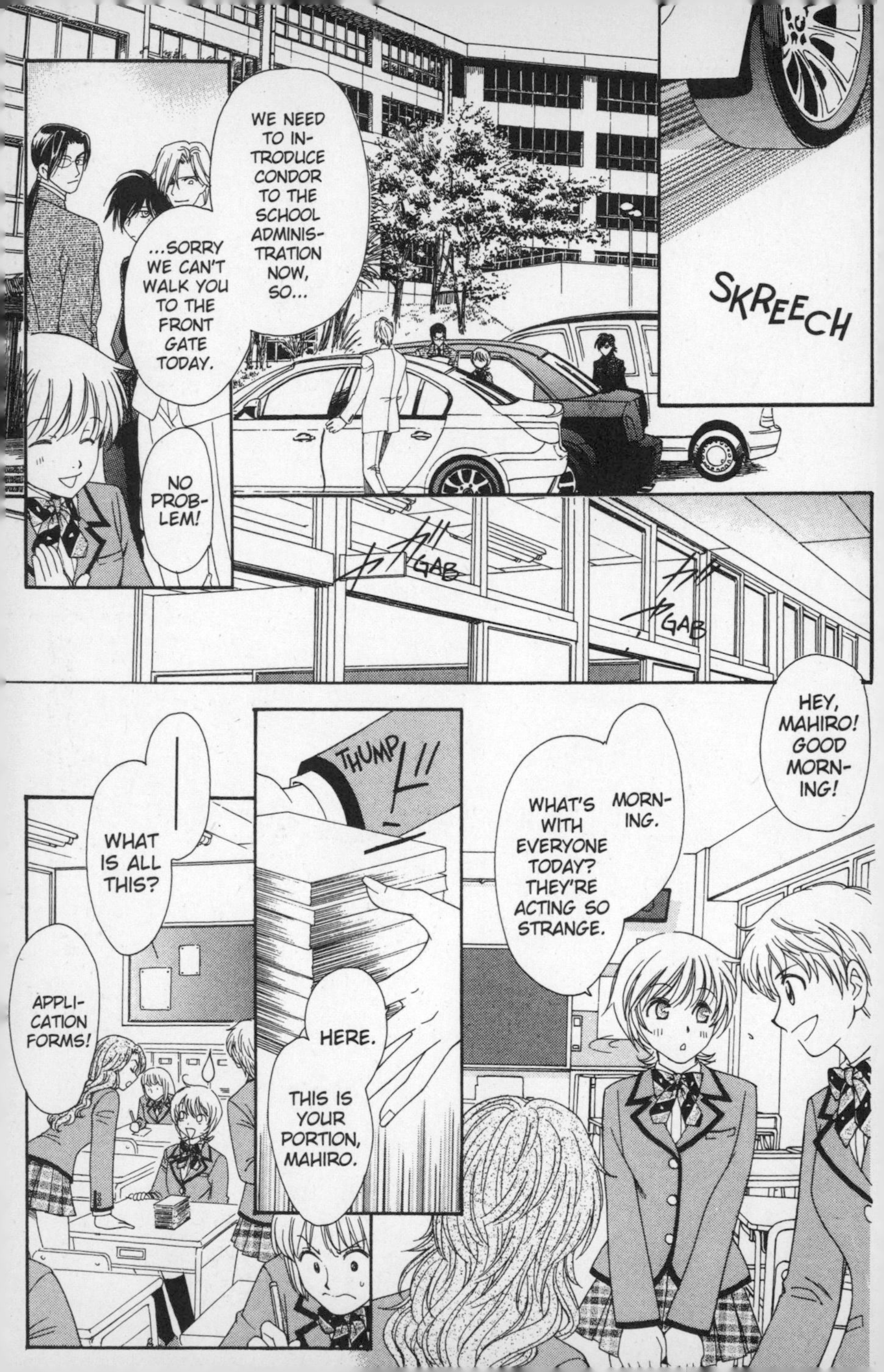
SKREECH
WE NEED TO INTRODUCE CONDOR TO THE SCHOOL ADMINISTRATION NOW, SO...
...SORRY WE CAN'T WALK YOU TO THE FRONT GATE TODAY.
NO PROBLEM!
GAB
GAB
HEY, MAHIRO! GOOD MORNING!
MORNING.
WHAT'S WITH EVERYONE TODAY? THEY'RE ACTING SO STRANGE.
THUMP
HERE.
THIS IS YOUR PORTION, MAHIRO.
WHAT IS ALL THIS?
APPLICATION FORMS!

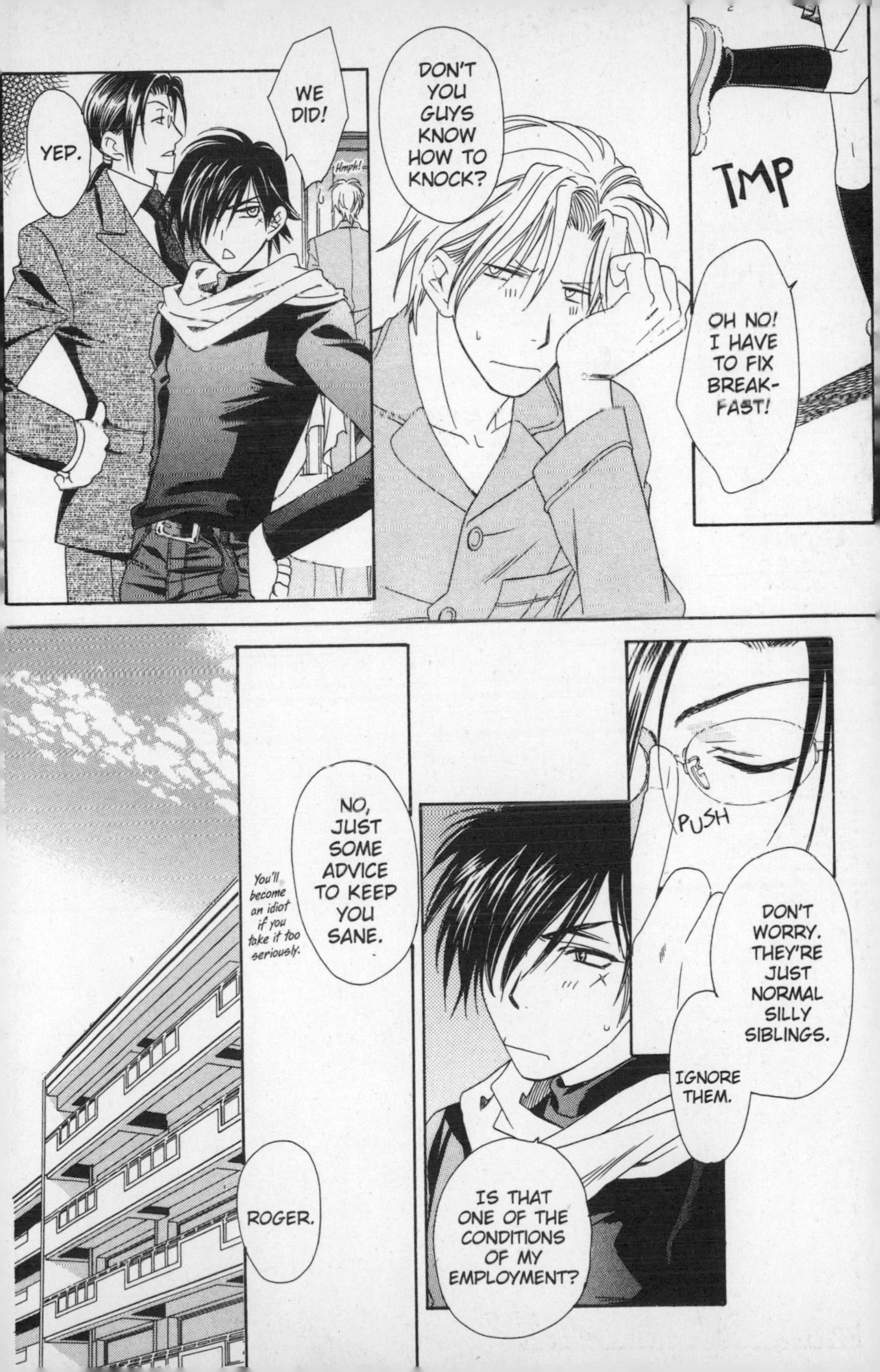
TMP
OH NO! I HAVE TO FIX BREAKFAST!
DON'T YOU GUYS KNOW HOW TO KNOCK?
WE DID!
Hmph!
YEP.
PUSH
DON'T WORRY. THEY'RE JUST NORMAL SILLY SIBLINGS.
IGNORE THEM.
IS THAT ONE OF THE CONDITIONS OF MY EMPLOYMENT?
NO, JUST SOME ADVICE TO KEEP YOU SANE.
You'll become an idiot if you take it too seriously.
ROGER.

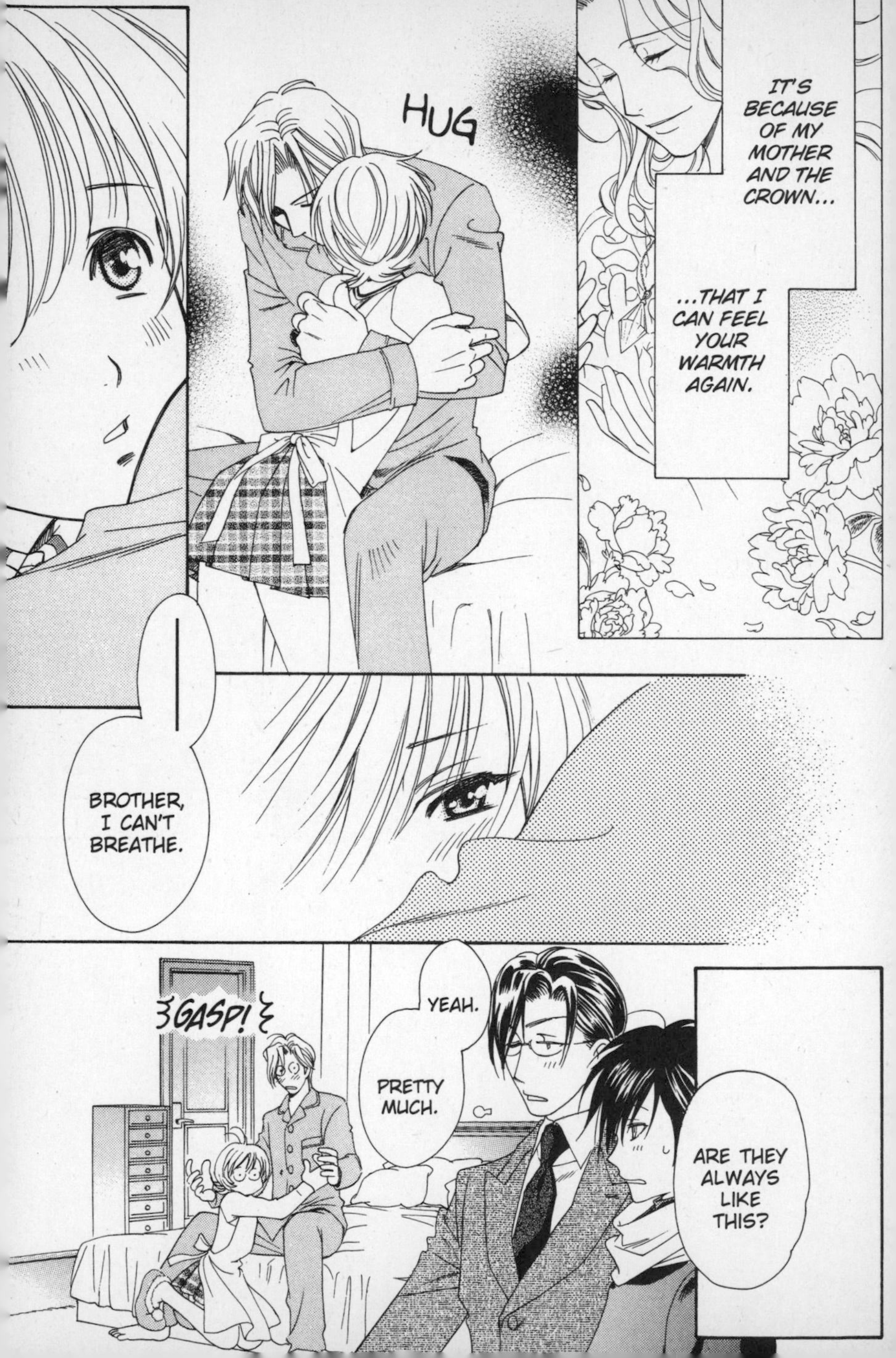
IT'S BECAUSE OF MY MOTHER AND THE CROWN...
...THAT I CAN FEEL YOUR WARMTH AGAIN.
HUG
BROTHER, I CAN'T BREATHE.
ARE THEY ALWAYS LIKE THIS?
YEAH.
PRETTY MUCH.
GASP!

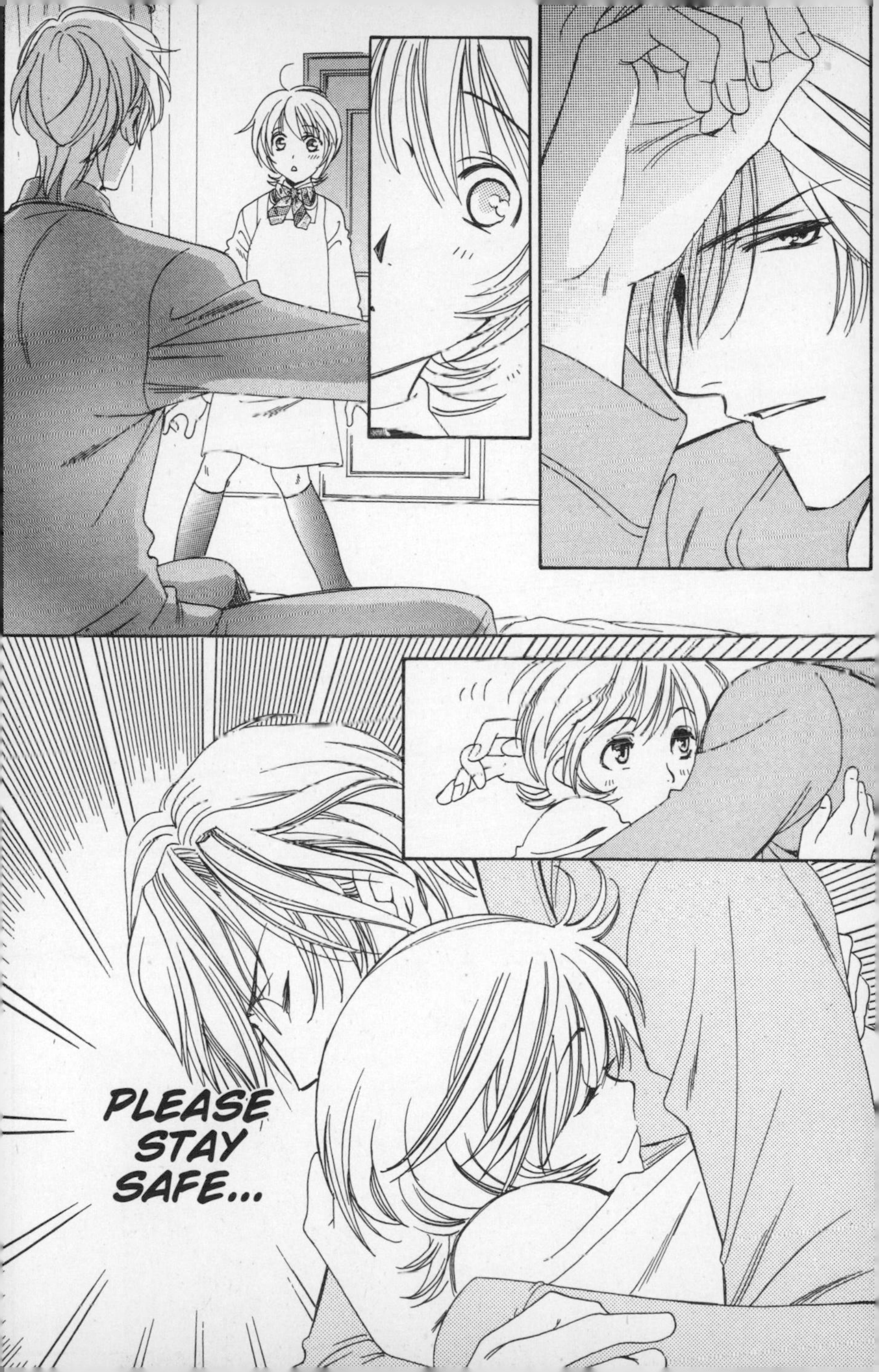
PLEASE STAY SAFE...

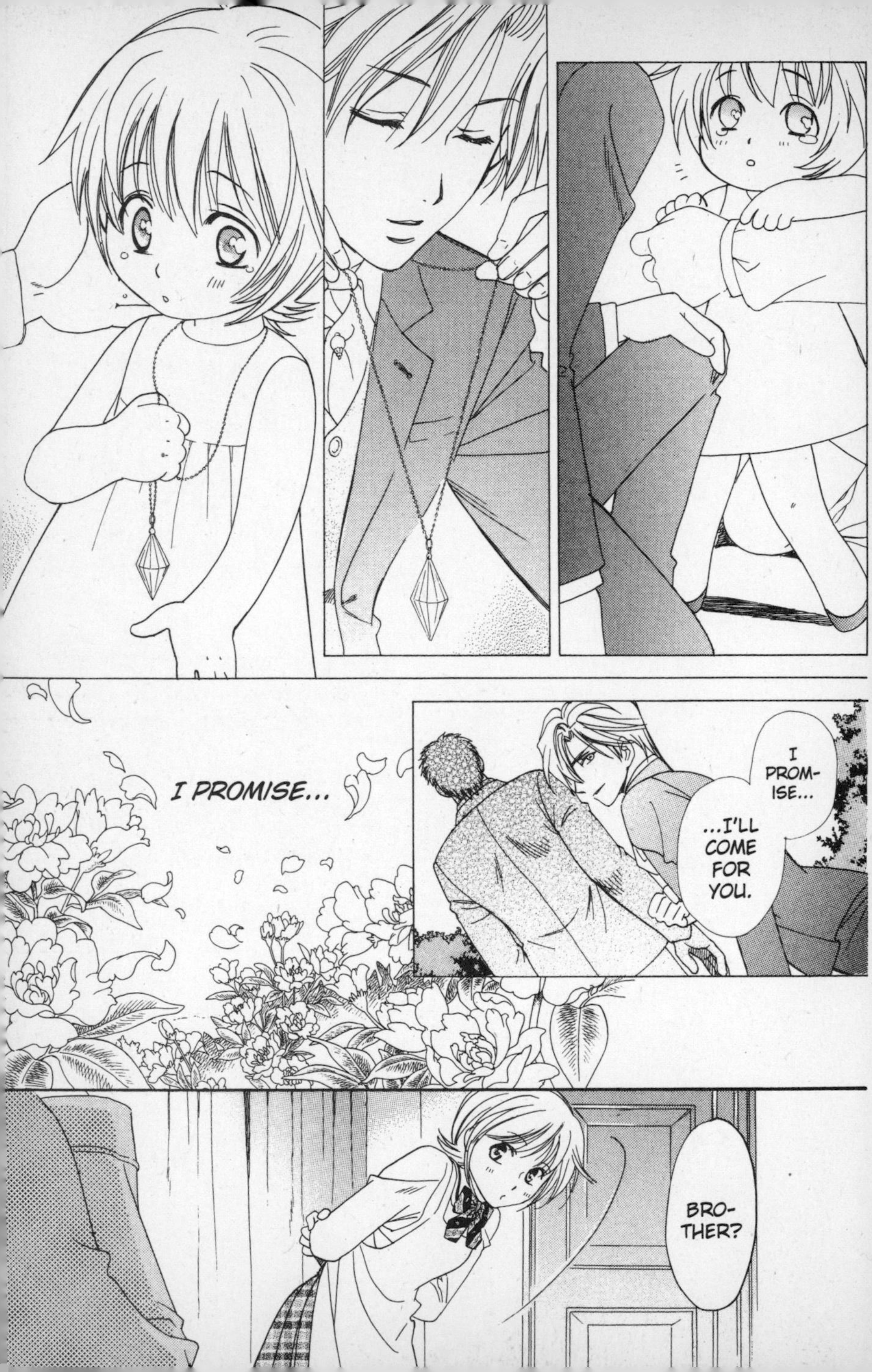
I PROMISE...
I PROMISE...
...I'LL COME FOR YOU.
BROTHER?

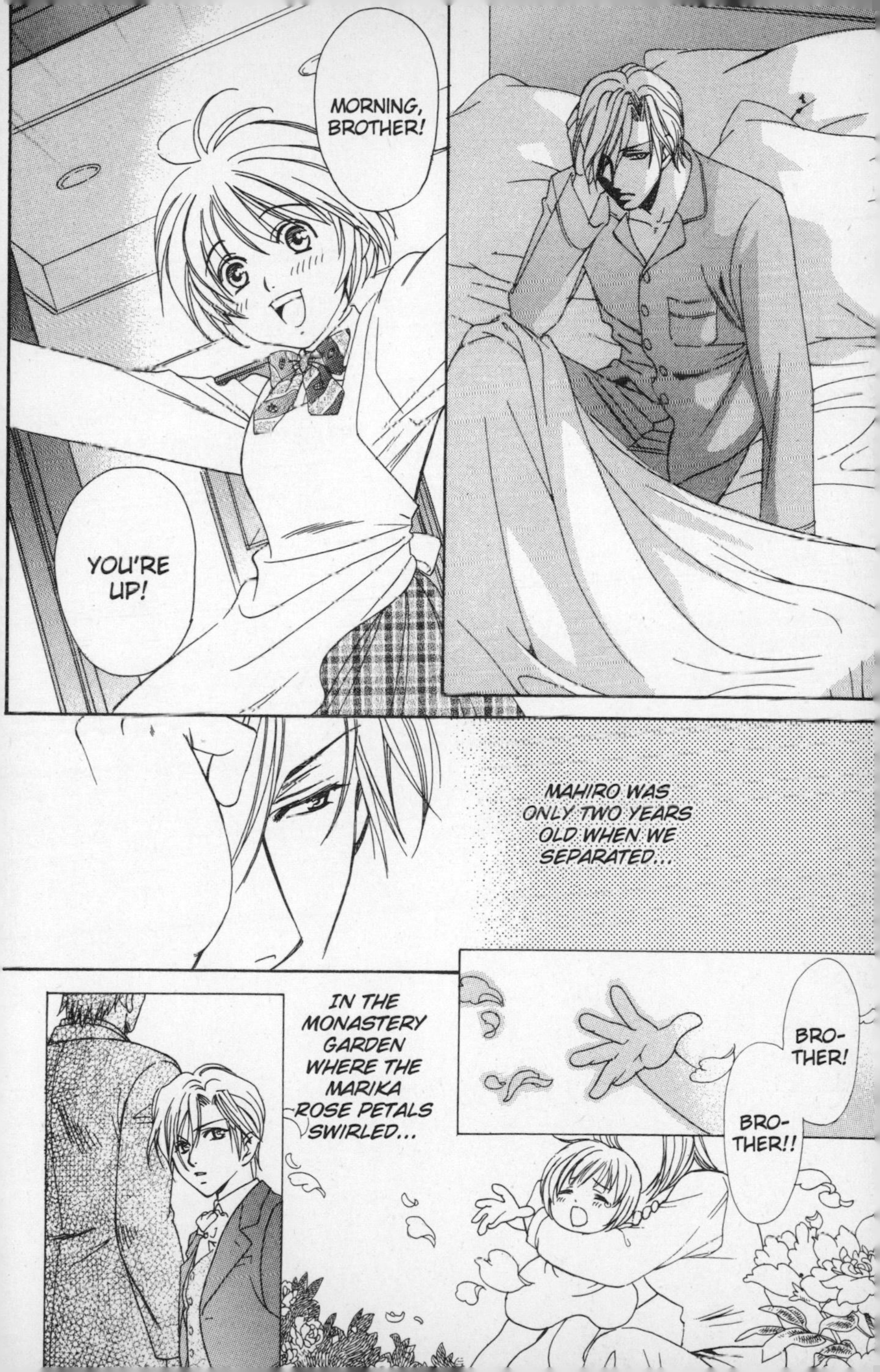

MORNING, BROTHER!
YOU'RE UP!
MAHIRO WAS ONLY TWO YEARS OLD WHEN WE SEPARATED...
BRO-THER!
BRO-THER!!
IN THE MONASTERY GARDEN WHERE THE MARIKA ROSE PETALS SWIRLED...

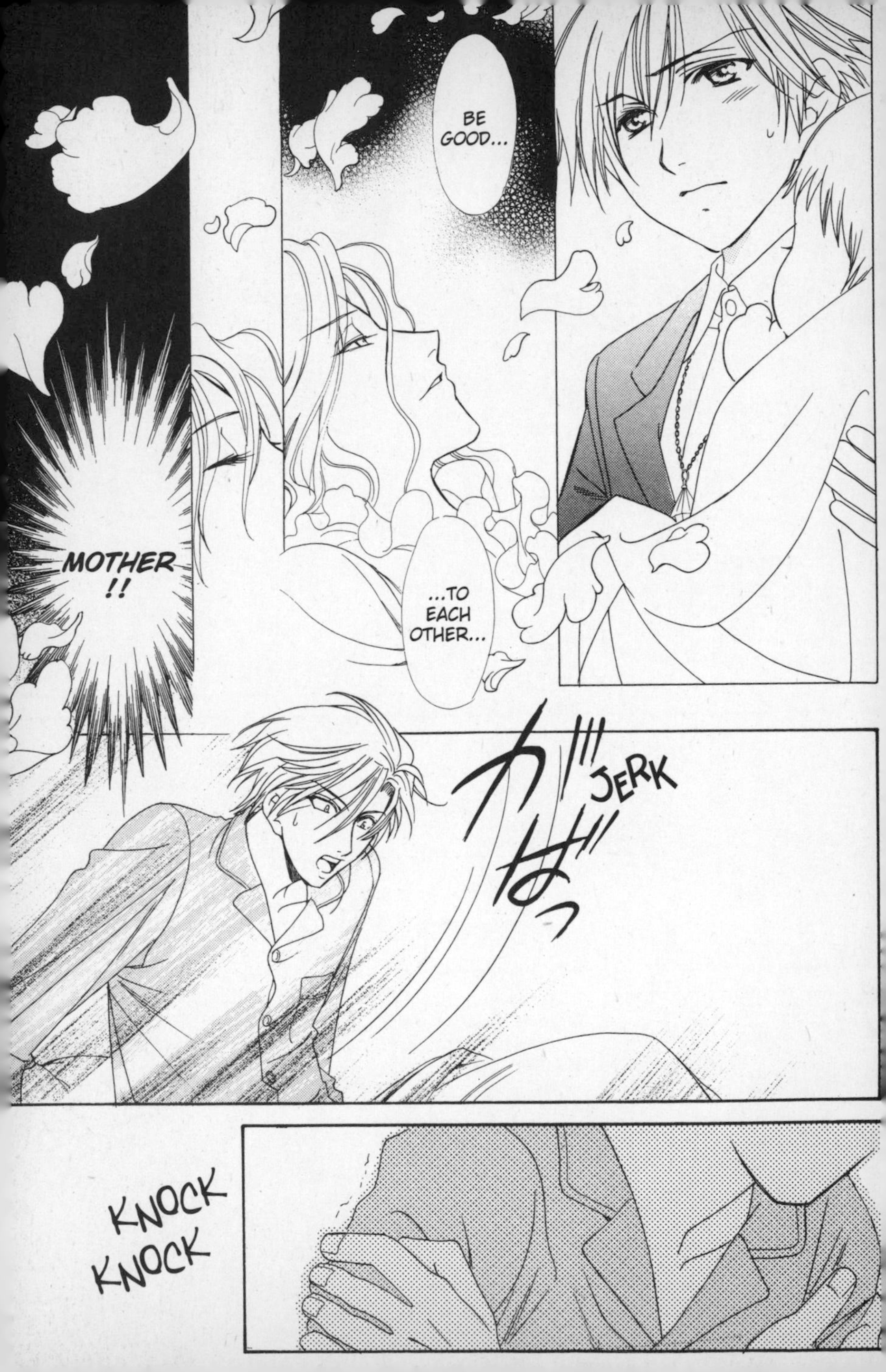
BE GOOD...
...TO EACH OTHER...
MOTHER !!
JERK
KNOCK KNOCK

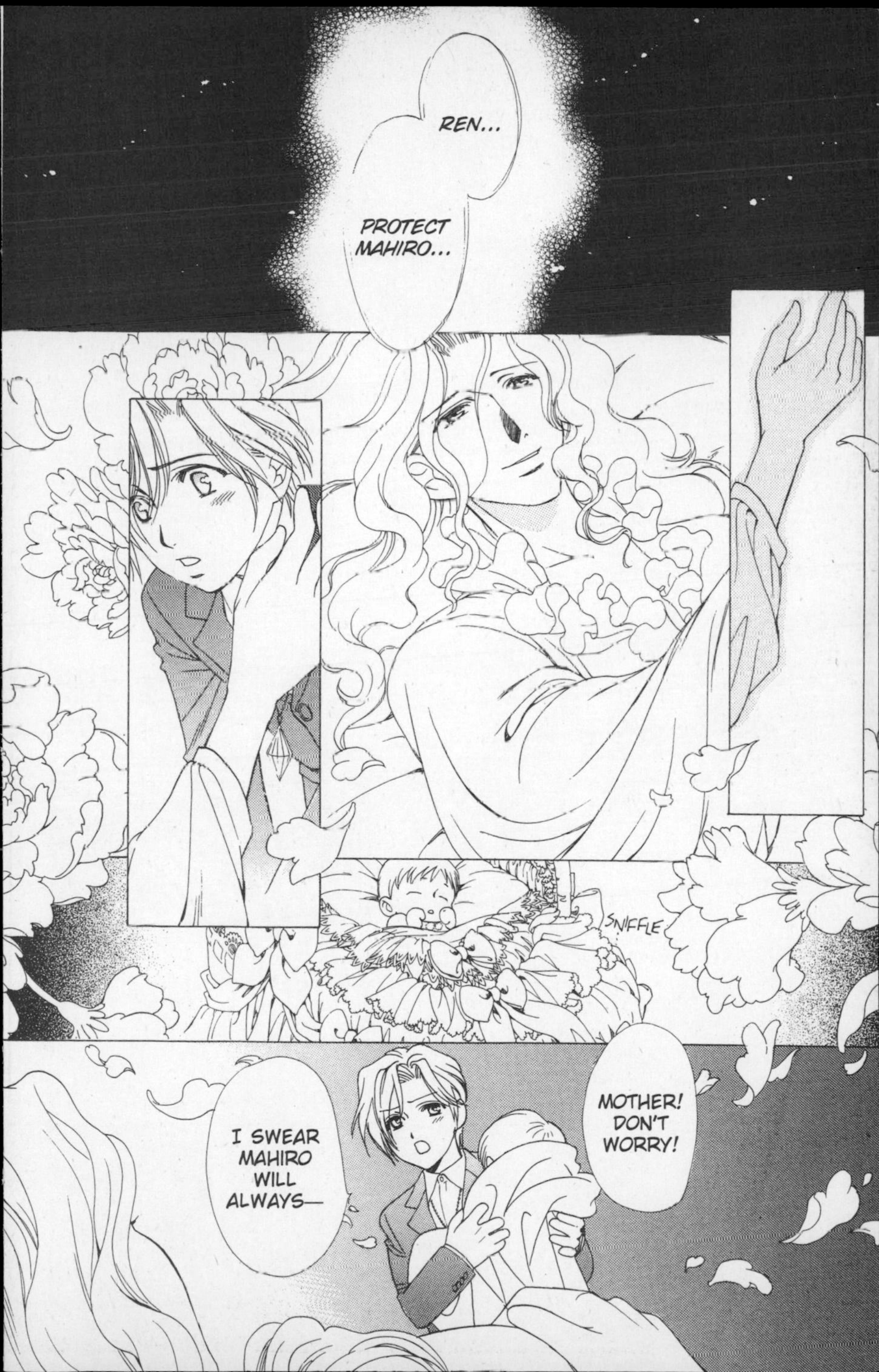
REN...
PROTECT MAHIRO...
SNIFFLE
MOTHER! DON'T WORRY!
I SWEAR MAHIRO WILL ALWAYS—

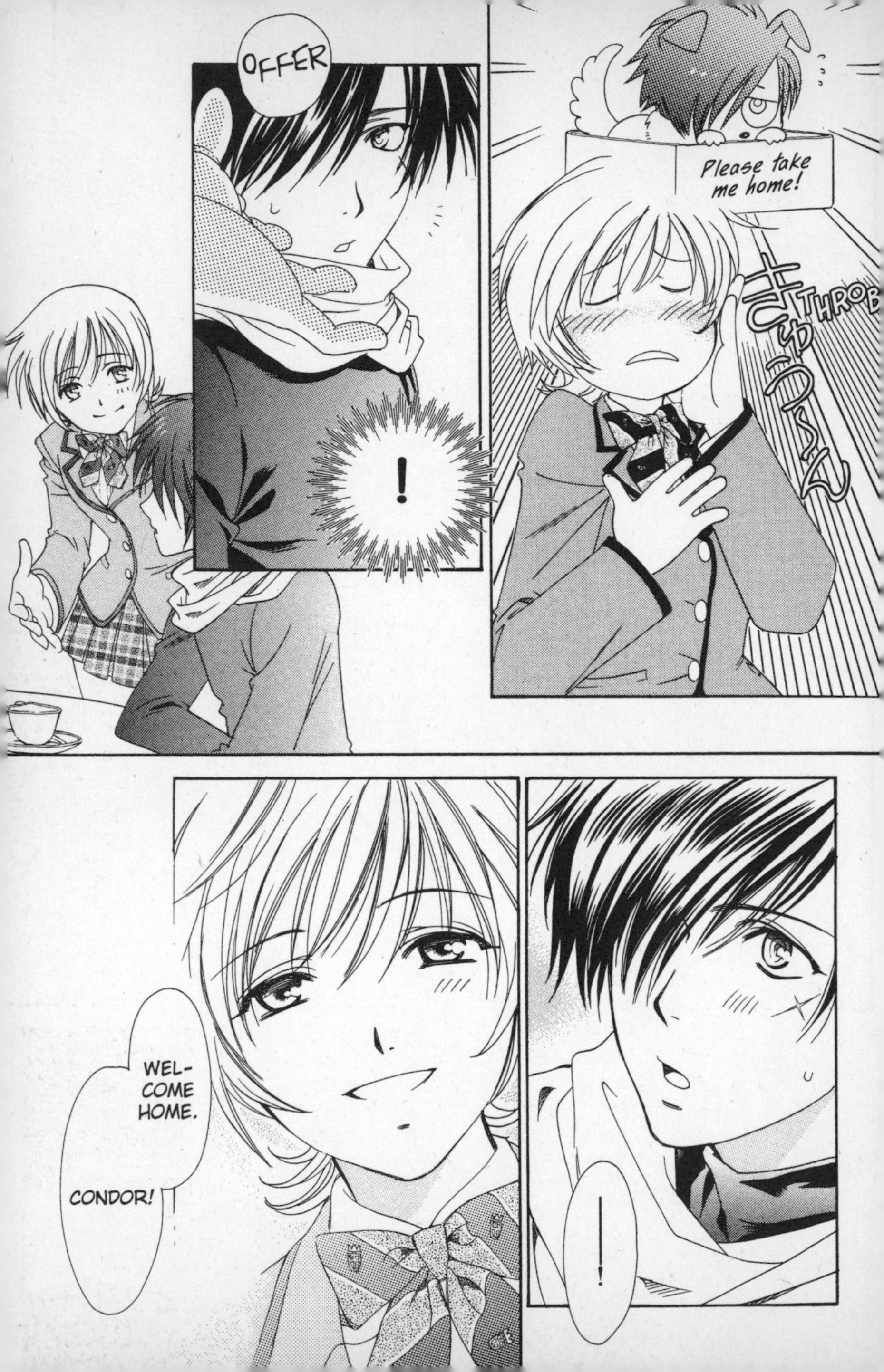
Please take me home!
きゅうぅ～ん
THROB
OFFER
!
WEL-COME HOME.
CONDOR!
!

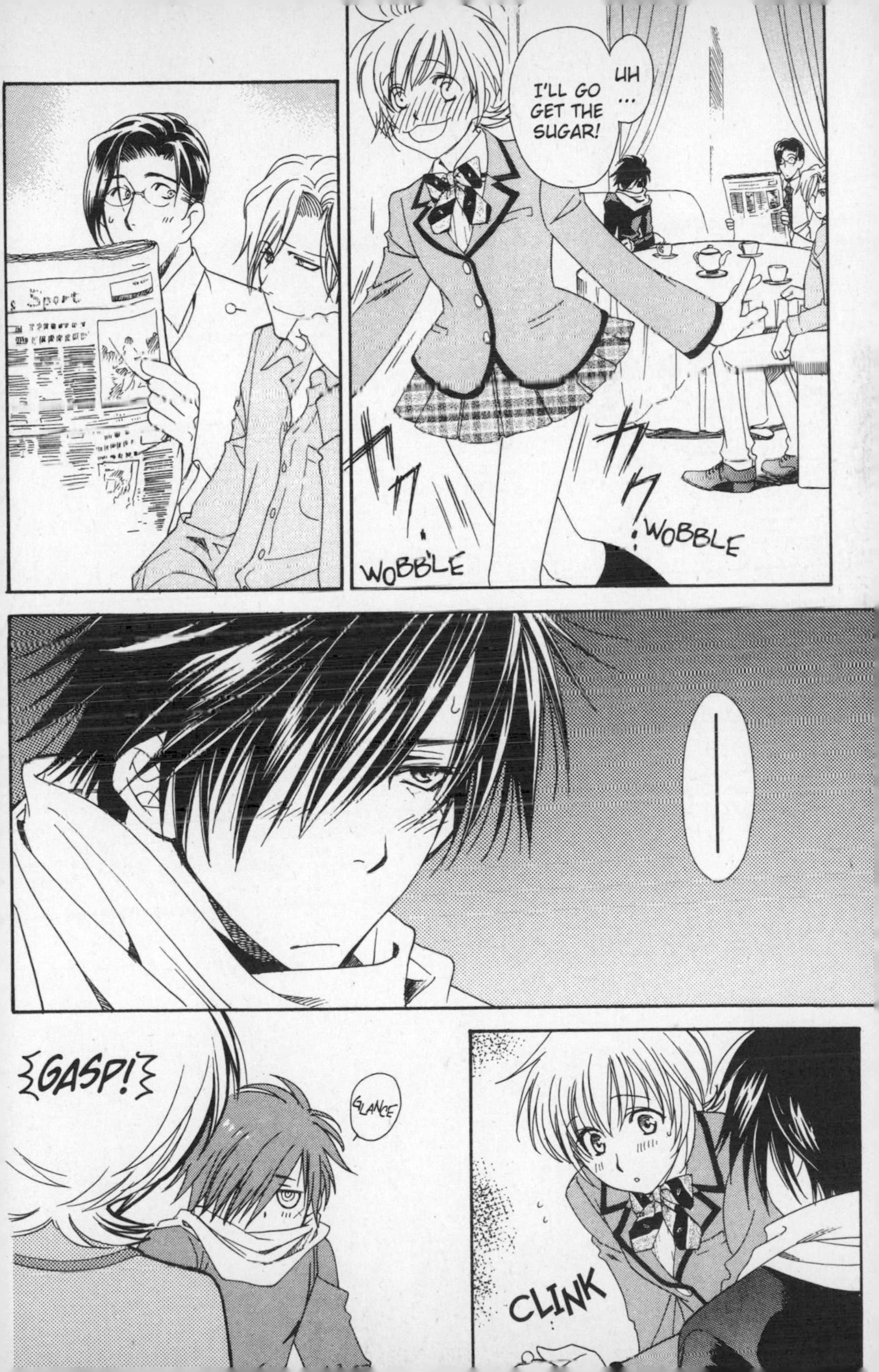

UH ...
I'LL GO GET THE SUGAR!
WOBBLE
WOBBLE
GASP!
GLANCE
CLINK

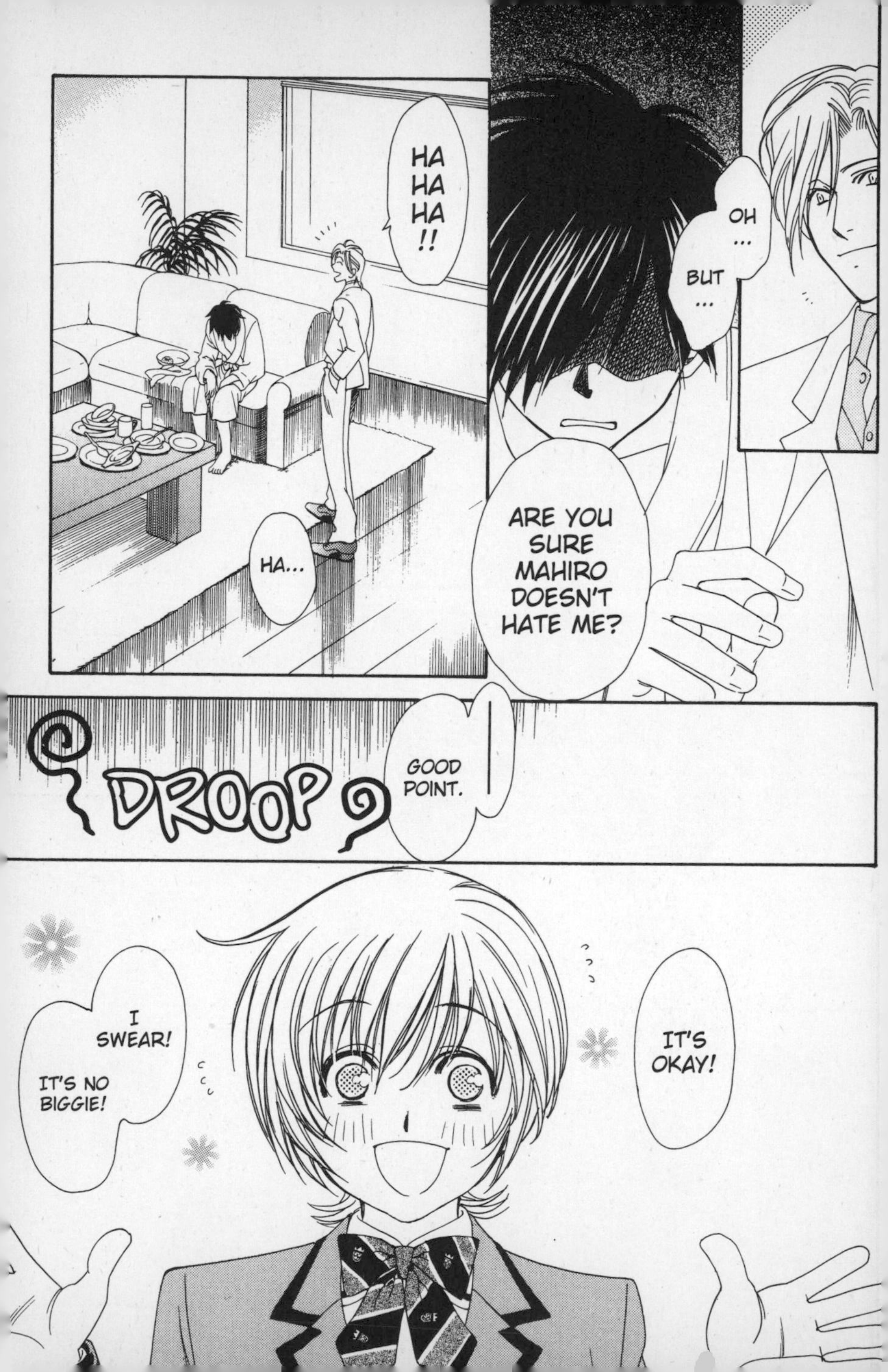
OH ... BUT ...
ARE YOU SURE MAHIRO DOESN'T HATE ME?
HA HA HA!!
HA...
GOOD POINT.
DROOP
IT'S OKAY!
I SWEAR!
IT'S NO BIGGIE!

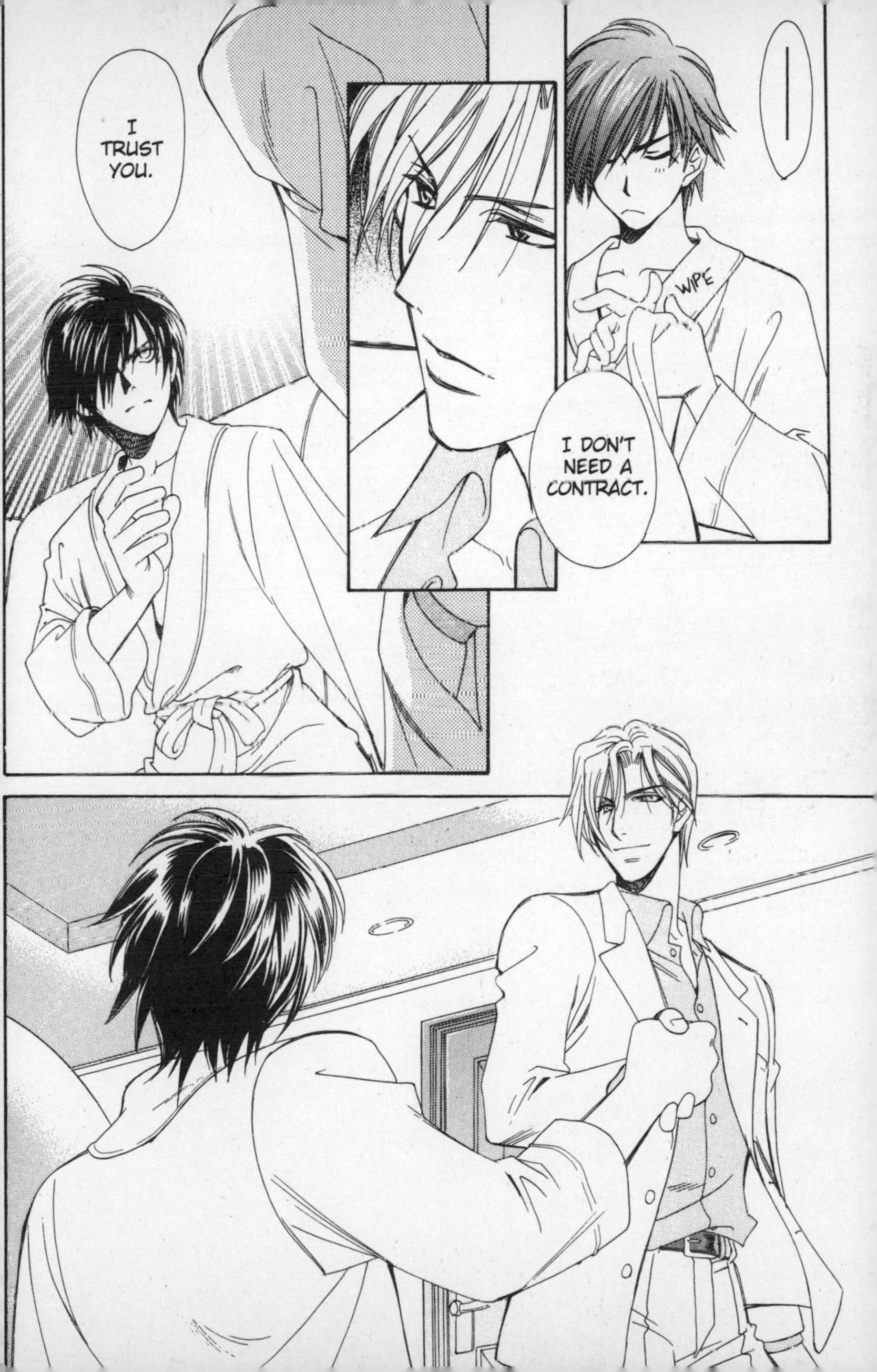
...
WIPE
I DON'T NEED A CONTRACT.
I TRUST YOU.

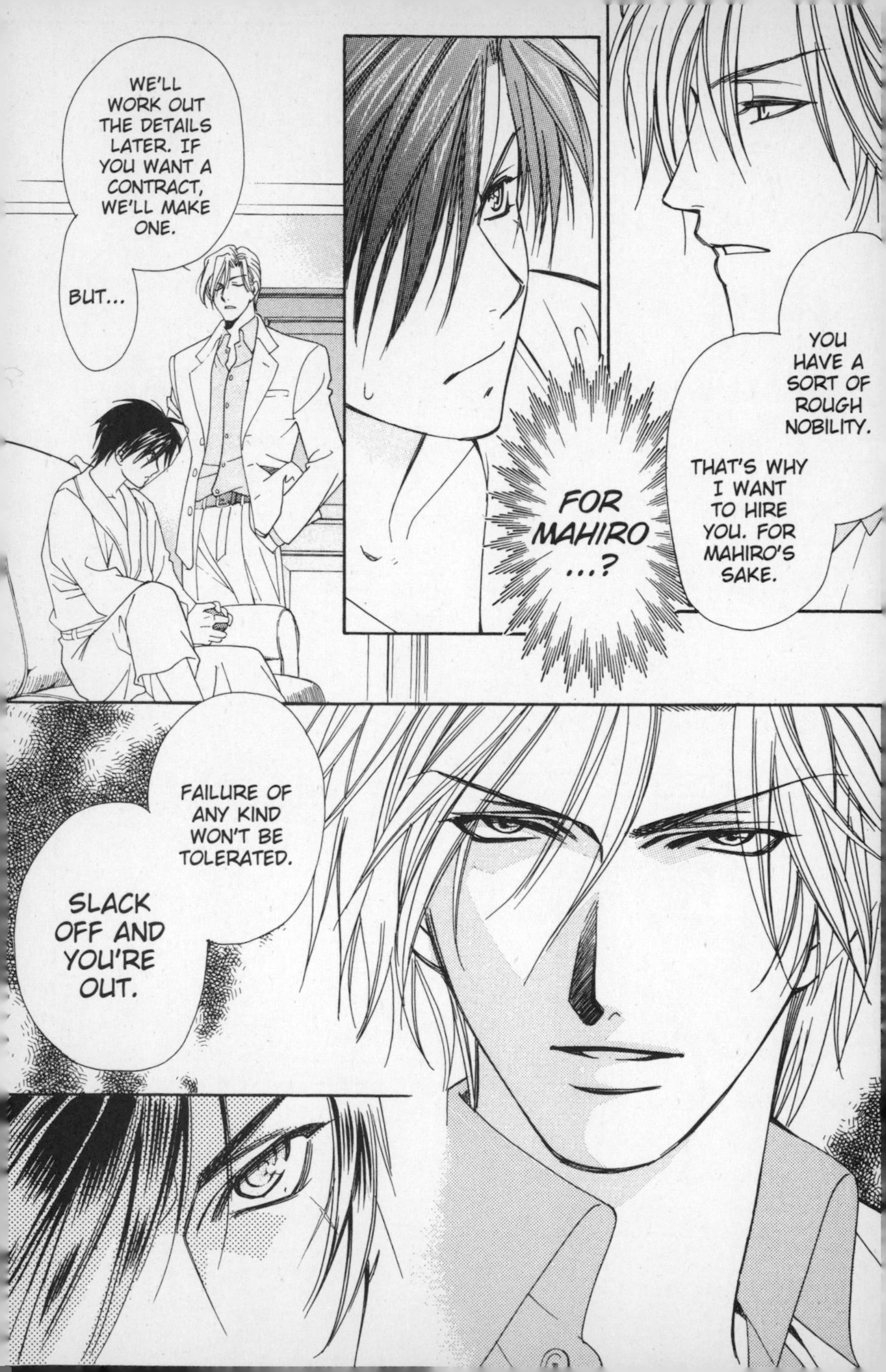
YOU HAVE A SORT OF ROUGH NOBILITY.
THAT'S WHY I WANT TO HIRE YOU. FOR MAHIRO'S SAKE.
FOR MAHIRO ...?
WE'LL WORK OUT THE DETAILS LATER. IF YOU WANT A CONTRACT, WE'LL MAKE ONE.
BUT...
FAILURE OF ANY KIND WON'T BE TOLERATED.
SLACK OFF AND YOU'RE OUT.

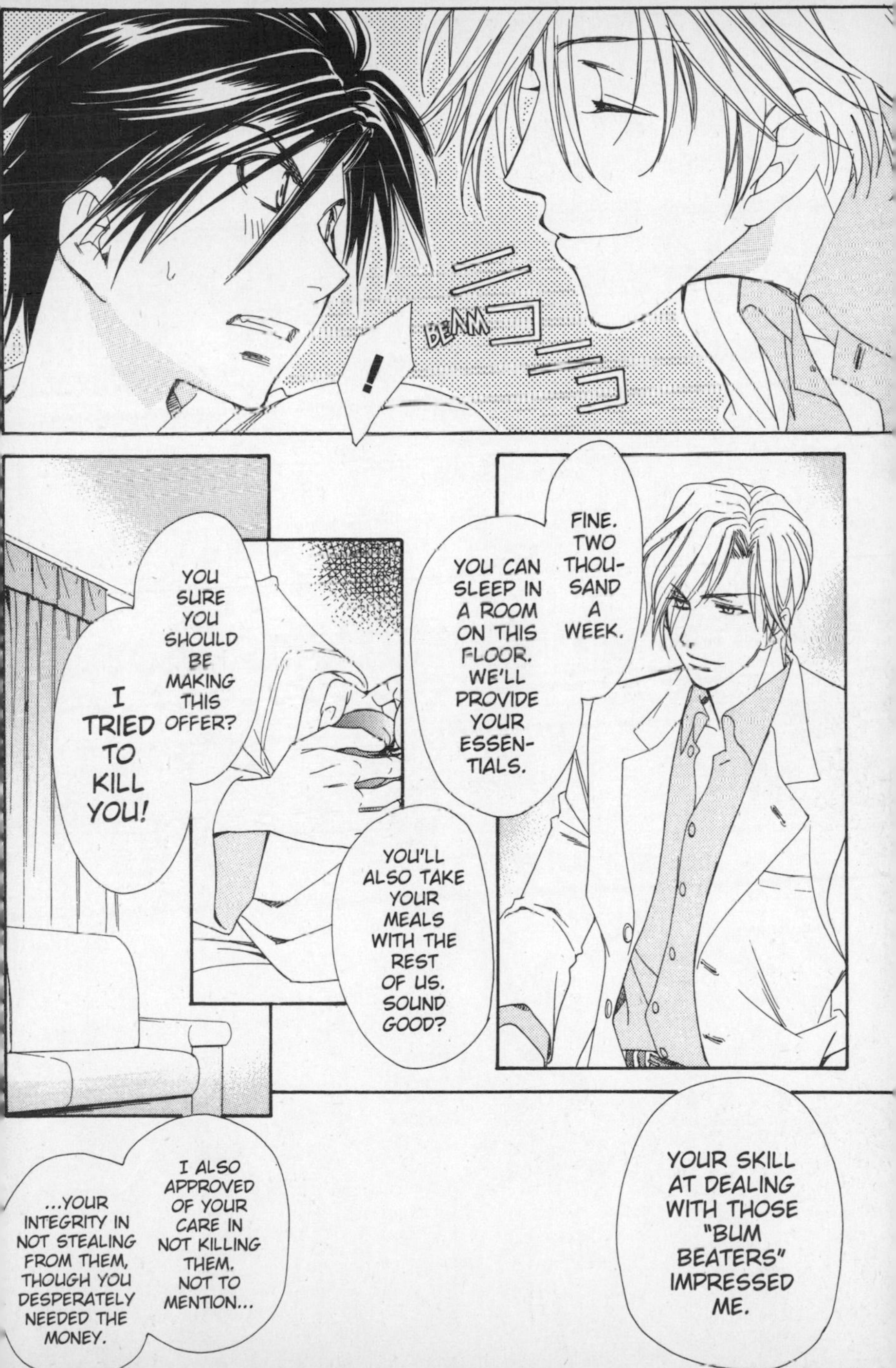

BEAM
!
FINE. TWO THOUSAND A WEEK.
YOU CAN SLEEP IN A ROOM ON THIS FLOOR. WE'LL PROVIDE YOUR ESSENTIALS.
YOU'LL ALSO TAKE YOUR MEALS WITH THE REST OF US. SOUND GOOD?
YOU SURE YOU SHOULD BE MAKING THIS OFFER?
I TRIED TO KILL YOU!
YOUR SKILL AT DEALING WITH THOSE "BUM BEATERS" IMPRESSED ME.
I ALSO APPROVED OF YOUR CARE IN NOT KILLING THEM. NOT TO MENTION...
...YOUR INTEGRITY IN NOT STEALING FROM THEM, THOUGH YOU DESPERATELY NEEDED THE MONEY.

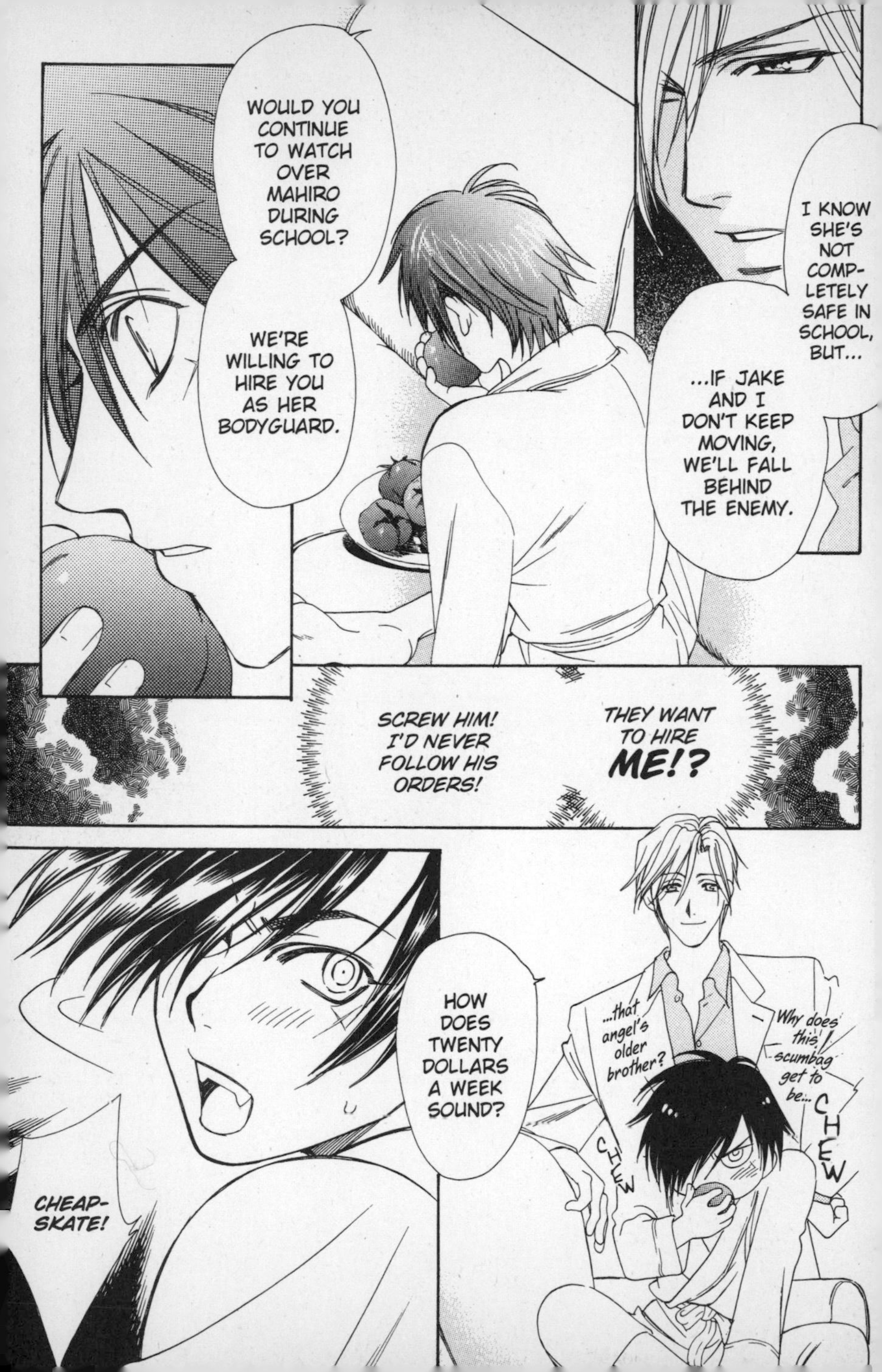
I KNOW SHE'S NOT COMP-LETELY SAFE IN SCHOOL, BUT...
...IF JAKE AND I DON'T KEEP MOVING, WE'LL FALL BEHIND THE ENEMY.
WOULD YOU CONTINUE TO WATCH OVER MAHIRO DURING SCHOOL?
WE'RE WILLING TO HIRE YOU AS HER BODYGUARD.
THEY WANT TO HIRE ME!?
SCREW HIM! I'D NEVER FOLLOW HIS ORDERS!
Why does this scumbag get to be...
...that angel's older brother?
CHEW
CHEW
CHEW
HOW DOES TWENTY DOLLARS A WEEK SOUND?
CHEAP-SKATE!

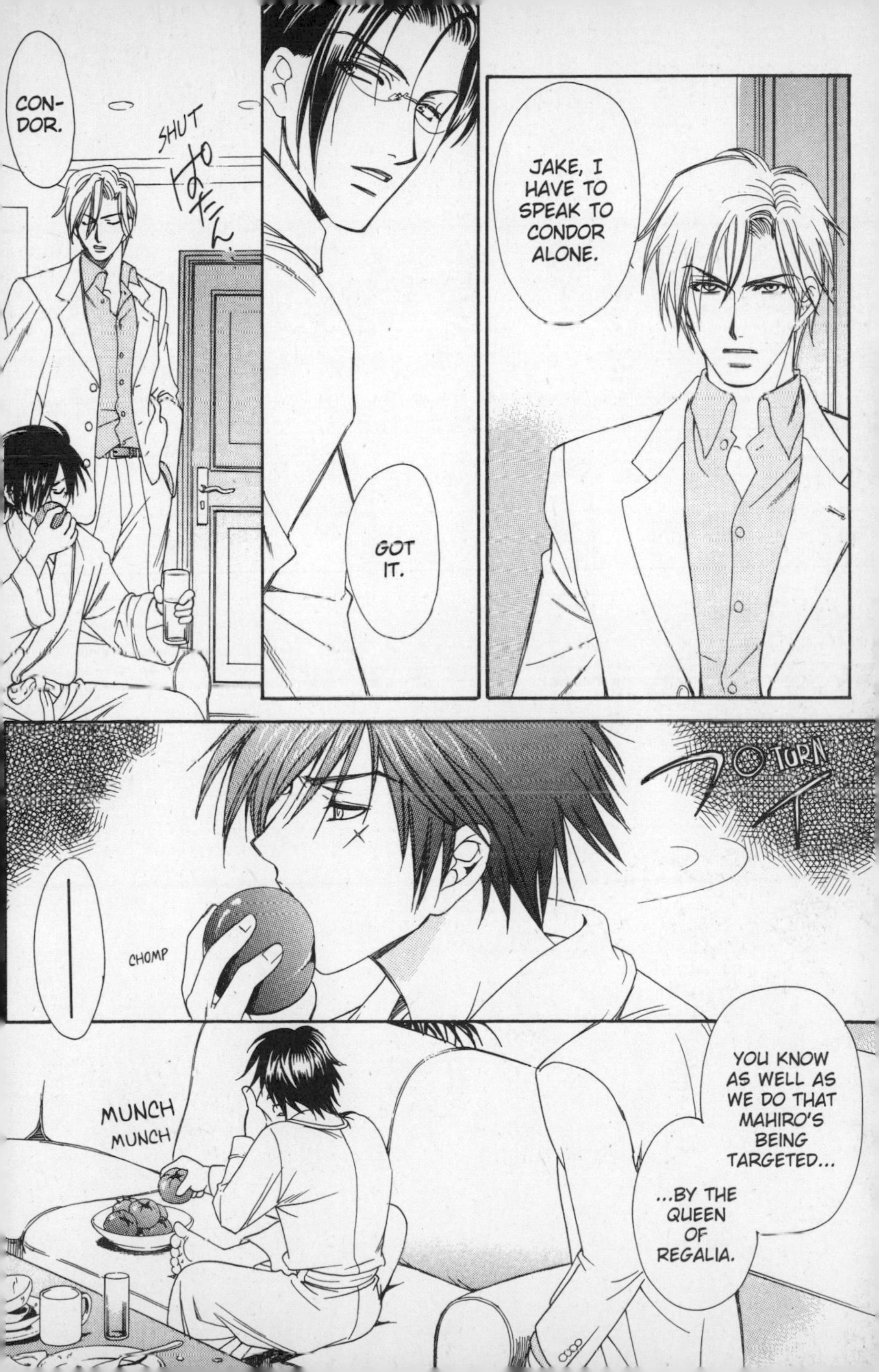

JAKE, I HAVE TO SPEAK TO CONDOR ALONE.
GOT IT.
CON-DOR.
SHUT
TURN
CHOMP
YOU KNOW AS WELL AS WE DO THAT MAHIRO'S BEING TARGETED...
...BY THE QUEEN OF REGALIA.
MUNCH MUNCH

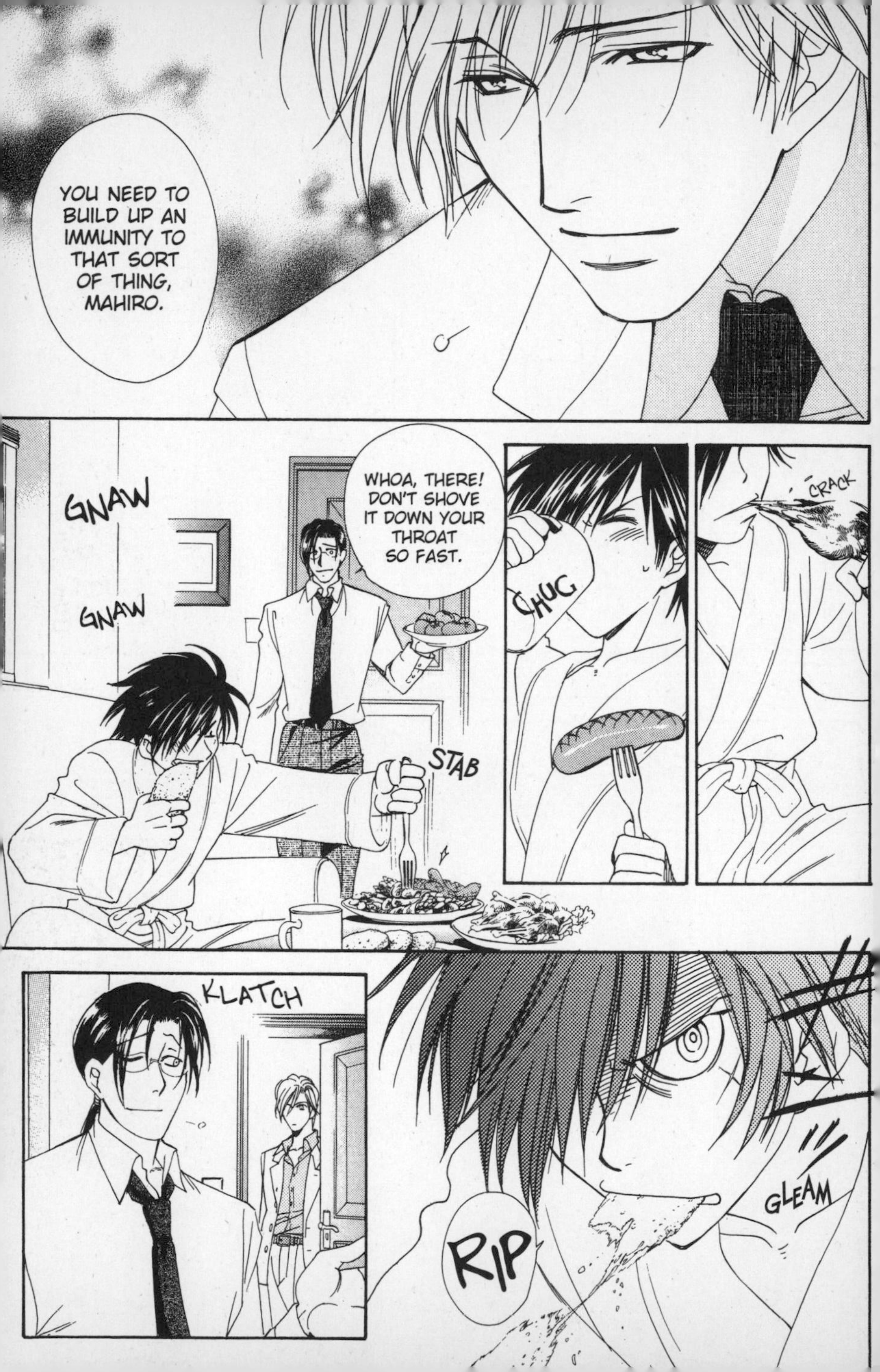
YOU NEED TO BUILD UP AN IMMUNITY TO THAT SORT OF THING, MAHIRO.
CRACK
CHUG
GNAW
GNAW
WHOA, THERE! DON'T SHOVE IT DOWN YOUR THROAT SO FAST.
STAB
GLEAM
RIP
KLATCH

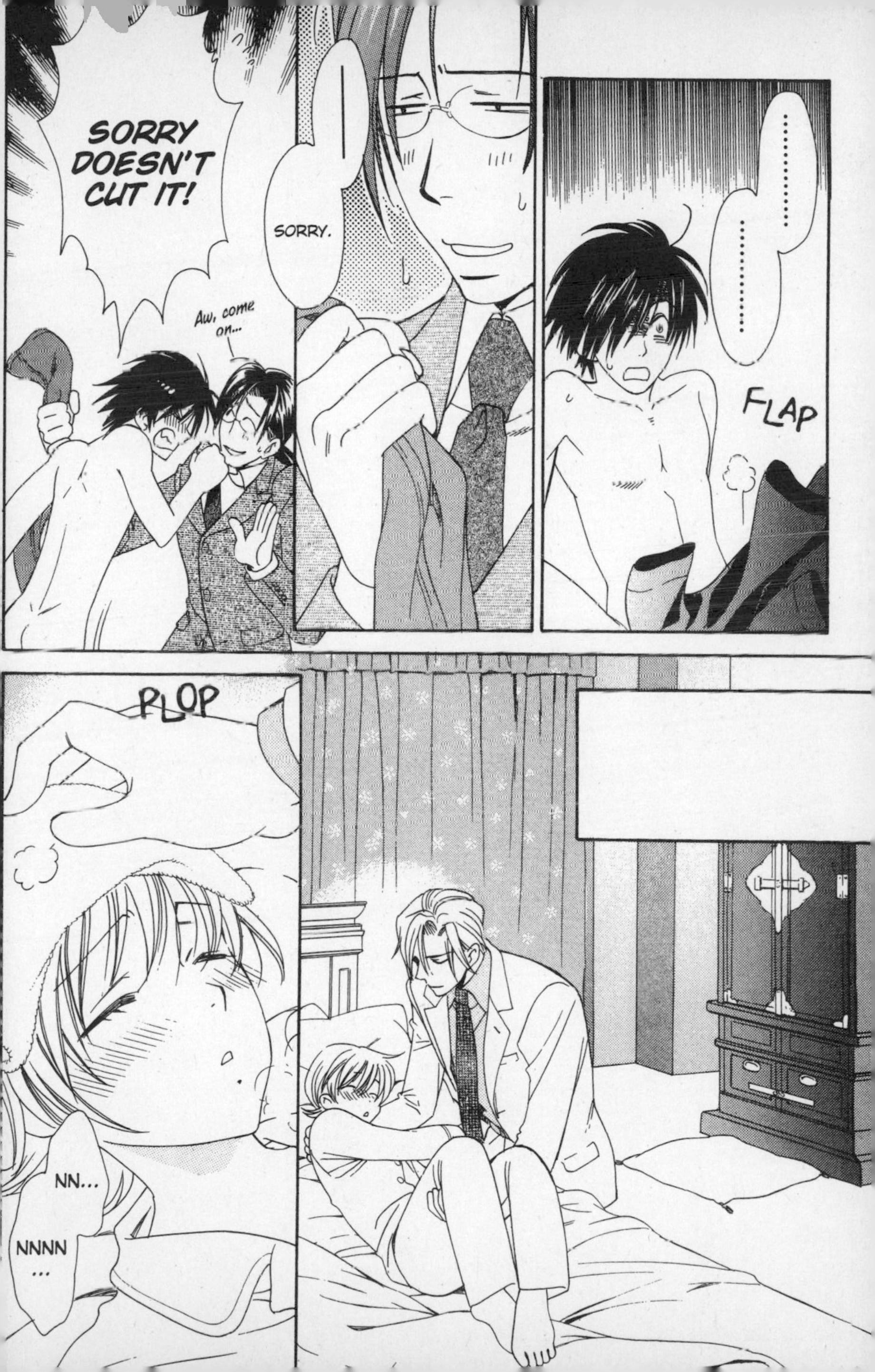
......
FLAP
SORRY.
SORRY DOESN'T CUT IT!
Aw, come on...
PLOP
NN...
NNNN ...

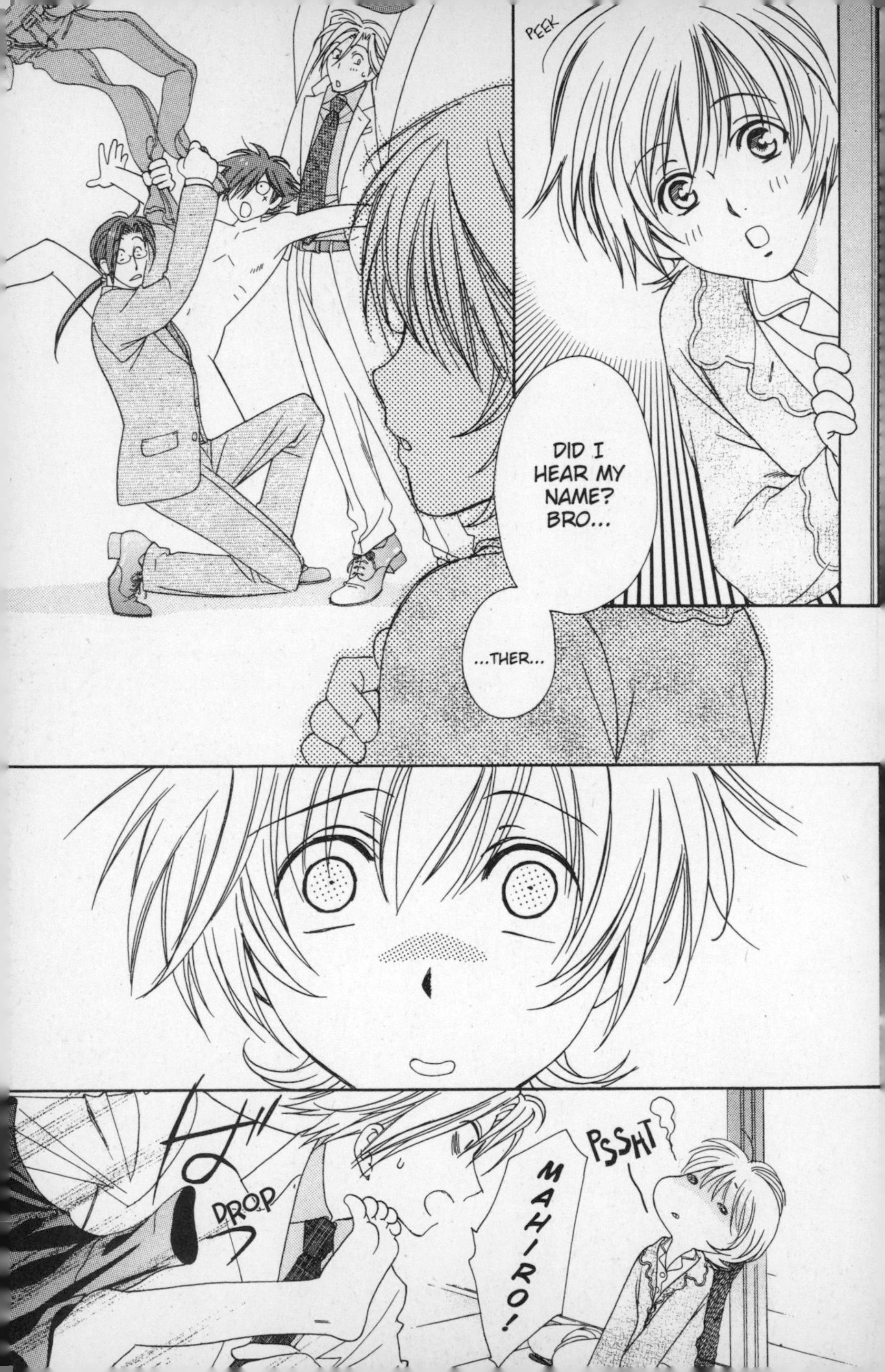
PEEK
DID I HEAR MY NAME? BRO...
...THER...
PSSHT
MAHIRO!
DROP

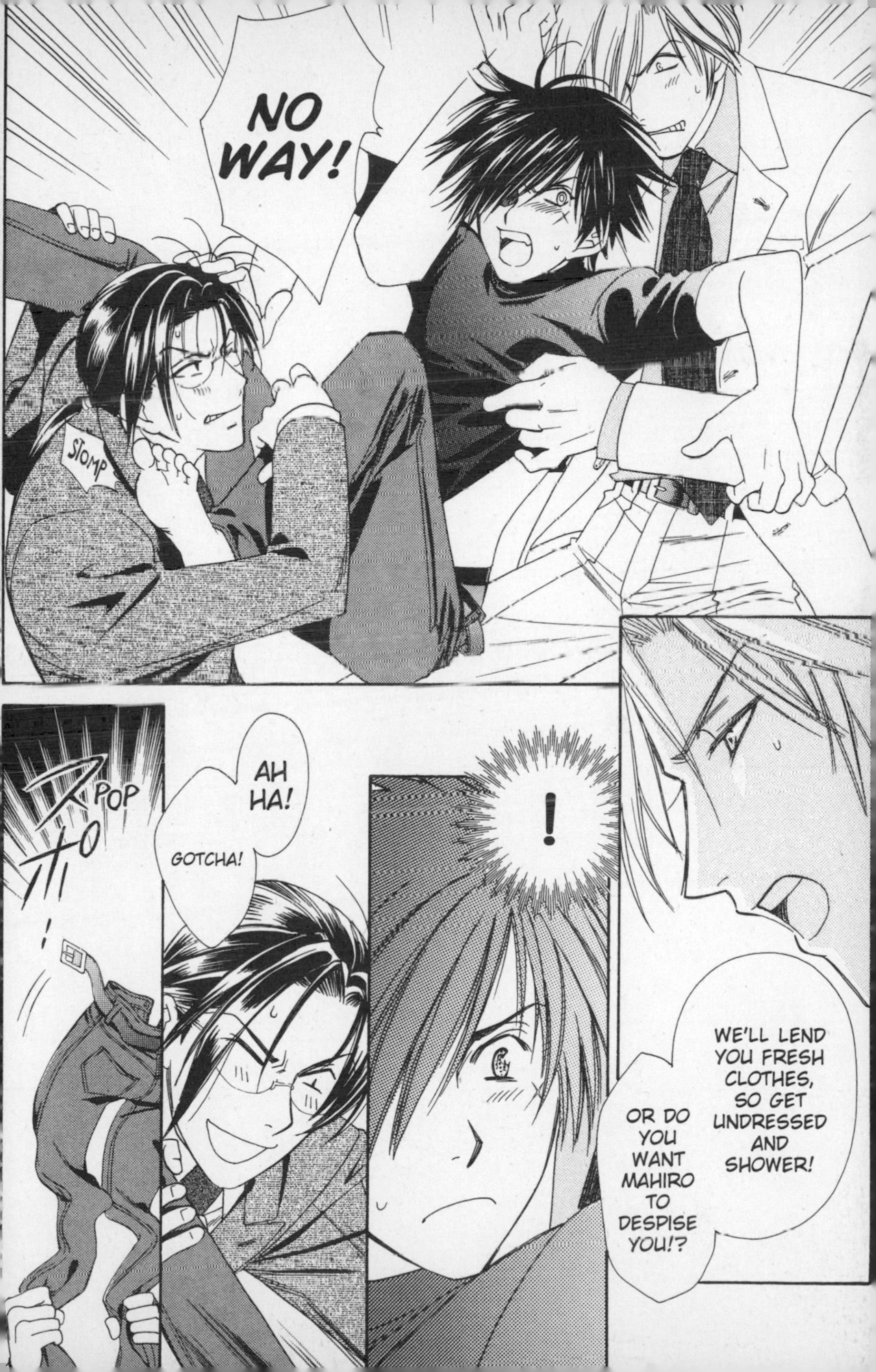
NO WAY!
STOMP
WE'LL LEND YOU FRESH CLOTHES, SO GET UNDRESSED AND SHOWER!
OR DO YOU WANT MAHIRO TO DESPISE YOU!?
!
AH HA!
GOTCHA!
POP

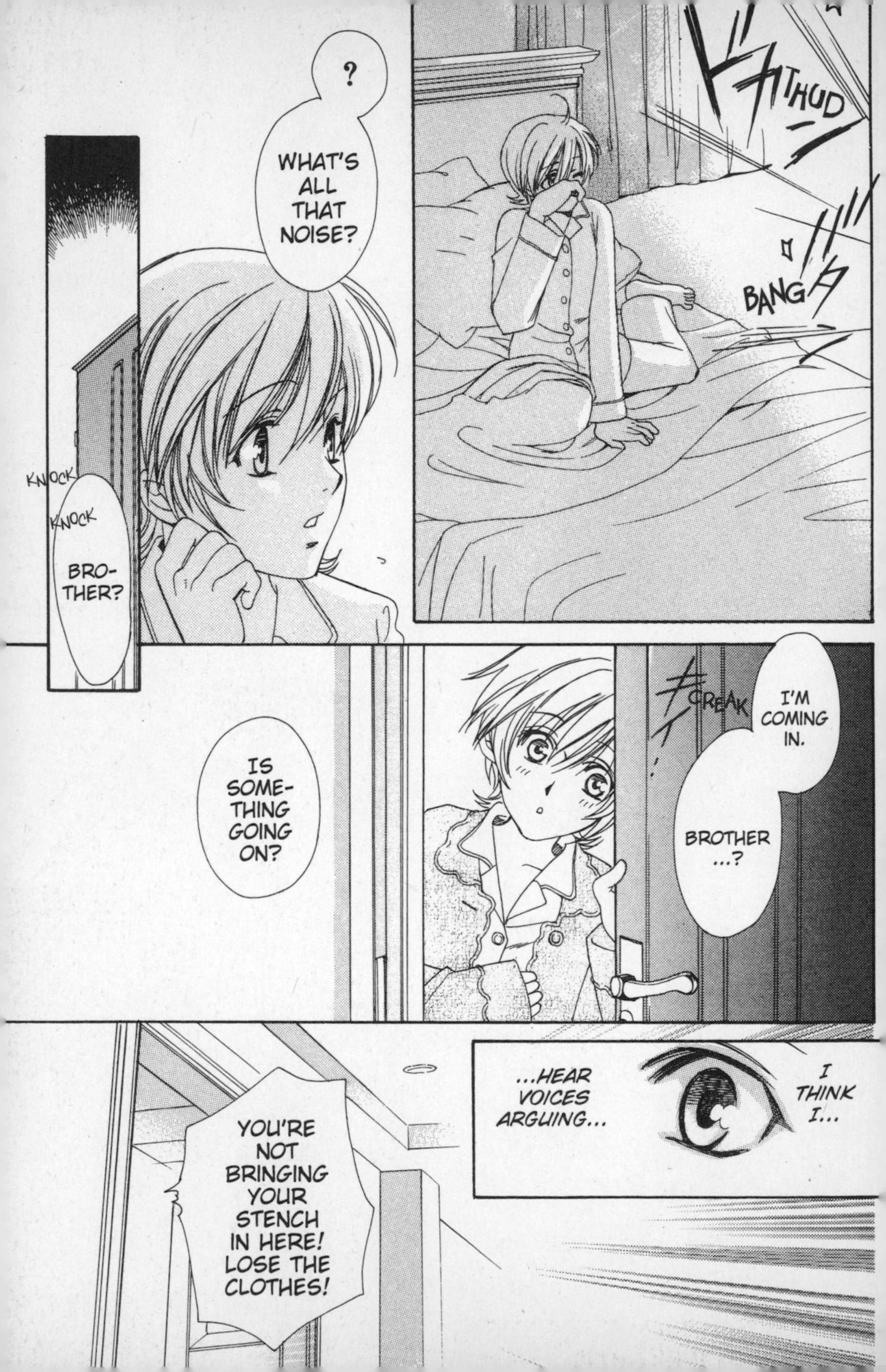
THUD
BANG
?
WHAT'S ALL THAT NOISE?
KNOCK KNOCK
BROTHER?
CREAK
I'M COMING IN.
BROTHER ...?
IS SOMETHING GOING ON?
I THINK I...
...HEAR VOICES ARGUING...
YOU'RE NOT BRINGING YOUR STENCH IN HERE! LOSE THE CLOTHES!

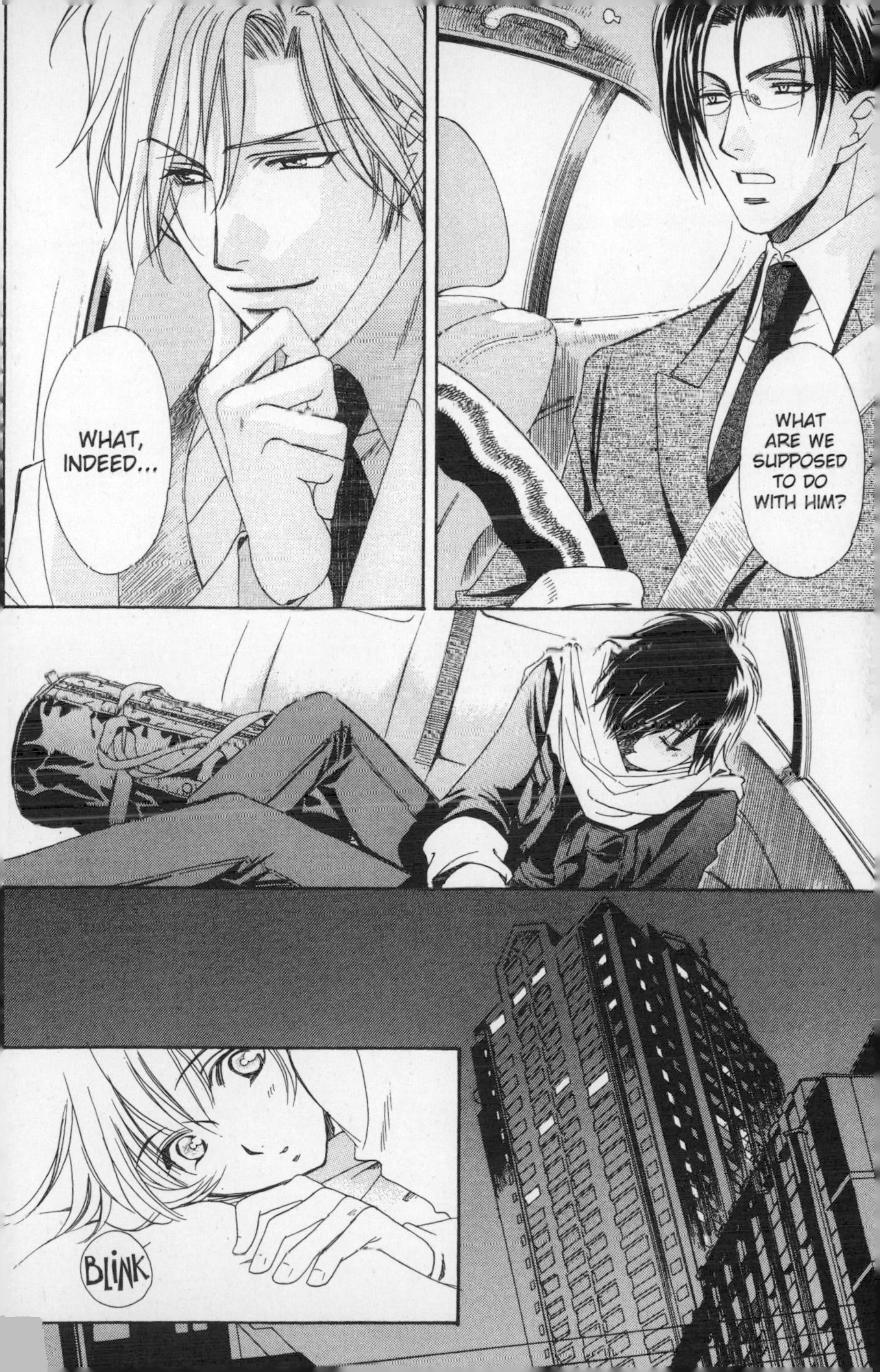
WHAT ARE WE SUPPOSED TO DO WITH HIM?
WHAT, INDEED...
BLINK

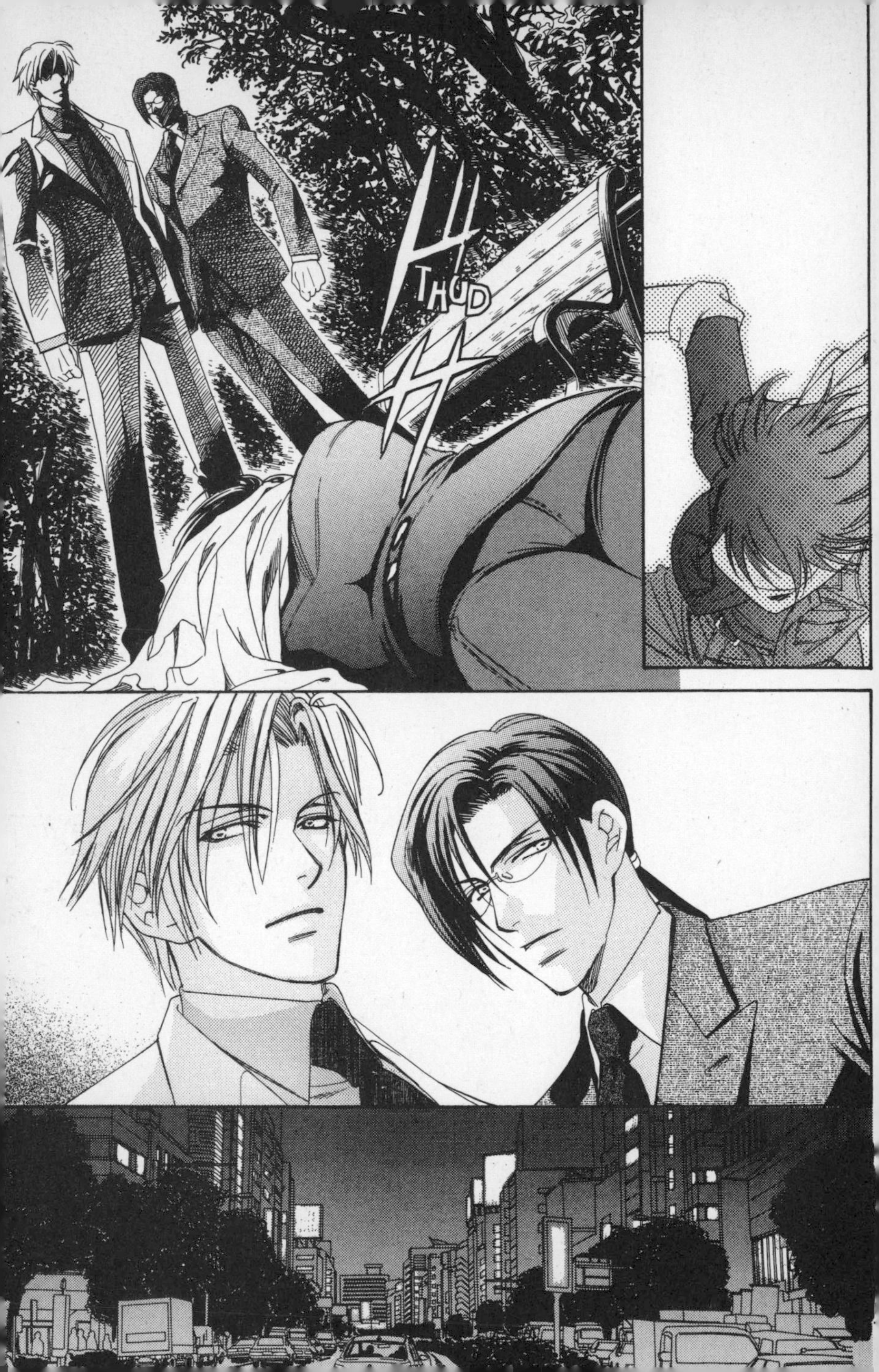
THUD

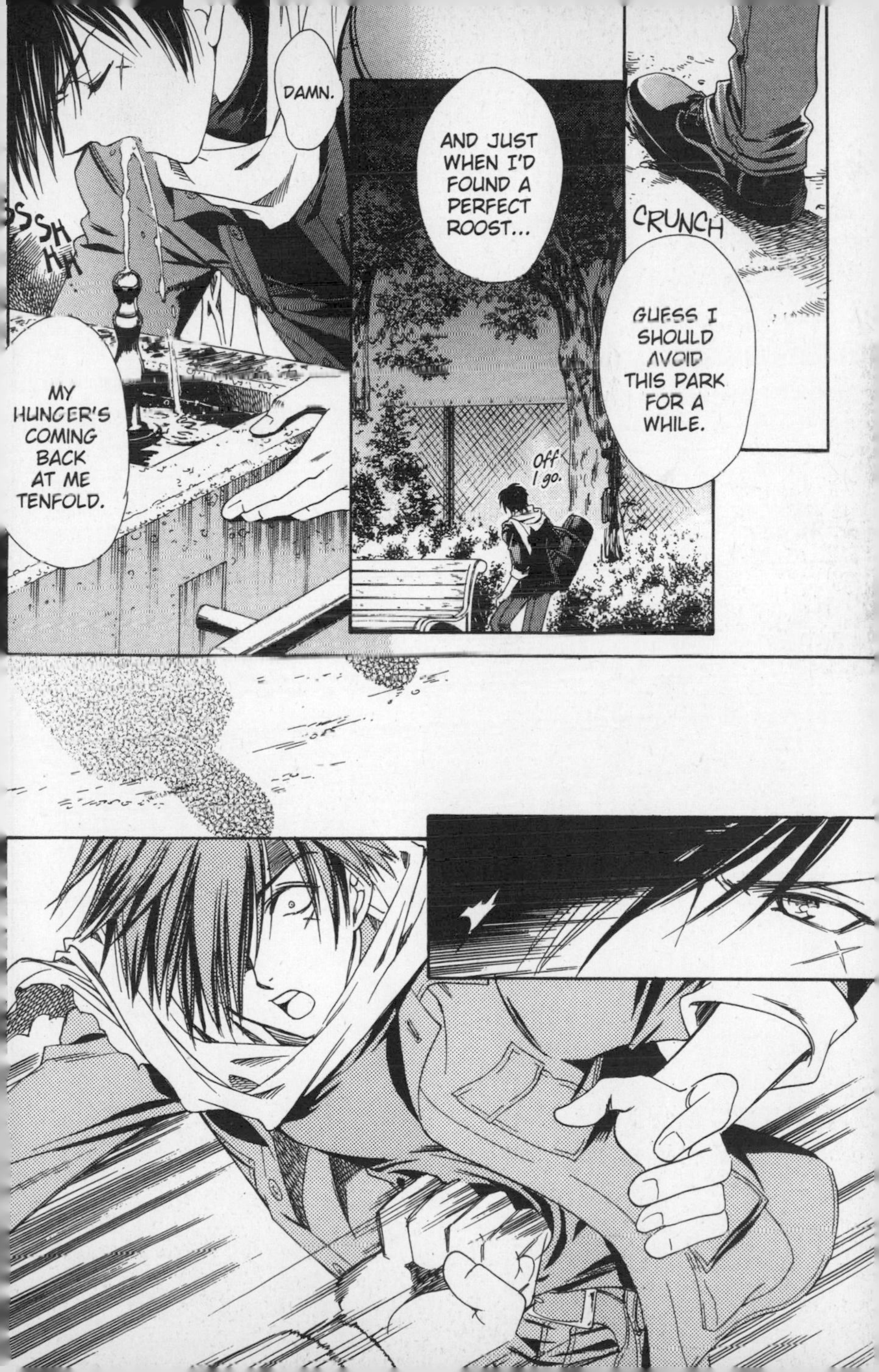
CRUNCH
GUESS I SHOULD AVOID THIS PARK FOR A WHILE.
AND JUST WHEN I'D FOUND A PERFECT ROOST...
Off I go.
DAMN.
SSSHHH
MY HUNGER'S COMING BACK AT ME TENFOLD.

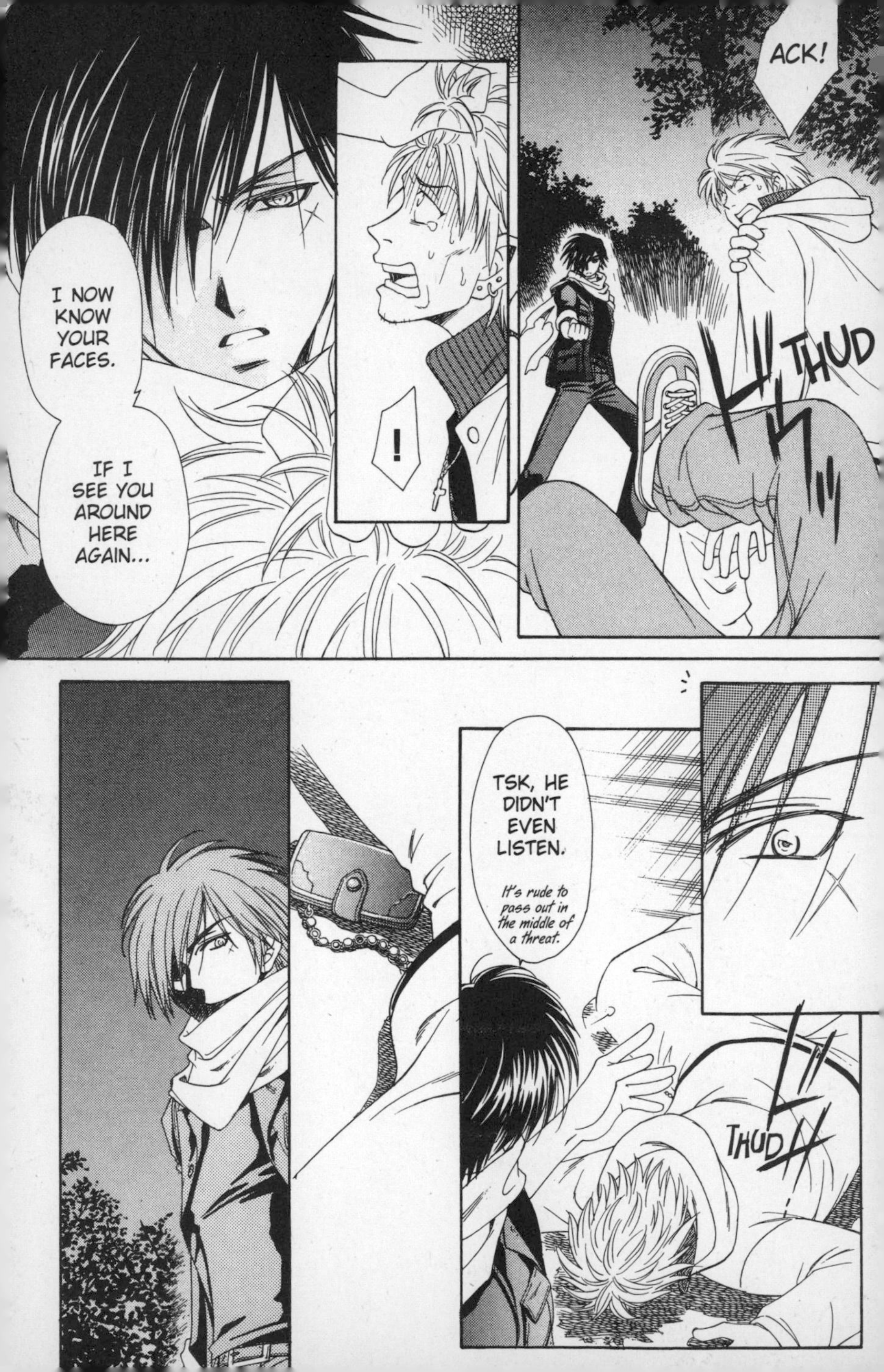
ACK!
THUD
!
I NOW KNOW YOUR FACES.
IF I SEE YOU AROUND HERE AGAIN...
THUD
TSK, HE DIDN'T EVEN LISTEN.
It's rude to pass out in the middle of a threat.

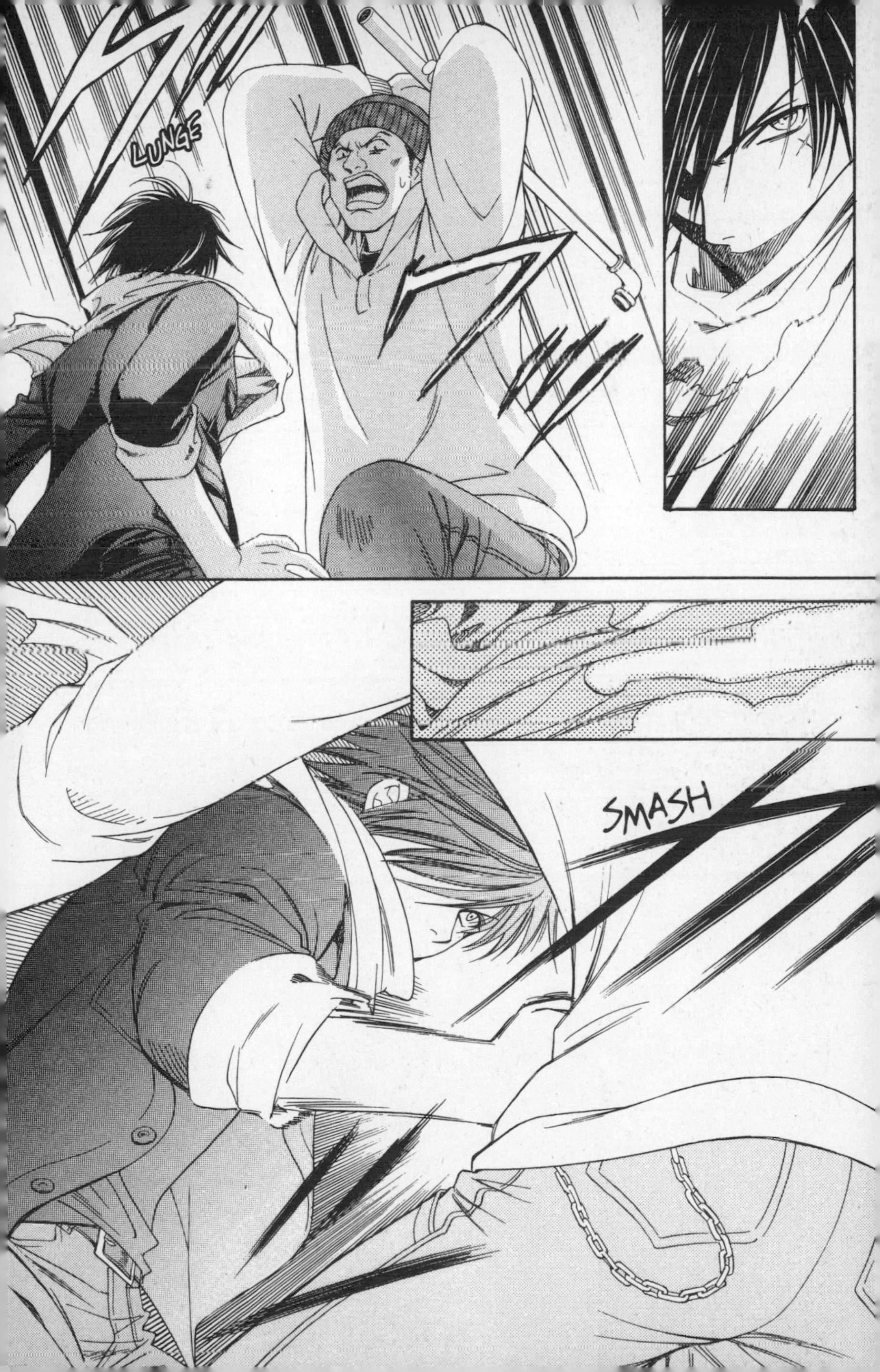
LUNGE
SMASH

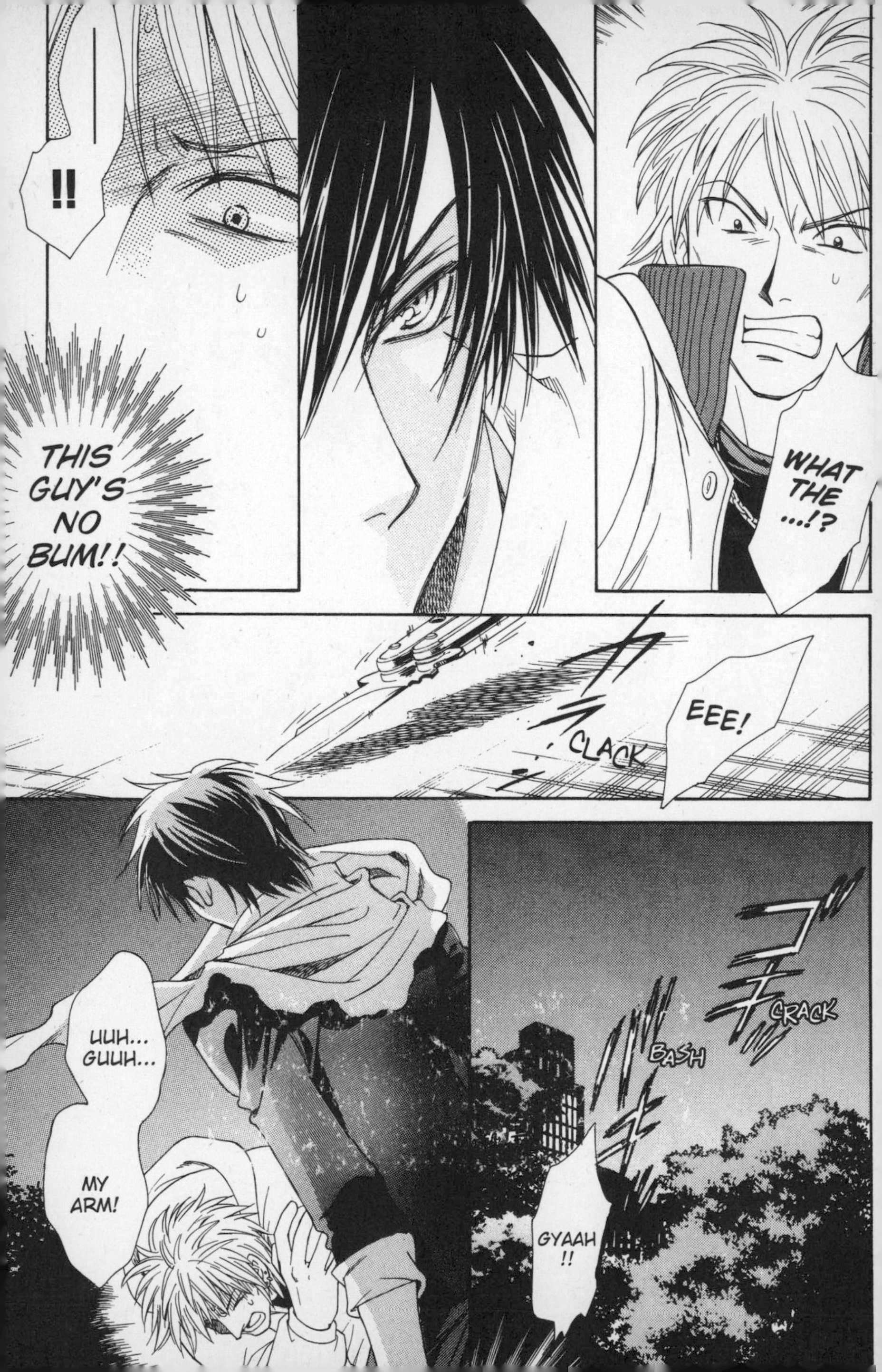
WHAT THE ...!?
!!
THIS GUY'S NO BUM!!
EEE!
CLACK
CRACK
BASH
GYAAH !!
UUH... GUUH...
MY ARM!

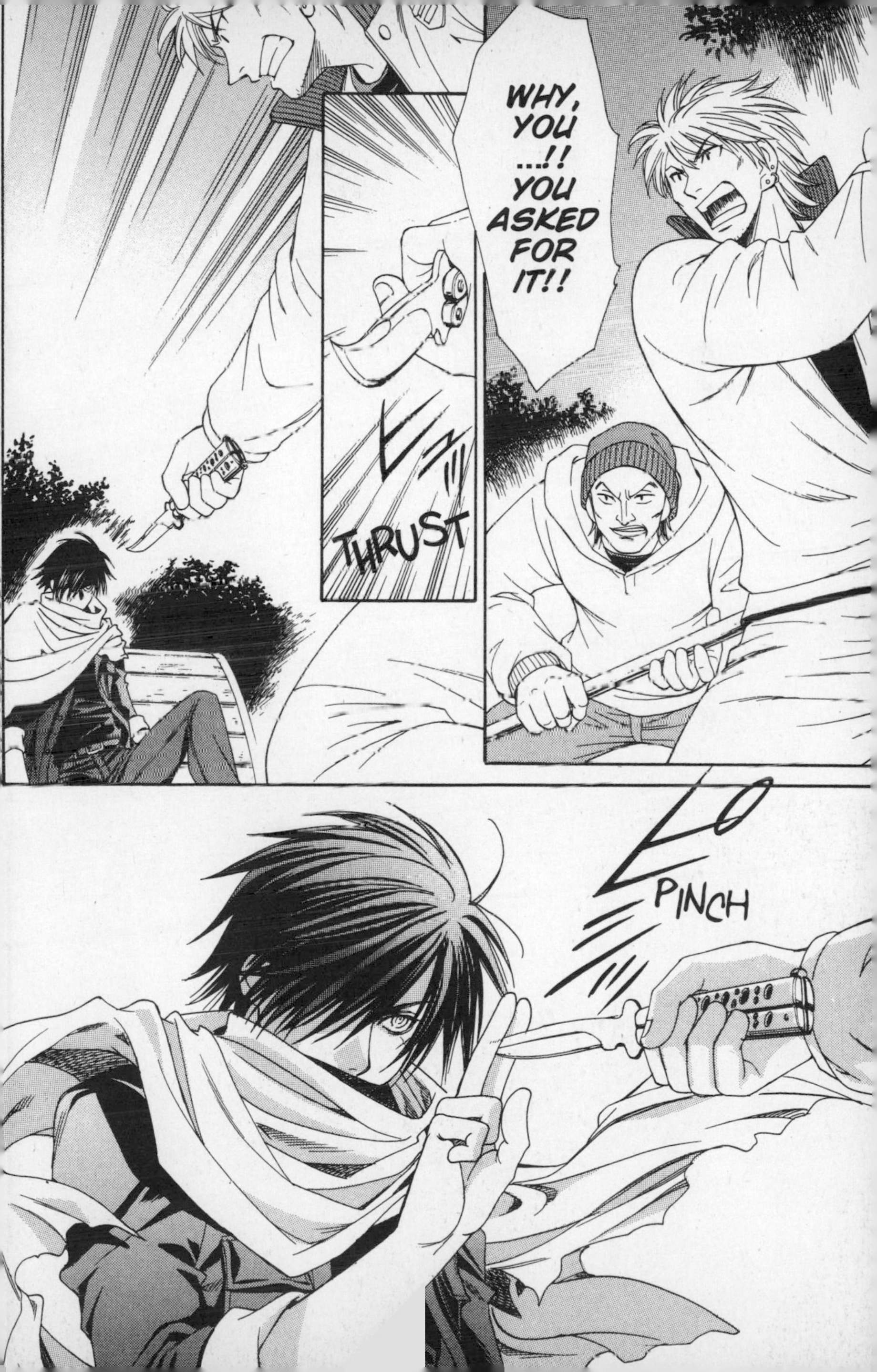
WHY, YOU ...!! YOU ASKED FOR IT!!
THRUST
PINCH

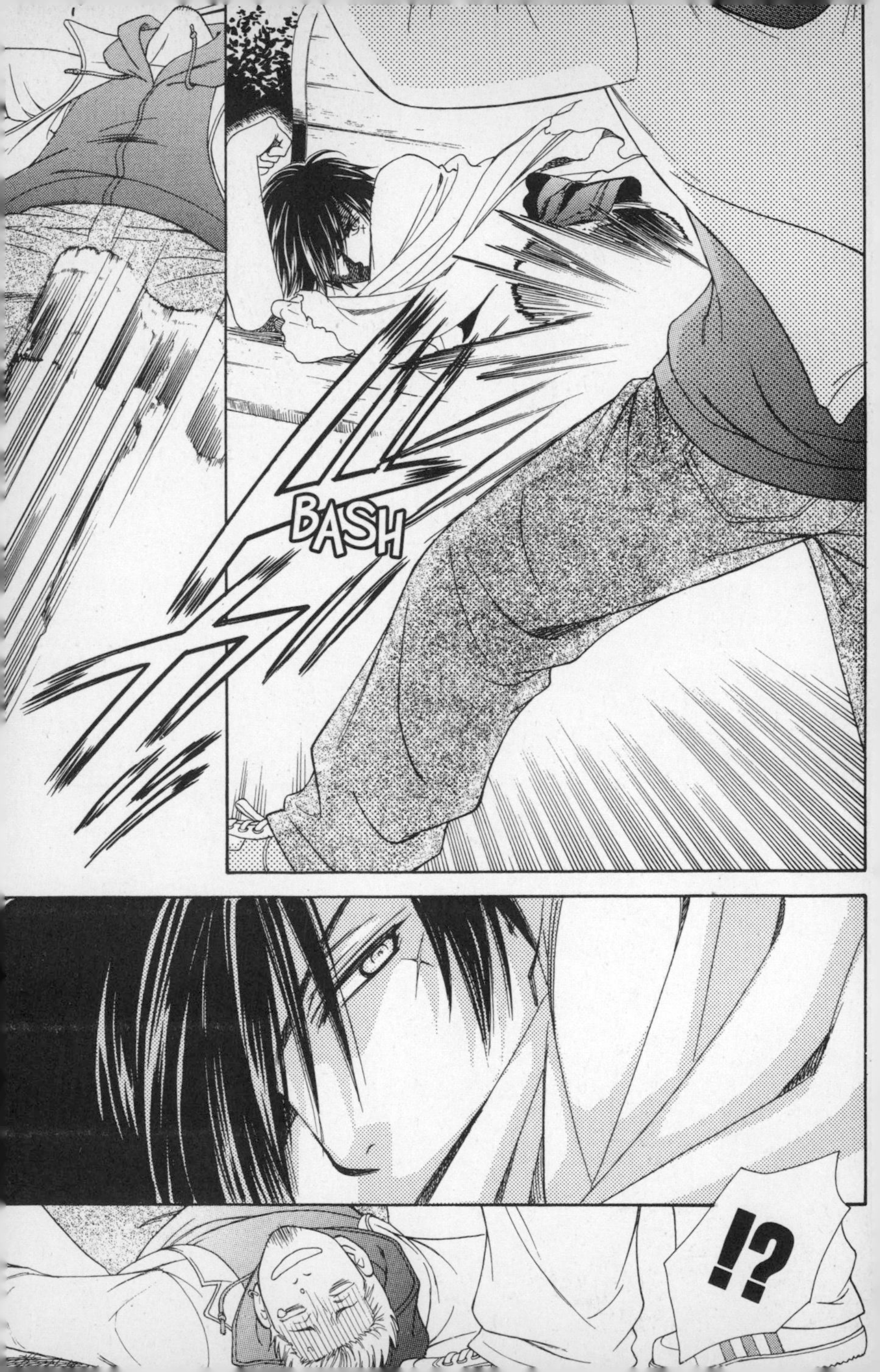
BASH
!?

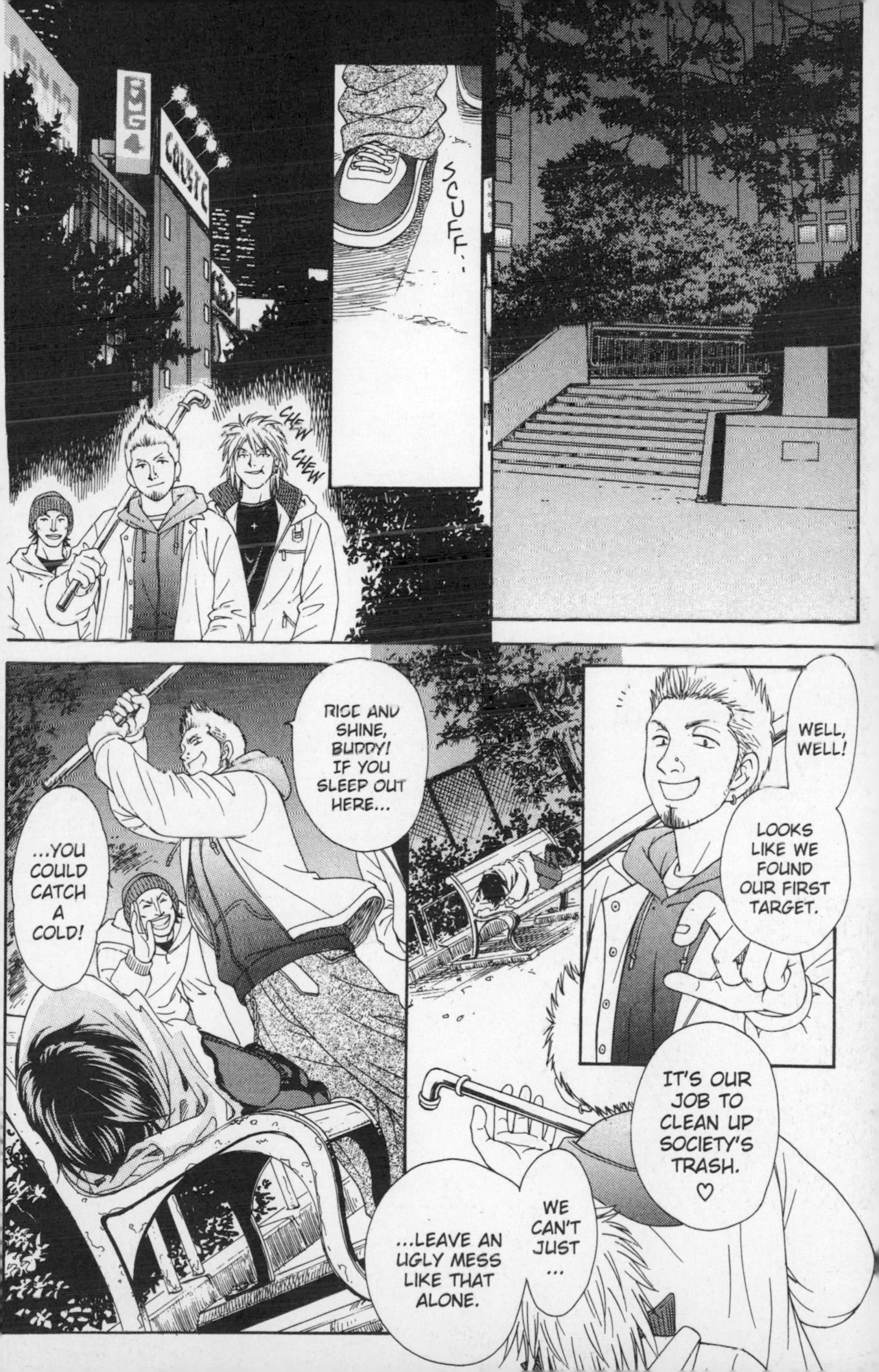
SCUFF..
CHEW CHEW
WELL, WELL!
LOOKS LIKE WE FOUND OUR FIRST TARGET.
IT'S OUR JOB TO CLEAN UP SOCIETY'S TRASH. ♡
WE CAN'T JUST ...
...LEAVE AN UGLY MESS LIKE THAT ALONE.
RISE AND SHINE, BUDDY! IF YOU SLEEP OUT HERE...
...YOU COULD CATCH A COLD!

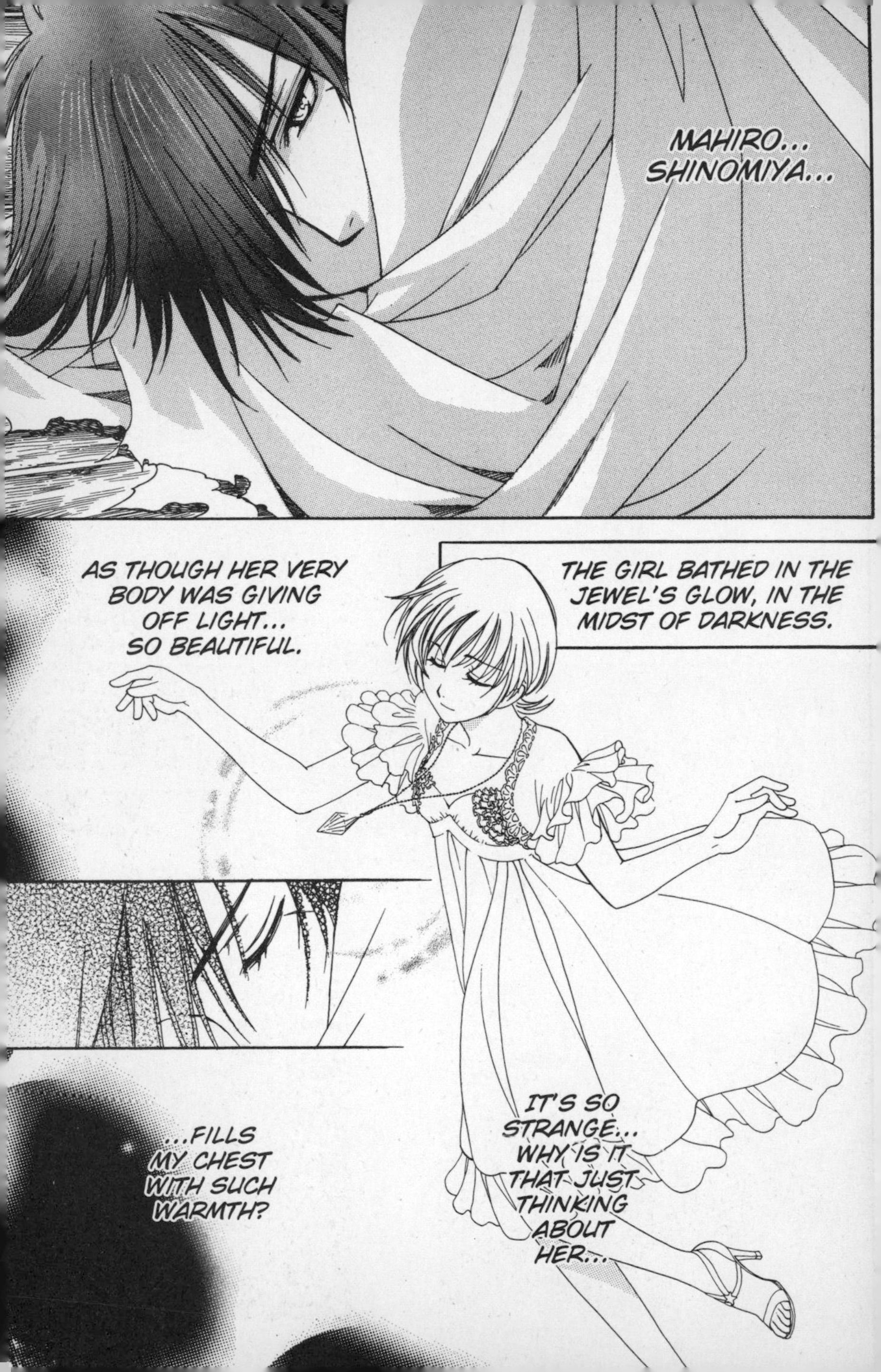
MAHIRO... SHINOMIYA...
THE GIRL BATHED IN THE JEWEL'S GLOW, IN THE MIDST OF DARKNESS.
AS THOUGH HER VERY BODY WAS GIVING OFF LIGHT... SO BEAUTIFUL.
IT'S SO STRANGE... WHY IS IT THAT JUST THINKING ABOUT HER...
...FILLS MY CHEST WITH SUCH WARMTH?

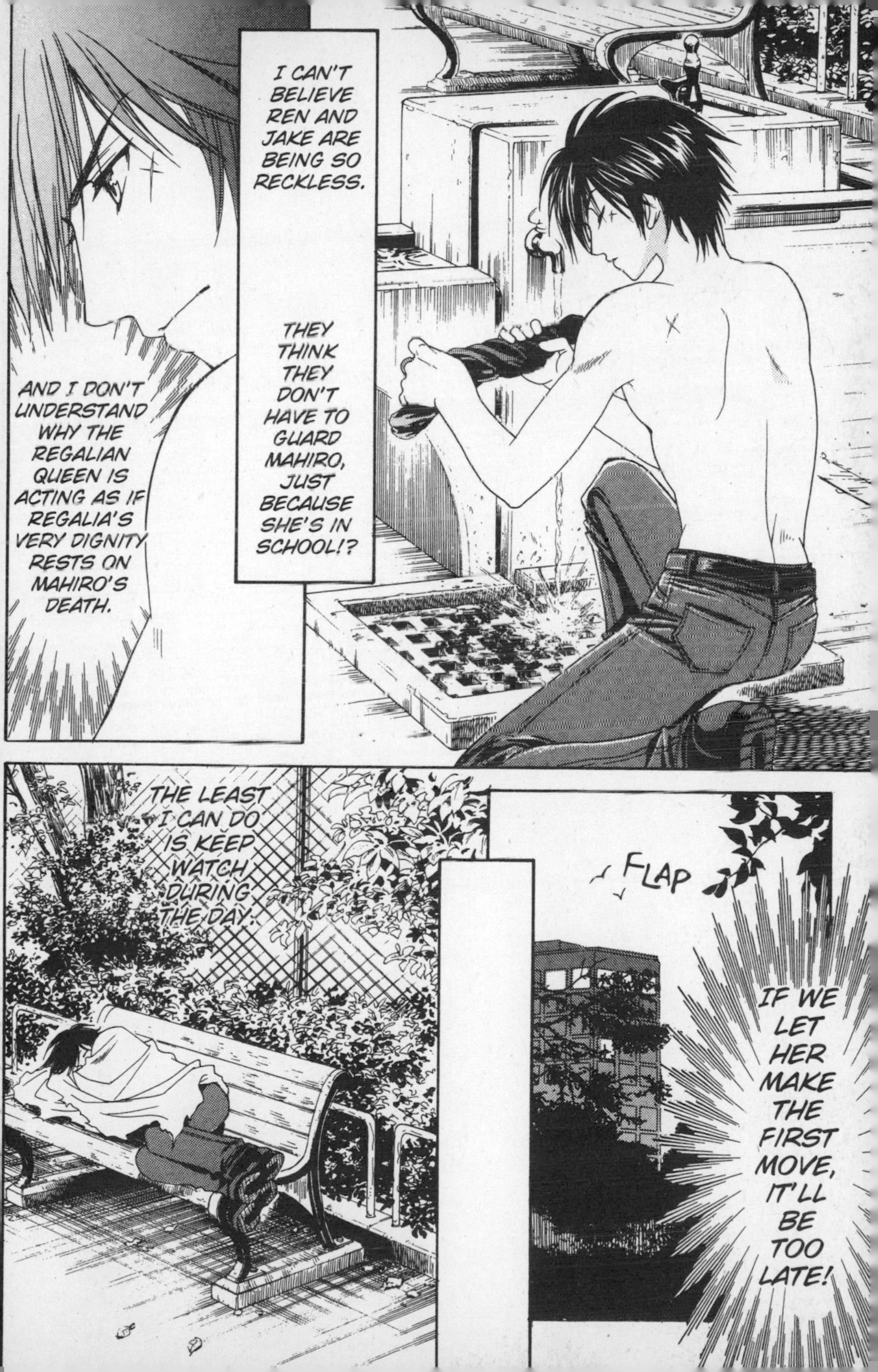
I CAN'T BELIEVE REN AND JAKE ARE BEING SO RECKLESS.
THEY THINK THEY DON'T HAVE TO GUARD MAHIRO, JUST BECAUSE SHE'S IN SCHOOL!?
AND I DON'T UNDERSTAND WHY THE REGALIAN QUEEN IS ACTING AS IF REGALIA'S VERY DIGNITY RESTS ON MAHIRO'S DEATH.
THE LEAST I CAN DO IS KEEP WATCH DURING THE DAY.
FLAP
IF WE LET HER MAKE THE FIRST MOVE, IT'LL BE TOO LATE!

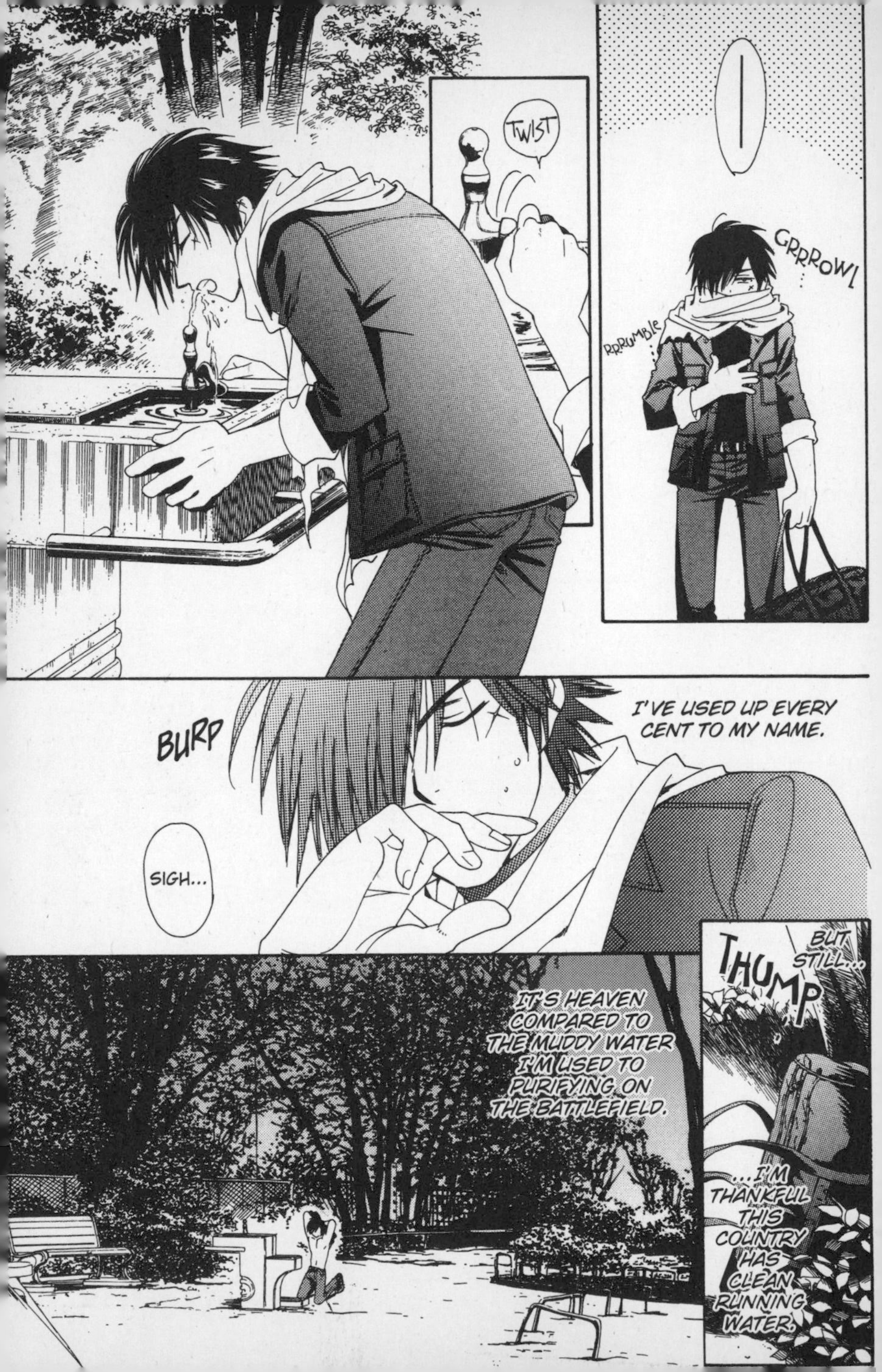
!
GRRROWL
RRRUMBLE
TWIST
I'VE USED UP EVERY CENT TO MY NAME.
BURP
SIGH...
BUT STILL...
THUMP
...I'M THANKFUL THIS COUNTRY HAS CLEAN RUNNING WATER.
IT'S HEAVEN COMPARED TO THE MUDDY WATER I'M USED TO PURIFYING ON THE BATTLEFIELD.

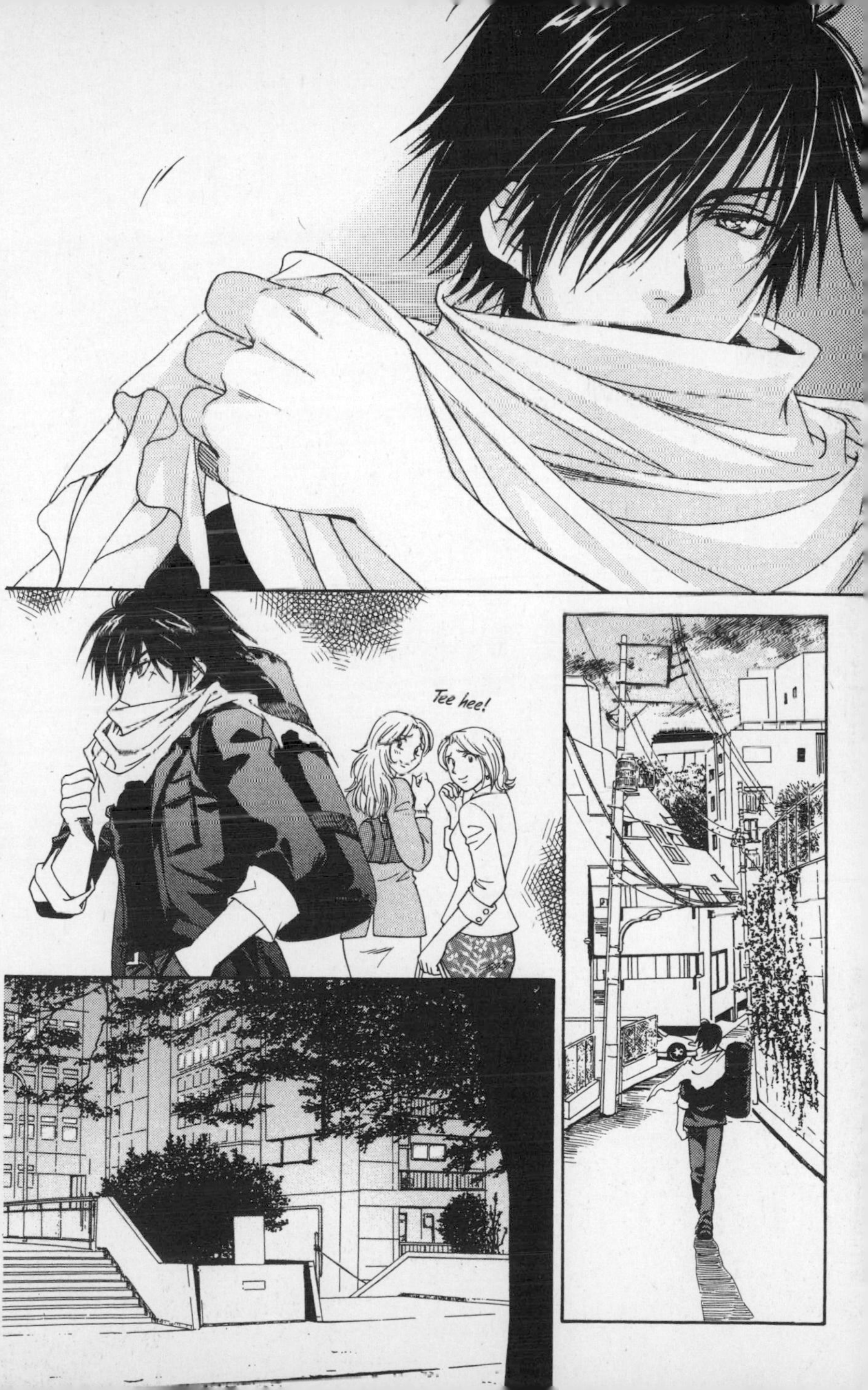
Tee hee!

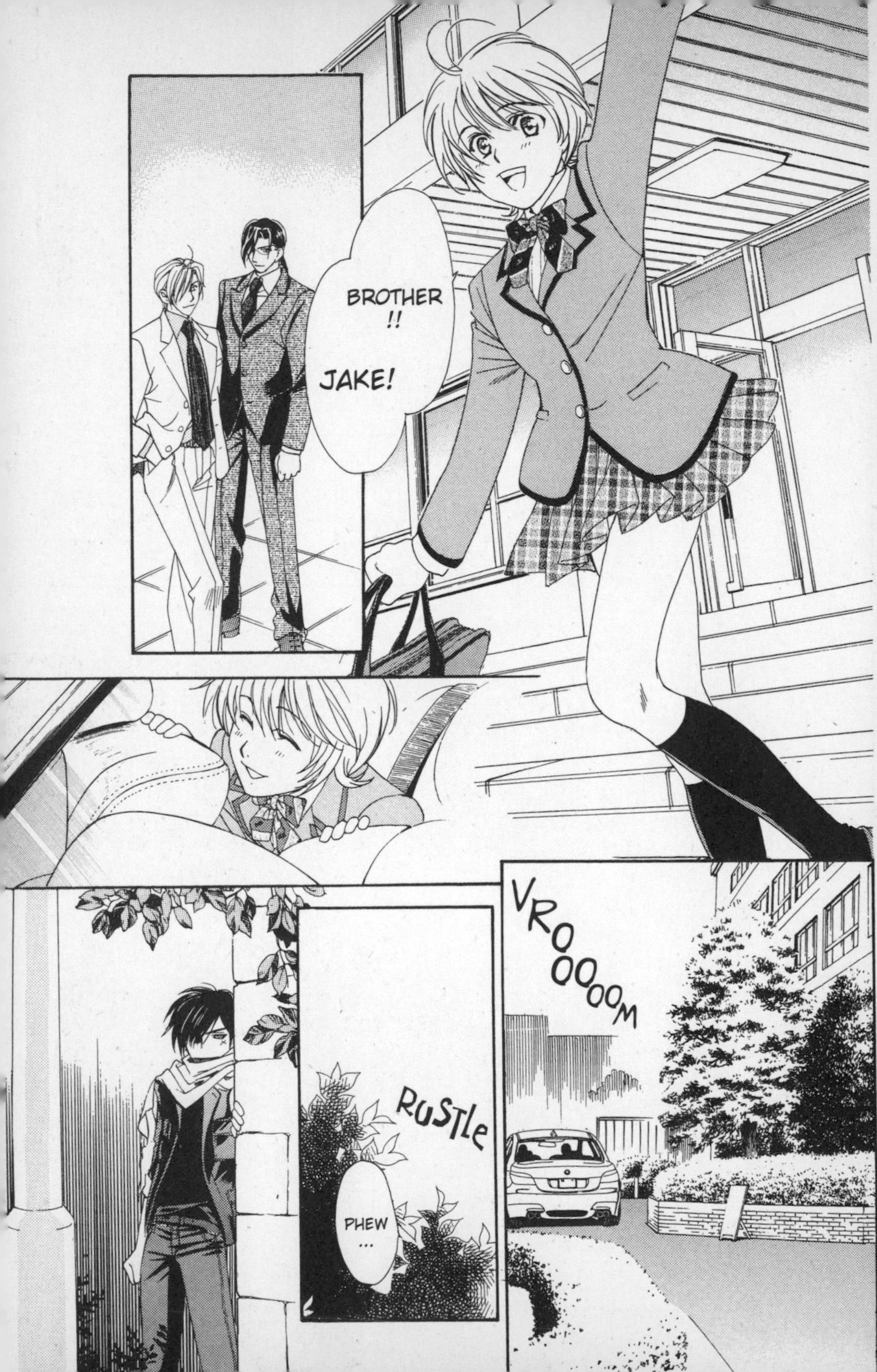
BROTHER !!
JAKE!
VROOOOOM
RUSTLE
PHEW ...

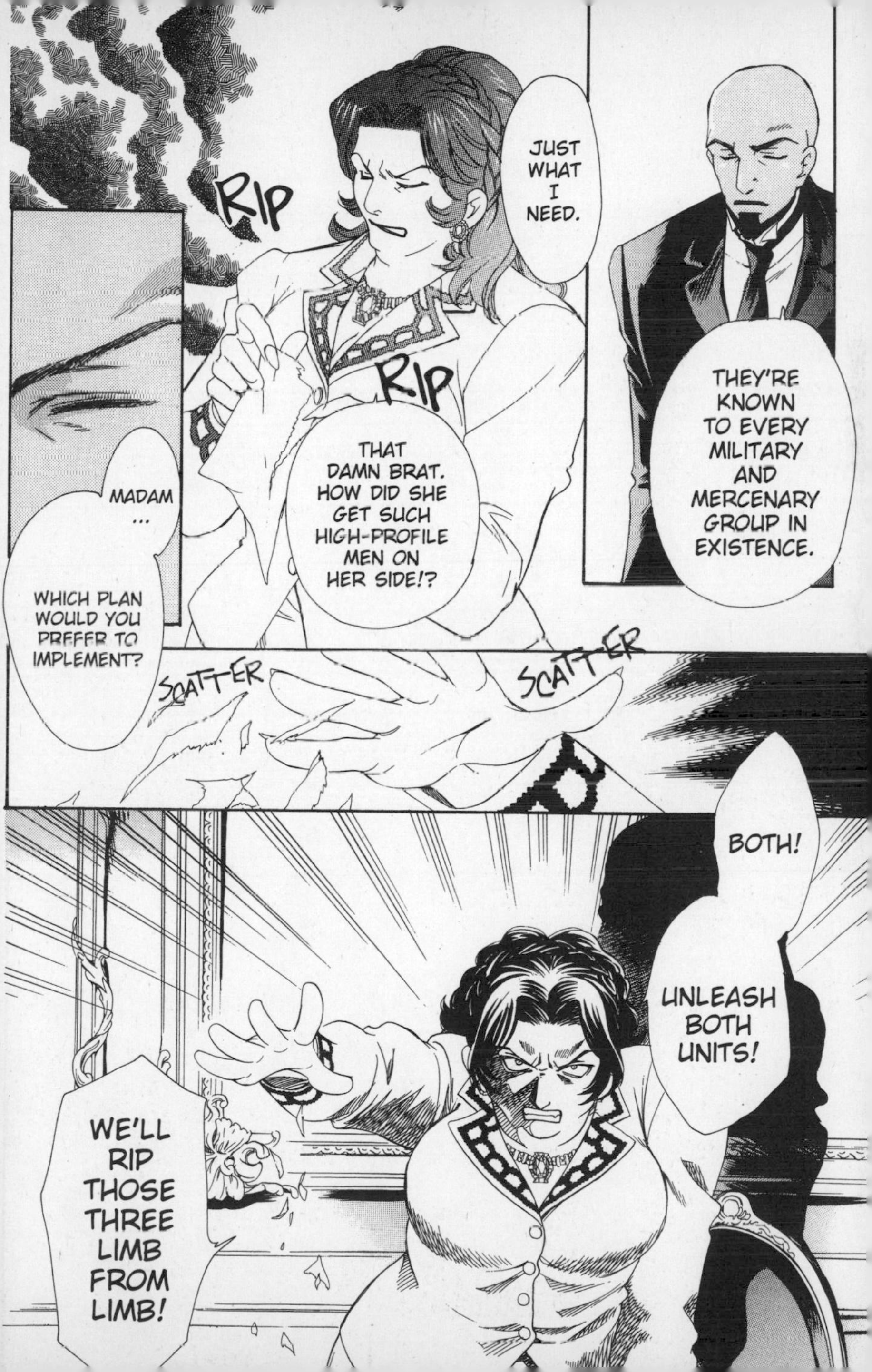
RIP
JUST WHAT I NEED.
RIP
THEY'RE KNOWN TO EVERY MILITARY AND MERCENARY GROUP IN EXISTENCE.
THAT DAMN BRAT. HOW DID SHE GET SUCH HIGH-PROFILE MEN ON HER SIDE!?
MADAM ...
WHICH PLAN WOULD YOU PREFER TO IMPLEMENT?
SCATTER
SCATTER
BOTH!
UNLEASH BOTH UNITS!
WE'LL RIP THOSE THREE LIMB FROM LIMB!

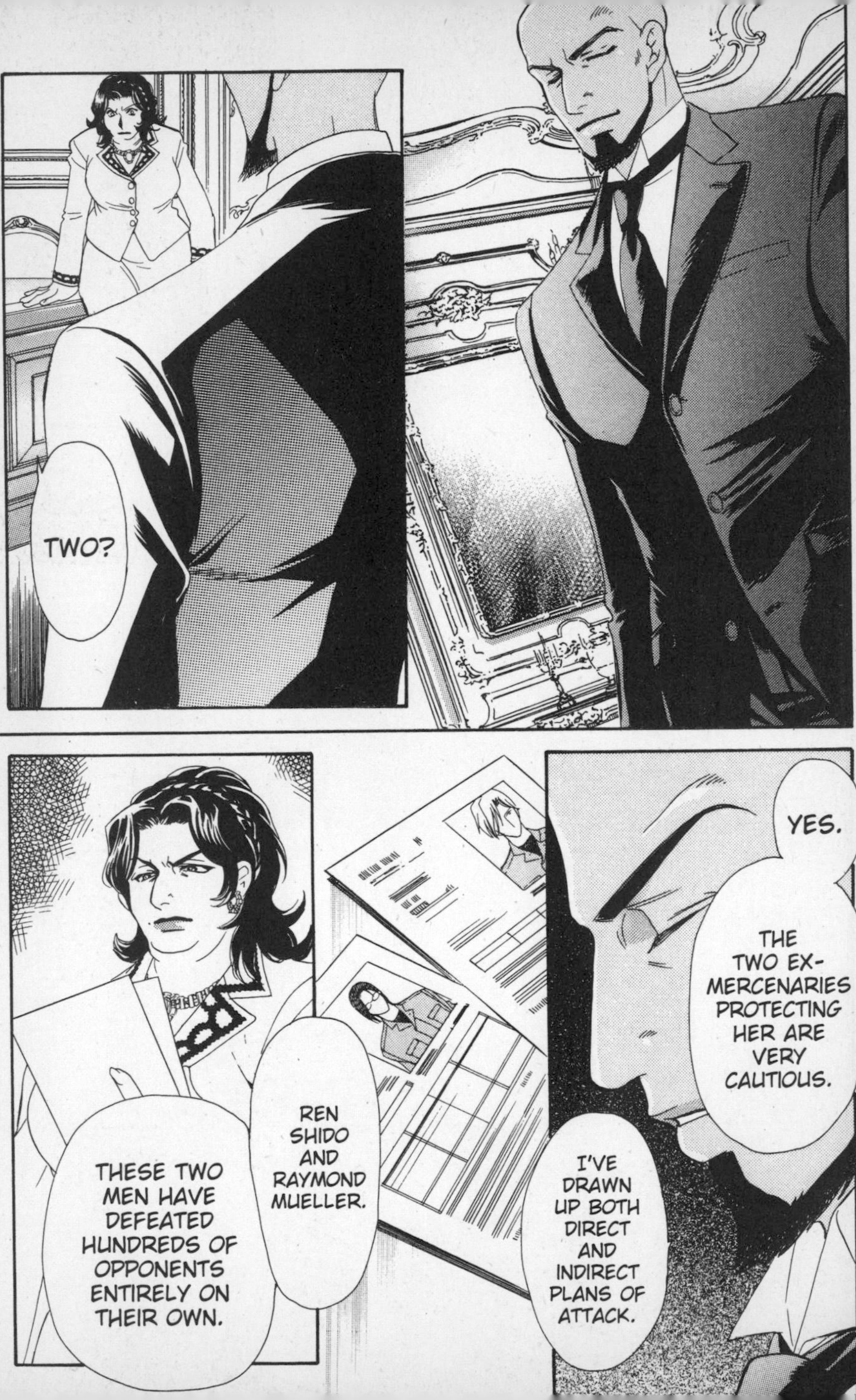
TWO?
YES.
THE TWO EX-MERCENARIES PROTECTING HER ARE VERY CAUTIOUS.
I'VE DRAWN UP BOTH DIRECT AND INDIRECT PLANS OF ATTACK.
REN SHIDO AND RAYMOND MUELLER.
THESE TWO MEN HAVE DEFEATED HUNDREDS OF OPPONENTS ENTIRELY ON THEIR OWN.

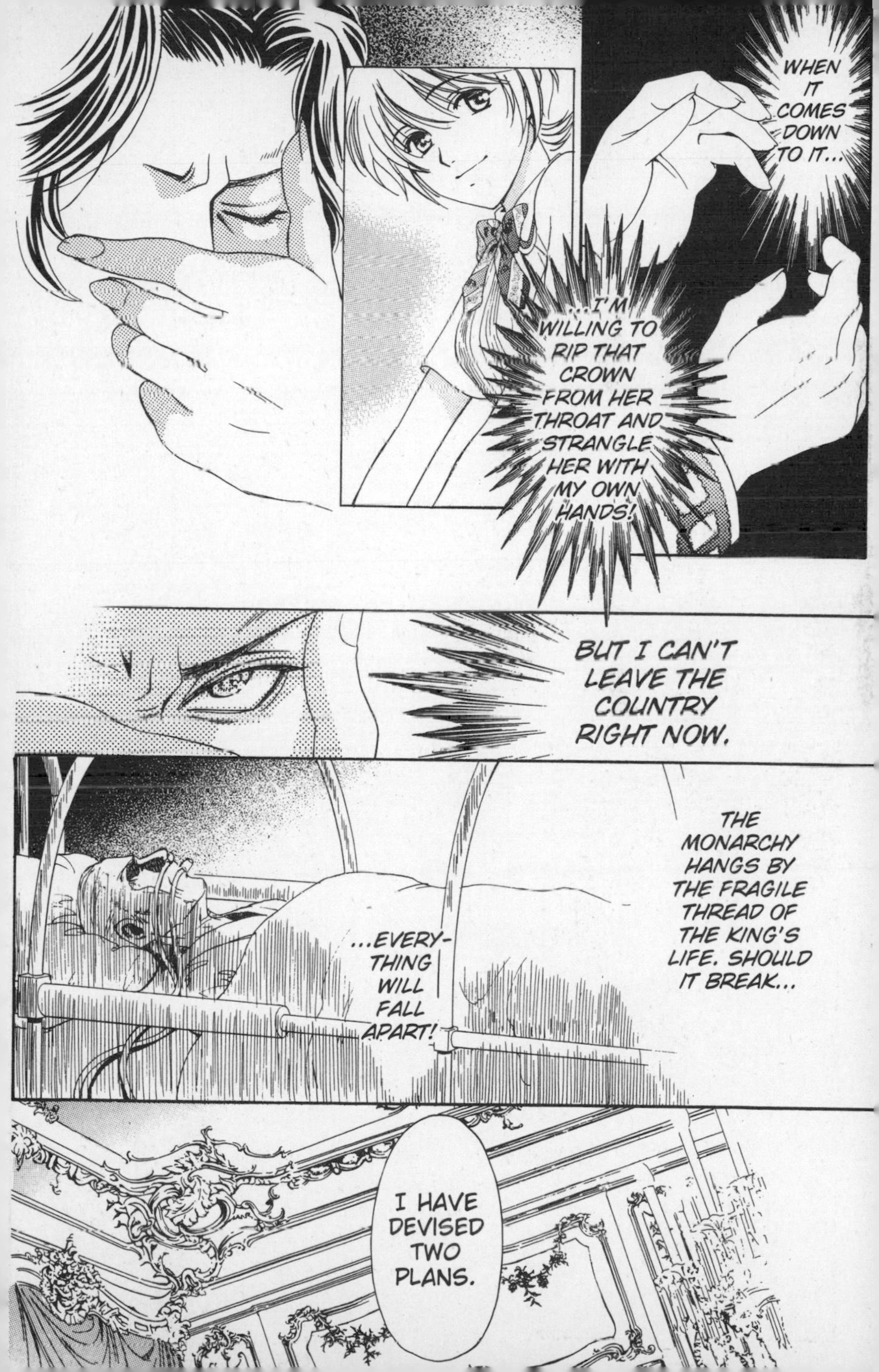

WHEN IT COMES DOWN TO IT...
...I'M WILLING TO RIP THAT CROWN FROM HER THROAT AND STRANGLE HER WITH MY OWN HANDS!
BUT I CAN'T LEAVE THE COUNTRY RIGHT NOW.
THE MONARCHY HANGS BY THE FRAGILE THREAD OF THE KING'S LIFE. SHOULD IT BREAK...
...EVERY-THING WILL FALL APART!
I HAVE DEVISED TWO PLANS.

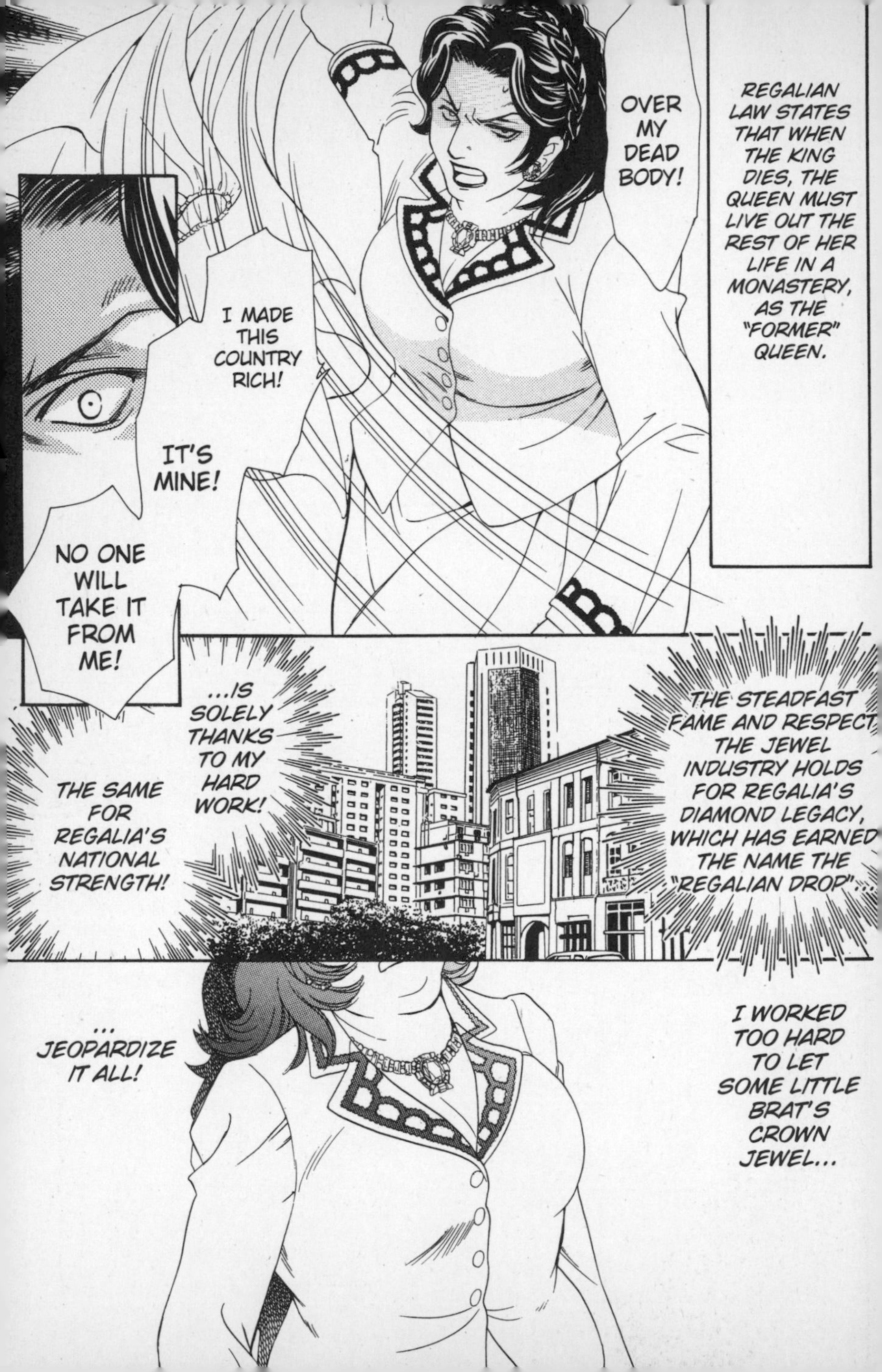
REGALIAN LAW STATES THAT WHEN THE KING DIES, THE QUEEN MUST LIVE OUT THE REST OF HER LIFE IN A MONASTERY, AS THE "FORMER" QUEEN.
OVER MY DEAD BODY!
I MADE THIS COUNTRY RICH!
IT'S MINE!
NO ONE WILL TAKE IT FROM ME!
THE STEADFAST FAME AND RESPECT THE JEWEL INDUSTRY HOLDS FOR REGALIA'S DIAMOND LEGACY, WHICH HAS EARNED THE NAME THE "REGALIAN DROP"...
...IS SOLELY THANKS TO MY HARD WORK!
THE SAME FOR REGALIA'S NATIONAL STRENGTH!
I WORKED TOO HARD TO LET SOME LITTLE BRAT'S CROWN JEWEL...
...JEOPARDIZE IT ALL!

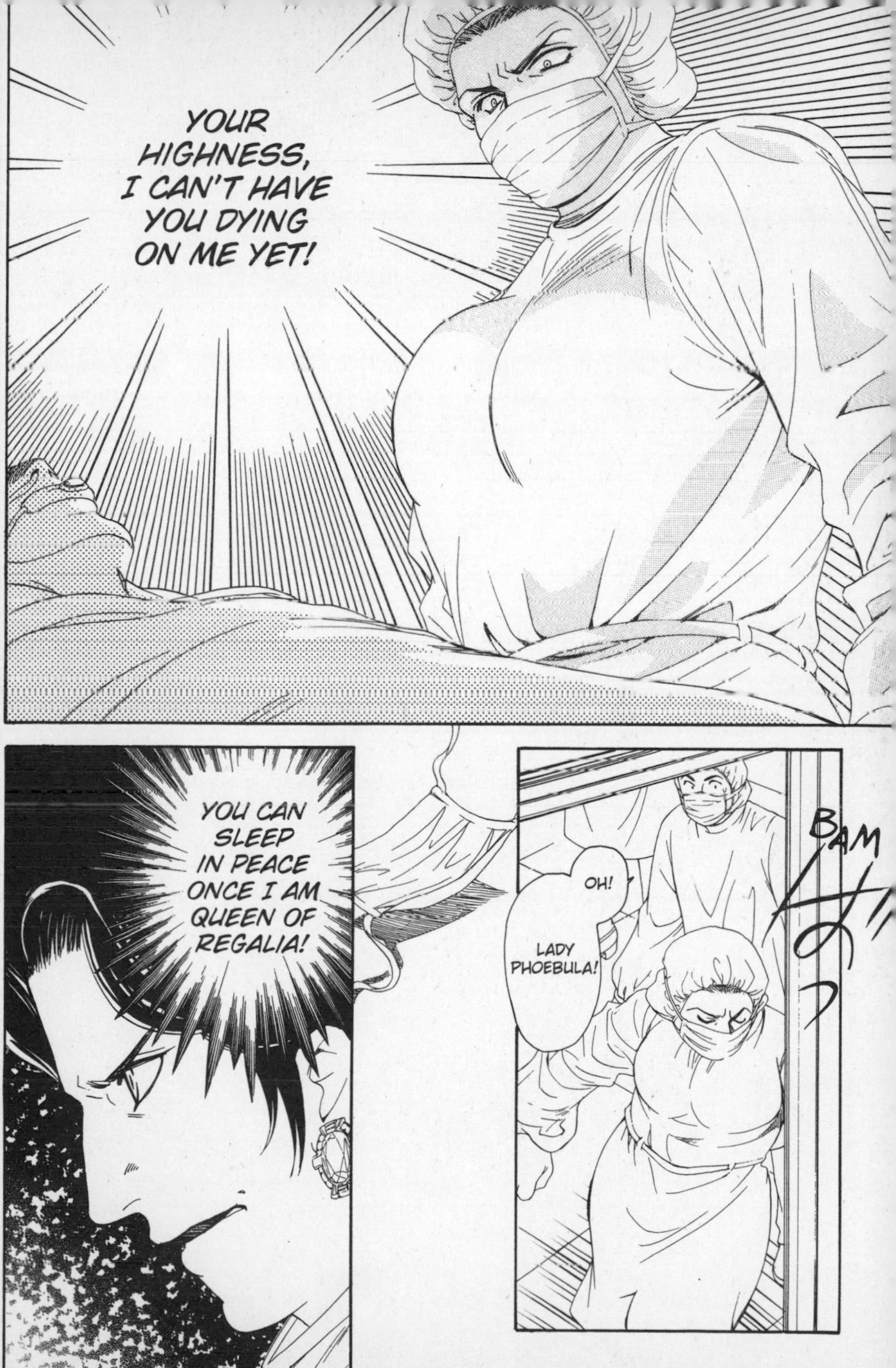
YOUR HIGHNESS, I CAN'T HAVE YOU DYING ON ME YET!
BAM
OH!
LADY PHOEBULA!
YOU CAN SLEEP IN PEACE ONCE I AM QUEEN OF REGALIA!

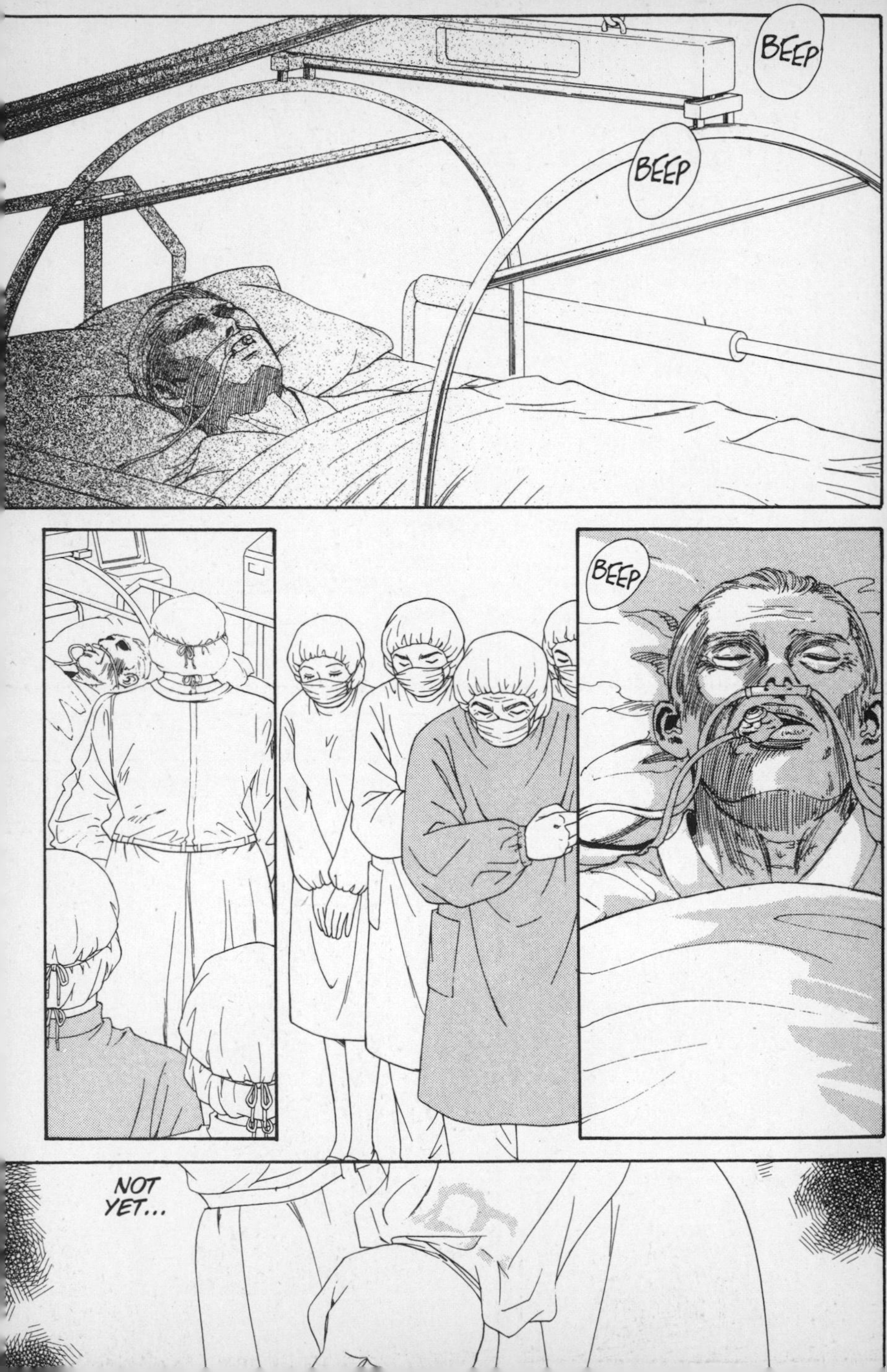
BEEP
BEEP
BEEP
NOT YET...

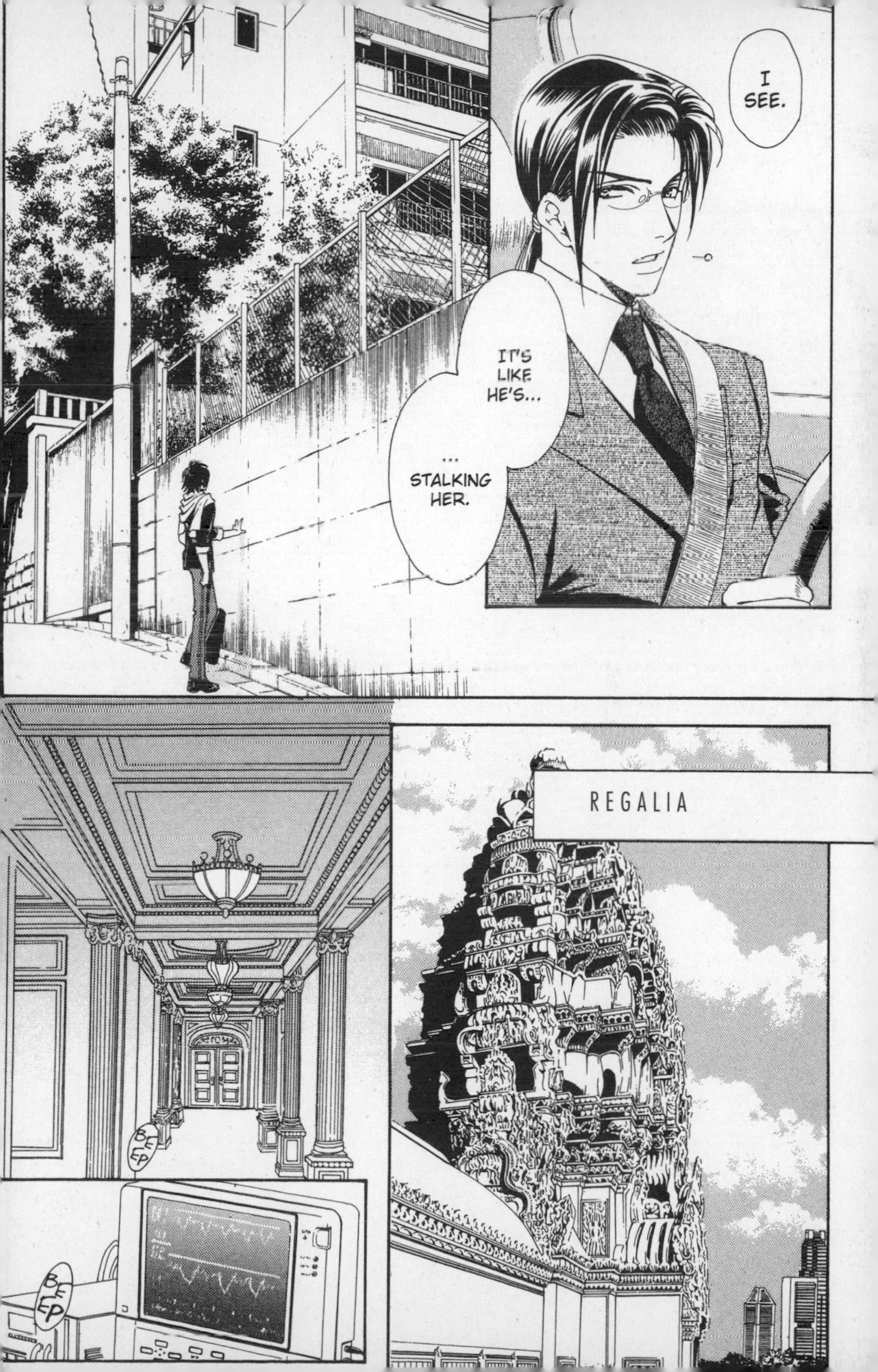
I SEE.
IT'S LIKE HE'S...
...STALKING HER.
REGALIA
BEEP
BEEP

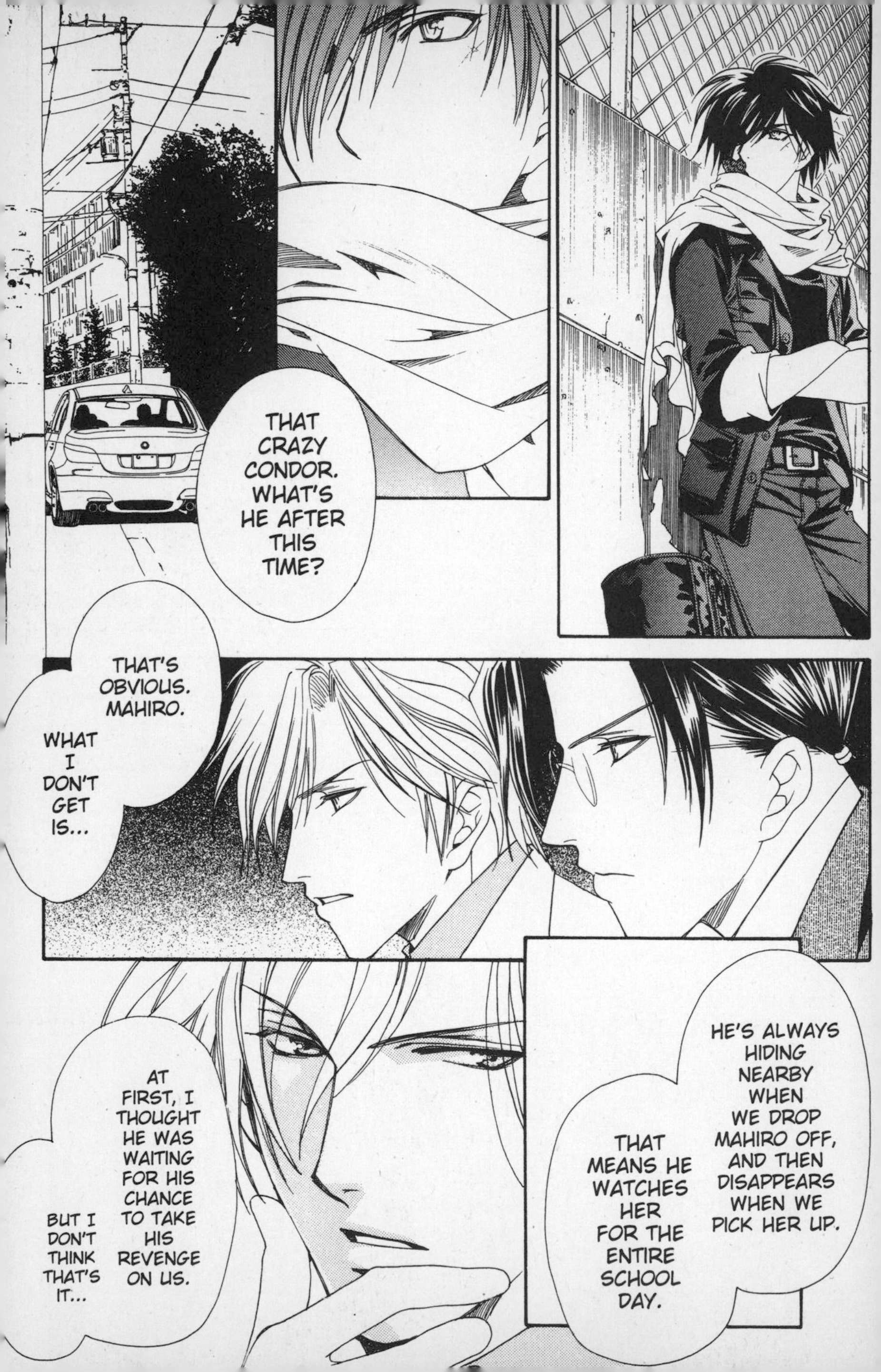
THAT CRAZY CONDOR. WHAT'S HE AFTER THIS TIME?
THAT'S OBVIOUS. MAHIRO.
WHAT I DON'T GET IS...
HE'S ALWAYS HIDING NEARBY WHEN WE DROP MAHIRO OFF, AND THEN DISAPPEARS WHEN WE PICK HER UP.
THAT MEANS HE WATCHES HER FOR THE ENTIRE SCHOOL DAY.
AT FIRST, I THOUGHT HE WAS WAITING FOR HIS CHANCE TO TAKE HIS REVENGE ON US.
BUT I DON'T THINK THAT'S IT...

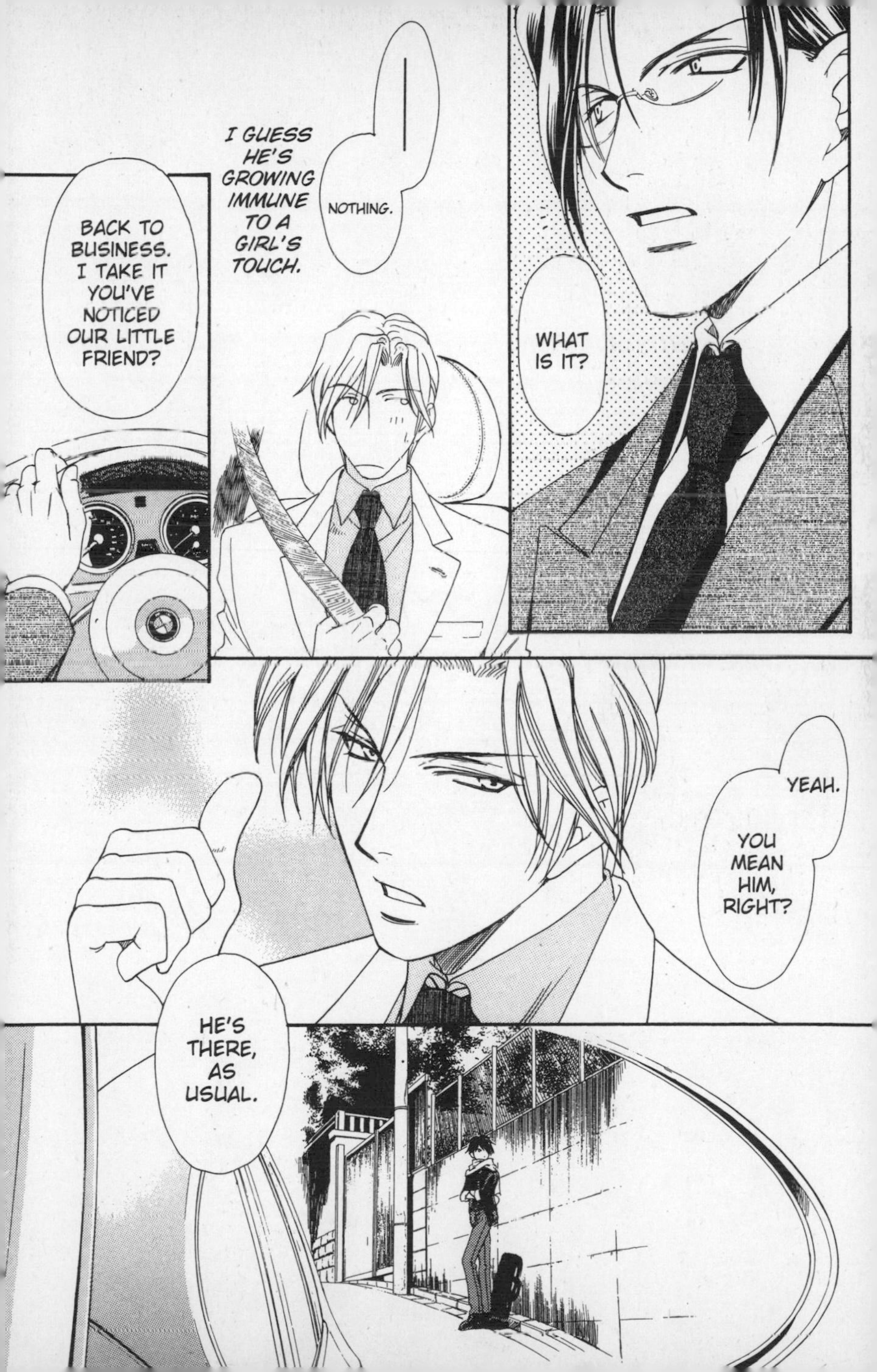
WHAT IS IT?
NOTHING.
I GUESS HE'S GROWING IMMUNE TO A GIRL'S TOUCH.
BACK TO BUSINESS. I TAKE IT YOU'VE NOTICED OUR LITTLE FRIEND?
YEAH.
YOU MEAN HIM, RIGHT?
HE'S THERE, AS USUAL.

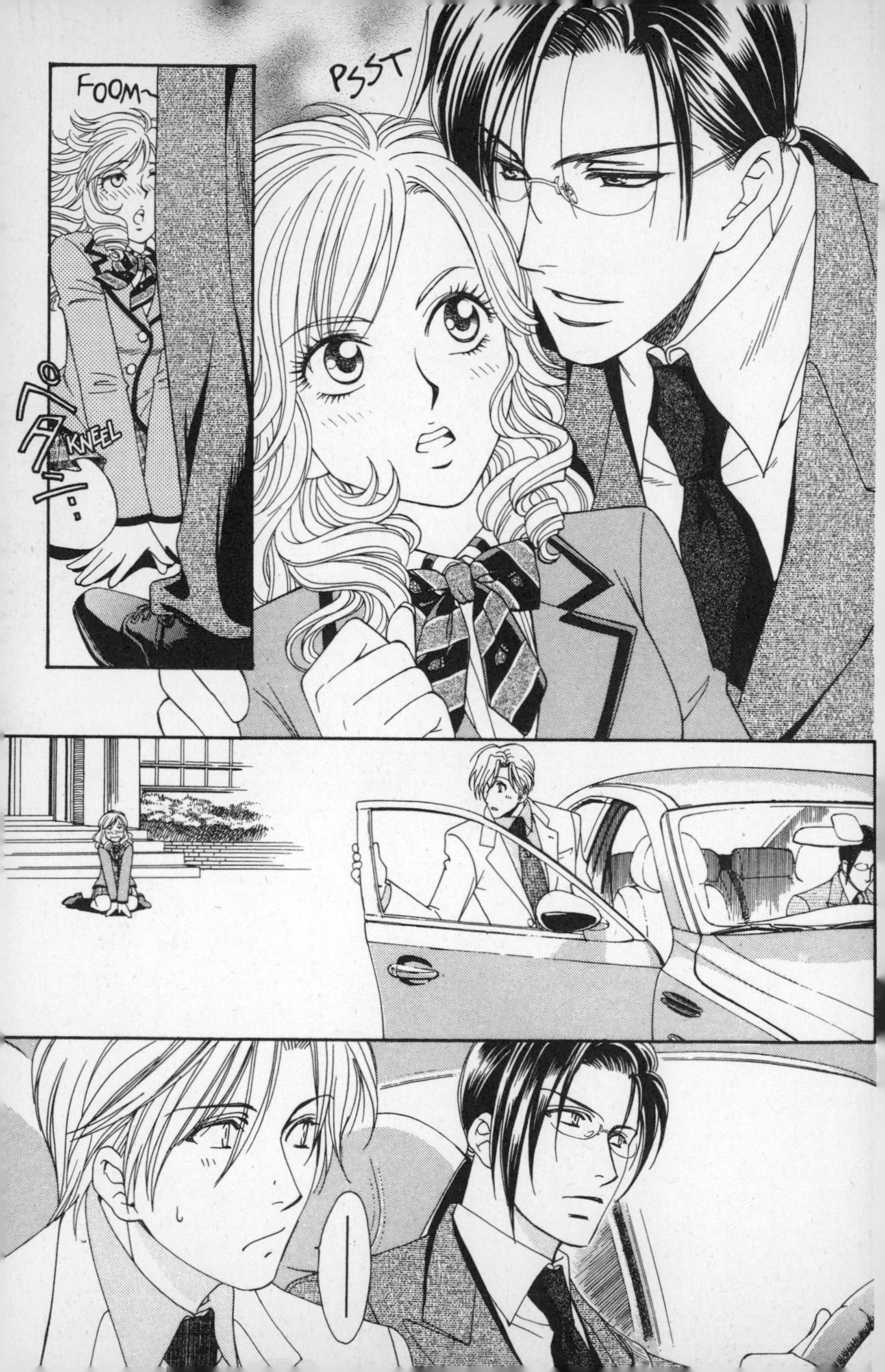
PSST
FOOM~
KNEEL

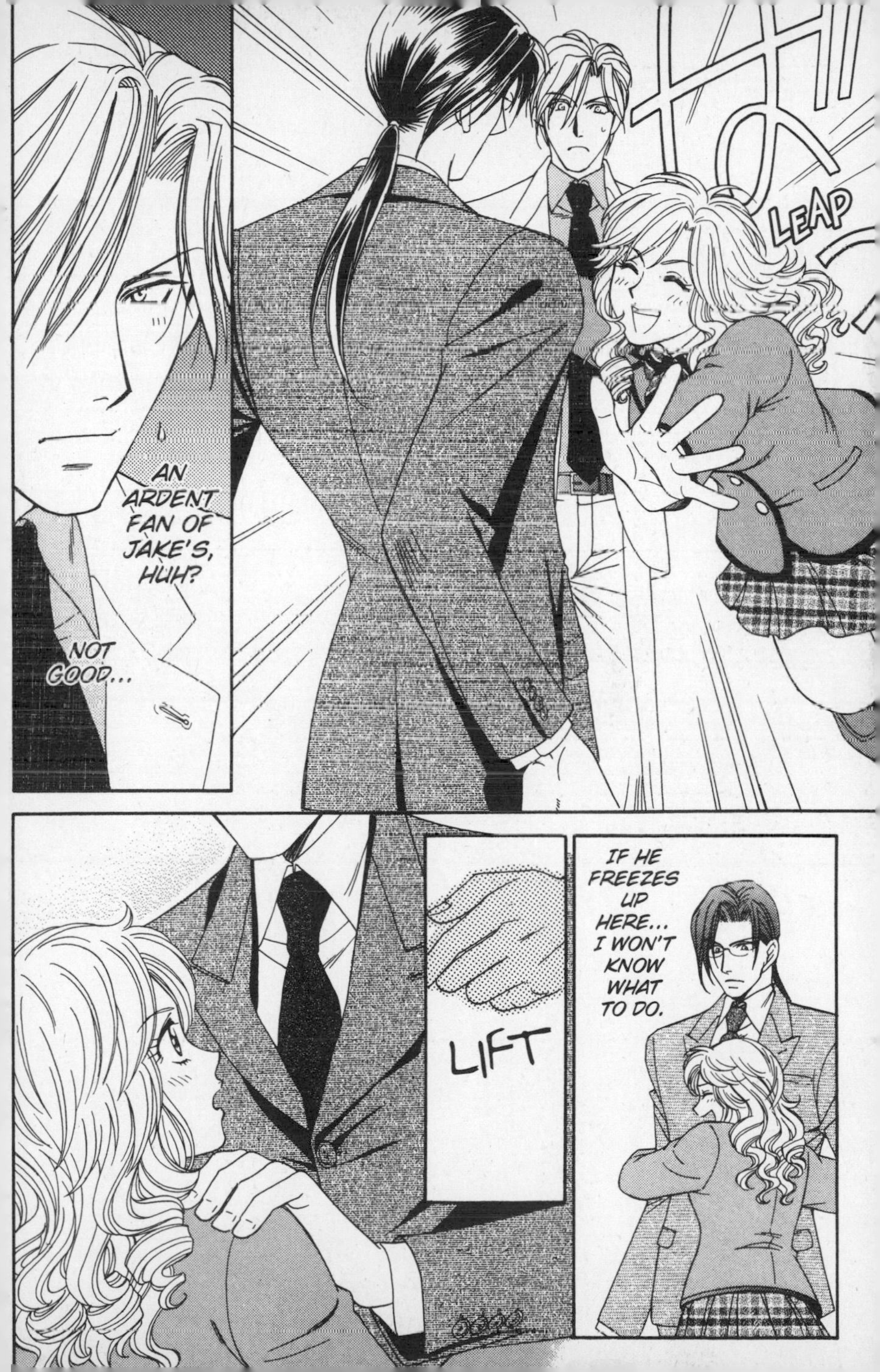
LEAP
AN ARDENT FAN OF JAKE'S, HUH?
NOT GOOD...
IF HE FREEZES UP HERE... I WON'T KNOW WHAT TO DO.
LIFT

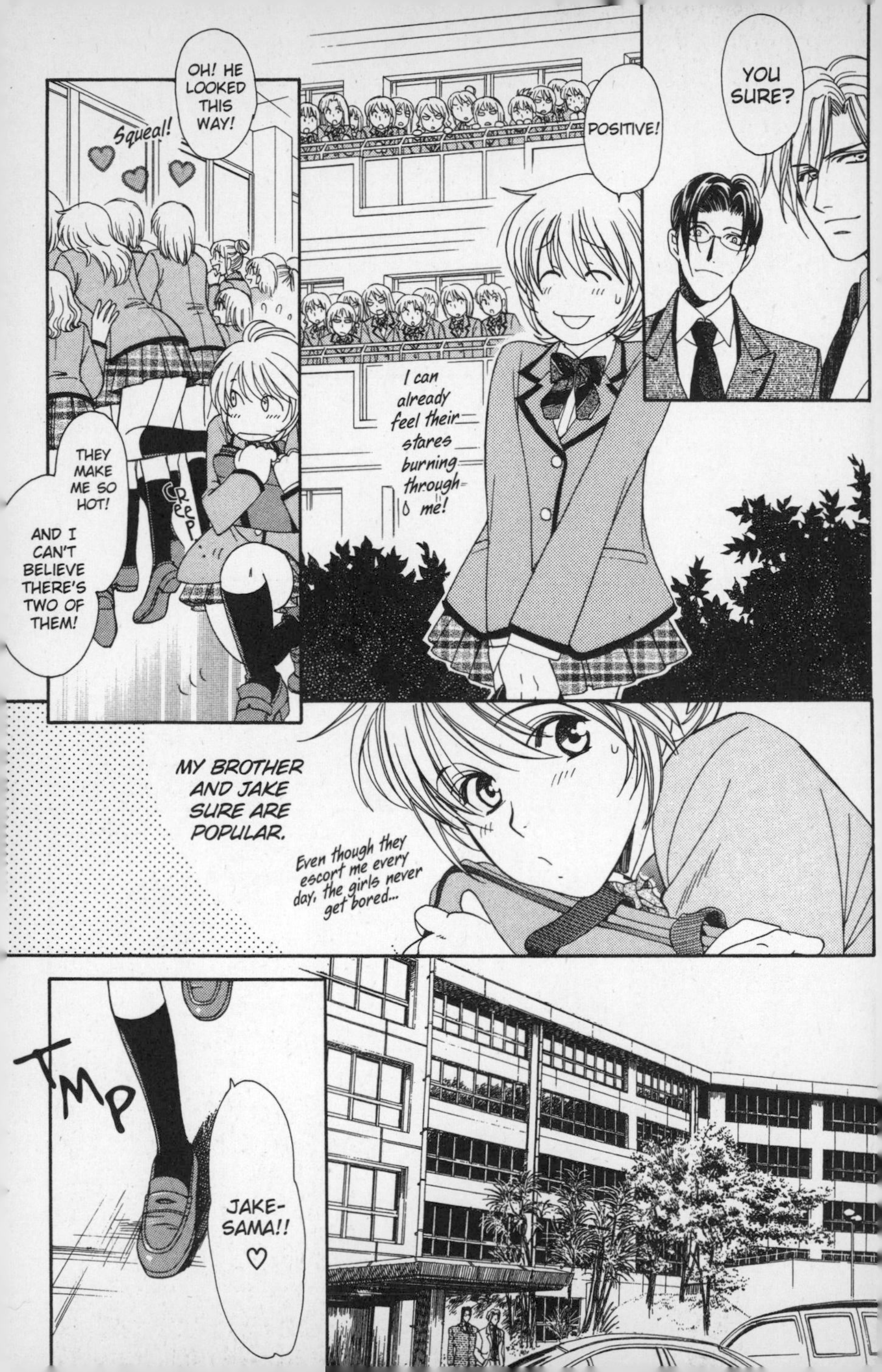
YOU SURE?
POSITIVE!
OH! HE LOOKED THIS WAY!
Squeal!
I can already feel their stares burning through me!
THEY MAKE ME SO HOT!
AND I CAN'T BELIEVE THERE'S TWO OF THEM!
CREEP
MY BROTHER AND JAKE SURE ARE POPULAR.
Even though they escort me every day, the girls never get bored...
TMP
JAKE-SAMA!! ♡

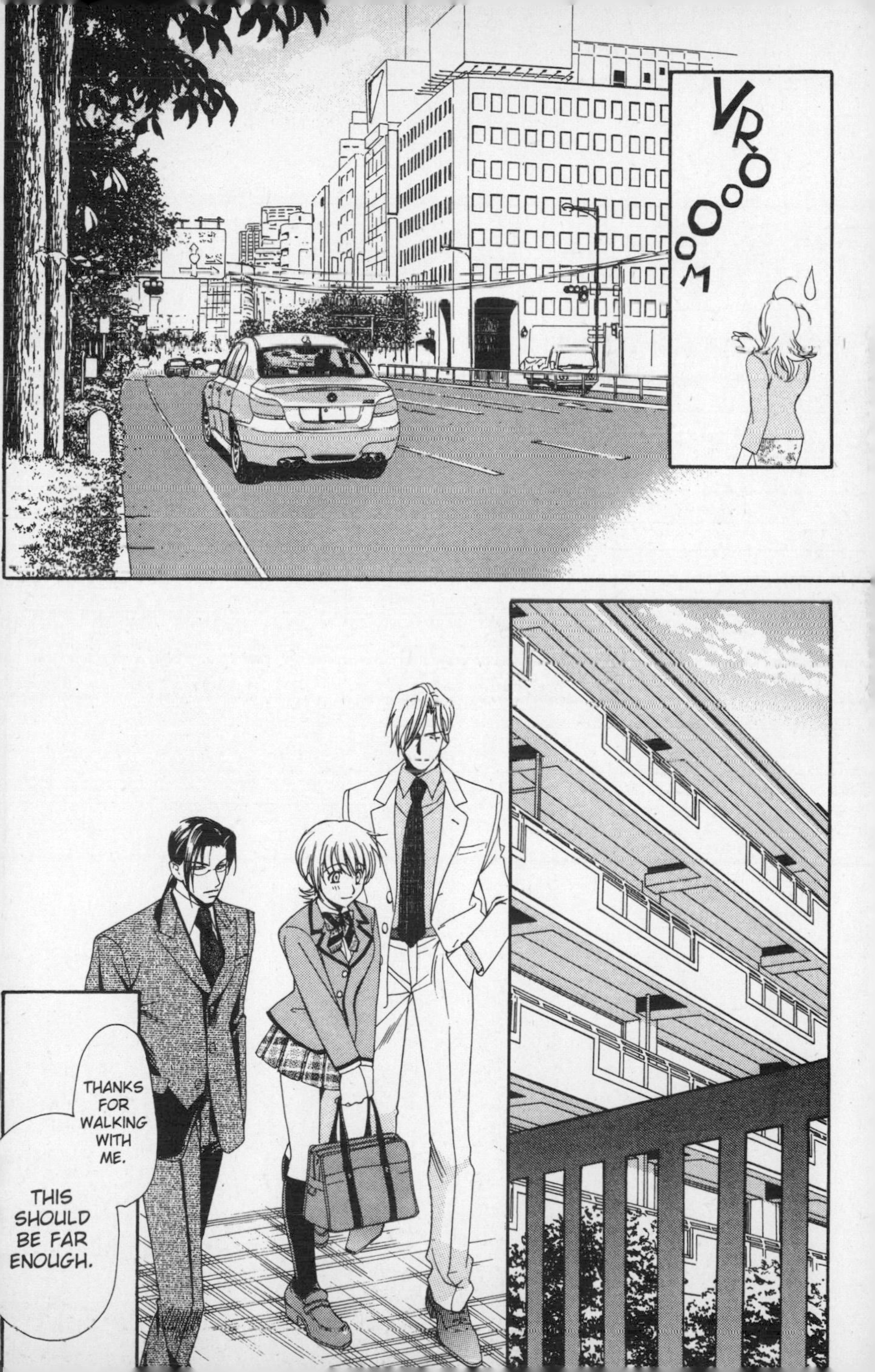
VROOOOOM
THANKS FOR WALKING WITH ME.
THIS SHOULD BE FAR ENOUGH.

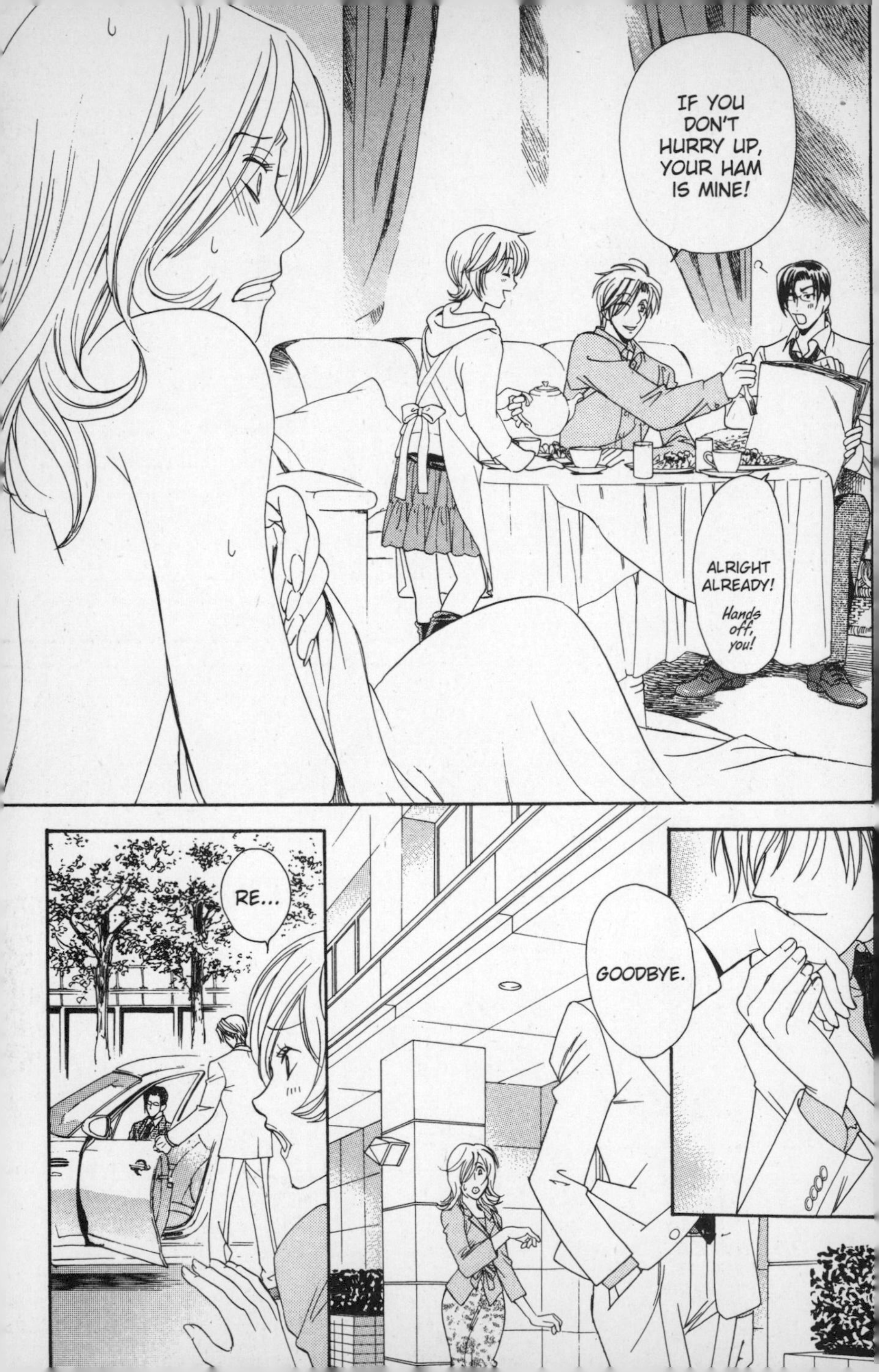
IF YOU DON'T HURRY UP, YOUR HAM IS MINE!
ALRIGHT ALREADY!
Hands off, you!
GOODBYE.
RE...

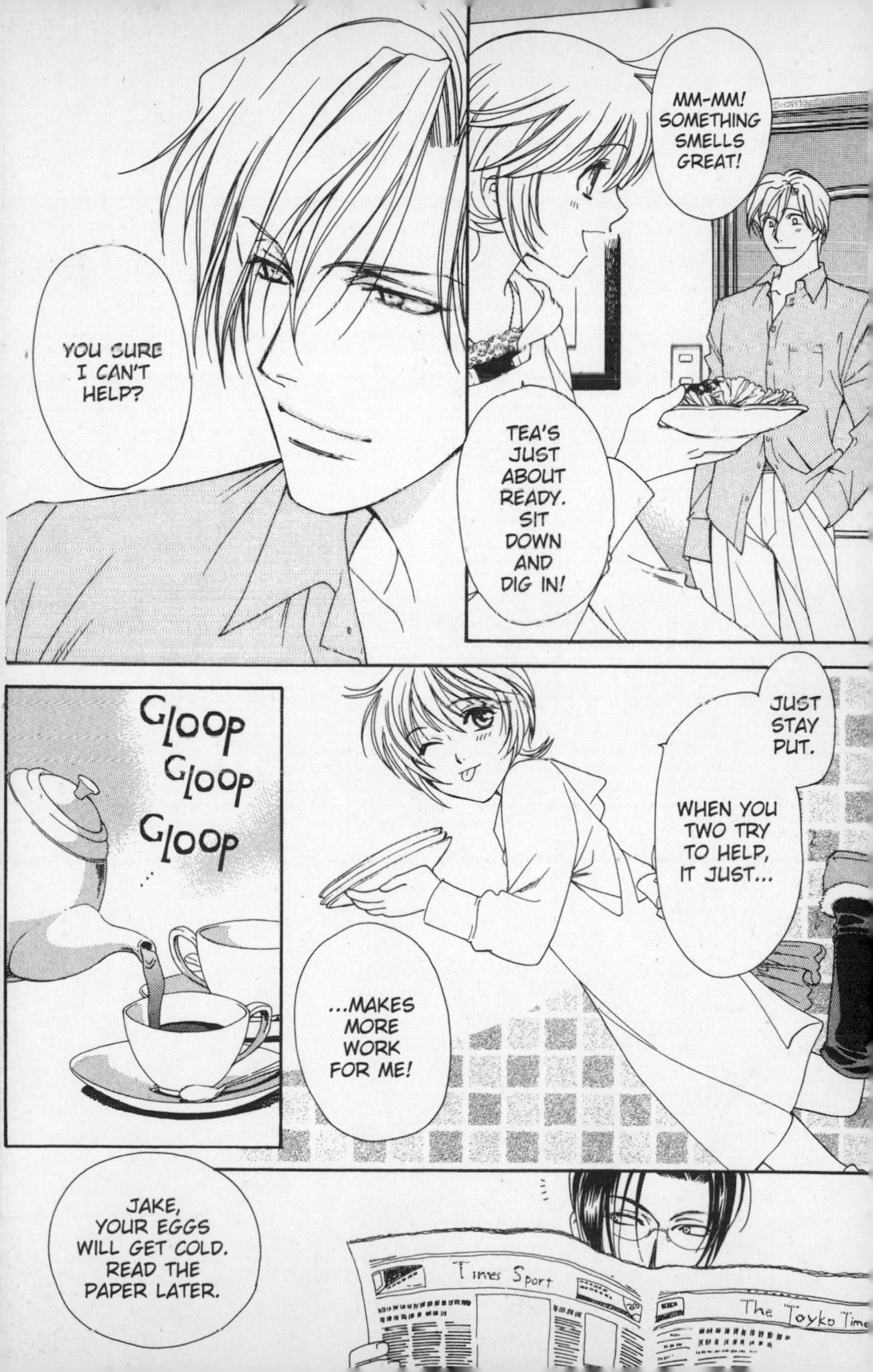
MM-MM! SOMETHING SMELLS GREAT!
YOU SURE I CAN'T HELP?
TEA'S JUST ABOUT READY. SIT DOWN AND DIG IN!
JUST STAY PUT.
WHEN YOU TWO TRY TO HELP, IT JUST...
GLOOP GLOOP GLOOP
...MAKES MORE WORK FOR ME!
JAKE, YOUR EGGS WILL GET COLD. READ THE PAPER LATER.
Times Sport
The Toyko Time

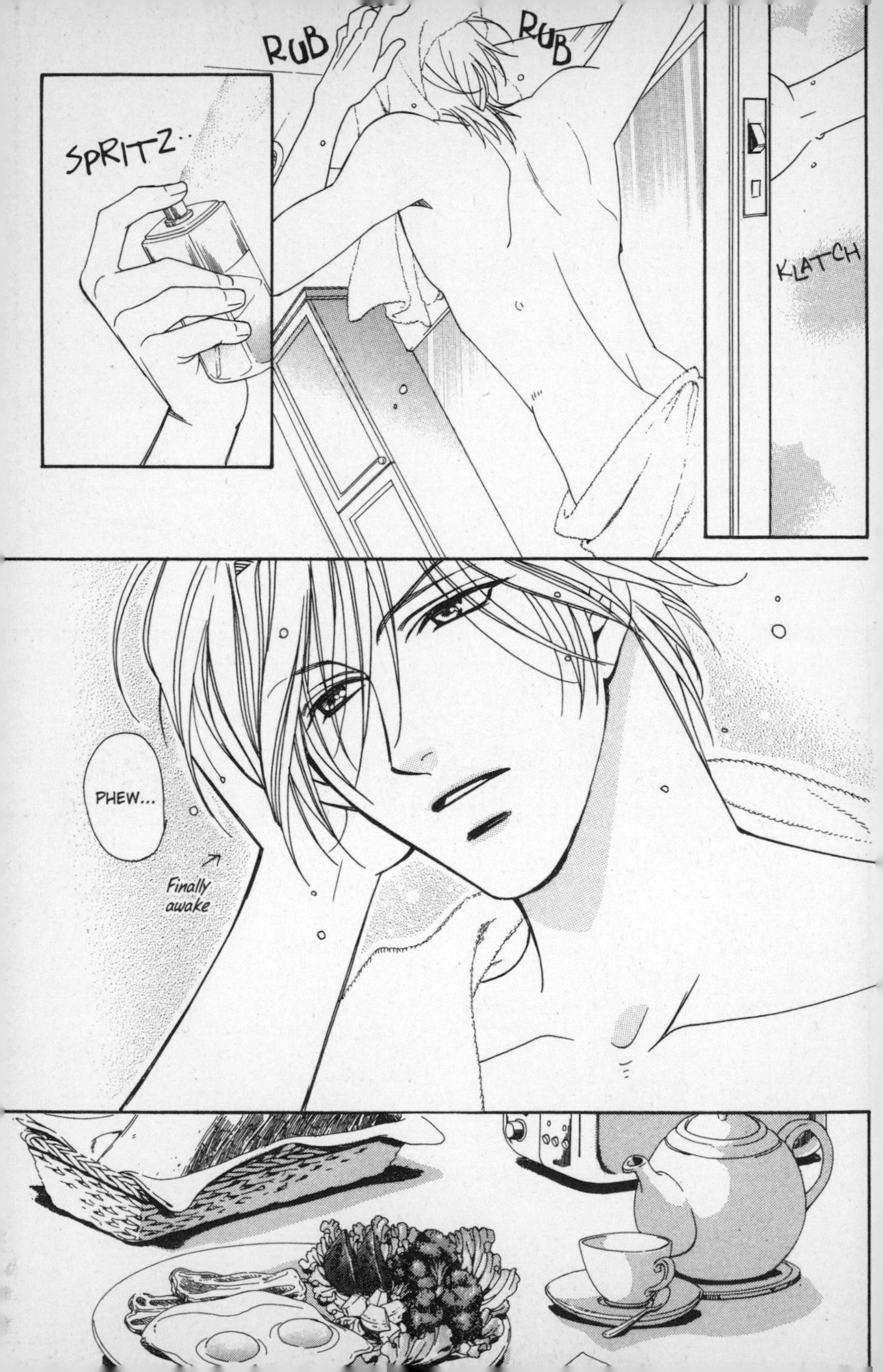
RUB
RUB
SPRITZ...
KLATCH
PHEW...
Finally awake

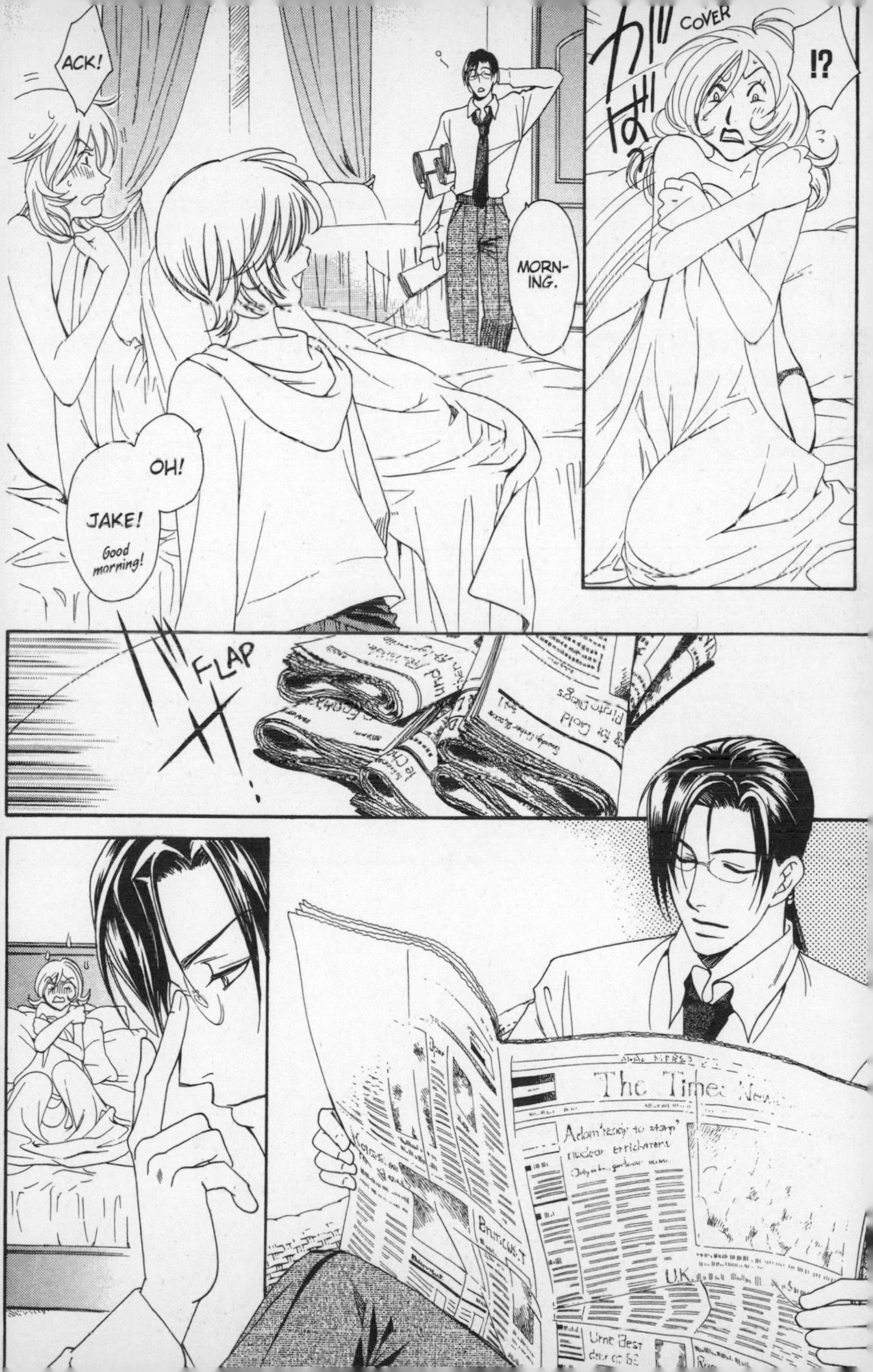

MORNING.
OH!
JAKE!
Good morning!
ACK!
がばっ COVER
!?
FLAP

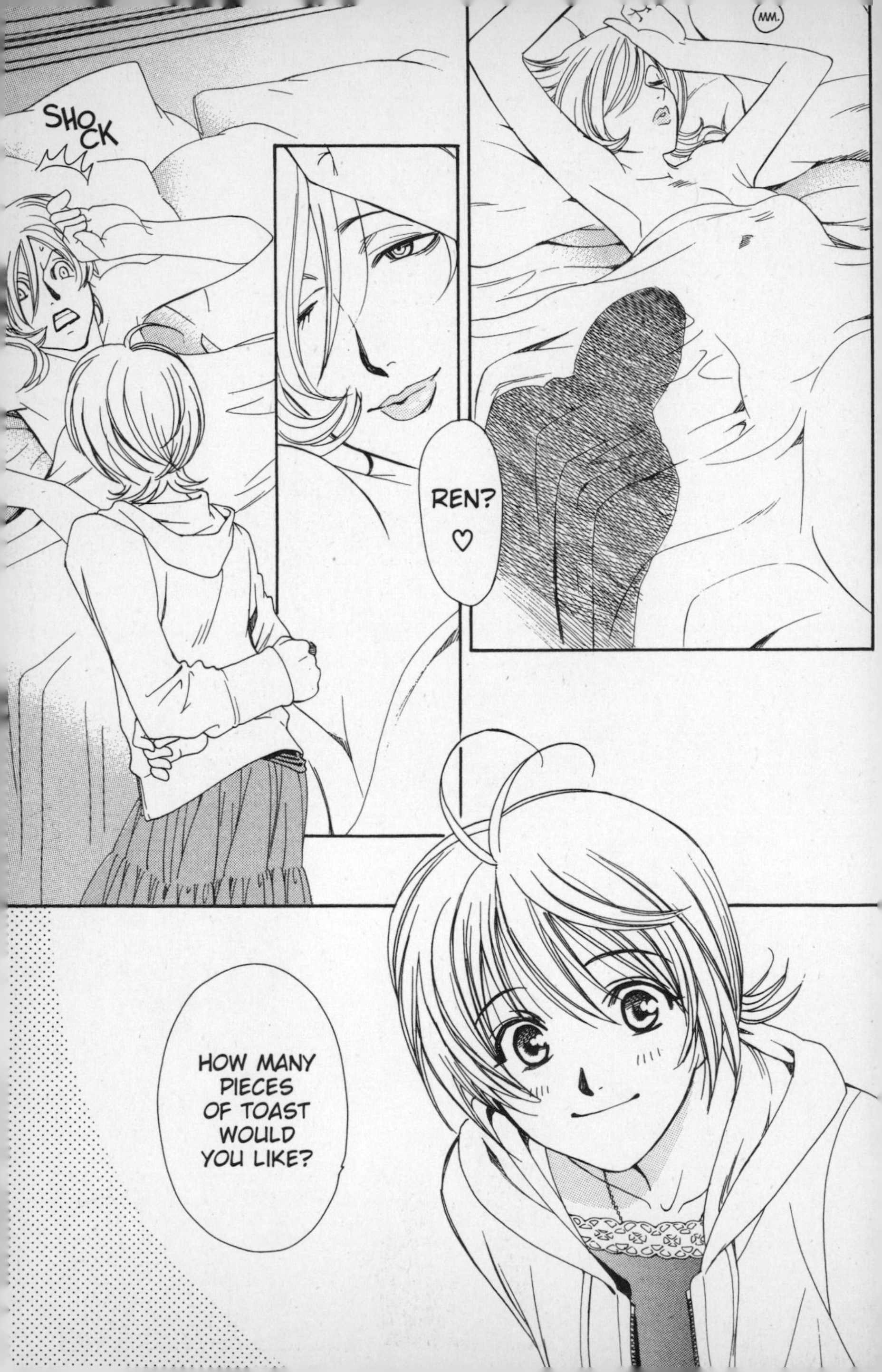
MM.
REN? ♡
SHOCK
HOW MANY PIECES OF TOAST WOULD YOU LIKE?

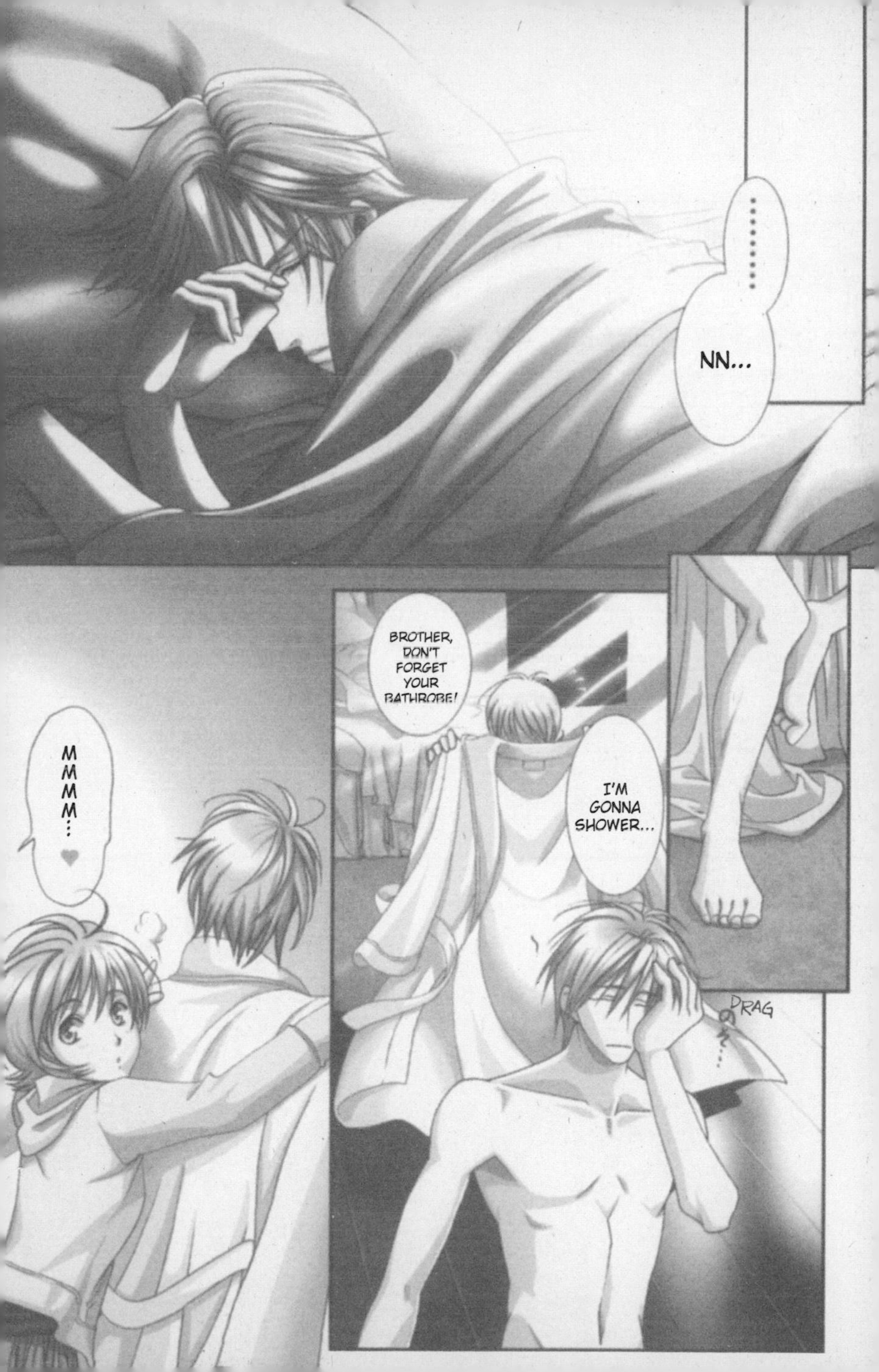

....
NN...
I'M GONNA SHOWER...
BROTHER, DON'T FORGET YOUR BATHROBE!
DRAG
MMMM...♥

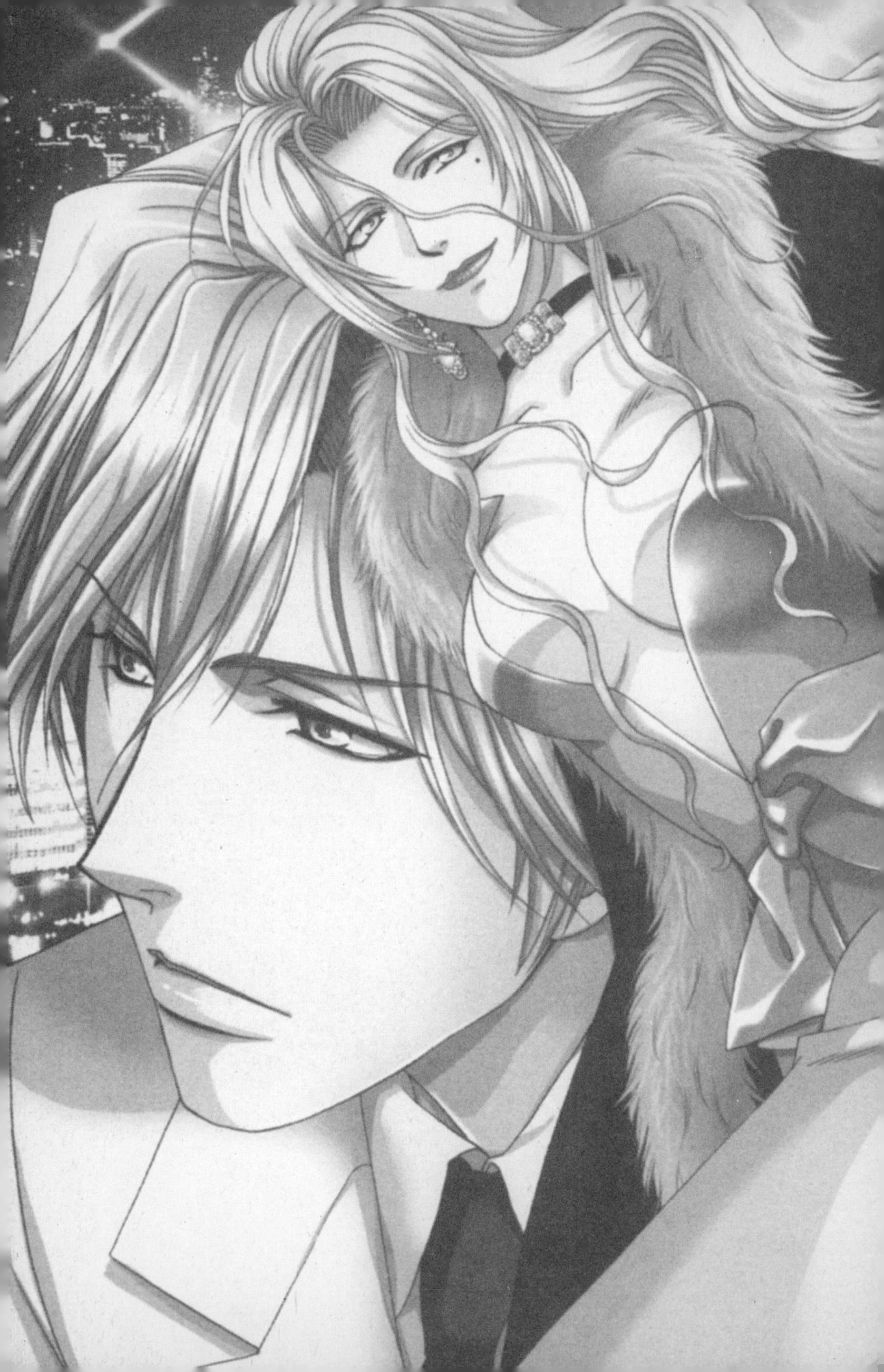

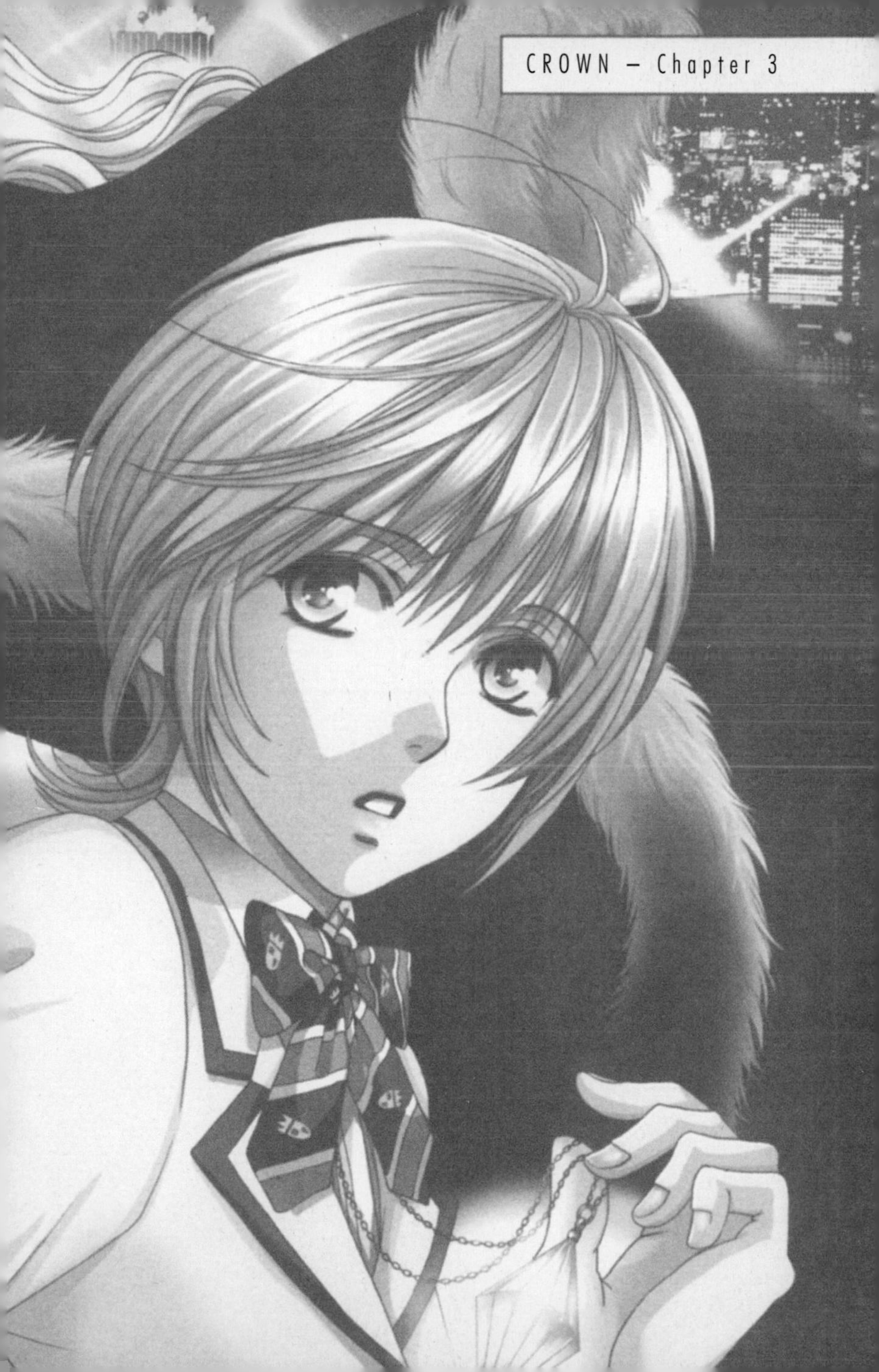
CROWN – Chapter 3

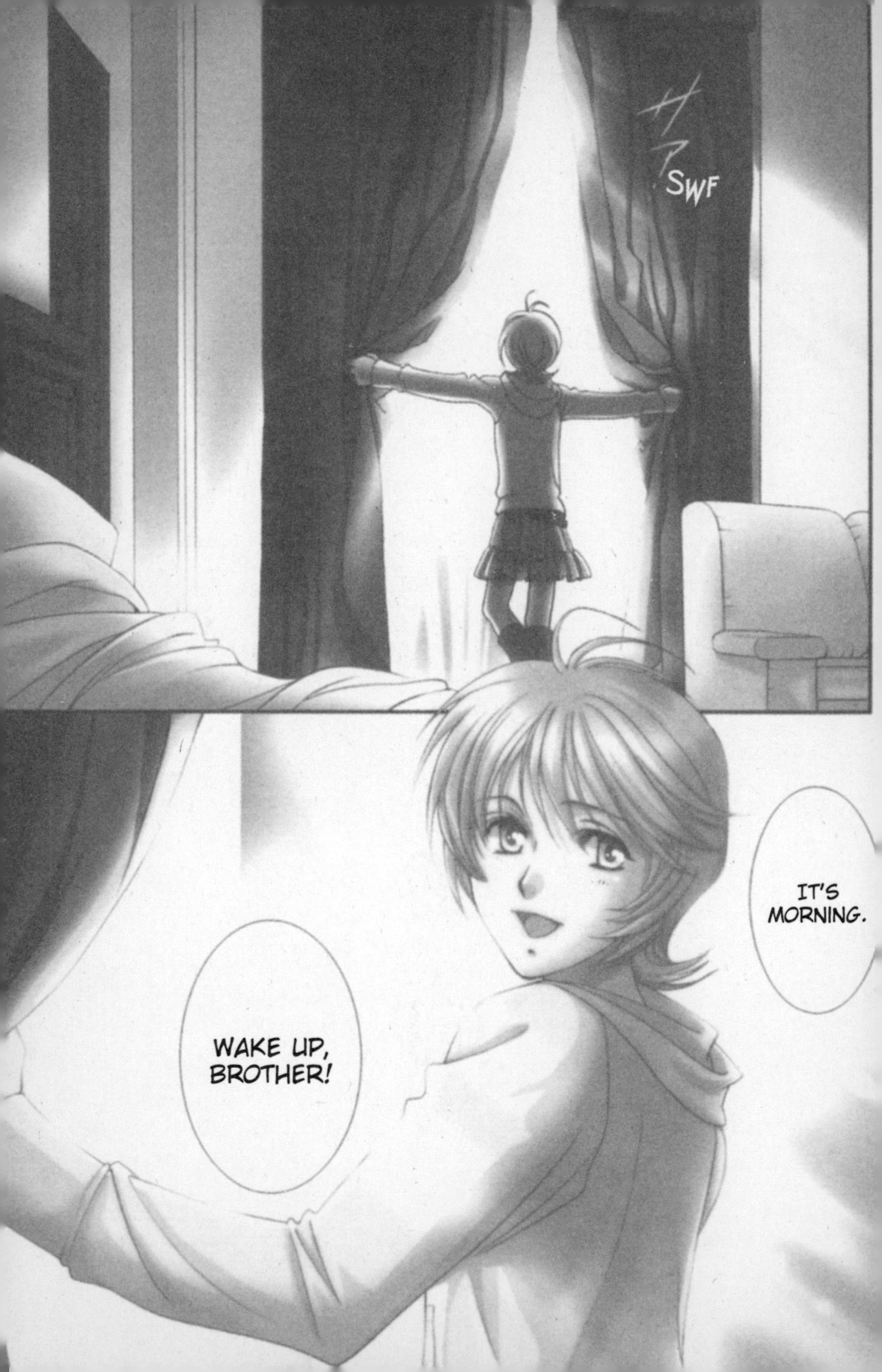
SWF
IT'S MORNING.
WAKE UP, BROTHER!

CONTENTS

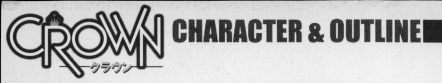

CROWN CHARACTER & OUTLINE

CHARACTER _____ 6

A skilled and dangerous mercenary who has fought Ren and Jake in the past.

● **CHONDRITE (CONDOR) BOURNE**

CHARACTER _____ 4

The unofficial Queen of Regalia. She's after the Crown...and Mahiro's life.

● **PHOEBULA**

KEY ITEM

The mystic jewel passed down through the Regalian royal family. Whoever possesses it is the rightful heir to the throne.

● **THE CROWN**

CHARACTER _____ 5

Phoebula's right-hand man. He masterminds her attack plans.

● **BARZAZ**

▮OUTLINE

Mahiro, a young girl who lost both of her parents, thought she was all alone in the world – until two hot men named Ren and Jake stormed into her life with the news that she was the rightful heir to the small Asian country of Regalia! Ren confessed that he was Mahiro's long-lost older brother and had come to protect her from the false Queen of Regalia, a cruel woman who has vowed to destroy the rightful heir and take her crown. With the country's wealth to play with, the wicked Phoebula has sent everything from the world's best assassins to a vast military force to attack our heroes. Ren and Jake have succeeded in protecting their innocent ward so far – but just how long can they keep it up? And what of Mahiro's budding feelings for Ren, taboo feelings for her brother which she can never confess?

CHARACTER 1

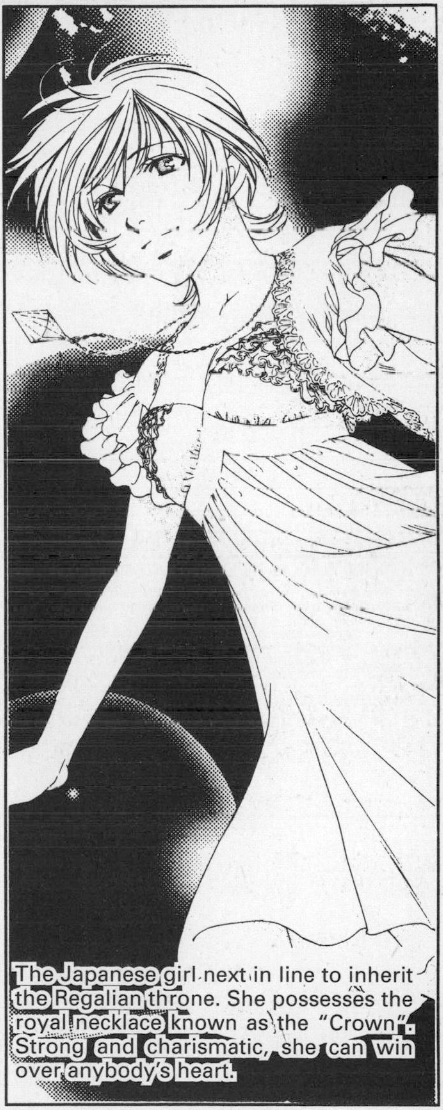
The Japanese girl next in line to inherit the Regalian throne. She possesses the royal necklace known as the "Crown". Strong and charismatic, she can win over anybody's heart.

MAHIRO SHINOMIYA

CHARACTER 2

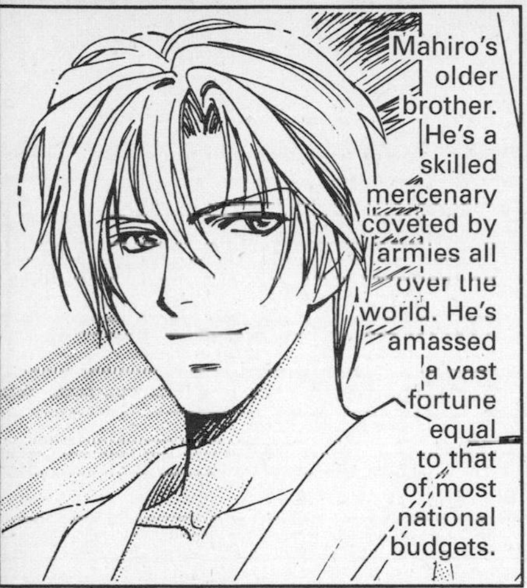
Mahiro's older brother. He's a skilled mercenary coveted by armies all over the world. He's amassed a vast fortune equal to that of most national budgets.

REN SHIDO

CHARACTER 3

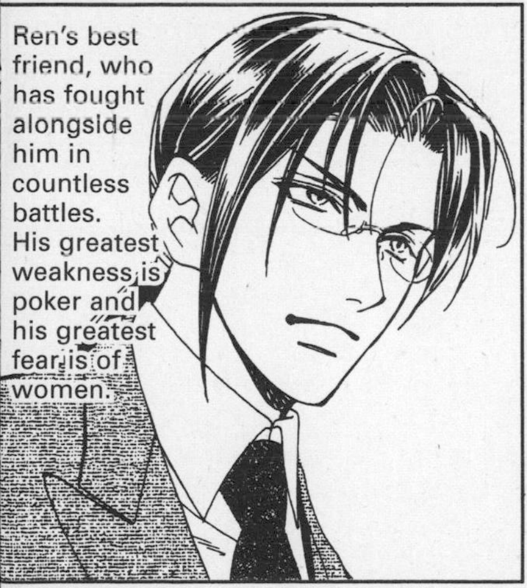
Ren's best friend, who has fought alongside him in countless battles. His greatest weakness is poker and his greatest fear is of women.

RAYMOND (JAKE) MUELLER

CHARACTER & OUTLINE

CROWN

SHINJI WADA   YOU HIGURI

CROWN

2

STORY: SHINJI WADA
ART: YOU HIGURI

PROPERTY OF BUC
VALTON COUNTY PUBL
LIBRARY SYSTEM

go!comi

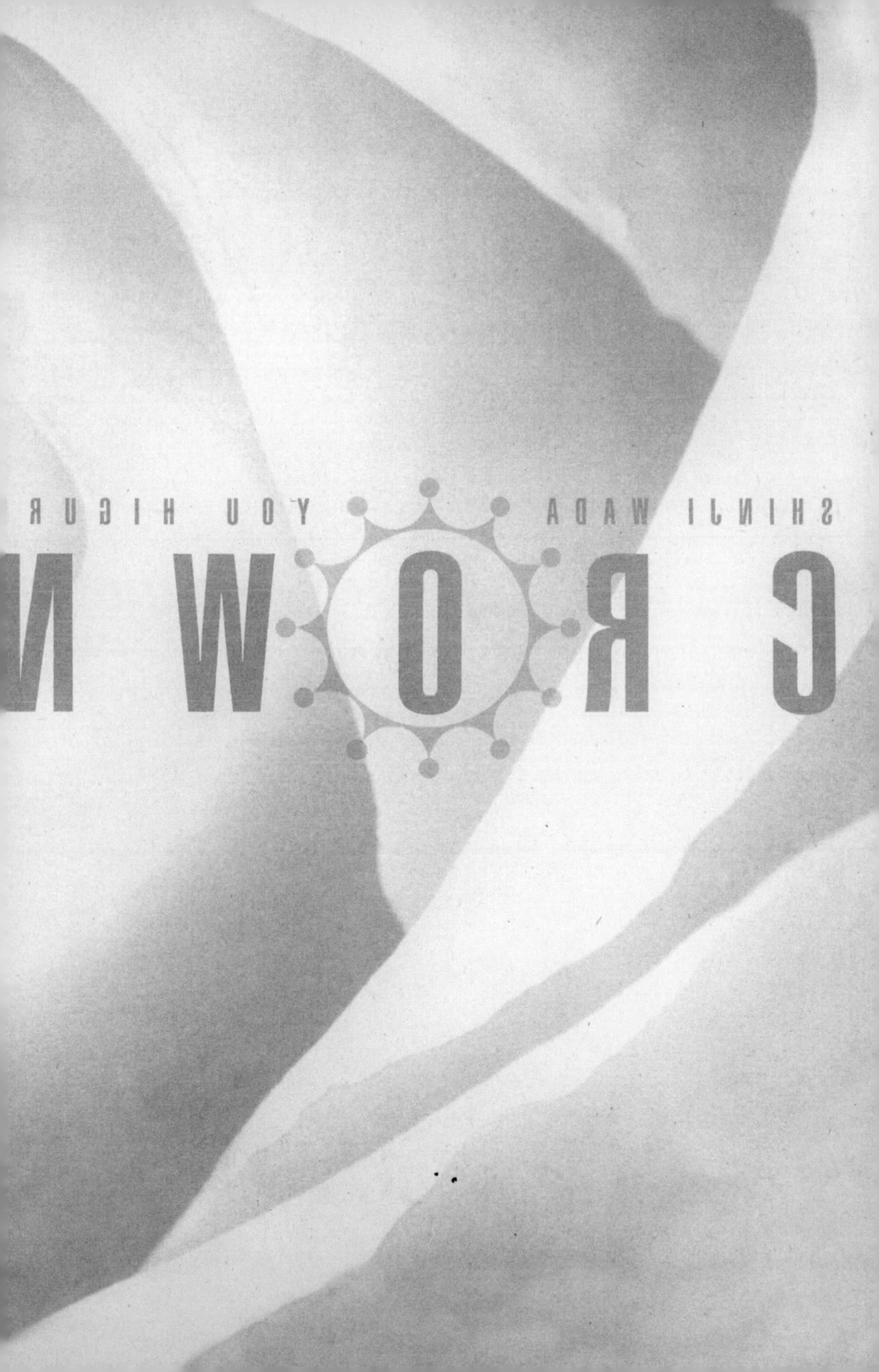
SHINJI WADA YOU HIGUR
CROWN

SHINJI WADA YOU HIGURI

CROWN

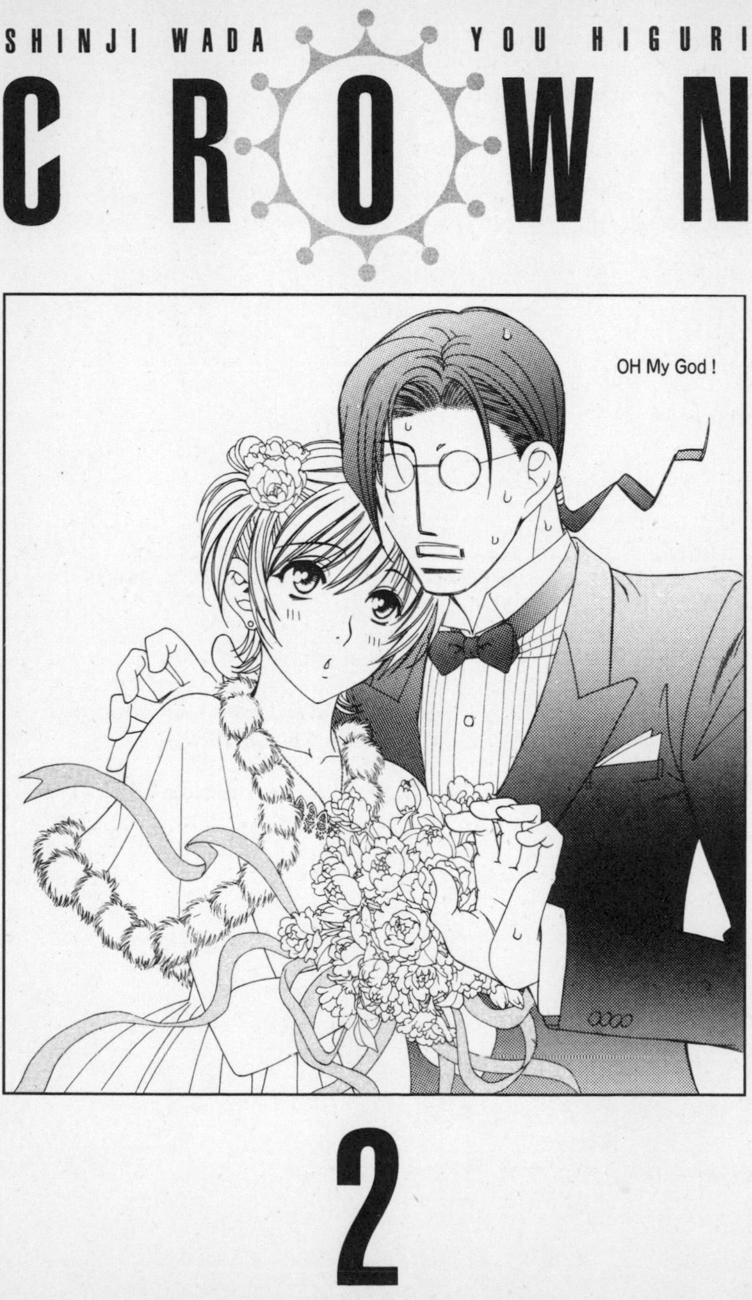
OH My God !

2

Translation – Christine Schilling
Adaptation – Brynne Chandler
Lettering & Retouch – Jose Macasocol, Jr.
Editorial Assistant – Christine Schilling
Production Assistant – Suzy Wells
Production Manager – James Dashiell
Editor – Audry Taylor

A Go! Comi manga

Published by Go! Media Entertainment, LLC

CROWN Volume 2
© SHINJI WADA/YOU HIGURI 2006
Originally published in Japan in 2006 by Akita Publishing Co., Ltd., Tokyo.
English translation rights arranged with Akita Publishing Co., Ltd.
through TOHAN CORPORATION, Tokyo.

English Text © 2009 Go! Media Entertainment, LLC. All rights reserved.

This book is a work of fiction. Names, places and incidents are either a
product of the author's imagination or are used fictitiously.

No part of this book may be reproduced or transmitted in any form or by any
means physical or digital without permission in writing from the publisher.

Visit us online at www.gocomi.com
e-mail: info@gocomi.com

ISBN 978-1-60510-006-7

First printed in April 2009

1 2 3 4 5 6 7 8 9

Manufactured in the United States of America.

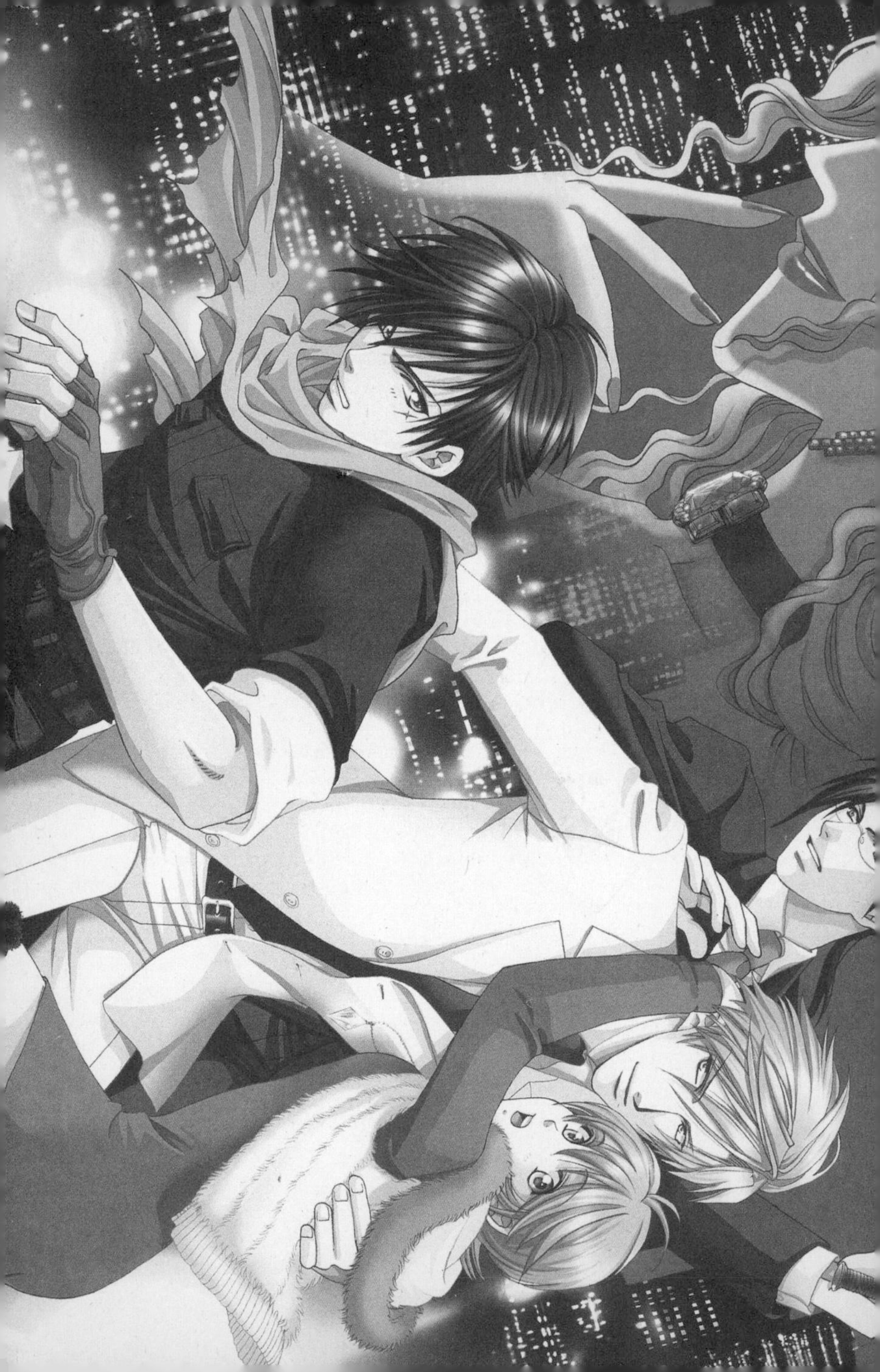